THE FAMOUS 41

NEW DIRECTIONS IN LATINO AMERICAN CULTURES

A series edited by Licia Fiol-Matta and José Quiroga

Published in 2003:

The Famous 41: Sexuality and Social Control in Mexico, c. 1901,
edited by Robert McKee Irwin, Edward J. McCaughan,
and Michelle Rocío Nasser

Velvet Barrios: Popular Culture & Chicana/o Sexualities,
edited by Alicia Gaspar de Alba,
with a foreword by Tomás Ybarra Frausto

Bilingual Games: Some Literary Investigations,
edited by Doris Sommer

New York Ricans from the Hip Hop Zone,
by Raquel Rivera

Forthcoming:

New Tendencies in Mexican Art
by Rubén Gallo

THE FAMOUS 41

Sexuality and Social Control in Mexico, c. 1901

Edited by

Robert McKee Irwin,
Edward J. McCaughan,
and Michelle Rocío Nasser

First published 2003 by
PALGRAVE MACMILLAN™
175 Fifth Avenue, New York, N.Y. 10010 and
Houndmills, Basingstoke, Hampshire, England RG21 6XS.
Companies and representatives throughout the world.

PALGRAVE MACMILLAN is the global academic imprint of the
Palgrave Macmillan division of St. Martin's Press, LLC and of
Palgrave Macmillan Ltd. Macmillan® is a registered trademark in the
United States, United Kingdom and other countries. Palgrave is a
registered trademark in the European Union and other countries.

ISBN 1–4039–6048–8 hardback
ISBN 1–4039–6049–6 paperback

Cataloging-in-Publication Data available from the Library of
Congress.

A catalogue record for this book is available from the British Library.

Design by Letra Libre, Inc.

First edition: February 2003
10 9 8 7 6 5 4 3 2 1

Printed in the United States of America.

CONTENTS

PART I: THE FAMOUS 41

PART II: SEXUALITY AND SOCIAL CONTROL IN MEXICO, C. 1901

Acknowledgments

This volume owes its existence to the sponsors of the symposium "Centenary of the Famous 41: Sexuality and Social Control in Latin American, c. 1901," which was held at Tulane University, November 15–17, 2001. We are particularly grateful to Tulane University's Roger Thayer Stone Center for Latin American Studies and its Executive Director, Thomas F. Reese, for their willingness to generously fund an event that was the brainchild of a new junior faculty member. Other generous cosponsors included: Tulane University's Center for Scholars, the Department of Spanish and Portuguese; the Georges Lurcy Fund of the Department of History; the Office of Lesbian, Gay, and Bisexual Life; the Office of the Provost; the Graduate School; Loyola University's Women's Resource Center and Women's Studies Committee; and the Consulate General of Mexico in New Orleans.

We also wish to thank the participants of the symposium. Due to the narrower focus of this volume, many excellent papers from the symposium are not included here; nonetheless, the dynamic interdisciplinary dialogue of the many participants whose work, taken together, reflects the current state of research on sexuality studies in Latin America of the late nineteenth/early twentieth centuries. These scholars include: Daniel Balderston, Peter Beattie, Pablo Ben, Katherine Bliss, Gabriela Cano, Scott Cooper, Débora D'Antonio, Héctor Domínguez, Licia Fiol-Matta, William French, Lilia Granillo Vázquez, James Green, Donna Guy, Wilfredo Hernández, Denilson Lopes, Magdalena Maíz-Peña, Oscar Montero, Luis Peña, José Quiroga, and Alfredo Villanueva Collado.

We also are grateful to the coeditors of Palgrave's New Directions in Latino American Cultures series, Licia Fiol-Matta and José Quiroga, for their enthusiastic support of and invaluable advice on this project, as well as to the helpfulness and efficiency of Gayatri Patnaik and the staff at Palgrave Macmillian, which has made our job as editors a pleasure.

Regarding the translations, the translators (Irwin and Nasser, for *Los 41* and the accompanying newspaper articles; and Aaron Walker for Carlos Monsiváis's article) gratefully acknowledge the help of Alessandra Luiselli, Patricia Walker, and Rafael Díaz.

Finally, we are grateful to the Tinker Collection of the Harry Ransom Humanities Research Center at the University of Texas at Austin for providing our cover illustration, taken from a 1901 broadsheet by José Guadalupe Posada.

LIST OF ILLUSTRATIONS

Sexuality and Social Control in Mexico, 1901

Robert McKee Irwin, Edward J. McCaughan,
and Michelle Rocío Nasser

Repugnante es el hecho que descubrió la policía el sábado en la noche en una casa de una de las calles de la Paz.
Celebrábase ahí un baile en el que se estaba produciendo más ruido del necesario en una diversión.
Acudió la policía y se encontró con que en el baile no había una sola mujer, pues la veintena que aparentemente estaba eran hombres vestidos con corpiños y enaguas y pintados con colorete y algunos hasta con aretes sobrepuestos.
Mujeres y hombres se encuentran en la cárcel.

[Repugnant is the only word to describe the incident that the police discovered Saturday night in a house on La Paz Street
A ball was being celebrated there that was producing more noise than necessary for merrymaking.
The police entered and discovered that there was not a single woman at this ball and that the 20 or so apparent women were actually men dressed in bodices and petticoats, made up colorfully, some even wearing earrings.
Women and men alike can now be found in jail] ("Baile de señores solos" Diario del Hogar, *11/19/1901 Spanish 35, English 21, this volume).*

On November 17, 1901, Mexico City police raided a private party and arrested 41 men, half of whom were dressed as women. This clandestine transvestite ball was apparently not an unheard of phenomenon at the time, although it was not normally something that would gain national attention. Mexican cultural trends in literature, in art, in the sciences, and in journalism, however, were inciting an atmosphere of sexual curiosity that was in search of the right turn of events to ignite a discursive explosion and focus interest on what was not a new phenomenon, but what was about to become a new concept: homosexuality.

The reign of Mexican president/dictator Porfirio Díaz (1876–1911) was a time of rapid modernization in Mexico. With technological advancement and industrialization came provocative new cultural trends, a range of new social problems, and the need for new mechanisms of social control to maintain order in an age of progress. "Order and progress," in fact, was the motto of the era, but the influx on information on the New Woman, on hysteria, on sexual inversion, on dandyism, on hermaphroditism, on transvestism, on degeneration, on decadence, etc. was stirring up all kinds of "disorderly" thinking and, in some cases, acts.

Extensive print media coverage of what quickly became known as the scandal of the Famous 41, including a series of lithographs by popular Mexican artist José Guadalupe Posada, helped to constitute what at the time seemed like just one more vulgar event of Porfirian excess, as Carlos Monsiváis argues, as the invention of homosexuality in Mexico. The one hundredth anniversary of "the famous 41" was the impetus for this book on sexuality and social control in turn-of-the-twentieth-century Mexico.

The weekend of November 17, 2001, the Roger Thayer Stone Center for Latin American Studies of Tulane University hosted the symposium "The Centenary of the Famous 41: Sexuality and Social Control in Latin America, 1901," which brought together investigators from all over the Americas to share their pioneering research on issues such as prostitution, rape, public hygiene, transvestitism, mental illness, sexually transmitted disease, degeneration, sex scandals, and homosexuality in late-nineteenth- and early-twentieth-century Latin America. In addition to the academic symposium, the centenary celebration also featured an exhibition, curated by Michelle Nasser, of Posada prints—including his various representations of the 41 as well as images of other sex crimes and scandals of the epoch— and reproductions of the original Mexico City newspaper stories of 1901 covering the 41 scandal. Tulane's exhibition ran concurrently with one in the Museum of the City of Mexico, which presented "la mirada satírica de 26 artistas" [the satiric view of 26 artists], contemporary artists to be sure, concerning the same theme, entitled "Muy Chulos y Coquetones" [very cute and coquettish] (*La Crónica de Hoy* 11/1/2001).[1] The events culminated the night of November 17, 2001, exactly one hundred years after the *baile nefando,* with a gala cocktail party and dinner attended by the symposium participants along with the ghosts of the 41 *maricones.*

It might seem ironic or even offensive for the event to have been called a centenary. A centenary or centennial is celebrated to honor an individual or a group or to remember an event of special significance on his, her, or its one-hundredth anniversary, not to mark the date of one's persecution or punishment. The ball of the 41 does have special significance in 2001, although it was not necessarily a new phenomenon in 1901, nor were its anonymous attendees probably any different from many other men who liked to dress up in drag in Mexico in November 1901 or before. What is original is that the clandestine queer underworld that produced the ball was exposed. The modern notion of homosexuality in Mexico is born not because of a new transvestitism or a new mechanism of sexual desire between men, but because there was a scandal that provoked a new discourse formulating the possibility of a certain eroticism existing between men.

The ball was raided and its attendees were arrested, publicly humiliated, and harshly punished, without so much as a trial or a chance to formally present a legal defense. A weekly newspaper of the era, *El Hijo del Ahuizote,* articulates the dilemma that the incident presents: "La depravación de los 'cuarenta y uno' no está calificada de delito en el Código; la falta a la moral que cometieron no fue pública y no hubiera llegado a las proporciones del escándalo sin la intervención de la policía que la reveló haciéndola notoria" [the depravation of the 'forty one' is not designated as a crime in the (Legal) Code; the moral fault that they committed was not public and would not have reached the proportions of a scandal without the intervention of the police that revealed and made it notorious] (12/1/1901). That is why it was the governor of the district and not a judge or a jury that found the 41 guilty and set their sentence. His condemnation of the men to hard labor was an attempt to appease a provoked and disapproving public, which made their punishment more of a lynching than an application of principles of justice.

The theme of the symposium was sexuality and social control. Does that mean, then, that it celebrated the punishment of homosexuality? Its criminalization? Invasion of privacy? The public humiliation of the transvestites? The homophobia of the press, the government, and the Mexican public? The 41's lack of recourse to a system of justice? Their lack of a public voice of any kind?

The symposium explored questions of sexual and social control not to celebrate them but to reveal the histories of their subtle mechanisms of efficacy and inefficacy. Homosexuality, prostitution, and other "abnormal" sexual behaviors have been manipulated by the discourses of religion, medicine, psychology, and "natural" law. Whereas today the rhetoric of alarm of a century ago may seem exaggerated to the point of being amusing, it is important to note how it was accepted—and how readily it was accepted—in that era, and also how sexual difference, so universally disdained, was used as a rhetorical arm in other battles: of gender, social class, race, nation.

The Centenary of the 41 celebrated not the repression of sexual subversion but its new visibility. With few exceptions, sexual acts were not discussed in nineteenth-century Latin America.[2] Monsiváis writes (referring specifically to Mexico), "Si en el virreinato se condena a los sodomitas a la hoguera porque 'mudan de orden natural', en el siglo XIX jamás se les menciona por escrito" [If during the viceroyalty sodomites were condemned to be burned at the stake because "they alter the natural order," in the nineteenth century they were never mentioned in writing] ("Ortodoxia" 197). As noted above, in Mexico, as elsewhere in Latin America, the new century experienced a new and sudden interest in all types of sexual desire, practice, and identity.[3] Positivist sociologists, criminologists, and psychiatrists examined cases of sexual "deviation" to better understand what they frequently perceived to be social degeneration. The popular press sensationalized sex scandals and crimes, inciting the interest of an apparently insatiable public curiosity. Naturalist and modernist literatures aestheticized, albeit in utterly distinct styles, a plethora of sexual behaviors never before imagined by literate Mexico. Sexuality had suddenly attained a new visibility that brought it to the forefront of the social and cultural debates of the era.

The irony is clear. As Foucault has argued so persuasively, the mechanisms of repression cannot function without inciting the discourse about that which they seek to repress, and this discourse is, in the end, productive. The discourse of repression incites the same desires and behaviors that it strives to repress. The Centenary of the Famous 41, the symposium, and this volume celebrate not the repression of transvestitism and homosexuality but the new proliferation of sexual dissidences that the discourses of sexual repression made possible.

The Tulane symposium brought together works on a range of related issues, many of the best of which are collected herein, although, whereas the symposium's participants addressed research on all regions of Latin America, this collection limits its scope specifically to Mexico. And although its essays treat a vast range of topics including literature, law, dandyism, consumption, advertising, political cartoons, criminology, and psychiatry, this is not to say that there do not remain significant epistemological gaps among the studies of Mexican sexuality and social control in this period. While scholars have begun to do careful rereadings of late-nineteenth- and early-twentieth-century Latin American literature and culture informed by recent developments in gender and sexuality theory, the age of the 41 in general has not received the attention necessary to put together a significant mass of the kinds of arguments necessary to fully reveal the relationship between sexuality and social control of the era. In Mexico, for example, a postrevolutionary tradition of political aversion for the Porfiriato has dissuaded the academy from focusing significantly on the era, and homosexuality, seen from a historical perspective, has only just begun to inspire academic inquiry. In addition, although feminist scholars have begun to assert the importance of women's writings and to reread patriarchal constructions of female sexuality of the era, lesbianism is a theme that remains largely unexplored.

The symposium of the 41 was a gathering of innovative researchers whose projects of investigation have led them into forgotten archives where they have found crumbling newspapers, dusty studies of the positivists, long-lost literary works of the *modernistas* and *naturalistas,* old legal codes and police registers, and the very infrequent testimonial writings, perhaps never before read by anyone, of the less than illustrious individuals who were confronted by the discourses and material forces of sexual repression. Some have reinterpreted well known texts from a fresh (queer studies) perspective. All benefited from the dialogue afforded by the symposium that brought them all out of the mustiest corners of Latin American archives to Tulane to share ideas, exchange data, and probe each other's arguments. This volume brings together many of the ideas that circulated among these scholars at the symposium. Because the symposium was organized around the Centenary of the 41, this book makes an especially important contribution to fleshing out a fuller understanding of sexuality and social control in early-twentieth-century Mexico. It is hoped that similar forays will soon be made into studies of other Latin American cultures from diverse disciplinary (or interdisciplinary) perspectives, particular with regard to the epoch in question, in which certain constructions of sexuality (most particularly male homosexuality and active female sexuality of any kind) were beginning to assume an important role in Latin American culture as the anathema that was needed as a rhetorical arm to construct and define an officially sanctioned national culture, and also as an integral aspect, albeit never officially acknowledged, of those same constructions and definitions.

The Famous 41

Part I of this volume is dedicated to the case of the Famous 41 and includes historical documentation of the scandal from 1901 Mexico City newspapers, published here for the first time in one hundred years, classic engravings depicting the 41 by Mexican popular artist José Guadalupe Posada (Illustrations 1–4), and excerpts of Eduardo Castrejón's until now lost and virtually unobtainable 1906 novel, *Los 41*.[4] The newspaper coverage and novel are provided in bilingual form, so that they may be consulted both by casual readers interested in reading about the 41 (whether in English or in Spanish) as well as by researchers who need to consult the original documents. The latter should be aware that the novel itself contained numerous errata, mostly spelling errors, which have been corrected for this edition.[5]

Since the 41 in particular and Mexican sexuality in general are rarely included in any Mexican historiography, it is important to get such materials back in circulation as well as to carry out, as Irwin and Monsiváis have done, the challenging task of analyzing the very limited data that has survived, if only to correct the many misconceptions that exist on the topic. For example, the limited scholarship on the 41 has until recently consistently cited Saturday, November 20, 1901, as the date of the notorious drag ball. Clark Taylor, Luis Mario Schneider, Monsiváis ("Ortodoxia"), and Carlos Bonfil are among those who have reported this date as that of the raid. However, November 20, 1901, was not a Saturday. Moreover, newspaper reports of the scandal commence as early as Tuesday, November 19. Journalistic accounts are inconsistent in pinpointing the date of the ball, some claiming it was Saturday, November 16, others Sunday, November 17. Most likely, the ball began the night of the sixteenth, while arrests were made in the wee hours of the morning on the seventeenth. This conclusion is confirmed by the dates reported in Castrejón's novel in Chapter XII. Why the common error? The newspapers in question are buried away in libraries and most researchers have not had access to them. Many can in fact be found in the Fondo Reservado of the Hemeroteca Nacional in Mexico City. Since they are not on microfilm, however, the materials published

Illustration 1. José Guadalupe Posada. "Los 41 maricones . . . Muy chulos y coquetones" [The 41 faggots . . . Very cute and coquettish]. Courtesy of Harry Ransom Humanities Research Center, The University of Texas at Austin.

Abanicos elegantes
Portaban con gentileza,
Y aretes ó dormilonas
Pasados por las orejas.

Sus caras muy repintadas
Con albayalde ó con cal,
Con ceniza ó velutina....
¡Pues vaya usté á adivinar!

Lievaban buenos corsés
Con pechos bien abultados
Y caderitas y muslos......
Postizos....pues está claro.

El caso es que se miraban
Salerosas, retrecheras
Danzando al compas seguido
De música ratonera.

Se trataba, según dicen,
De efectuar alegre rifa
De un niño de catorce años,
Por colmo de picardías.

Cuando más entusiasmados
Y quitados de la pena,
Se hallaban los mariquitos
Gozando de aquella fiesta

Púm! que los gendarmes entran
Sorprendiendo a los *jotones*!
Y aquello sí fué de verse....
¡Qué apuros y que aflixiones!

Algunos quieren correr,
O echarse dentro el *común* ...
Otros quieren desnudarse
A otros les dá el patatús.

Una alarma general....
Lloran, chillan, y hasta ladran,
¡Qué rebumbio! ¡Qué conflictos!
Pero ninguno se escapa.

A todos, uno por uno
La policía los recoje,
Y á Tlapisquera derecho
Se los va llevando al trote.

Illustration 2. José Guadalupe Posada. "Abanicos elegantes . . ." [Elegant fans . . .]. Courtesy of Harry Ransom Humanities Research Center, The University of Texas at Austin.

herein are based on coeditor Irwin's manual transcriptions, carried out in 1995 on a research trip generously funded by New York University's Center for Latin American and Caribbean Studies. Some of these newspapers undoubtedly can be found in other archives, but the fact that they are so rarely consulted was a major factor in our deciding to publish highlights from them here, in English and in Spanish. Space limitations prevent us from including them all. However, researchers wishing to study this material in detail hopefully will soon be able to consult them, thanks to a project in the works by Alejandro García.

Apparently the primary source that kept the memory of the 41— chronologically distorted as it may have been—alive during the twentieth century were the several broadsheets of the infamous *maricones* illustrated by José Guadalupe Posada, one of which erroneously reports the date of the arrest as November 20, 1901. Its headline reads "Los 41 maricones. Encontrados en un baile de la Calle de la Paz el 20 de Noviembre de 1901" [The 41 *maricones*. Discovered at a ball on La Paz Street on November 20, 1901], and is then followed by a *corrido* whose well-known title is "Aquí están los maricones, muy chulos y coquetones" [Here are the *maricones,* very cute and flirtatious] (Illustration 1). Republishing the wonderfully humorous Posada images here, despite their relative availability, is essential to our project of making this the definitive text on the Famous 41.

This is the same reason why we are thrilled to reprint for the first time an abridged version of Castrejón's long lost novel. *Los 41* is a queer text in several ways. It is a text virtually unmentioned in any literary history, and was written by an author whose name appears in no critical or philological sources on Mexican literature. Coeditor Irwin first stumbled on a copy in 1995 when looking in the card catalogue of Mexico's Biblioteca Nacional for Paolo Po's milestone 1964 novel *41, o el muchacho que soñaba en fantasmas,* which is sometimes cited as Mexico's first "gay novel." He read *Los 41* in a single afternoon, and was quite excited at his archaeological fortune. He soon discovered, however, that he was not the first to unearth it as mention of it appeared soon after in an article by Monsiváis ("Ortodoxia"). Later, Irwin obtained a photocopy from Ben. Sifuentes-Jáuregui, who also beat him to it, if only by a few weeks. The Biblioteca Nacional's copy is apparently the only one that has survived, making this novel one of those classics of the academic underground that circulate only in the form of photocopy. While it was not possible to include the whole novel in this volume, we are fortunate to be able to present a sizeable piece of it (over 60 percent) in bilingual form. Because of space limitations, we have chosen to publish only the parts of the novel that address the Famous 41, leaving out the author's second plotline about two ex-girlfriends of the transvestite protagonists. This was a painful decision: even though the novel may not be a great literary work, it is a rare and important historical document on homosexuality in Mexico in the early twentieth century. Still, we believe that the chapters that have been cut are of substantially less historical interest. In addition, its shorter length makes it an easier read, and a more convenient pedagogical tool for professors of history, literature, cultural studies, and the social sciences.

Following the novel, the section concludes with two critical articles by the two scholars who have done the most to revive interest in the 41 in recent years, Monsiváis (see, for example, "Ortodoxia") and Irwin (see "The Famous 41"). Here we include new essays by each that reconstruct the events surrounding the 41, locate them within their historical context, and analyze the long-term impact of the case in defining popular notions about homosexuality in twentieth-century Mexico.

For Monsiváis, organizing a transvestite ball in 1901 Mexico City was almost the equivalent of organizing a Gay Pride March in 2001, given the centrality of machismo in the national culture:

> Only in the second half of the twentieth century is homosexuality in Mexico approached from a scientific perspective, or one that claims to be such. Before then, *the masculine* is the singular and living substance of *the national* and *the human,* with *the masculine* understood as the code of absolute *machismo* which does not require a definition, *the human* as the fulfillment of obligations towards the mythology of the species, and *the national* as the catalog of possible virtues, which are exemplified by heroes and, in daily life, by the *muy machos.*

The arrest of the 41, writes Monsiváis, "broke the silence of traditionalism and its hatred" for those creatures not even worthy of being named.

Irwin focuses on the ways in which the "repressive discourse" surrounding the 41 case "not only makes possible and in some ways promotes its counterdiscourse, but also incorporates it, albeit unintentionally." From his reading of the press accounts, Posada illustrations, and Castrejón's novel, Irwin concludes:

> In the end, the apparent discourses of censure often turned out to foment if not homosexuality itself, at least a curiosity about sexual diversity. Their desire to wipe out homosexuality muddled itself with another contradictory desire to explore it and know it. Their eagerness

EL GRAN VIAJE DE LOS
41 MARICONES PARA YUCATAN,

Las impresiones de viaje—Resaladas
cual no hay más—De todos los maricazos
Que mandan á Yucatán.

Sin considerar tantito
A nuestro sexo tan casto,
Ni el estado interesante
Que casi todas guardamos,

Hechas horrible jigote
A todas nos encajaron
En un carro de tercera
Del *trensote* Mexicano.

Revueltas cual chilaquiles
Fuímos con jergas soldados
Que injuriaban leperotes
Nuestro pudor con descaro.

Al pobrecito Sofío
Le dieron muchos desmayos
Con los continuos meneos
De este tren tan remalvado.

Illustration 3. José Guadalupe Posada. "41 maricones para Yucatán" [41 faggots to the Yucatan]. Courtesy of Harry Ransom Humanities Research Center, The University of Texas at Austin.

to denigrate it with humor ended up celebrating it. Finally, their insistence on rejecting it and suppressing it from national culture failed. . . . [I]n Mexico homosexuality placed itself agilely into the national landscape and the 41 became national myths.

SEXUALITY AND SOCIAL CONTROL IN MEXICO, 1901

The case of the 41 also introduces broader themes related to sexuality and social control addressed in the multidisciplinary essays that make up Part II of this volume.

Porfirian Mexico was, of course, a contested nation about to explode in the first great social revolution of the twentieth century. Robert Buffington's examination of the construction of homophobia in Mexico City's satiric working-class penny press from 1900–1910 reminds us of Nira Yuval-Davis's warning: "Nations are situated in specific historical moments and are constructed by shifting nationalist discourses promoted by different groupings competing for hegemony. Their gendered character should be understood only within such a contextualization" (4). The dandy may have served as a symbol of civilization, modernization, and even patriotism for Mexican upper classes of the era, but he also became a symbol of bourgeois corruption and decadence for Mexico's incipient revolutionary forces. According to Buffington, penny press editors "sought to subvert the masculinity of all bourgeois men by portraying them as parasitic *catrines* who dozed in a narcissistic haze of self-congratulation and conspicuous consumption while working-class patriots struggled to protect and nurture *la patria*." His study of these popular journals shows how the 41 scandal played out in their political satire. Men who in the late 1800s had been mocked as despicable but largely harmless indolent fops were now sexual deviants whose degeneration threatened national culture itself. Male effeminacy, which had long been an arm of Mexico's political satirists and cartoonists, suddenly became lethal.

Víctor Macías-González uses advertisements in gentlemen's magazines from the Porfiriato, as well as diaries, novels, and correspondence of the era, to examine the role of elite males as consumers and arbiters of taste. Taking what for Buffington had been a largely rhetorical figure, he turns to the real-life models for the penny press's lampoonery, noting the contradictions of dandyism for the dandy and for the elite who sought to imitate him: "[I]n their consumption practices that proclaimed elite males' patriotism and modernity, as

Tomo V. Epoca II.   México, Julio 25 de 1907.   Año V. Número **41**

LA GUACAMAYA

DEL PUEBLO Y POR EL PUEBLO.

SEMANARIO INDEPENDIENTE DEFENSOR DE LA CLASE OBRERA.

Director Propietario: **FERNANDO P. TORROELLA**

El feminismo se impone

Mientras la mujer asiste
al taller y á la oficina,
y de casimir se viste,
y de la casa desiste
y entra airosa á la cantina,

el hombre barbilampiño
queda haciendo el desayuno
cose, plancha y cuida al niño,
y todos con gran cariño (?)
le llaman **cuarenta y uno.**

Illustration 4. José Guadalupe Posada. "El feminismo se impone" [Feminism imposes itself]. Courtesy of Benson Latin American Collection, The University of Texas at Austin.

well as their class and racial superiority, also lurked the sinister specter of moral danger, for the devotion of dandies' time and resources to conspicuous consumption perilously mimicked what society then considered a strictly feminine behavior."

Pablo Piccato shifts attention back to Mexico's lower classes, or "criminal classes" as Porfirian elites so often referred to them. Mexico's positivist criminologists, in their quest to carry out the mandate for order and progress, sought to link the social problem of crime to the sexual degeneration of the lower classes. Piccato's research shows how Mexico's prison system served as a correctional institution for deviant sexuality. The author delves into the reality of prison life in turn-of-the-century Mexico where "sex was both part of prison labor and the most prestigious way to profit from power." He discusses the treatment of prisoners and the power hierarchies that were inspired by sexual favors. By using interviews of prison inmates conducted by the famed criminologist and journalist Carlos Roumagnac, Piccato is able to offer a view into the minds of the prisoners and to begin to document "el infierno de los homosexuales," as described by the inmates themselves.

The next chapter turns our attention from the prison system to the medical institutions, which also played a key role in efforts to rehabilitate those considered to be social and sexual misfits. Cristina Rivera-Garza invites a more intimate reading of the General Insane Asylum *La Castañeda,* "the largest state institution devoted to the care of mentally ill men, women, and children in late Porfirian Mexico, where prospective inmates and medical interns first faced one another, exchanging information that substantiated or questioned accepted notions of mental illness and mental health in which the issue of sexuality played a prominent role." Rivera-Garza examines the testimonial writings of one patient, Luz D., regarding her life and experiences in *La Castañeda.* She further explores the relationship that ensued between Luz D. and the asylum's Dr. Agustín Torres, who encouraged the patient's innovative writings as an approach to advance his career in medical research. Social control, according to Rivera-Garza's analysis, operated not as a discourse of absolute power imposed on passive victims but as a dialogue in which hierarchies were not erased but might be constructed on relations of mutual dependency.

Sylvia Molloy's chapter, "Sentimental Excess and Gender Disruption: The Case of Amado Nervo," treats, rather unexpectedly, the kitschy poetry of Mexican Amado Nervo, "the most popular of [Latin American] *modernistas,*" as well as Nervo's public persona. She examines the role of the feminine in the work of a poet who appears both to have written for women and to have treated relations with women as shameful, "resort[ing] to the rhetoric of 'the love that dares not speak its name' when referring to a woman." Her rereading of Nervo's excessively sentimental poetry and his personal letters to his beloved friend Luis Quintanilla reveal a profound gender trouble at the heart of the work of one of Latin America's most revered (and most mocked) poets.

CONCLUSION

These essays taken together aim to reevaluate the Porfiriato in terms of the emergence of modern notions of sexuality and of the initial discourses that attempted to shape and control these notions. Sexuality and social control were not issues marginal to supposedly more important questions of class conflict, political struggle, nation building, cultural production, scientific development, and popular culture during the Porfiriato. New preoccupations with sexuality had begun to inflect all aspects of Mexican culture by the last decade of the Porfiriato, and were a major source of anxiety.

The Mexican Revolution itself, it could be said, was part of its aftermath. Whereas it would perhaps be frivolous to attribute a major social revolution to sexual anxiety, it becomes clear by the 1920s that Porfirian sexual angst had turned into an underlying obsession of national cultural discourse. When, in the 1920s, the new generation of postrevolutionary intellectuals went about debating what Mexico's new national culture would look like, virility (and its opposite term, effeminacy, and, by implication, male homosexuality) was the key term of contention. And the constant struggle to ward off the contamination of Mexican machismo by the ever-threatening presence of homosexuality comes to be a crucial aspect of Mexican national character in its canonical expression, most particularly in the work of Samuel Ramos and Octavio Paz.[6]

This book attempts to shed more light on the importance of questions of sexuality and social control in turn-of-the-century Mexico, and to do so in the spirit of Sylvia Molloy's challenge to scholars to produce a more sophisticated history of Latin American nationhood with attention to gender and sexuality. In her provocative article, "La flexión del género en el texto cultural latinoamericano," Molloy calls, for example, for a rereading of José Enrique Rodó: "una lectura desde el género de Rodó . . . para elaborar, desde ese mismo género, la noción de vergüenza y de redención en Rodó para luego relacionarlas con su férreo proyecto de una ciudadanía sublime" [a reading of Rodó from

a perspective of gender . . . to elaborate, from this same perspective, the notion of shame and redemption in Rodó in order to then relate them to his ferrous project of a sublime citizenship] (56). She also asks, "¿Qué doblez o qué flexión añadiría a las ideas recibidas de esa crítica sobre ateneos o cenáculos latinoamericanos . . . , qué doblez añadiría, repito, la inclusión de la utópica Colonia Tolstoyana de Augusto D'Halmar, claramente disidente en términos de género y sexualidad, como un lugar otro donde pensar la homosociabilidad que es la base misma de los proyectos de nación?" [What fold or flexion would be added to the ideas received from the criticism on Ateneos[7] or Latin American cenacles . . . what new fold would be added by the inclusion of the utopian Tolstyoyan Colony of Augusto D'Halmar, clearly dissident in terms of gender and sexuality, as a place of otherness from which to think the homosociability that is the very basis of the projects of nationhood?] (56).

Molloy's vision with respect to the discourses of social control is then quite complex. Her aim is not to seek out the lost voices of Latin American queers, nor to examine cases of sexual oppression per se, but instead to reread carefully the very canonical discourses of social control, of nation building, of Latin Americanism[8] that are typically assumed to be (and often are blatantly) sexist and homophobic. She calls for critics to show how these texts have always been contaminated by the subversive sexuality they pretend and seem to repress, as well as how this grand Latin Americanist tradition has dealt with the queer skeletons long hidden away in its closet.

This volume, with its essays on journalism, political satire, consumption, literary and intellectual history, criminology, and psychiatry, is ambitious in this regard: its goal is not to draw attention to the margins of turn-of-the-century Mexico but to disrupt mainstream constructions of nation, of history, of collective identity by reexamining the notions of sexuality that lay behind them and the discourses of social control that sought to reify them.

Notes

1. This phrase comes from the famous Posada engraving that comes accompanied by the *corrido* that opens "Aquí están los maricones, muy chulos y coquetones" [Here are the faggots, very cute and coquettish] (Illustration 1).
2. A notable exception is Brazil; see, for example, Beattie.
3. The body of work in the fields of history, literature, and cultural studies on this topic has been growing remarkably in recent years. Some

examples that treat the epoch of the 41: Sylvia Molloy (various articles), Jorge Salessi, Francine Masiello (various articles), Pablo Ben, James Green, Peter Beattie, Oscar Montero (various articles), Robert Buffington, and the anthology edited by Tina Escaja.

4. We are grateful to Ben. Sifuentes-Jáuregui for helping obtain a copy of the novel.
5. Although errors reflect sloppy editing of the text's original Spanish, foreign (usually French or English) terms were more frequently misspelled.
6. See Balderston, "Poetry, Revolution, Homophobia." For a more complete view of gender rhetoric and Mexican national discourse, see Irwin, *Mexican Masculinities;* for a look at more recent culture, see McCaughan.
7. Formal cultural clubs, common among elite intellectuals in Latin America in the nineteenth and early twentieth centuries.
8. On Latin Americanism, see Moreiras, De la Campa.

BIBLIOGRAPHY

Balderston, Daniel. "Poetry, Revolution, Homophobia: Polemics from the Mexican Revolution." Sylvia Molloy and Robert McKee Irwin, Eds. *Hispanisms and Homosexualities*. Durham, NC: Duke University Press, 1998: 57–75.

Beattie, Peter. "Conflicting Penile Codes: Modern Masculinity and Sodomy in the Brazilian Military, 1860–1916." Daniel Balderston and Donna J. Guy, Eds. *Sex and Sexuality in Latin America*. New York: New York University Press, 1997: 65–85.

Ben, Pablo. "Muéstrame tus genitales y te diré quién eres. El 'hermafroditismo' en la Argentina finesecular y de principios de siglo XX." omar acha and Paula Halperin, Comps. *Cuerpos, género, identidades: estudios de historia de género en Argentina*. Buenos Aires: Ediciones del Signo, 2000: 61–104.

Bonfil, Carlos. "Los 41." Enrique Florescano, Coord. *Mitos Mexicanos*. Mexico City: Aguilar, 1995: 219–224.

Buffington, Robert. *Criminal and Citizen in Modern México*. Lincoln: University of Nebraska Press, 2000.

La Crónica de Hoy 11/01/2001.

De la Campa, Román. *Latin Americanism*. Minneapolis: University of Minnesota Press, 1999.

Escaja, Tina, Comp. *Delmira Agustini y el modernismo: Nuevas propuestas de género*. Rosario: Beatriz Viterbo, 2000.

García, Alejandro. "Los 41: Crónica hemerográfica de un baile prohibido." Unpublished manuscript.

Green, James Naylor. *Beyond Carnival*. Chicago: University of Chicago Press, 1999.

Guy, Donna J. *Sex and Danger in Buenos Aires: Prostitution, Family, and Nation in Argentina*. Lincoln: University of Nebraska Press, 1991.

Irwin, Robert McKee. "The Famous 41: The Scandalous Birth of Modern Mexican Homosexuality." *GLQ: A Journal of Lesbian and Gay Studies* 6:3, 2000: 353–376.

———. *Mexican Masculinities*. Minneapolis: University of Minnesota Press, Forthcoming.

Masiello, Francine. "Estado, género y sexualidad en la cultura del fin de siglo." Josefina Ludmer, Comp. *Las culturas de fin de siglo en América Latina*. Rosario: Beatriz Viterbo, 1994: 139–149.

———. "'Gentlemen,' damas y travesties: ciudadanía e identidad cultural en la Argentina del fin de siglo." Lelia Area and Mabel Moraña, Comp. *La imaginación histórica en el siglo XIX*. Buenos Aires: UNR Editora, 1994: 297–309.

McCaughan, Edward J. "Gender, Sexuality, and Nation in the Art of Mexican Social Movements." *Nepantla: Views from South* 3:1 (2002): 99–143.

Molloy, Sylvia. "La flexión de género en el texto cultural latinoamericano." *Revista de Crítica Cultural* 21, 11/2000: 54–56.

———. "His America, Our America: José Martí Reads Whitman." Betsy Erkkila and Jay Grossman, Eds. *Breaking Bounds: Whitman and American Cultural Studies*. New York: Oxford University Press, 1996.

———. "The Politics of Posing." Sylvia Molloy and Robert McKee Irwin, Eds. *Hispanisms and Homosexualities*. Durham, NC: Duke University Press, 1998: 141–160.

———. "Too Wilde for Comfort: Desire and Ideololgy in Fin-de-Siècle Latin America." Monica Dorenkamp and Richard Henke, Eds. *Negotiating Lesbian and Gay Subjects*. New York: Routledge, 1985: 35–52.

Monsiváis, Carlos. "Ortodoxia y heterodoxia en las alcobas." *Debate Feminista* 6:11, 1995: 183–210.

Montero, Oscar. "Julián del Casal and the Queers of Havana." Emilie Bergmann and Paul Julian Smith, Eds. *¿Entiendes? Queer Readings, Hispanic Writings*. Durham, NC: Duke University Press, 1995: 92–112.

———. "Modernismo and Homophobia: Dario and Rodo." Daniel Balderston and Donna Guy, Eds. *Sex and Sexuality in Latin America*. New York: New York University Press, 1997: 101–117.

Moreiras, Alberto. *The Exhaustion of Difference: The Politics of Latin American Cultural Studies*. Durham, NC: Duke University Press, 2001.

Salessi, Jorge. *Médicos, maleantes y maricas*. Rosario: Beatriz Viterbo, 1995.

Schneider, Luis Mario. "El tema homosexual en la nueva narrativa mexicana." *Casa del Tiempo* 49–50, 1985: 82–86.

Taylor, Clark. *En el ambiente: Male Homosexual Life in Mexico City*. PhD Dissertation. University of California at Berkeley, 1978.

Yuval-Davis, Nira. *Gender and Nation*. London: Sage Publications, 1997.

PART I

THE FAMOUS 41

The Famous 41

Newspaper Scandal of 1901

*Translated by Robert McKee Irwin
and Michelle Rocío Nasser*

November 19, 1901
El Diario del Hogar[1]

Men-Only Ball

Repugnant is the only word to describe the incident that the police discovered Saturday night in a house on La Paz Street.

A ball was being celebrated there that was producing more noise than necessary for merrymaking.

The police entered and discovered that there was not a single woman at this ball and that the 20 or so apparent women were actually men dressed in bodices and petticoats, made up colorfully, some even wearing earrings.

Women and men alike can now be found in jail.

November 19, 1901
El Universal

Ball of Effeminate Men

The gendarme on duty on the fourth block of La Paz Street noted that in an annex to one of the houses on the block, a ball was being held behind closed doors, and he knocked on the door to request a proper permit. An effeminate type answered the door dressed as a woman with his skirt gathered up, his face and lips full of makeup, and a very sweet and affected way of speaking. At this sight, which turned the stomach of even this most hardened sentinel, he entered the annex, suspecting what might be going on, and found there 42 such couples, some dressed as men and the others as women, dancing and merrymaking in that lair.

The watchman felt an urge to tackle the matter by using his night stick and by slapping those scoundrels, but instead, containing his justified ire, he took everyone in to the station, and from there they were remitted to Belem Prison.

November 20, 1901
El Popular[2]

Clandestine Ball Raided; 42 Men Apprehended, Some Dressed as Women

Last Sunday night, the police of the Eighth Precinct were informed that in the house located at number 4 La Paz Street, a ball was being held without the corresponding permit.

They immediately moved in to surprise the culprits, and after having encountered numerous difficulties in trying to get the partygoers to open up, the police broke into the house's patio where they found 42 individuals who were dancing to the excessively loud music of a local street band.

When they noted the presence of the police, some of those who were dressed in women's clothing attempted to flee in order to change out of the clothes of the opposite sex; but as the police understood the gravity of the situation, they did not allow anyone to leave, and all 42 including those still dressed as women were taken to the station, from which they were then sent to Belem Prison, charged with attacks on morality, and put at the disposition of the District Governor.

As a complement to the previous report, we will say that among those individuals dressed as women, several were recognized as dandies who are seen daily on Plateros Street.

These men wore elegant ladies' gowns, wigs, false breasts, earrings, embroidered shoes, and a great deal of eye makeup and rouge on their faces.

Once the news hit the boulevards, all kinds of commentaries were made, and the conduct of those individuals was censured.

We will not provide our readers with further details as they are summarily disgusting.

November 22, 1901
El País[3]

*Catholic
conservative
anti-liberalist*

THE NEFARIOUS BALL

The state of immorality to which the execrable influx of impiety has led revealed itself in yesterday's news story, in which we reported the men's only ball that the police raided on La Paz Street. The public good needs to register bad news, just as truth requires taking note of evidence of the ravages of error with facts. Just as one abyss leads to another, it happens that the authorization of libertinage—fundamental abyss of liberalism—leads, by an ineludible logic, to the abysses of aberrations, which seem at first glance to be incredible. One of these occupies us presently. With a practical authorization of sensuality in public culture, from the distribution of certain cigarette brands to what culminated with Zaza (we speak only of the speakable), with youth led into the most unbridled licentiousness, whether at the consent of pagan parents who attend mass or by the liberalism that desires nothing other than degeneration of the greatest proportions in order to dominate, the fruits can only be nefarious. In the men's ball, at which many were dressed as women, society must see a symptom of the depravity into which it has descended, and even more so when many of these men are known figures. Now, we must add today to our news of yesterday that they have already been sent to Yucatán [. . .]

In Veracruz they will be boarded onto the steamship José Romero on its way to Yucatán where they will render service as soldiers.

More than a few of those identified have submitted false names.

Yesterday, many influences and connections were put into motion by some to avoid the horrible but well deserved legal proceedings; but authorities have been inflexible, to the applause of all society.

As a complementary note, we will say that the punishment of these repugnant men began in the barracks to which they were assigned. As many of them were still wearing curls on their foreheads and some of the womanly accessories the police had caught them in, the soldiers made cruel fun of them. We were told that they sang "Where Are You Going in a Manila Shawl?" and "Oh, What a Look!"

But ignoring these comical details, the fact is that numerous people of a society that considers itself honorable have been caught on ground that marks the limits of depravity, and they were only discovered by chance. Would it be difficult to deduce everything that has not been discovered?

What accounts are the progressives giving of all this?!

November 22, 1901
La Patria[4]

THE 41 DANCERS

Our readers already know that Sunday night in a house on the fourth block of La Paz, 41 individuals and an old woman were caught having a party in which the men were enjoying themselves, 19 of them in women's dresses.

That night, the watchman who was on duty at the corner of the above mentioned street observed that carriages were continually arriving and dropping off couples.

Moved by curiosity, he approached the door of the house observing that the patio had been turned into an indecent ballroom.

He remained for a moment in observation and was able to ascertain that all attendees were men, which he duly reported to the Eighth Precinct.

Commissioner Manuel Palacios sent several undercover policemen to the location where they remained until three in the morning.

Among those dressed as women, there were many with faces made up in black and carmine, with black eyeliner, false breasts and hip pads, low heeled shoes with embroidered stockings, several of them with diamond earrings and with short silk dresses tightly fitted to the body with corsets.

On the inspector's arrival, the police, with the night reserve assisting, apprehended 41 individuals, some dressed as men, others as women, and an old woman who was taking care of the house and who had been a witness for the police to the ball that has inspired so much talk among all classes.

It is shameful and highly irritating that among those arrested, there were many who frequent Plateros boulevard and are from good families.

The governor of the district in which they were being held resolved, ignoring all influences in motion, that the 22 men dressed as men be sent to the barracks of the 24th Battalion where they were registered and given haircuts yesterday.

As for the 19 dressed as women, they can be found for the moment in the Montada barracks, from which they will be conscripted into armed services.

November 23, 1901
El Popular

THE BALL OF THE 41:
19 OF THOSE BEING HELD SENT TO YUCATÁN

Yesterday, Thursday, in the morning, 19 of the individuals apprehended at the ball that was raided in a house on the fourth block of
La Paz were conscripted into one of the units operating in the east-
ern end of the Yucatán Peninsula.

All of them were brought Wednesday before the Secretary of War so
that they could be registered and once that requirement was fulfilled,
the recruits were sent to one of the Battalions at war with the Mayans.

At six in the morning they were removed from the barracks of the
24th Battalion and taken to the Mexican Railroad's Buenavista Station, from which they would depart for Veracruz.

At the station, pitiful scenes played out: the families of the conscripted men escorted by soldiers of the 24th Battalion took seats
aboard a third-class wagon.

The 19 individuals will be loaded onto the first steamship that
leaves for Yucatán.

[. . .]

As many of these individuals belong to well-known families of
good social standing, there have been abundant influences to get the
district governor to mete out a less severe punishment; but that vigorous official has shown himself to be inflexible.

We offer to publish in *El Popular* all details relating to the subject,
as well as to frankly state what people are involved, as it is high time
to prevent such indecent scenes from recurring.

November 23, 1901
El País

THE MEN-ONLY BALL:
FOUR INDIVIDUALS REQUEST CLEMENCY
REAL NAME OF ONE DETAINEE

The men-only ball that was raided by the police continues provoking
talk in all social circles, by virtue of the fact that many of those detained are perfectly well known, since among them are men who

stroll day after day down the boulevards showing off their stylish and perfectly tailored suits and wearing sumptuous jewels.

As we stated in yesterday's issue, 12 of those captured in the house on the fourth block of La Paz were sent to Veracruz along with seven thieves who also were conscripted into the armed services.

At 5:30 in the morning, the hour at which attendance is taken in the 24th Battalion (that of those being remitted to the Port of Veracruz), those called on first were the 12 individuals who had been at the famed ball, and after number 13, who was a *pelado*,[5] was called, he replied on hearing his name, "Present, my Captain, but let me go on record as saying that I am being conscripted as a thief; but I'm not one of them," and he pointed to the group of dancers.

This provoked the laughter of those present, because not even a thief was willing to be confused with the perfumed boys, as they are called by the soldiers of the barracks.

A very amusing scene developed in the barracks of the 24th Battalion when the repugnant ones arrived wearing their magnificent overcoats, along with hats and fine patent leather shoes. The captain of the recruits had them all undress without delay, and then handed out the rough but honorable articles of clothing that are given to recruits.

With tears in their eyes, they stripped off all their clothes, some of them begging that they be allowed to at least keep their fine silk undergarments, a request that the captain denied, since, he told them, there they were just the same as everyone else. He didn't even allow them to keep their socks and they all began to cry when they put on the shoes that would replace their pretty patent leather ladies' shoes.

Four of those detained have requested clemency, or rather their closest relatives have done so.

Alejandro Pérez did so for his brother Esteban of the same last name, who had called himself Juan López at the Precinct House, and is one of those being sent off to Veracruz according to yesterday's report.

Felipe Martínez's mother also sought clemency, manifesting that her son is in the barracks of the 24th Battalion against his will, earning one *real* per day, and in addition suffering mistreatment at the hands of the officers who beat him all day long.

Rather strange, moreover, is the clemency that Lamberto Sandoval appealed for in the name of his brother Juan B. Sandoval, who is also on his way to the Yucatán Peninsula.

He says he was invited by his brother Juan to an exotic diversion, a costume ball, whose costumes encompassed both clothing and physical features.

What a pretty ball!

And, lastly, Saúl Revilla's wife also has requested clemency to prevent his conscription into armed services.

Revilla is among those who accompanied Esteban Pérez or Juan López and Juan B. Sandoval to their destination, Yucatán.

We don't know when another group will be remitted and why the individuals who were dressed as women can still be found in the Barracks of the Mounted Police. They have already been given haircuts and therefore no longer have the curls across their foreheads that they had worn to attend the ball.

It is said that two or three of them who occupy good social position will not be sent to Yucatán but will instead be stiffly fined.

We believe that the governor, without worrying about social courtesies nor special considerations of any kind, will apply the law equally for all individuals who have fallen under his jurisdiction and whom the police found dancing on La Paz Street; therefore, we expect that all of them will be eliminated from the capital, as ordered by the aforementioned governor.

That is democracy: equal responsibility under the law.

November 23, 1901
El Imparcial[6]

THE SCANDALOUS BALL

A repugnant tale has been running through the press concerning a scandalous men-only ball raided by the police in which individuals of bad habits took part.

Public curiosity and the muffled references of the press have given rise to the circulation of more or less fantastic versions of events. There are those who affirm that among the individuals apprehended were capitalists and others of exalted social standing belonging to very distinguished families. It also has been said that the prisoners were conscripted into the armed services.

We believe it necessary to rectify those opinions. The truth is that at the aforementioned excessively immoral and scandalous party there was found only to be a group of over 40 men, well known for their depraved customs and who more than once have figured in similar scandals. Most of them changed their names on being apprehended; but the police have been able to identify many of them, among whom count a young Zozoya, an individual who practiced dentistry, and another who it is said was a lawyer.

All prisoners have been sent to Yucatán, but not—as it has been said—to join the ranks of the valiant soldiers taking part in the campaign; they will be employed instead in such tasks as digging trenches, opening breaches, and raising temporary fortifications.

November 24, 1901
El Popular

THE BALL OF THE 41:
THOSE SENT TO YUCATÁN

We have been informing the readers of *El Popular* about everything relating to the ball of La Paz where the police caught 41 attendees, some dressed as women, with ladies' shoes, silk embroidered stockings, padded hips and breasts, wigs with braided extensions, faces painted white, with the obligatory picaresquely made-up eyes, in short, their disguises so well done that it was difficult to tell at first sight whether those individuals were men.

The authorities, proceeding ahead with all their energy, have been severe in meting out punishments, and first of all determined that those accountable for the dance would sweep the streets in their characteristic dress, and afterward, the district governor, with a zeal that we applaud, resolved to conscript some of them into armed service, with the Secretary of War establishing that they would be sent to Yucatán, not as soldiers, but rather as mess hall staff [. . .]

In Veracruz they should have boarded the steamship José Romano, which would take them to Yucatán where they will render their services.

A reporter affirms, in a newspaper published yesterday morning, that the moral anguish of the dancers began in the barracks where they were consigned.

As many of them were still wearing curls across their foreheads along with the feminine attire in which the police caught them, the soldiers cruelly mocked them. We were told that they sang to them, "Where Are You Going in a Manila Shawl?" and "Oh, What a Look!"

Considering the above together with our information acquired from a good source, we know, and this we declare because it is honorable to do so, that among those apprehended by the police on the fourth block of La Paz, were several individuals who were victims of a veritable trick because in the early hours of Sunday night, cards signed by a Señora Vinchi, which were invitations to a ball in the aforementioned house that same night, were given out.

As was natural, there were some who supposed that this concerned one of so many balls that are held in certain houses and they went only to be tricked, which they now must profoundly regret.

May it go on record then that the harsh commentaries that we make and have made are directed to those who, utterly lacking in shame, have stooped to dressing as women and dancing with other equally shameless men, many of whom have been described as effeminate, and have been known as such at Police Headquarters since the era of Don Eduardo Velázquez.

November 29, 1901
El Popular

The Voyage of the 41
Collective Diary

Our special envoy, charged with filling us in on the impressions of the trip of the unfortunate young ladies of the hybrid ball of La Paz Street, has managed, with great skill, to get ahold of a copy of the *Travel Diary of the 41* that has attained the celebrity status of *The Three Musketeers.*

Here is the *Diary:*

Monday

Without consideration for our sex and the interesting status of several of the young ladies who are victims of male barbarity, we were put, all jumbled together, in a third-class Mexican rail car, mixed in among those uncivilized soldiers who constantly insulted our modesty with filthy obscenities.

Sofío, shaken by the train, suffered several fainting spells.

Beatrizito complained that the seat was too hard, since it was plain wood, and that it hurt the most enchanting section of his personality.

Herlindo asked for pulque and they gave him . . . a kick in the posterior.

Pepito began to abort . . . obscenities; but we covered his little mouth, telling him: "Be quiet, cutie, for the love of God, because these big lowlifes are going to continue harassing us as if we were streetwalkers."

Tuesday

Yesterday we were left without dinner. The mighty soldiers invited us to the mess hall. Yuck!

We spent half the night with a penny's worth of aged cheese and a half a rusk.

We brought along a few oranges; but we didn't want to try them because the doctor has forbidden us acidic foods.

Wednesday

We arrived in Veracruz, asking God to give us yellow fever.

Soon Lucrecio felt the need to vomit and we were all overcome with a horrid fear; but a compassionate person told us that this was not yellow fever.

It is likely that Lucrecio is very embarrassed[7] about what is happening to him and the proof is that every so often he would say, "You see, Pepe, what your mischief has caused."

Thursday

Today we embarked in a huge boat, very jiggly, like Carolino, and the sailors began to say many ugly things to us.

They asked some of us if we were mermaids, and others if we were meat or fish.

Finally they put us in the boat's cargo hold and the odor of tar, machine oil, and sea water, together with the rolling of the ship was killing us.

Accustomed as we are to being spoiled with things like perfumes or a feathered mattress, we suffered atrociously. If these very manly types wrinkle up with seasickness, what wouldn't we poor pretty ones have suffered?

The worst thing is that this travesty will last three days from here to Progreso, and we don't know what those sailors might try when they find out that we are women traveling alone, and with the certainty that we have no mother.[8]

In the midst of this solitude, we were able to entertain ourselves by playing games; but we just ended up rolling on top of each other, showing our legs, and not finding a comfortable position.

A curse on the ball of La Paz that has been such a nuisance!

And a curse on the men who abandon poor girls in the middle of the sea, in peril of shipwreck!

Here end the fragments of the Travel Diary. Tomorrow we will publish copies of some of the letters of the travelers.

December 1, 1901
El Popular

THE LETTERS OF THE 41

Respecting original spelling, we are publishing below a few copies, provided by our correspondent, of the letters of the Mimí's, victims of free love like Manon and Desgrieux.

First Letter

Alfredo of my intestines:

Ay! There is no woman in the world more disgraced than me. Uy! How my heart and my posterior hemispheres ache! Ever since that nefarious and murky day when I was torn from your side, I have felt you aching like a molar; but aside from the cruel absence, what hurts me most is that today you are going to batter me even worse with that ugly and shameless Abelardo. Of course! Now that I can no longer spy on you at night in Alameda Park and the Zócalo[9] like I used to, drinking in my subsequent tears.

It helps that no damage lasts a hundred years. One day we'll see each other.

I am sending you a petal from the gardenia that I wore in my hair the night of the ill fated ball, and a little kiss.

Speaking of little little things, please send me the two pesos you owe me.

Yours, yours, yours,
Concho

Second Letter

My golden Luiz[10]

Now its tru, there's no way out![11] Their treeting me like an asasin, and you no that my wite hands have never bin staind with blud.

I beleve that from now on will never sea each other agen. Be brave and don't kill me by comiting suiside.

Try to send me my underdrors with the little holes and lace that I left in the dresser. Take good kare of my little berd.

Goodbuy! I dont have the nerve to rite any more.

Your disgraceful,

Lolito

Third Letter

Dear Mister Tricky:

If only because you were the first one to throw me into the world, I beg you to do whatever you can to bring me back to Mexico.[12] I can't bear being away from my son. Because he cost me ten pesos and I bought him, by making many sacrifices, in the La Palma toy store. You still don't know what it is to be a mother.

By your pretty eyes, I beg you on my knees to plead for my clemency and get them to let me go home to the hart[13] of my family. I swear to you that I will do what ever you want to make you happy.

Do it for yore mother and the rest of yore relatives.

Just say that I was tricked and they will believe everything.

Fare well, my cute Licenciado.[14] Remember the thymes that I gratified you in everything and don't snub me now that I don't have any honoraria to offer you.

Yore unhappy

Carolino.

NOTES

1. Opposition newspaper.
2. Newspaper known for its sensationalism.
3. Conservative Catholic journal opposed to the "liberalism" of Porfirio Díaz's regime.
4. Newspaper with federal subsidies, edited by Ireneo Paz.
5. Slang term for a lower-class, poorly educated urban macho.
6. Semiofficial newspaper of the Díaz government.
7. A *double entendre:* "embarazado" translates as both "embarrassed" and "pregnant."
8. The expression, "no tener madre," in Mexican slang, means "to be utterly shameless."
9. Large square and symbolic center of the city; Alameda Park is located a few blocks away and continues to be a gay cruising ground today.
10. This greeting is a pun on "Mi adorado Luis," "My dear Luis" that literally translates as "Golden piss Luis."

11. Spelling errors have been added to show phonetical ambiguities in an attempt to mimic the spelling errors in the original Spanish text.
12. To Mexicans, Mexico City is usually known as just Mexico. With respect to the particular case of Yucatán, the region was so isolated from centralized Mexican culture that many considered it to be culturally distinct. Separatist movements have not been uncommon there, and it the region is frequently referred to as "Sister Republic of Yucatán."
13. A few minor spelling errors mimic similar errors in the original.
14. Title for holder of undergraduate college degree whose approximate equivalent in the United States is the Bachelor degree.

Los 41

El escándalo periodístico de 1901

19 de noviembre de 1901
El Diario del Hogar[1]

Baile de señores solos

Repugnante es el hecho que descubrió la policía el sábado en la noche en una casa de las calles de la Paz.

Celebrábase ahí un baile en el que se estaba produciendo más ruido del necesario en una diversión.

Acudió la policía y se encontró con que en el baile no había una sola mujer, pues la veintena que aparentemente estaba eran hombres vestidos con corpiños y enaguas, y pintados con colores y algunos hasta con aretes sobrepuestos.

Mujeres y hombres se encuentran en la cárcel.

19 de noviembre de 1901
El Universal

Baile de afeminados

Notó el gendarme de la 4ª calle de la Paz que en una accesoria se afectuaba un baile a puerta cerrada y para pedir la licencia fue a llamar a la puerta. Salió a abrirle un *ajembrado* vestido de mujer, con la falda recogida, la cara y los labios llenos de afeite y muy dulce y melindroso de habla. Con esa vista, que hasta al curtido guardián le revolvió el estómago, se introdujo éste a la accesoria, sospechando lo que aquello sería y se encontró con cuarenta y dos parejas de canallas de éstos, vestidos los unos de hombres y los otros de mujer que bailaban y se solazaban en aquel antro.

Ganas le dieron al sereno de emprenderla a palos y bofetadas con los bribones aquellos, pero conteniendo sus justas iras, cargó con ello a la Comisería, de donde fueron remitidos a Belem.

20 de noviembre de 1901
El Popular[2]

Un baile clandestino sorprendido:
42 hombres aprendidos,
unos vestidos de mujeres

La noche de domingo último, tuvo conocimiento la policía de la 8ª Demarcación, de que en la casa número 4 de la calle de la Paz, se efectuaba un baile sin la licencia correspondiente.

Inmediatamente se procedió a sorprenderlo, y después de haber tropezado con muchas dificultades para conseguir que los bailadores abrieran, la policía penetró al patio de la referida casa, en donde encontró a cuarenta y dos individuos que bailaban una danza al son descompasado de una murga del barrio.

Al notar la presencia de la policía, algunos de ellos que estaban vestidos con ropas de mujer, pretendieron huir para quitarse los vestidos del sexo contrario al suyo; pero comprendiendo la policía que se trataba de algo grave, no dejó salir a ninguno y a los 42 aún los vestidos de mujeres fueron llevados a la Comisaría respectiva, de donde pasaron a la Cárcel de Belem, por ataques a la moral, a disposición del Gobernador del Distrito.

Como complemento de la noticia anterior, diremos que entre algunos de los individuos vestidos de mujeres, fueron reconocidos algunos de los pollos de Plateros que diariamente se ven por ahí.

Esos vestían trajes elegantísimos de señora, llevaban pelucas, pechos postizos, aretes, choclos bordados y en la cara tenían pintadas grandes ojeras y chapas de color.

Al saberse las noticias en los boulevards, se hacen toda clase de comentarios y se censura la conducta de dichos individuos.

No damos a nuestros lectores más detalles, por ser en sumo asquerosos.

22 de noviembre de 1901   catholic
El País[3]

El baile nefando

El estado de inmoralidad a que ha conducido el execrable influjo de la impiedad se revela en el suceso de que hemos dado noticia en nuestro número de ayer, referente al baile de sólo hombres, que sorprendió la policía en la calle de la Paz. El bien público necesita registrar las notas del mal, así como la verdad requiere fijar con hechos la prueba de los estragos del error. Como un abismo llama a otro abismo, sucede que la autorización del libertinaje,—abismo fundamental del liberalismo—conduce por lógica ineludible, a los abismos de aberraciones, a primera vista increíbles. Uno de ellos es el que nos ocupa. Autorizado prácticamente el cartel de la sensualidad, desde la que difunden ciertas marcas de cigarros, hasta la que coronó en apoteosis con Zaza, (hablamos de lo narrable); encauzada la juventud en la más desenfrenada licencia, ora por el consentimiento de los padres paganos que oyen misa, ora por el liberalismo que no desea otra cosa que la degeneración de lo más para dominar, los frutos tienen que ser nefandos. En el baile de hombres, muchos de ellos vestidos de mujeres, la sociedad tiene que ver un síntoma de la depravación a que se va descendiendo, tanto más cuanto que muchos de ellos son personas conocidas. Ahora bien, a nuestras noticias de ayer debemos agregar hoy, que han sido ya remitidos a Yucatán . . .

En Veracruz serán embarcados en el vapor «José Romano», con rumbo a Yucatán, en donde prestarán servicios de soldados.

No pocos de los nombrados, se han cambiado de nombres.

Ayer se movieron muchas influencias para evitar, respecto de algunos, el terrible cuanto merecido procedimiento; pero la autoridad ha sido inflexible, con aplauso de toda la sociedad.

Como nota complementaria diremos que el castigo de los repugnantes, comenzó en el cuartel a que fueron consignados. Como muchos llevaban aún los «chinos» sobre la frente y parte de los atavíos femeniles con que los sorprendió la policía, los soldados se burlaron cruelmente de ellos. Nos dicen que les cantaban el «¿A dónde vas con mantón de Manila?» Y otros el «¡Ay! ¡qué facha!»

Pero desentendiéndonos de estos bufos detalles, el hecho es que numerosas personas de una sociedad que se considera honorable, han sido sorprendidas en un terreno que marca el extremo de la depravación, y sorprendidas por casualidad. ¿Será fácil deducir todo lo que queda sin ser sorprendido?

¡Qué cuenta van dando los progresistas! . . .

22 de noviembre de 1901
La Patria[4]

Los cuarenta y un bailarines

Ya saben nuestros lectores que la noche del domingo fueron sorprendidos en una casa particular de la 4ª calle de la Paz, cuarenta y un individuos y una vieja en un baile en que los hombres se divertían vestidos diez y nueve de ellos con trajes de mujer.

La noche referida, el gendarme que estaba de punto en la esquina de la mencionada calle, observó que llegaban continuamente carruajes conduciendo algunas parejas.

Movido por la curiosidad se acercó a la puerta de la casa observando que el patio había sido convertido en salón de un baile indecente.

Permaneció un momento en observación y pudo convencerse de que todos eran hombres, por lo que fue a dar parte a la 8ª Inspección.

El Sr. Comisario Manuel Palacios, determinó que acudieran al lugar algunos gendarmes disfrazados que permanecieron hasta las tres de la mañana.

Entre los vestidos de mujer había muchos pintadas las caras de blanco y carmín, con negras ojeras, pechos y caderas postizas, zapatos bajos con medias bordadas, algunos con dormilonas de brillantes y con trajes de seda cortos ajustados al cuerpo con corsé.

La policía aprendió a la llegada del Inspector, con la imaginaria de la comisaría, a 41 individuos entre vestidos de hombre y de mujer y a una vieja que cuidaba la casa y que había sido testigo con los gendarmes, del baile que tanto ha dado que decir en todas las clases.

Lo vergonzoso y altamente irritante es que entre los aprehendidos hay muchos que han figurado en el boulevard de Plateros y son hijos de buenas familias.

El Señor Gobernador del Distrito, a quien fueron consignados, resolvió, desoyendo todas las influencias, que se han movido, que pasaran 22 de los bailadores, los vestidos de hombres, al cuartel del 24º Batallón, donde fueron filiados ayer rapados.

En cuanto a los 19 vestidos de mujeres, se encuentran por lo pronto en el cuartel de la Montada, para ser consignados al servicio de las armas.

23 de noviembre de 1901
El Popular

El baile de los 41:
19 de los consignados remitidos a Yucatán

Ayer, jueves, por la mañana, fueron consignados a uno de los cuerpos que operan en el extremo Oriente de la Península de Yucatán, diecinueve de los individuos aprehendidos en el baile sorprendido en una casa de la 4ª calle de la Paz.

Todos ellos fueron llevados el miércoles a la Secretaría de Guerra, para que los pasaran por cajas y una vez llenado este requisito, los filiados fueron destinados a uno de los Batallones que pelean contra los mayas.

A las 6 de la mañana fueron sacados del Cuartel del 24º Batallón y llevados a la Estación de Buenavista del Ferrocarril Mexicano, por cuya línea salieron para Veracruz.

En la estación desarrollaron las escenas más lastimosas: las familias de los consignados custodiados por soldados del 24º Batallón, tomaron asiento a bordo de un wagon de tercera clase.

Los 19 individuos serán embarcados en el primero vapor que salga para Yucatán.

. . .

Como muchos de estos individuos pertenecen a familias conocidas y de buena posición, han abundado las influencias para conseguir del Sr. Gobernador del Distrito que sea menos severo su castigo; pero tan energético funcionario se ha mostrado inflexible.

Nosotros ofrecemos publicar en *El Popular* todos los pormenores que se relacionen con este asunto, así como decir con franqueza de qué personas se trata, pues es tiempo de impedir que escenas tan indecentes se repitan.

23 de noviembre de 1901
El País

El baile de sólo hombres:
Cuatro individuos piden amparo
Verdadero nombre de un consignado

El baile de sólo hombres sorprendido por la policía, sigue dando qué decir en todos los círculos sociales, en virtud de ser muchos de los consignados perfectamente conocidos, pues que entre ellos hay jóvenes que día a día paseaban por los boulevards ostentando sus trajes perfectamente pagados a moda y llevando ricas joyas.

Como dijimos en nuestro número de ayer, doce de los capturados en la casa de la 4ª calle de la Paz fueron enviados a Veracruz, juntos con 7 rateros que también van consignados al servicio de las armas.

A las 5:30 de la mañana, hora en que se pasa la lista del 24º Batallón de los remitidos al puerto de Veracruz, fueron llamados primero los doce individuos que estaban en el célebre baile y después al tocarle su turno al número 13 era un pelado, contestó al oír su nombre: "Presente mi Capitán, pero hago constar que yo voy consignado por ratero; pero no soy de esos," y señaló el grupo de los bailadores.

Esto provocó la risa de cuantos estaban presentes, porque ni el ratero quiso confundirse con los *perjumaos*, como les dicen los soldados en el cuartel.

Una escena muy chusca se desarrolló en el cuartel del 24°, cuando llegaron los repugnantes, los cuales llevaban magníficos abrigos, así como sombreros y choclos de fino charol. El Capitán de reemplazos hizo que todos se desnudaran a la mayor brevedad y les fue repartiendo las toscas pero honrosas prendas de ropa que se les de a los reclutas.

Con las lágrimas en los ojos, fueron despojándose de todas sus prendas, suplicando algunos, que se les dejase siquiera sus ropas interiores de fina seda, a lo cual se opuso el Capitán, pues les dijo que allí eran iguales a los demás. Ni los calcetines les permitió y todos comenzaron a llorar cuando se calzaron los zapatos que iban a reemplazar a los monos choclos de glace pasia y charol.

Cuatro de los consignados han pedido amparo, o mejor dicho sus parientes más cercanos.

Alejandro Pérez, por su hermano Esteban del mismo apellido, quien se puso Juan López en la Comisaría y es uno de los que han marchado a Veracruz, según noticia que dimos ayer.

La madre de Felipe Martínez también pidió amparo, manifestando que en el cuartel del 24° Batallón está su hijo sin su voluntad ganando un real diario, y además está sufriendo el maltrato de los oficiales porque todo el día le están dando de golpes.

Curioso por demás está el amparo que interpuso Lamberto Sandoval, a nombre de su hermano Juan B. Sandoval que también va ya rumbo a la península yucateca.

Dice que fue invitado su hermano Juan, a una diversión exótica, a un baile de disfraces, junto en la indumentaria como en los rasgos fisionómicos.

¡Bonito baile!

Y por último, la esposa de Saúl Revilla también ha pedido amparo contra la consignación de éste al servicio de las armas.

Revilla es de los que acompañaron a Esteban Pérez o Juan López y a Juan B. Sandoval para su destino, Yucatán.

No sabemos cuando salga otra remesa y el por qué los individuos que estaban vestidos de mujer aún se encuentran en el Cuartel de Gendarmería Montada. Estos están ya rapados y por consiguiente no llevan en la frente los rizos que se hicieron para concurrir al baile.

Se dice que 2 o 3 que ocupan buena posición, no serán enviados a Yucatán, pues se les aplicará una multa fuerte.

Creemos que el señor Gobernador, sin fijarse en miramientos sociales ni consideraciones de ningún género, aplicará el castigo por igual a todos los individuos que han caído bajo la acción de la justicia y que la policía encontró bailando en la calle de la Paz; así es que esperamos que todos ellos sean eliminados de la capital, como lo dispuso el mencionado señor Gobernador.

Esa es la democracia: la igualdad de responsables ante la ley.

23 de noviembre de 1901
El Imparcial[5]

El baile escandaloso

Ha corrido por toda la prensa una historieta repugnante relativa a un baile escandaloso de hombres solos que sorprendió la policía en el cual tomaban parte individuos de malas costumbres.

La curiosidad pública y las embozadas referencias de la prensa, han dado motivo a que circulen versiones más o menos fantásticas. Hay quienes aseguran que entre los individuos aprehendidos había capitalistas y otras personas de posición encumbrada pertenecientes a familias muy distinguidas. También se ha dicho que los presos fueron consignados al servicio de las armas.

Creemos necesario rectificar esas opiniones. La verdad es que en la referida reunión, excesivamente inmoral y escandalosa, sólo se encontraba un grupo de más de 40 hombres, muy conocidos por sus costumbres depravadas, y que más de una vez han figurado en escándalos por el estilo. La mayor parte, cambiaron de nombre al ser aprehendidos; pero la policía ha podido identificar a muchos, entre quienes se encuentra un joven Zozaya, un individuo que ejercía como dentista, y otro que se decía abogado.

Todos los presos han sido enviados a Yucatán, pero no—como se ha dicho—a formar parte en las filas de los valientes soldados que hacen la campaña; sino que se les empleará en trabajos de zapa, como abrir brechas, rellenar bajos, abrir fosos y levantar fortificaciones pasajeras.

24 de noviembre de 1901
El Popular

El baile de los 41:
Los enviados a Yucatán

Hemos estado informando a los lectores de *El Popular* de todo el relativo al baile de la Paz donde fueron sorprendidos por la policía 41 concurrentes, algunos de ellos vestidos de mujer, con choclos, medias bordadas de seda, caderas y pechos postizos, pelucas con trenzas, pintados los rostros de blanco, con las picarescas ojeras de ordenanza, en fin, el disfraz tan bien hecho, que era difícil al primer golpe de vista, saber si aquellos individuos eran hombres.

La autoridad, procediendo con toda energía, ha sido severo en su castigo, y primeramente determinó hacer que barrieran la calle en tan típico traje los afectos al baile, y después el Sr. Gobernador del Distrito, con un celo que aplaudimos, resolvió consignar a algunos de ellos al servicio de las armas, determinando la Secretaría de Guerra, que fueron enviados a Yucatán, pero no como soldados sino como rancheros de la tropa . . .

En Veracruz deben haber tomado ayer pasaje en el vapor «José Romano» que les conducirá a Yucatán donde prestarán sus servicios.

Un «reporter» asegura, en un diario que vio la luz pública ayer en la mañana, que el suplicio moral de los bailadores comenzó en el cuartel a donde fueron consignados.

Como muchos llevaban aún los «chinos» sobre la frente a parte de los atavíos femeniles con que los sorprendió la policía, los soldados se burlaron cruelmente de ellos. Nos dicen que les cantaban el: «¿A dónde vas con mantón de Manila?» Y otros el «¡Ay! ¡qué facha!»

Ya escrito el anterior, y con datos adquiridos de buena fuente, sabemos, y esto declaramos porque es honrado hacerlo, que entre muchos de los aprehendidos por la policía en el baile de la 4ª calle de la Paz, había algunos individuos que fueron víctimas de un verdadero chasco pues que, en las primeras horas de la noche del domingo se repartieron en varias cantinas unas tarjetas firmadas por una Sra. Vinchi en las que se invitaba a un baile en la casa citada esa misma noche.

Como era natural, hubo algunos que se supusieron se trataba de uno de tantos bailes que se dan en ciertas casas y acudieron para llevarse el gran chasco que ahora deben lamentar hondamente.

Conste, pues, que los comentarios severos que hacemos y hemos hecho van dirigidos a aquellos que perdiendo toda vergüenza han descendido hasta vestirse de mujer y bailar con otros tanto desvergonzados, muchos de los cuales están retratados como afeminados conocidos en la Inspección General de Policía desde la época de D. Eduardo Velázquez.

29 de noviembre de 1901
El Popular

EL VIAJE DE LOS 41
DIARIO COLECTIVO   *Comedia*

El enviado especial nuestro, encargado de darnos cuenta de las impresiones de viaje de las infelices señoritas del baile híbrido de la calle de la Paz, ha podido, con suma habilidad, apoderarse de copia del *Diario de viaje de los 41,* que ha alcanzado la celebridad de los *3 Mosqueteros.*
He aquí el *Diario* referido.

Lunes

Sin consideración a nuestro sexo y al estado interesante de varias de las señoritas, que somos víctimas de una barbaridad masculina. Nos metieron, hechas bola, en un carro de tercera clase de ferrocarril mexicano, revueltas con esos mecos soldados que, a cada rato, insultaban nuestro pudor con palabrotas muy cochinas.

Sofío sufrió algunos desmayos, con motivo de que el tren lo maneaba.

Beatrizito se quejaba de que el asiento era muy duro, por ser pura tabla, y le lastimaba la sección más encantadora de su personalidad.

Herlindo pedía pulque y le dieron . . . un puntapié en la trastienda.

Pepito comenzó a abortar . . . malas palabras; pero le tapamos la boquita, diciéndole:

—«Cállate, chulita, por el amor de Dios, porque estos *leperotes* nos van a seguir tratando peor que si fuéramos clandestinos»

Martes

Ayer nos quedamos sin cenar. Los soldadotes nos convidaban al rancho ¡Fuchi!

Nos pasamos media noche con un centavo de queso añejo y medio bisote.

Traemos unas naranjas; pero no las quisimos probar porque el médico nos ha prohibido los ácidos.

Miércoles

Llegamos a Veracruz, pidiéndole a Dios que nos diera el vómito.

A poco le dieron ganas de vomitar a Lucrecio y a toditas nos entró un miedo espantoso; pero un compasivo nos dijo que eso no era el vómito. Probablemente Lucrecio está muy embarazado con lo que le pasa y la prueba es que cada rato decía «Ya lo ves, Pepe, por tus tarugadas.»

Jueves

Hoy nos embarcaron en un buquezote muy meneador, al estilo de Carolino, y los marineros nos empezaron a decir muchas cosas muy feas.

A unas les preguntaban si eran sirenas, y a otras si eran carne o pescado.

Por fin nos metieron en la bodega del buque y el olor del alquitrán, del aceite de la máquina y del agua del mar, además del balanceo de la embarcación, nos pusieron a la muerte.

Acostumbradas a los perfumes, al chiqueo, a un colchón de plumas, sufrimos una atrocidad. Si los muy hombres se cerrugan con el mareo ¿qué no habremos sufrido nosotras; pobres Monomas?

Lo malo es que esta travesía durará tres días, de aquí a Progreso, y no sabemos a lo que se atreverán esos marineros, al saber que somos mujeres y solas, y con la seguridad de que no tenemos madre.

En medio de esta soledad nos podíamos entretener a jugar a pipis y gañas, a la momita, al pan y queso; pero nada más rodamos las unas sobre las otras, enseñando las piernas y sin encontrar un lugar cómodo.

¡Maldito baile de la Paz que nos ha dado tanta guerra!

¡Y malditos los hombres que así abandonan a las pobres muchachas en medio del mar y sujetas al naufragio!

Aquí acaban los fragmentos del *Diario de viaje*. Mañana publicaremos las copias de algunas de las cartas de las viajeras.

1 de diciembre de 1901
El Popular

LAS CARTAS DE LOS 41

Respetando la ortografía publicamos a continuación, unas copias que nos proporcionaron nuestro corresponsal, de algunas de las cartas de las Mimís, víctimas del amor libre como Manon y Desgrieux.

Primera Carta

Alfredo de mis intestinos:

¡Ay! No hay en el mundo mujer más desgraciada. ¡Uy! ¡Cómo me duelen el corazón y los hemisferios posteriores! Desde el día nefasto y nebuloso en que me arrancaron de tu lado, sentí que dolías como una muela; pero aparte de la cruel ausencia de lo que más me duele es que hoy me vas a pegar más fuerte con ese feote y sin vergüenza de Abelardo. ¡Claro! Como ya no puedo andar espiándote de noche en la Alameda y en el zócalo como antes lo hacía bebiéndome mis respectivas lágrimas.

Vale que no hay mal que dure cien años. Algún día nos veremos.

Te mando un pétalo de la gardenia que tenía yo en la cabeza la noche del baile infausto y un piquito.

A propósito de piquito haz por mandarme los dos pesos que me debes.

Tuyo, tuyo, tuyo,
Concho

Segunda Carta[6]

Mea dorado Luiz

¡Ora si que no ay, remedio! Me yeban como un hasesino, y vien zabes que mis blancas manos nunca sean manchado con sangre.

Llo creo que desta echa no nos bolbemos a juntar. Ten balor y no vallas a zuicidarte con un suisidio que me mate.

Procura mandarme mis calsones de piquitos y encajes que dejé en la cómoda. Ciudame mucho a mi pararito.

¡Hadios! No tengo balor para escrivirte más.

Tu desgraciado
Lolito

Tercera Carta[7]

Señor Licenciado Triquiñuelas:

Siquiera porque usted fue el primero que me echó al mundo le suplico que haga lo que pueda porque me regresen a México. No puedo estar sin mi hijo. Por señas que me costó diez pesos y lo compré, con muchos sacrificios, en la juguetería de la Palma. Usted no sabe to da vía lo que es ser madre.

Por sus lindos ojos le ruego de rodillas que me pida amparo y logre que pueda volver al seno de mi familia. Yo le juro que aré lo que más le guste para dejarlo contentito.

Agalo usté por su madre y demás parientes.

Solamente con que diga usté que fui engañada lo creerán todo.

Adios, remonono Licenciado. Acuérdese de las beses que te di gusto en todo y no me desaire ora que no tengo honorarios que ofreserle.

Su infeliz
Carolino.

Notas

1. Periódico de oposición.
2. Periódico conocido por su sensacionalismo.
3. Periódico conservador y católico, en contra del liberalismo del regimen de Porfirio Díaz.
4. Periódico con subsidios federales, editado por Ireneo Paz.
5. Periódico semioficial del porfiriato.
6. Errores de ortografía en el texto original.
7. Errores de ortografía en el texto original.

The 41:
A Novel of Social Criticism [1906]

Eduardo Castrejón

*Translated by Robert McKee Irwin
and Michelle Rocío Nasser*

A Few Words

The author of this book, counting on the public's good will, handed over to this publishing house his first attempt at the genre of the novel; and the house is publishing it for the reasons set out below.

With the exception of geniuses such as Victor Hugo, whose first work was a success, as *Our Lady of Paris* is read with ever growing interest, it can be said after a century that all writers—in their initial more or less fortunate efforts—have counted on the help or advice of authors already experienced in the genre they cultivate.

Such has been the sequence in the unending chain of men and of eras: generations learning lessons from past history of progress and advancement; putting themselves in the social sphere in order to develop; and literature taking on the exploitation of the new ideas, the ideals, and the tendencies of an era. Each society in its historic moment has a particular taste; and in this way we have passed extemporaneously from classicism to romanticism, and today to realism, without being able to explain the reason for this evolution with much certitude, since unforeseen factors, anomalous circumstances, and other determining causes may intervene.

But a few things on which all epochs are in agreement, whether we speak of history or of literature, are the rectification of social customs, the condemnation of social vices, the anathema of all corruptions, the exaltation of morality, and the censure of the perversion of human sentiment. On most occasions, the writer who uses his pen as if it were a lightning bolt to annihilate social crimes is the victim; but souls tempered in the sacred fire of truth must face all vicissitudes and persecutions of hypocrisy to enter the social sphere victorious. The "Mexican Thinker," in his immortal work the *Periquillo*, put the olden society on the operating table, performed the autopsy and discovered all the gangrene that was devouring that annihilated body, confronted the customs, and then with a resonant word or with bitter satire, threw philosophical reproaches into the terrain of reason and truth.[1] Excommunicated, persecuted, anathematized, and killed in the struggle, history has done him justice and his book will forever stand as a monument that will endure longer than his ashes, which have been forever lost. Eugene Sué struck a blow against the Jesuits with his *Wandering Jew*, from which they will never recover, just as the trilogy of Emile Zola dropped lightning bolts of political and religious indignation on their heads.[2] In Europe, these works yield a profit that doesn't thrust the writer into the abyss of misery; but in our country the situation is the opposite: they lead to social persecution, and later to the fall into misery, the hospital, and death. Fortunately, in current times, fanaticisms have faded to a certain point; freedom has taken its place, and anything can be written of without fear, leaving society as judge of what is written.

The author of the novel we publish today has fulfilled a social duty, regardless of the success or failure of what he calls his novel but actually is the faithful historical rendering of an act that produced scandal and left in the flames of satire a memory that will last for many years. The book's author lets the force of his imagination be felt, presents detailed images, and flagellates in a horrible way an execrable vice, on which society itself spits, as the corruptor of generations. The author begins his career today and there is no need to demand that he be compared to the authors with whom we have been educated, particularly in this era in which literature has taken a gigantic step forward, as evidenced in that multitude of beautiful novels that charm countless readers.

In our own culture, literature has begun to cultivate itself into a genre and because it is in its infancy, we must offer it maximum protection. We are just barely beginning to have novelists: Mateos, Rabasa, Salado Álvarez, and a few others who have gained public favor and whose works are sought with eagerness and read with satisfaction.[3] It is now time that letters come to blossom in our country; we will begin with deficiencies, as is the case everywhere, but we will lay the cornerstone of the future. It is now time to initiate the competition, not only in history, in theater, but in the novel for whose struggle our race and our character possess sufficient energy. We believe in the future, and encourage Mexican writers in their arduous work; we are willing to publish all works that their ingenuity may produce and that their learning and intelligence may offer us in the vast sphere of national literature.

The Editors

I.

The afternoon was fading! . . . The sun hid its immense blondness and on the horizon banks of clouds took on a bronze tint . . .

Through Mimí's aristocratic house, adorned with exquisite feminine taste, and in the elegantly furnished parlor, disseminated waves of delicious perfumes.

Mimí is alone!

In his perfectly fitted suit, cut in American style, an exquisite elegance is noted; his hands, smooth and white, toy with his gloves, and he impatiently looks at his watch, which appears many, many hours slow.

It is seven in the evening.

In the vast parlor, the innumerable electric light bulbs that illuminate the room make a harmonious artistic ensemble together with the screens of capricious forms, as well as various statues of Carrara marble on bronze pedestals.

A fifteen-year-old footman—handsome, blue-eyed, with a voluptuous and melancholic expression—announces to Mimí with a melifluous and ceremonious voice that several young men wish to speak with him.

"Let them in, let them in!" Mimí responded eagerly.

The footman opened the leaves of the stained glass partition, pulled the silk curtains to the side, and several adolescents whom we shall refer to by the names, Ninón, Star, Modesty, Virtue, Carola, Blanca, and Margarita, paraded in.

Each was dressed with a masculine elegance.

They embraced Mimí effusively, exchanged erotic kisses, and seated themselves in the velvet armchairs.

Mimí had changed: his infinite sadness was transformed into pleasure; and Ninón, a Hercules, of seductive and manly countenance, took Mimí's hand, depositing on it an osculation of love, a sonorous osculation full of fire, rhymed by an interminable murmur.

"Has the modiste arrived with the gowns?" asked Modesty.

"Not yet," responded Mimí, "We made an appointment for eight o'clock and it will not be long before she brings the finished outfits."

The footman entered with a tray of fine cakes and several bottles of champagne that the guests began to drain.

The high-pitched voices of the adolescents, forming an immense din, ran the gamut of tones of sweetness; their effeminate manners gave the scene a cloying and scurrilous tint, the gathering seeming more like one of young ladies chitchatting in the drawing room than one of dapper young gentlemen.

"Do you love me?" Ninón asked Mimí.

And Mimí, caressing Ninón's cheeks, enthusiastically swore that he did.

"Did you go to the opera last night?" Star asked Margarita.

"Ay . . . of course I did!!"

"And you, Blanca, didn't you?"

"No, dear!!! I was a trifle ill and didn't want to leave the house."

"What precious little waves you have in your hair, Margarita! Did you curl it?"

"No, my dear, they are natural . . ."

"And your shoes, Virtue, are they American?"

"Yes, Star, they look lovely with my open-work stockings, don't they?"

"Gorgeous, Virtue, and most elegant!"

Only Modesty and Carola didn't speak; flung into an amorous embrace, they contemplated one another, entranced with life's delights, and from time to time sipped their glasses of champagne to refresh their burning lips.

At precisely eight o'clock the footman announced that the modiste had arrived.

As if impelled by an electric spring, they all rose from their seats at the same time and ran to the door.

Señora Charmanti, who was the modiste hired to make the outfits to which Modesty had referred, entered the parlor preceded by a servant, who deposited several cardboard boxes containing women's dresses on the table.

"Are they finished?" Mimí asked her with a feigned sweetness and a seductive expression.

"Yes, sir," the modiste responded with dignity, "if you find anything that displeases you, I will come back tomorrow to take care of it."

They had barely seen off Señora Charmanti when the young men threw themselves upon the boxes and, opening them up, they precipitously took out some skirts, a low-cut bodice, a silken slip with very fine and exceedingly chic lace.

And, like vain females whose chances for happiness lay in the carriage and adornment of a womanly dress, they turned to a lovely dressing room; and removing their jackets, vests, shirts, and ties, they began dressing themselves up in supremely elegant and artistically fashioned corsets.

Mimí tried on a Sevillian style skirt; Margarita a very low-cut ballet dancer's bodice and a blonde Louis XV - era wig; Carola some open knit patterned stockings stuffed with cotton; Blanca some shoes embroidered with a gold trimming; Star a sheer baby outfit; Modesty and Virtue serpentine gowns; Ninón made up his face with white and vermilion powder and perfumed the curly locks of his black hair.

The enthusiasm was indescribable!

They felt overjoyed, fulfilled, excited, plethoric with happiness, seeing themselves dressed up as women.

Oh! And what erotic transports, what fortune, what raptures . . . trading in their men's suits and turning themselves into delicious girls (?), into enchanting houris of soft curves and undulant seductive lines.
. . .

The degenerate hearts of those young prostituted aristocratic men palpitated in that immense Bacchanal.

The overwhelming joy originating out of the possession of women's clothing on their bodies, the womanly postures, the carnivalesque voices, made the dressing room seem like a chamber of fantasies; the disseminating perfumes, the embraces, the sonorous and feverish kisses recalled degrading paintings of those scenes of Sodom and Gomorrah, of those orgiastic parties of Tiberius, of Commodus and Caligula, where the explosive fire of savage passion devoured the flesh, consuming it in desires of the most unbridled prostitution.

And into that insatiable whirlpool of brutal pleasures have fallen young men who, at the height of crudeness and prostituted degradation, contribute to the bastardization of the human race, gravely injuring Nature itself.

II.

Mimí was splendid!

Because of his physique, that of a truly feminine beauty, as well as of his affected manners, he was the only one who resembled a delicious female; his dark eyes, with artistic and skillfully applied eyeliner, were the *non plus ultra* of the young ladies (?) gathered there.

From the dressing room they all went into the living room, and Star, who was a good musician, without wasting any time, masterfully executed a Shubert serenata with such delicious tenderness and such deep sentiment that his playing inspired feigned tears in our lovely ladies (?).

Next he played a bright two-step, performed with great speed, as if driven by a Satanic inspiration.

And the pleasure was immense!

Carola, Blanca, and Margarita reclined languidly in elegant *chaises longues* and Modesty and Virtue, Ninón and Mimí, enlivened, joyfully took each other's arms, throwing themselves into the whirlwind of the dance, outlining extravagant, exaggerated silhouettes until falling spent with pleasure and full of crazed and fecund jubilance.

The young footman announced that dinner was served and that everything was ready for the guests.

And lifting their skirts and imitating the demeanor of triumphant queens, airily swishing their bodies, two by two, arm in arm, they paraded into the dining room where a sumptuous dinner and a fine and magnificent selection of wines awaited them to conclude those moments of pleasure.

Each one took a random seat around the table, except for Ninón and Mimí, who seated themselves at the head of the table, presiding over the gathering, with their chairs closely placed together as if to fuse their bodies into a single soul.

They dined gobbling down each course of exquisite dishes and emptied wine into their mouths of hearty drinkers.

The alcoholic effect triumphed and those faces of such pretty delicate boys gesticulated into drunkenness as they sang bits of the operas "La Bohème" and "Tosca."

Hebe, standing upon an altar of erotic flowers, smiled maliciously; Bacchus blessed that exalted orgy; and Cupid, the little trickster, wounded those mawkish hearts with his darts.

The toasts, imbued with fire, with infinite vehemence, came one after another without interruption.

The good, the accommodating Bacchus, put all his charms and all his powerful fantasy into the glasses of wine, and everyone felt satisfied forging amorous visions in his feverish imagination.

And that disgusting phalanx of ruffians of the aristocracy, worthy imitations of Heliogabolus, possessed of a colossal joy in the midst of the most nauseating drunkenness, reached the culminating period of obscene delirium.

Mimí, full of great joy, and such haughty pleasure, contemplated in ecstasy, voluptuously squinting his eyes to caress the seductive face of Ninón with his gaze.

Modesty felt inspired; those moments of bestial degeneration were not enough to satiate his desires; a whole heaven of joy, a whole world of sensual pleasures, and new gratifications; he imagined himself transported to the land of eternal happiness creating interminable pleasures of nefarious aberrations.

Carola, Blanca, Star, Virtue, and Margarita, entangled among each other at the same level of lowness, in that sad degeneration, in incredible debasement, embraced each other, inflamed each other with the contact of their soft skin, anointed each other with perfumed oils, and deflowered each other's hands with smacks of ardent and sonorous kisses.

Ninón's eyes lit up with pleasure; that succulent dinner, those aged wines and the painted faces of his friends delighted and satisfied him.

Mimí's effeminate face, his beauty, his curled hair falling over his sloppily painted cheeks forming silken ringlets, his low-cut neckline with his very tight-fitting ladies' dress emphasizing the curves of his body; he was the craved and glorious goal of Ninón's most cherished ideals.

Ninón, debased, in a state of brutality, oblivious to honor and duty, opened the enormous gates of his feverish imagination to foolishly dissipate in what for him were the intoxicating caresses of Mimí's body.

Wretched laxity . . .

The young footman, with his sweet and languid gaze, bending at the hips, solicitously refilled the wine glasses.

The height of disorder reigned; empty bottles and broken glasses lay strewn all over the floor; tablecloths, stained with wine, looked like they were soaked in blood.

And that nucleus of idlers and libertines, yawning, with lewd expressions and postures, they drunkenly quarreled, sang, and laughed obscenely.

Only Mimí had remained quiet, indolently slumped against the back of his chair, biting his lips, playing with the tablecloth, content with that pleasant orgy, and dreaming delicious adventures in a world full of ineffable joys, like the exalted and venerable bliss of heaven.

His posture, hair, and makeup resembled those of *cocottes de toilette á la pompadour* and he seemed at Ninón's side to be the favorite of the harem of her lord, and first harlot in the emporium of debauchery, whereupon initiating himself in it, the human being loses his dignity and shame to dwell in the gangrened heart of that cynical and abject community, of that wretched community, usurper of the functions reserved only for women.

He had the extraordinary idea to propose that a regal and elegant ball be organized, that it be a landmark in the magnificent history of depraved men, and that the entire caravan of those bastard beings participate, that they come dressed elegantly as women, and that they also invite the most disgraceful guests to give greater excitement and glitter to the soirée.

And this nonsensical proposition was accepted.

The effeminate physiognomies of the young men became ardently animated; their enthusiasm surged forth in all its splendor; and a burst of applause and a hosanna of drunken pleasure spread throughout the dining room.

Mimí was imposing; he had untied the laces of his transparent bodice of blue silk, covered with diamonds, and showed off his naked shoulders, provoking desire in the languid eyes of his footman.

He proposed that they rent the house located at number 000 La Paz Street, which he would appropriately decorate, while the others would take care of hiring a first-rate orchestra and printing up invitations to be handed out to trustworthy neighbors.

And those parasites that dreamed of flirtations arose staggering from their seats, changed back from women's to men's clothes; and with groveling and weak voices, amid kisses and embraces, squeezing of hands and oaths of abominable perversion, they parted ways satisfied in the wee hours of the morning, while the city slept lethargically and only once in awhile the whistle of somnolent night watchmen could be heard in the asphalt streets.

A man, the fold of his cape drawn up over his eyes, stepped out from the threshold of a door near Mimí's house, where he had been hiding, and with a rapid gait, he went up to one of the drunken fops, and the youngster, believing him to be a friend of the group, offered him a cigarette and told him all their projects of filthy bastardy without thinking that he was the nuncio of their civil death and the author of the righteous prologue of those inflammable youths, repudiated young men, hated by the future and by all generations, scum of society and discredit to honorable men who are fervent lovers of the fecund beauties of women.

III.

Chapultepec Forest was swollen with an elegant and splendid gathering of hundreds of luxurious carriages, which were circulating on its leafy avenues, carrying within them aristocratic ladies, giving a majestic splendor to the crepuscular human hubbub.

In a luxurious open coach, Estela and Judith launched piercing stares at a coupé where a happy couple gently reclined.

"How happy Leopoldo and Rosaura are! Don't you think so, Judith?" said Estela.

"Yes, Estela," responded Judith, excited, "their honeymoon has been a delicious spring where love has settled in, bearing its fruit in the florid orchard of infinite joy."

"Are you envious, Judith?"

"Envious, Estela? . . . No, don't you believe it; when my eyes contemplate the happy couple of an incipient marriage, I feel a satisfaction that floods my soul with joy to think that very soon I will be happy."

"I think differently from you," responded Estela, with a touch of envy and hate in her voice, "upon contemplating, like you, a couple full of candor and joy, in my soul a tempest of jealousy, of envy, of egoism rumbles, and I suffer terribly to think that Mimí, who proclaims so often that he adores me, is cold when at my side, his words are icy, grossly indifferent! When in my meditations his figure and face seduce me, I adore him enthusiastically, I forge myself dreams of so many pleasures that I want to give life to his heart and infuse into his body virile and untamable energies of youth, that vigorous youth that so impassions ardent women."

"Well, in that case," replied Judith, "I don't envy you, Estela; my burning heart that spills over with the dreams of a volcanic passion, in which my desires seek a perfect ideal, a sublime ideal, have found it in Ninón, who is all love, all goodness and heart.

"Young, vigorous, lover of strength that he is, he has whispered into my ears divine and poetic words of an enchanting tenderness; he has made me a visionary in my nights of vaporous fantasies, and in my solitary vigils, where in each thought of the future, he is there, to satisfy my desires and to crown the success of my future reveries.

"His strong voice seems like the sound of the entrancing harmonies of a viola; his very fine manners enchant me and his graceful and Herculean figure utterly relieves the anxiousness of virgins like me who dream of marriage.

"Nonetheless, Estela, like you, I am also an unhappy woman who begs for his caresses; I have felt a volcano of jealousy in my soul and, more cautious than you, I'm paying a man who was formerly a police detective to follow Ninón's every step in order to completely enlighten me as to what is going on with him.

"This morning my maid gave me a letter from the detective and I have been too cowardly to dare to open the envelope; I wanted to consult you and depending on the content of the letter, I wanted both of us to agree to work as a team.

"Ay, Estela! There are great pains in life that are incurable, and I don't wish to succumb because I detest pain. . . . I have a deer-like fear about opening the letter. . . . In the most intimate place in my soul I foresee a horrible cataclysm."

"Don't be afraid, Judith! Aren't I here at your side? Do you want me to open it?"

"Yes, Estela," responded Judith, visibly overwrought, "but let's go home soon; there we'll give it a read and overcome this horrible anxiety once and for all."

Estela gave orders to the coachman to return home with haste; the horses, goaded by the whip, threw themselves into a vertiginous sprint along Reforma Avenue and arrived promptly.

Estela and Judith got out of the carriage and entered the perfumed and elegant boudoir of Estela, anxious as they were to reveal to each other their impressions and find out the result of the letter.

. . .

The living room, tenuously lit by the last rays of late afternoon sunlight, took on a melancholically poetic look.

Seated face to face in fluffy chaises longues, and agitated by a most animated conversation, Estela and Judith, made desperate by mixed feelings of fatalism, disgrace and the ruins of a love that both had believed to be lasting, plotted out their projects.

"And if in the letter," interrupted Estela, "we are presented with irrefutable, condemning proof against Mimí and Ninón, would you hesitate to take revenge, Judith?"

"I don't know, Estela," Judith responded gravely, "Open the letter, read it, and once we know its content I will reply appropriately."

So, Estela, with a premonition of great pains, tore open the envelope, unfolded the letter, and with a vibrant voice, with that feminine virility that a woman possesses in an endeavor of rage, she read clearly and deliberately:

"My respectable lady:

Your fears have not been groundless.

Step for step I have been following the movements of Sr. Ninón, making myself into his most implacable pursuer. You are paying me well for my news and I hope you will compensate me liberally for this information, which will surely be of great interest to you.

I have had to go through great difficulties to investigate the life of Sr. Ninón and I have used up all my sleuthful wiles, spending money whose sum you will find in the detailed note which I have attached.

In Chapultepec Forest, in the 'Maison Dorée,' in the theaters, in the casinos, and in the gatherings of greatest renown among the aristocracy, it caught my attention that Sr. Ninón is inseparable from Sr. Mimí, whom you know.

Piqued by curiosity, I have learned that Sr. Mimí and Sr. Ninón have a bad reputation among their friends and servants, except for a few who like to use the following pseudonyms, if they can be called that, and they are the Señoritos Blanca, Star, Virtue, Modesty, Carola, and Margarita.

Not missing any detail of his life, and drawing conclusions from the manners and tastes of those gentlemen, I have come to understand that Sr. Ninón appreciates them too much, much too much, I mean . . . he fancies them with great fire, with so much fire that I fear he is burning himself and that he is descending into a vice from which some young prostituted men suffer in that society in which you live.

I am neither a liar nor a contemptible informer in my sad profession, as are many of my colleagues. No, Srta. Judith. Nor do I belong to the dregs of wretches who stain and smear honorable reputations; but in this case, given that you are paying me splendidly, I believe and assure you affirmatively that Sr. Ninón and Sr. Mimí were not born to adore you and Srta. Estela.

Believe this truthful letter: Sr. Ninón loves Sr. Mimí with all the power of his heart.

Am I seeing things? . . . Am I an imposter? . . . No, young lady, I tell the truth in all its nakedness.

They embrace, they kiss, they have an affection that is too fraternal, that transcends all limits of friendship.

And there is still more, Señorita.

On Sunday, the little gentlemen, Sr. Ninón and Sr. Mimí, met; they dined gaily, drank a lot of wine, and . . . prepare yourself to believe this: they dressed up as women, improvised a little dance with the young Star playing the piano, the little party ending at a very advanced hour of the night.

Faces painted, they came stumbling—because of the effects of alcohol—out of Mimí's house when the dawn began to stretch in its astral bed.

I spied on them in front of Mimí's house, hidden in the dark threshold, and when they came out I followed them in the street, and when one left the group to take a different route, I came out to meet him and we chatted.

He thought I was one of the brotherhood and he told me that he had been carousing and they had been dancing dressed up as women, and that within a few days they will be throwing a grandiose ball in the house at number 000 on La Paz Street, which is unoccupied, and that there will be an Art Nouveau raffle, yielding a happy prize to the winner.

If only you had heard the enthusiasm with which he spoke, and Sr. Mimí was going in full feminine gala along with Sr. Ninón in rigorous formal wear.

It's not too much to tell you that I am invited and that I will do my best to attend in order to inform you of the outcome.

If I can offer you anything at all, I beg you to feel free to ask your humble servant, who respectfully kisses your hands,

Scorpion Claw"

"Is such ignominy possible, Estela?" asked Judith, indignant, "Mimí, that young man so full of life, of happiness, of money, is it possible for him to change roles from man into beast, by means of filthy and degrading debauchery?"

"I conceive," said Estela, desperately, "that a man like Mimí, spoiled by fortune, accepted into our high aristocracy, might be fickle with women, but to say that he has exchanged woman's caresses, man's fundamental source of delight, for the gross aberrations of pederasts, that, Judith, never passed through my ardent and visionary mind.

"In my fantasies, in the reveries of my imagination, he has always figured as the man who would fulfill the world of my desires and my grand aspirations.

"His seductive face filled me with pride when I was with my friends, and I thought I had found a superiority without limits dreaming of an earthly paradise where only he was the God of my pleasures.

"Yes, I dreamed only of him. . . . I thought that my life intertwined with Mimí's would be eternal kismet, that it would be serenaded with psalms by a chorus of archangels the day that at the altar, with my body in an elegant white gown covered in orange blossoms, I would exhibit my gallant fiancé like a sublime acquisition before the multitude . . .

"Oh, what shame I will have to experience! What whispers will come to invade my ears, and what caustic satires will lash at me! And my pride will fall tearfully beaten down from the pedestal of its grandeur.

"Into the underworld of shame and desperation, my pleasant daydreams will fall, mutilated, and the lush roses of the most sublime ideals of my existence will fall plucked of their petals into the mud where debauched infamy wallows!

"Ah! But his civil death will be eternal; in my soul, vengeance rumbles, a huge vengeance that reduces to impotence that imposter who erected a senseless passion in the depths of my soul.

"My moral fall will see its rehabilitation, and his fall. . . . His fall will be the most degrading and shameful!

"Everyone will know, Judith; I will show them, if they want, the letter from the detective; I will circulate his degeneration throughout our society until he is reduced to impotence, until he emigrates from the city and then, only then, will my vengeance be satisfied.

"How we women err in our flirtations! We admire the exterior, adore a seductive face, glitter dazzles us, and we fall vanquished when we should be the victors.

"I, the eminently erotic woman; I, who guarded my amorous day-dreams to enjoy them by his side; I, whose whole world of fortune was for him . . . for a pansy who spurns my supreme tenderness for that of those repulsive and shameful creatures!

"It makes me nauseous to think of the disgusting behaviors of Mimí, and I will not stoop so low as to meet with him. I will write him definitively to conclude these indecorous relations, locking myself up in a profound silence, and my determination from now on is inalterable!"

. . .

"And you, Judith," asked Estela in conclusion, after a short moment of silence, "will you avenge yourself, too? Shall we unite to unmask those scoundrels?"

"We'll soon speak at length about the subject, my dear Estela," responded Judith with a hushed and sinister voice, "I am quite nervous, and the best thing I can do is go home. We will meet tomorrow afternoon; I will tell you the result of my decision then."

"Are you leaving, Judith?"

"Yes, Estela, I'm leaving; and I only ask that, in these moments of tribulation in which our spirit wrestles with disgrace, we try to be titans in our force of will, to defeat those monsters who branded with a blot of ignominy our beautiful life, which surges splendidly forth in the spring of our youthful reveries."

IV.

We have arrived like a gnome from a mythological legend in the splendid boudoir of Judith to bear invisible witness to her painful grief and her vengeful thoughts.

An ostentatious bedroom, cheerful, gay, and beautiful, with that suggestive beauty, white like a serene and limpid dawn; a bedroom like a fairy mansion, like the heaven of the cherubs of our fantastic reveries.

A boudoir decorated in Louis XV style; carpets and draperies of white satin; a nickel-plated bridal bed dispersing scintillating luster into the light; and on the surface of the mattress, a white quilt and overstuffed feather pillows with blue silk cases and huge lilac bows. A little dresser with a Venetian mirror; a coffee table artistically carved with filigree figurines; an exquisitely upholstered armchair, adorned with a white silk canopy; and a mahogany writing desk holding numerous love letters from her fiancé Ninón.

The nearby church clock has struck nine o'clock . . .

Judith has entered her bedroom and is alone, tearful and sad.

And underneath the transparent canopy, simulating the silvery mist of the night of a full moon, seated, her delicate white elbow resting on the plush arm of the easy chair, her expression vague, and a bitter smile painted on her carmine lips, Judith was spellbound by the arabesques of the carpet as she contemplated from time to time a porcelain flower pot from Saxony that adorned the room with lovely begonias.

Her dress embroidered in silvery grey accentuated the curves of her graceful princesslike body.

From her eyes fell ardent tears, and her moist pupils rose up to look at the golden framed portrait of Ninón, imagining him to be smiling amorously.

And . . . one by one, with vertiginous speed, like an overflowing torrent, the tears came pouring out, interspersed with muffled sighs and virginal laments.

And as if swept by a hurricane, all her memories of the past, her dreams of pleasure and innocent love came rushing through her feverish imagination.

Her present was invaded by massive thick clouds, dimming the sky of her fortune; in the depths of her soul resonated painful laments and interminable sighs as tears of fire rolled from her eyes.

And the future, her dream future full of enchantments and fulfillments of happiness, died sterilely, with an agonic, harrowing death rattle, without a new dream, nor a hope, nor a wave saturated in faith sprouting in its place.

The spring of her ideals faded to a close and soon turned to winter preceded by phantasms of lugubrious deliriums, killing the triumphs and glories of her ardent soul, extinguishing in a single blow the resplendent light that illuminated the Eden of all her happiness.

Ah!! . . . but in her soul rumbled an Etna, which formidably erupted, covering the ignominious past with candescent ashes.

She would send for Ninón immediately, and there, alone, face to face, she would repudiate him, she would expel him, slapping him in the face with her vengeance and her contempt.

And determined to put an end to that relationship, she rang the bell, and after a few minutes, her maidservant appeared.

Judith went to the desk and took out a perfumed card, and wrote to Ninón asking him to come and see her immediately; and handing it to her servant, she said, "Have one of the footmen take this to Sr. Ninón's house and tell him he will wait to accompany him here."

When the maid left, Judith sat down again in her easy chair, and holding her head in her hands, she sobbed bitterly, with that painful weeping of a vain woman whose lofty heart senses the impossible, the irremediable, and curses her bad luck, her life, the incurable pain that would make anyone whose soul is filled with a fictitious grandeur sob like a child.

V.

It is eleven P.M.!

A serene night, its ethereal curvature splashed with diamantine stars, the moon standing out in its paleness.

In the poetic quarters of Judith, there is a torrent of electric light; she has taken pains to ensure that there be a profusion of light and has lit every lamp, as is her custom on days of grand receptions.

Ninón and Judith are face to face!

"You have summoned me urgently, Judith," Ninón was saying, looking on her with tenderness, "and here you have me, my dear, as always, loving and ready to prove that I adore you."

"That you adore me, Ninón?" Judith replied ironically.

"Do you doubt it, Judith, when you know that you are my only creed, my sole dream?"

"Liar, liar, Ninón!" exclaimed Judith in the paroxysm of choler.

"I'm lying, Judith?" responded Ninón with hypocrisy, "Have I not given you a thousand proofs of my ineffable fondness? Haven't I deposited on you and only you everything of the most noble, of the most grandiose, of the most venerable that I had stored in my soul?"

"You are an imposter, Ninón; you believed that because of the love that I profess for you, you would accomplish what you proposed, and that you would barter my nobility and pride for the love of the streetwalker who sells her caresses for one of your smiles, for one of your sighs, and for one of your incendiary gazes.

"But you were wrong; neither have I fallen from my lofty position in society, nor have I lost my dignity nor my pride; nor have I felt for you nor for anyone else the yearning desire that is woman's perdition, and stain on her purity, no; I worshiped you, yes, as few women, no matter how ardent, know how to love; but I am looking for a man who has never fallen into the precipice of vileness.

"And you are unworthy, miserable, degenerate; your instincts are criminal and bastardly.

"You seek, infamous Ninón, in orgiastic dinners, affections like that of Mimí, Modesty, Virtue, Star, and I don't know how many more men, who have brought to the world a sign of disgrace and who serve as passive instruments for you, for you who are in the vigor of a youthful existence.

"And you tarnish and profane that life with men like you, with men . . ."

"But, what are you saying, Judith?" interrupted Ninón, "Have my enemies, those who appear to be friends and who know I love you, perhaps prejudiced you? But no . . . no, Judith; I don't know what men you are talking about, not even their names. . . . Why are you telling me this, my dear?"

"Because, I repeat," answered Judith, "you are an imposter, Ninón; because everything noble that you have has turned into vile baseness."

"Judith!" whispered Ninón, pleadingly.

"Yes, Ninón," Judith went on, "I'm going to be frank once and for all with you.

"When we met and began our love affair, I believed you to be worthy, good, and noble.

"I knew that you had been wild and that you enjoyed Don Juan style excitement, and although I felt jealousy boiling in my breast, I allowed you everything because I assumed that one day, tired of your adventures and philandering, you would come to me, submissive and amorous, and your caresses and thoughts would be only for me.

"And I loved you, I adored you, Ninón; at your first insinuation, your first pained complaint, I would have kissed your forehead and wiped away your tears; with my tenderness I would have quieted the beasts of your heart, disappointed and weary from so much drunken pleasure.

"The first kiss you gave me I felt on my lips like an ardent, erotic, immaculate balm; it reverberated in the most intimate corners of my soul, making it tremble with joy, I believed that it would be the symbol of the insoluble union of our souls.

"How many times in my powerful reveries did my mind break through the gates of reality on the wings of a fantasy turning this room into a royal palace while, wrapped in white gauze, a consoling angel dropped down to me bringing you to my side, escorted by a group of cherubs who planted the most chaste kisses on my forehead, and sang in a beautiful chorus, tremulous and melodious like a nuptial hymn?!

"But you broke the mysterious enchantment of my innocence with your bastardly actions of impurity.

"You have swarmed in the midst of vice and crime, exhibiting yourself grotesquely among actresses and streetwalkers, and not satisfied, you prostituted yourself to the point of plunging into the swamp where pigs are ashamed to wallow for fear of soiling themselves.

"And not only Mimí and those young degenerates whom you claim not to know have satisfied your venal desires, but you have even prostituted your servants, initiating them into that life of depravity in which man loses decorum, dignity, and pride.

"You, Ninón, are the agent of those disgraceful usurpers of womankind, and the stigma of dishonor will fall upon you . . ."

"Listen to me, Judith," begged Ninón ashamedly, "but I love you, it is all a lie!"

"You repeat that you love me, Ninón?" snapped Judith, "But I know you too well; you are so hypocritical and so prostituted that you need armor to shield you, and the victim sacrificed on an altar of shame would be me.

"You wanted to join your name to mine in order to enter into a matrimony that could only end with your treasuring my millions only to squander them with those knaves while using my honorable name to keep up appearances in the society in which we live and which, disgracefully, is just as prostituted and hypocritical as you are.

"Yes, you wanted us to appear radiant with happiness for the masquerade of this demanding blue blooded society; while at home where intimacies are amalgamated, where passions are unleashed, where free rein is given to pain and pleasure, where good souls caress each other, no, Ninón, at home there would be nothing but damnation; there, my pride would be beaten down by fear of social scandal; there, there would be only unhappiness, adultery, degradation! . . ."

"Listen to me Judith, hear me out! I need to prove to you that all this is a lie . . . that I adore you . . . that . . ."

"Enough, Ninón, enough of this comedy; it is useless for you to try and convince me; from this instant, everything is over between us. . . . Get out, get out, Ninón!"

"Judith, my love, listen to me!" Ninón begged anew.

"Get out of here you miserable man! Get out of here right now or I will call my servants to throw you out with a whipping," said Judith arrogantly while her eyes shot him a sinister look.

And Ninón, shamed, trembling, and pale, left that apartment with the burden of scorn on his shoulders, and on taking the last step through the threshold of the door, he turned his face back and his eyes met those of Judith, which emitted glaring rays of inextinguishable hatred.

VI.

Judith had barely left Estela's house when Estela went to a stylish desk and wrote a long letter to Mimí in which she told him everything she knew, and ended by repudiating him and breaking off their love affair forever.

Once she had sent the letter off to its destination, she dropped into an armchair and raised her hands to her bitterly crying eyes.

The light from the electric bulbs fell full across her face, and rays of moonlight penetrated through the window of her room, poetizing that most elegant abode.

She suffered immensely. The recently opened wound seemed incurable to her.

A torrent of Luciferian thoughts of vengeance against that bloody joke of her destiny sprouted from her haughty aristocratic breast.

The strophes of the poem of her love life, those sweet and tender strophes, vanished from her life, as tyrannical phrases surged in their place; the cry of the mocking mob of friends who had envied her before wounded her ears.

Her opulent and splendorous fantasies extinguished themselves at the spate of reality, and their mysterious magnificence withered like flowers in that terrible winter of supreme deceptions.

And like a phantom came the tedium, covering up the jealous pachyderm of pain, thirsty from gloomy disillusionments.

Her vanity, that stupid women's vanity, fell mutilated at her feet; and in the immense pain of her soul, she damned that society, a thousand times phony, a thousand times hypocritical and disloyal, that appeared radiant before the demanding multitudes of noble birth, while in its intimacies it hid its miseries, its bloody dramas, its tragedies, and its crimes.

She cursed the miserable human condition with fury.

In her social contact with the elegant world, she had met Mimí; her friends had vouched for him enthusiastically and everyone knew she adored him.

And now, the most crude mockery, the most piquant whispering, and the gossip of those snobbish despots would fall on her, infesting her sick heart with their infectious breath.

That society pardons nothing because it has neither feelings nor shame.

Ay! and the emptiness would take form around her. But she resolved to overcome her pain by herself; she would suffer less that way; she would see herself excluded from that caravan of vain women who hide their horrible misery beneath lace silken dresses; and in whose every facet of joy lurk a perfidy and a crime.

On learning of her disgrace, that swarm of harlequins and boulevard vagabonds, of ignorant dandies who pestered her with their insensitive pretensions, would disappear as well.

But she was grand, energetic, relentless, vengeful.

She would understand that Mimí would never return to the flock of honor because everyone who prostitutes himself in the fountain of depravity suffers the consequence of laziness, egoism, and unbridled passions that shake and palpitate with vibrations of impotence . . .

Estela, beautifully pale, with the reflection of her rage and of her lofty vengeance in her face, looked like an apocalyptic angel who foresaw Mimí's shameful end.

And in the hazy atmosphere of these fantasies of a dethroned princess, she bore a mystery of indefinable desperation that made her launch a copious cry, injurious screams like the howl of a helpless hyena, sublimated by the ire of her vengeance.

VII.

The house marked number 000 on La Paz Street was decorated festively within.

On the patio of the house there are two lateral stairways with a third in the center that leads into the house, which is divided into two large rooms; in the middle of the patio there is a fountain made of Chiluca stone; the house's interior rooms are spacious and pleasingly decorated.

The banisters of the stairways are adorned with garlands, and the larger interior room, with crowns of gardenias and *panneaux* of daises and white roses, as well as innumerable colored bandoleers spread over the walls.

Ninón and Mimí, the party's organizers, were extremely happy and waited impatiently for the happy moment when the din of the soirée would begin.

They spoke excitedly and promised each other ineffable joys and exalted sensations.

"Have you arranged everything, my Ninón?" Mimí asked him tenderly.

"Everything, Mimí." Ninón replied amiably, "The orchestra, which is one of the best, will be along shortly; I gave the invitation cards for our intimate friends to Star; and I gave the others to your manservant for him to hand out in cantinas among strangers who, attracted by the novelty, won't have any problem about coming and enjoying themselves for awhile."

"And the wines and sandwiches, are you having them prepared?" Mimí asked.

"Everything is ready," answered Ninón, utterly satisfied.

"So, only our personal touch is missing," said Mimí,

"Oh! And how elegant you will look in your princess's skirt with its low cut silk bodice. You will look like a queen, my lovely Mimí," said Ninón with a flattering tone.

"And have you decided not to wear a woman's dress, handsome Ninón?"

"No, my dear. Don't you know I'm your little husband?" responded Ninón with a grotesque grin.

"But you will perfume your hair and your silky moustache, won't you, little one?" asked Mimí eagerly.

"Yes, Mimí, to make you happy, I'll do whatever you want . . ."

"Promise, Ninón?" asked Mimí coquettishly.

"Don't I love you," asked Ninón, "as one loves a virgin under an infinite smiling sky, full of inexplicable pleasures?

"Haven't I," he went on, "given up everything for you? Even the hand of Judith, who adored me so? . . . Aren't you satisfied, my precious Mimí?"

"Ay! My God what a barbarity!" responded Mimí, blushing, "I don't deserve all that, Ninón; but you know that my love for you is inalterable, immense, delicious . . ."

"That's why I adore you," said Ninón, "That's why I make you happy; that's why on this happy night you will be the only little partner I'll take in my arms, you will be the only one who receives the tenderness I feel for you; but if you smile at, if you glance at, if you speak to anyone else . . . , then, Mimí, . . ."

"Are you jealous, Ninón?"

"And do you expect me not to be?" asked Ninón, "if from now on you are the only love remaining for me? Women are evil, vain, selfish; in exchange for a smile, they ask for the sky; for a kiss, a treasure; and later when they have us imprisoned in their webs and we are their slaves, our heads buried and our freedom tossed away, we trade our love for hatred! . . . You aren't like that Mimí, you are constant, loving, sincere and noble; for a kiss you want another in return, for a smile another smile; for my love you give another bigger, more eternal, more real, more powerful love.

"Poor women! Proud, deluded women who seek only slaves and beggars of love!" Ninón finished, full of wrath.

"Ay, Ninón!" Mimí said to calm him down, "For holy God's sake, don't get angry, don't get riled up. I'm at your side as always, with the answer to your every whim."

And while a hypocritical tear trickled out of Mimí's eyes, he furiously embraced Ninón, feeling happy to be in the arms of his fiancé(?).

VIII.

Modesty, Virtue, Blanca, Margarita, and Carola are in Star's elegant bedroom preparing their toilette for the ball of La Paz Street.

Modesty was dressed up in a magnificent women's outfit of red silk with black lace, showing off, with a low-cut top, his skinny neck with its prominent Adam's apple protruding, and from his back, like a promontory, his naked shoulder blades daubed with base powder, his blonde powdered wig, an enormous wide-brimmed hat, with a museum of birds falling over his left shoulder.

Virtue wore a white outfit of Spanish leather with a long skirt covered in orange blossoms, a black wig that contrasted with his blue eyes, a lace hat, and his hands played with a finely crafted fan.

Blanca wore a cream colored dress, transparent and covered with lilac ribbons and lace, slippers embroidered in gold, black gloves, blonde wig, and braids, and a black hat; his chubby dark-skinned shoulders, his beady eyed face, his mouth of a thick-lipped African, and his Roman nose, gave him the air of a female gorilla, riotous and disturbing.

Margarita wore a blue silk dress, a beautiful robe, under which the toe of a foot shod in slippers of the same color with silver plated buckles and a little bow *à la mignon* barely visible; the low-cut neckline was interesting, revealing a prominent breast, utterly white (because of excessive makeup), with two large ribbons hanging from either side, and his enormous eyes, his columbine nose and his diminutive mouth standing out, his face painted with great artistry, with that masterly artistry customary in harlots, which made him look like a low-class circus clown.

Carola had on a very simple but elegant muslin dress; behind his black wig could be seen a white bonnet; he also wore a white bibbed apron with blonde laced edging; his very short skirt showed off well-shaped calves, his fretted hose stuffed with cotton, patent leather high-heeled shoes, and well-placed false hips; his feminine voice and manners made him so ridiculous that on looking at him one couldn't help laughing and recalling some comic scene from San Balandrán Island.[4]

We have intentionally saved the description of the toilette and clothing of the spiritual and nubile Star, the pale little duke, as his friends called him, for last; the wretched youth was coming out for the first time that night to the society of the degenerated, the prostituted, and the shameless.

A black wig covered his curly hair, gracefully adorning his face. His limpid black, shining, and lively eyes gave him the charming air of an immaculate virgin. His thick-lipped mouth featured two rows of clean white teeth, and his cheeks, two seductive dimples, that beardless fifteen-year-old adolescent was most effeminate looking. His dress was fitted tightly to his small and vigorous body. He wore a white baby dress; a small and high-cut robe, fretted with Brussels lace; a silken bonnet laden with transparent lace; a ribbon tied at his neck and another wider one at his waist tied into a great bow; white hose and black shoes with silk pompoms; expensive rings on his fingers and a pear necklace at his throat.

His look was that of a virtuous little girl, playful, innocent, and spoiled.

Now, the young men all ready, covering their bare shoulders with large elegant feminine cut overcoats, they stepped outside and got into elegant carriages that awaited impatiently to take them to La Paz Street, to number 000, where pleasure, applause, and caresses lay in wait and smiling Bacchus, Cupid, and Priapus prepared to solemnize that great initiation of the spiritual (?) Star.

IX.

Don Pedro de Marruecos!

His name alone indicates the magnitude of his popularity.

Tall, strapping, white skinned, with an abundant blonde moustache, turned up at the ends, he was a distinguished gentleman.

Immensely rich and married to a beautiful lady of noble stock, he was one of the most prominent figures of our tale.

He spent money lavishly and magnificently; his lofty coach was one of the most elegant in the Metropolis; his pure-blooded horses were the best and most splendid in the Hippodrome of Peralvillo.

In France he had provoked the admiration of the Parisians, and in his extravagances, in exotic Bacchanals, he learned a great deal, of the most unbridled prostitution.

He began with the conquest of the humble *grisette*[5] on whom he threw away a great deal of money.

He continued climbing the heights of pleasure and he imparted luxurious lifestyles and magnificent houses to his exploitative *cocottes*.[6]

He went to Italy and there, in the land of art and music, he procured the caresses of notable feminine artists. He improvised soirées where the sopranos of an archangel's voice delighted his ears, while he, delicately sprawled under a canopy, looked on, entranced, with his half-opened eyes, at the seductive movements of his sopranos, while at times he closed them with indolence to hear the voice of his nightingales, leaving his imagination to fly to other worlds of great pleasure.

He visited Spain: Andalucía evoked in his ardent imagination the delights of the paradise he created, and the voluptuous dances, the charm, the gaiety of the Iberian girls excited him and he died, slowly died of disappointment, satisfying his venal desires and his drunken ecstasies, and ruining his organism with the excess of lewd pleasures.

Tired of contemplating the splendid light of art, weary of pleasure of the highest degree, he came to Mexico, bearing the disillusionment and premature death of his ideals, after having lived so fast.

Life was unbearable for him.

He saw women as useless and despicable beings, incapable of creating new pleasures for him, and cursed Nature because feminine delights were so short lived and insatiable.

His impotent body screamed for more pleasure, more excitement, more inconceivable delights.

And all was in vain; from the top of the ladder, he was descending to the lowest level of lowness, to the level of brutes.

Now for him women were nothing more than laughable and despicable sarcasm.

And failing to live up to his duties, his dignity, his mission as a civilized man, he was a slave to his passions and his unruly appetites.

New delights germinated in his heart; he saw the frightful ruins of the past as steamy, pestilent, and there surged up in him the gorged beast of vengeance, blind and irascible, and he plunged down the criminal slope into an endless abyss of blackness and pain.

He began frequenting secret circles of degraded beings and believed he found himself a new world.

And then . . . and then he degenerated, inevitably degenerated . . . and fell into that whirlpool that pulled at him like vertigo . . . he prostituted himself and reached the bottom of the abyss.

On the night that concerns us, gleaming with elegance, perfumed, his blonde moustache curled up at its ends, he had himself driven from his property to the house on La Paz Street to dispel his boredom and to fall into execrable debauchery, while his grand and noble wife slept innocently dreaming of him in a world of holy illusions and of a delicious future on the glorious road of her happiness.

X.

In the best and most popular cantinas of the Metropolis, several local residents were given invitation cards for a ball and raffle by a young man with languid eyes, winsome, effeminate, and ceremonious.

The novelty consisted of an Art Nouveau raffle and an elegant ball.

Many of the youthful regular revelers, attracted by the ballyhoo of the cards, amid joke after joke, with drink after drink in their stomachs, took the local coaches bound for the famous La Paz Street.

The orchestra, not the best but, rather, on the mediocre side, composed of various somnolent professors (?), filled the air of the ballroom with varied pieces of music for dancing.

In the next room, comfortably equipped, was the bar, with a rickety counter, well stocked with good wines, various cases of champagne, and a good provision of sandwiches.

It must have been around ten o'clock when several luxurious carriages arrived at the door, out of which what appeared to be ladies in showy, fancy dresses descended.

They were the young men, Star, Modesty, Virtue, Carola, Blanca, and Margarita.

In the ballroom there arose a murmur of curiosity and many of those present turned their attention to the entrance to contemplate the faces of the ladies (?).

The seductive ladies (?) had barely passed through the doors of the ballroom when the drunken and Bacchic court of erstwhile admirers greeted them with an enthusiastic round of applause and a guttural "viva" that spread in sonorous waves through the room; at that instant some of the orchestra members played a salute worthy of the most enthusiastic Punch and Judy encore.

A rattan bridal chest was reserved as the place of preference for the ladies to sit.

After that, at various intervals, other ladies (?) arrived, although not dressed up with the same elegance.

The little servant, for his part, also an enthusiast, and in close contact with all the servants of those men, among whom there were many initiates into the secret love, had also formed his squadron of effeminate beings.

They arrived in rickety old coaches, with coachmen, lackeys, and especially manservants and table servants, who were going to share democratically with their masters the venerated pleasures of their heaven forged from the joys of the new earthly paradise, from which they partook as sterile plants for the good seed, but nonetheless producers of immorality and savagery.

Poor degraded beings!

None of the attendees invited by the cards handed out in the cantinas had noticed that they had had the wool pulled over their eyes, the dresses being so well made, and the feminine manners so well mimicked.

But until then no movement had been so out of the ordinary in the ballroom as the arrival of an interesting and popular personage.

"Don Pedro de Marruecos!" pronounced a strong and sonorous voice.

And with that cry, all leaped from their seats and gathered into two groups, opening up a path for Don Pedro who entered majestically, investigating the ambiance of the room with his eyes, turning toward the ladies (?) and greeting them with amorous affection.

But despite the arrival of Don Pedro de Marruecos, a longing invaded everyone's countenance; the ladies (?) performed comically and the Pierrotesque laughter spread in gay murmurs.

Something was missing from the party.

The queen (?) of the party was there, with her modest baby dress, courted by a caravan of gallant young men.

But Ninón and Mimí, the hosts of the party were missing.

Star was admired with curiosity; his virginal candor was irresistibly attractive and there was no lack of gallant young men offering him drinks of spiritual champagne.

Don Pedro de Marruecos went and sat down at his side, greedily caressing his hands, and staring into his eyes as if wishing to hypnotize him with a gaze impregnated in burning fire, in that volcanic fire that makes the heart palpitate and comprehend the inspiration of a man vitiated in all its horrors.

XI.

As the electric lights were twinkling in their colored bulbs and candelabras with a multitude of stearin candles were giving off magnificent light; as the *panneaux* of gardenias and daisies dispersed their waves of perfume and the orchestra was playing the prelude to a march, the Herculean Ninón and the timid Mimí entered triumphantly into the ballroom.

Of the most unanimous, uproarious, prolonged, and spontaneous enthusiasm was the ovation with which they were received, as the orchestra, enthusiastic and playful, played a military salute.

Mimí, carrying himself like a princess, softly swinging his padded hips, and tenderly languishing with a sylph-like gaze, seized Ninón's arm, making friendly remarks.

He was the most elegant in his dress and his hairdo; the long train of his skirt overloaded with Brussels lace, he gathered it up with his left hand, pulling it tightly to his body in order to exhibit his curves, and leaning on Ninón, he toured the room smiling at his little friends with a graceful demeanor.

The ball had begun!

The conductor, standing in the center of the room, announced the first number, a sonorous, rhythmic, and lively waltz.

Don Pedro de Marruecos offered his arm to Star, while Ninón and Mimí, swift and light, mixed in with the other dancers, twirling vertiginously.

Carola, Blanca, Modesty, Virtue, and Margarita, affectedly making their suitors beg for their attentions like chaste young ladies, ceded their hands to a thousand requests of friendly enthusiasts of their class.

And the pleasure was infinite, sweet, satisfying.

There they danced with immense insanity, ridiculous in all their gross falseness.

The ballroom was swollen with spectators; those who had come from the cantinas, avid for novelty, were departing for the most part, annoyed, leaving just a couple of stragglers here and there, incoherent and drunk, more interested in drinking wine than in having fun with the apocryphal pretty faces.

The ballroom, having cleared out a little due to those departing, now was left with mainly birds of the same feather, the community content to be among its own, and the soirée went on at its absolute climax, resembling a Pompeian ball of Roman decadence.

Fanning the fire in which the young men burned, they made extravagant movements in the dance, and inflamed like brazen strumpets, they exhibited their false charms with captivating vehemence amidst scandalous impudicities.

The interval between dance numbers was covered primarily by bawdy songs; some, accompanied by the leading bassist, sang their immodest songs, which upon the final note were greeted by a round of applause.

Mimí, excited, sang as well; his high-pitched voice performed a heartfelt and ridiculous romantic ballad that the audience felt merited an encore.

Ninón felt satisfied; from time to time he contemplated Mimí with delight, and his robust youth shuddered; and violating all modesties, he embraced him effusively, placing his lips of fire upon the fresh lips of his companion. Ninón was famished, voracious for caresses and kisses.

Don Pedro de Marruecos, the elegant *amateur*,[7] felt a wave of pleasing harmonies upon hearing the clear and well toned voice of the young Star, carefully embellished with his modest baby's dress.

He squeezed Star's hands with fervent vehemence; he felt a Satanic attraction when the youth dressed up as a baby let the morbidities of his body peek out.

And with elegant style and harmonious voice, Don Pedro asked him tenderly, "Would you love me, Star?"

And Star, like a shy nymph, responded weakly, "Ay! Don Pedro, who knows?!"

"Do you think I won't make you happy?" insisted Don Pedro.

"No, Don Pedro," replied Star, "I need to consult my heart, and aside from your having your merits . . ."

"I will love you very much, Star; I will adore you to the point of delirium; you will have a house, a coach, luxury, so much luxury, many comforts. . . . Swear to me that you will love me. I promise you whatever you yearn for, whatever you want, my love."

And dialoguing into Star's ear with soft and cadenced whispers, Don Pedro was given over into ardent transport, sweetly grasping Star's hands as she listened to his declarations as a chant of adoration.

The honored page of Don Pedro's life disappeared below a chlamys full of pauperisms, and a corrupting page arose, full of delinquencies, full of twitches of his impotent nerves, amid the crumbling of his shame and his dignity as he fell once more from the lofty pedestal of his existence and his social position.

Whither lead the vices of men?

He kissed Star's fluttering eyelids, and in a delirious outburst, drew his burning lips to the young man's face and cheeks, and with his passion even more heated, Star lost himself in a long embrace, very long, ineffable, intoxicating, and histrionic like the affectation of his manners.

Meanwhile, in the ballroom, the excitement mounted.

Phosphorescent eyes, lewd eyes, languid eyes; false hips, undulant, slender, with their irreproachable curves; powdered painted faces; wigs marvelously adorned with ornamental combs encrusted in gold and fine jewels; calves well chiseled by dint of cotton and authentic amorphous leanness; false breasts, prominent and enormous, struggling to burst out of their prison; grotesque faces and feigned voices; all this together gave the orgy a macabre and fantastic air.

The hour of the raffle was near, the hour awaited with such impatience, with true impatience.

The prologue of the party had been splendorous; the apotheosis would be the most beautiful, the most practical, the most satisfactory, and the epilogue would close with a golden broach of their Bacchic orgy . . . at least that was how the revelers imagined it.

In the paradise of love, the thousand gradations of the brilliant ideals of their dreams sparkled ostentatiously.

XII.

It was early Sunday morning, November 17, 1901.

The supreme and solemn moment of the eagerly awaited raffle had finally arrived.

A bronze amphora placed on a table contained various little rolled up pieces of paper which would be removed one by one, leading up to the grand prize, and one by one every winner would give ardent kisses to the young man dressed as a baby, the spiritual Star. . . . The pen resists describing the twelfth prize.

The orchestra was playing *danzones* of Veracruz when the voice of Ninón announced that the raffle was commencing.

Everyone stopped dancing and lined up in two rows while Don Pedro prepared to pull out the winning numbers.

The "Art Nouveau" raffle announced in the invitations that had been handed out had nothing to do with any object of art, let alone . . .

The prostitution at its lowest degree let itself be mutilated ignominiously and closed its ears to the protests of men of conscience.

What to men of honor appears to be the filthiest, the most unbridled, the most miserable of vices, to those young men and their servants was the feast of the gods, and they had no scruples about sacrificing their modesty, their dignity, their shame to the dishonest vice that, like a sarcasm, insulted the law, the life, the civilization, the progress of all humanity along with Nature itself!

For every winning number that came out and that Don Pedro announced to those present, Star received as many kisses as were written on the piece of rolled-up paper.

There remained only one more number to be pulled: the grand prize, the number 12, and everyone's countenance was livid.

Here and there a drunk danced with pleasure in his place and looked at the number in his hands.

Star was pale, serene, and satisfied; he waited with resignation for the joyous hour in which they would play to his glory and in which the applause, the *viva*'s, the military salutes, and the toasts would rise crepitantly up like a triumphant symphony of his degradation.

To the tumult of pleasure and happiness was added the tumult of terror.

Don Pedro was slowly unrolling the last number when several coachmen and lackeys entered frightened, screaming, fear painted on their faces.

"The police!! The gendarmes are knocking at the door!!!"

A stick of dynamite tossed into the ballroom would not have caused so much panic among the revelers.

There were 44 people in the room who took not a single step to remedy the situation, nor daring to open the outside door of the house.

The police meanwhile were knocking loudly, violently, waiting for someone to open the doors and show them the permit for the party.

Don Pedro, without saying goodbye to anybody, and followed by two of his servants, sought an exit from which to escape, and found a ladder propped up against one of the patio walls; they climbed up to the roof and then he and one of his servants climbed down the same ladder onto the patio of the building next door that housed the workshops of the Lithographic Union, and disappeared into the darkness.

In the meantime, the other servant went back up the ladder to return it to its place and remained on the roof under the Valencian moon, after having saved his master, awaiting the outcome of the police's inquiries.

With such pounding on the door by the police, one of the less timorous resolved to open it, full of fear, his teeth chattering and his legs trembling.

The police finally entered and the majority of the revelers dispersed into the rooms of the other part of the house.

Some hid behind doors, others in the lavatories, others under an overturned tub; some attempted to climb into a stove, and others into the chimney.

Mimí's servant, utterly repentant, crossed himself and twisted a rosary in his hands.

Mimí sobbed bitterly; Ninón pouted and cracked the knuckles of his gloved hands.

Star, cynical, unabashed, waited calmly, impassively for the end of the comedy.

Everyone opened his eyes wide and proffered effeminate and grotesque exclamations in the following tenor: "Oh my God, what a state they have found us in! . . . Holy virgin of Miracles! . . . Miraculous child of Atocha! . . . Holy mother of Sorrow, save us! . . . Saint Pascual Baylon, Saint Nycomed, Saint Cyprian, hear us oh Lord!"

A drunk who was laid out across some chairs, half asleep, upon being wakened by one of the gendarmes, threw his arm around him, saying, "Another drink, my dear, my little heart of gold?"

The musicians, startled and confused, took their hats and picked up their instruments to leave.

But as the senior officer of the gendarmes saw that they had caged the cat, he ordered the gendarmes to apprehend everyone; the police sent reinforcements from the night reserve and a few moments later they had searched the house down to the last corner, apprehending 41 individuals, several of whom were dressed as women, and all of whom were conducted to the Police Station.

Don Pedro's servant had remained on the roof observing everything and when the police climbed up the same ladder that had saved his master, he had no choice but to take a cold bath, plunging into a tank that supplied water to the house, thereby miraculously saving himself.

XIII.

Dawn, that fantastic princess, half shadow, half soft and vague light, stretched haughtily with its divine tones of daybreak.

In the bluish curve of the horizon, millions of pale stars sadly blinked out and the moon, with its whiteness of a newly-wed bride, stood up straight with the last flashes of its greatness.

The vigorous loftiness of daylight triumphed brightly.

Winter, that implacable assassin of life, began to extend its cold cloak of north wind and snow.

The opulent inauguration of the filthy bacchanal of the house on La Paz Street had its sad epilogue in the filthy prison of the police precinct.

What an enormous transition! From the atmosphere saturated with perfume, from the decorated ballroom, from the hum of music, from the ardent kisses and caresses, to a vitiated and foul microbicide of an atmosphere; sinister rumors, deep sighs, and copious cries of immense pain.

A sad and grotesque scene; an image of vacant masculinities damning and detesting Priapus and Lampsacus, smoking cigarettes to console themselves, their smoke rings carrying up with them so many memories of the past . . . so many erotic desires consumed in desperation.

One by one they were called to make a statement, objects of laughter and contumely on the part of the guards who led them from the prison to the office.

There were those who dared to cry in front of the scribes whom they begged for mercy.

The spiritual Mimí cried his heart out as well; having confessed and been convicted, he had no choice but to suffer enormous shame and derision. He changed his name at the precinct house and awaited, numb and somnolent, the fatal outcome.

Star, the raffled virgin, laughed stupidly like those brazen harlots who have exercised their profession for so long in the immense emporium of prostitution.

A number of those who had stayed behind at the ball and those who were taken for such were those who had come with the invitations that had been given out in the cantinas, and though they protested energetically, it was no use, they had to prove it.

Ninón was the one who suffered most. He regretted his errors; he recognized that his ambition for luxury, his soft living, and the pernicious influence of his friends dragged him into dishonor.

He was sliding downward, impelled by his unbridled and furious desires, striving in vain to fulfill his pleasures, and it seemed to him to be too late to cleanse the impurities from his life; he felt his eyes haze over in tears, and in each burning teardrop, the regeneration of his existence was lost in the void of the unknown.

In his imagination, as if in a kaleidoscope, all his memories flashed by, and he saw the faces of his parents who, although proud and ridiculous in their dreams of pedigree and nobility, always loved him with infinite tenderness.

His mother, who adored him so, how she was going to weep; how she would suffer the shame and the whispers at the High Life.[8]

And Judith, the haughty courtesan who had loved him so, how she would enjoy his miseries and moral ruin; she would avenge herself terribly as wounded and proud women avenge themselves by repudiating the men they hate.

Then the future presented itself to him and it frightened him, he felt dread . . . yes, the future waved the black flag of his irremediable disgraces, and the spectral destiny of his fears sank in its insatiable hyena teeth . . . the most infinite desperation paralyzed him and he fell into a senseless lethargy, weakened by cowardice, by the fear of the rod of justice, that rod that flagellates the perverse in the name of a sacred law, the law that honorable society upholds so that it be respected.

This time the manly, incorruptible energy of the governor, who knew to punish the imposters who spurned good society and good habits, deserved the true praise of both the metropolitan press and society as a whole.

At approximately ten in the morning, in fancy dress, those pretty young men who had masqueraded in elegant ladies' garb, some provided with good brooms, others with barrels of water and steel watering buckets, went out chaperoned by a good number of police officers to clean a block of Arts Street near the police precinct.

And they were a sight to see, doing their job so well. A young lady would not have been able to do it with such art and such haste.

The most grotesque physiques were exhibited in the street, with their swollen eyes, looking downward, immodestly in some cases; they had taken off their wigs and earrings of brilliant stones, and they made people laugh looking at their sullied faces with their little twisted moustaches, their skirts gathered up, their embroidered high-heeled shoes; and with each movement of the broom, they exaggeratedly swung their hips, thereby powerfully provoking some of the spectators' satire and the sharpest of puns.

"You! Isn't your broom heavy for you?" one spectator said to another to ridicule those who were sweeping.

"Yes, you!" responded the other.

"Where do you live, lover boy?" one shouted.

"On Hydrangea Street, number Carnation!!" replied a ruffian with feigned glamour.

And in this tenor the immortal 41 were the butts of the most festive and cruel jokes.

Once they finished sweeping the street they were led to jail for registration, and the governor judged them with the promptness that their case demanded in order to quiet the voice of indignation of an outraged society.

Some who proved their innocence and that they had only gone with the desire to dance, ignorant of the scandalous presence of the effeminate men, were given their liberty after many negotiations.

Thanks to the exacting energy of justice, the others were con-signed into armed service, the Secretary of the Armed Forces determining that they were to be sent to Yucatán, not as soldiers, but instead as mess hall workers, or laborers assigned to do light fortification work.

In effect, all those consigned were taken on Wednesday, the twentieth of the same month to the same secretary's office to be registered and once they had fulfilled that requisite, they were sent off for one of the battalions engaged in the campaign against the Mayan Indians.

XIV.

On Thursday, November 21, 1901, at seven in the morning, on board a third-class train car, chaperoned by soldiers from the 24th Battalion, 19 of the individuals from the ball on La Paz Street were heading to Veracruz to be boarded onto the first steamship leaving for the Yucatán coast.

At Buenavista Station of the Mexican Railroad, which would take the *maricones* to Veracruz, a sizable group of curious onlookers had come early to see them go.

Our citizens are extremely curious; any topic that has caused a sensation preoccupies them and they only abandon it once their curiosity has been satiated and they have learned all the last details.

Star, Virtue, Modesty, Blanca, Margarita, and Carola marched among the other recruits, sad, heads bowed.

They bid farewell to their adored Mexico, to their families who were also crying, and upon their last goodbye, they spilt authentic and copious tears.

They left their comforts, their luxury, their pleasure emporium, their filthy sewer . . .

They would no longer cruise through Chapultepec Forest in their luxurious carriages, nor would they attend their laughable formal balls, nor would they park along Plateros Street in order to be seen in the company of aimless dandies who occupy themselves with whisperings, waving right and left to show off their fashionable outfits and demonstrating with huge grins that they are the ruin of the privileged classes.

Ninón and Mimí, also dejected, marched along mechanically.

When the train departed, Ninón heard a painful, suffocated scream, and turning around, he could barely make out the lovely face of Judith who held a handkerchief to her eyes to dry her tears.

Ninón came to hate his past of ignominy; he convulsively gritted his teeth, and his eyes burned with anger as he looked at Mimí, who was at his side, with a fiery, Mephistophelean look in which the most enormous belated, irremediable contempt sparked.

They arrived in Veracruz and were led to the Fortress of San Juan de Ulúa where they were isolated from the other prisoners in order not to rile up the cellblock with the obscene scandal of their crime.

In a few days, the second boat of the crew of the corvette Zaragoza took them aboard and brought them to the Norwegian cargo steamer Mercator, which was to sail then for Yucatán.

In the Port of Progreso, the Isla de Mujeres, the Port of Morelos, where the Mercator refueled, the Isla de Cozumel, and at the end of their journey at the Ascención bays, they were the objects of limitless curiosity of the simple folks of the coast.

Once they had arrived at the camp where the army was stationed in its struggle against the rebels, they were handed over to the Corps that were undertaking the campaign and were distributed among several companies to prepare food in the mess halls for the soldiers in some cases, and to dig trenches in others.

The exuberant vegetation, the ancient trees, the multitude of coconut palms and banana trees that gave the coastline its sublimity and of which an artist might dream consoled the young 41.

The sea, with its immense blue waves, softly bathed the shores at high tide, while a multitude of ships seemed to lose themselves plying into the immensity and among the waves.

The palm huts, some springing upward, others sunken in amid the thickest groves of trees, gave the flavor of cities of the ancient epoch in which Columbus discovered our young America.

Intermittent fevers, malaria, and vomiting were the incessant nightmare of the little men who upon remembering the bacchanal of deviation cried tears of blood and ironically cursed their fate.

The excessive heat and the plague of the gadflies made life unbearable for them.

Their squalid, famished, and sickly faces had nothing in common with the appearance they had in the Metropolis.

The sailors of the Zaragoza protected them, giving them their clothes to wash for ten cents, and always followed with insults.

Mimí was unrecognizable, demoralized; he had written first to his parents and they had remained silent. He then wrote a letter to Don Pedro de Marreucos, telling him of his tender pains, his insupportable suffering and his horrible martyrdom, but Don Pedro had died in an orgy as a consequence of alcoholic congestion; he turned to Ninón to make his captivity less unbearable, but was repudiated; Ninón, in contrast, had gone through a metamorphosis; he seemed to be the most resigned, but he regretted his deviations in the depths of his soul, deplored the first demonstration of brutishness that he had inflicted and promised to regenerate, ashamed of the vileness of his past life of orgies.

The captain trusted him to a detachment, which, sympathetic to him, separated him from the 41, assigning him to desk work for the troop.

His only idea was to escape; to look for an opportunity and go back home to his parents who were writing him very sad letters of sane advice.

When he contemplated the white clothing of the coastal dwellers, with their blue or red embroidered robes, their white headdresses with immense brims, so full of friendliness, charm, and grace, he thought of Judith, that ardent woman, so full of fire, and he, so full of regret, withdrew into a profound meditation.

He madly adored Judith and became desperate upon contemplating her in his imagination, so pure and lovely, lover and heroine; his eyes clouded over in tears and he recalled her final Olympic disdain and that infernal look of incommensurate hatred.

Translators' Interlude

At this point, the focus shifts inexplicably to the lives of Estela and Judith. Estela ends up falling in love with a working-class youth, to the chagrin of her parents, that is until he saves her life in a freak fire accident. She then marries him with parental approval and presumably lives happily ever after.

Meanwhile, Judith's life takes a different turn, as will be seen below. Her downfall allows the author to continue using the hyperbolic language of debauchery and perversion that he so enjoys.

As for the famous 41, once shipped off to Yucatán, they essentially disappear from the narrative. Despite the book's title, they are not its focus after Chapter XIV, with the exception of Ninón, whose name reappears in Chapter XXII, when Judith receives a letter from him.

XXII.

. . .

"Dearest Judith," Ninón said in the letter.

"Thanks to the sailor who so graciously offered to deliver this letter, I have been informed that you are in Veracruz, with your parents, for a brief time.

"I received the souvenirs you sent me, and believe me I am most grateful.

"The bread of exile, my love, is the bitterest of dishes.

"The language of sadness is my only confidant in these solitudes heated by ardent temperatures; the bays are very sad: many trees, many mountains, suffocating heat, and some terrible frights because I think often of the Maya Indian attacks.

"I have sought oblivion from my remembrances in my pain, and I have found it; I have suffered so much and believe that I am becoming purified.

"You can't comprehend what I suffer and what I have suffered; first your anger, your scorn, your loss; then revenge, degradation and misfortune.

"At all hours your image is engraved in my mind with indelible, sidereal features and I love you; yes, love you, Judith, with all the sincere expression of my soul. I love you because I know that virtue nests in your unblemished heart.

"If I didn't believe in the nobility of your actions and your modesty, I might have become mixed up into the rabble of the perverse, of the drunken, or believe it or not, I might have sought relief in suicide.

"But your heart is so big, so sincere and so loyal, that I have no doubt that you will forgive my youthful mistakes.

"My punishment has been immense, but my regeneration is even more immense.

"For you and only you I will be good; forgive my follies, my brutishness of times past . . . they were the blindness of my spirit, of my inexperience, of my disgrace.

"I will be your slave, I will be whatever you want me to be, provided that your forgiveness, impregnated of immaculate purity, be my salvation. If you forgive me, I will believe myself to be in the hands of God's Divine Justice, which redeems all men when pain and misfortune purify them in the asphyxiating atmosphere of the cruelest martyrdoms.

"You, who are so good, such a dreamer, and so sublime in your acts of forgiveness, please tear out the black page of the past and open your arms and your heart to the unhappy man whose only wish is to see himself illuminated by the sacrosanct dawn of your eternal redemption.

"The union of our beings will be the delightful life of my soul. Don't crumble my castles of grandness, don't turn the temple where I've deified you to dust, don't abandon the sterile land where I vegetate, where with your forgiveness my yearnings for transfiguration will bear the fruit of my happiness, and the rehabilitation of my dignity and my honor . . .

"Ninón."

. . .

Once she had finished reading the letter, Judith remained pensive for a moment; Ninón was regenerating, of that there could be no doubt; but she, pushed by destiny, had fallen into prostitution, preferring obscene pleasures over an honorable rehabilitation.

That night, after having been with various individuals, drinking wine, before going to bed, nearly drunk, she answered Ninón with the following letter:

"Ninón,

"Proud, like any blue-blooded woman, I will never forgive you.

"With Antonio, your most intimate friend, I eloped from my parental home, and when I sent you my ironic souvenirs, I was with him, in his arms, feeling the irresistible current of the flood of his caresses.

"Remembering you and reading your letter to me, I broke out in raucous guffaws of laughter because I hate you with all the powerful strength of my soul.

"The Judith that you knew has fallen and her lauded pureness has broken into a thousand splinters; I needed a man to mitigate my anxieties; you were loathsome, so I had to cede to the first impulse of Antonio's exhilarating passion.

"I needed a different atmosphere; I parody that life of dissipation that you led and that gave you pleasure, forging in your brain interminable gaieties, drunken binges of love, joining your arms with those of brazen courtesans, toasting with glasses overflowing with frothy wine, I needed an atmosphere that would warm my body and spirit . . .

"The cherub wings with which you dressed my ivory shoulder blades in your exalted imagination have been plucked out by impassioned hands that have left me drained and satisfied with divine delight.

"I've sought oblivion in everyday orgies and with wine I have erased the memory of our insipid love.

"The interminable poem of my sorrow burnt out amid shouts from the insatiable mob of buyers of my burning kisses.

"That is why I celebrate my fall with bacchanals of love, fever, and wine.

"I am the sinner who avenges you; I'm the one who indulges herself to the limit and afterwards returns to the fold so that some imbecile or shameless man who covets my assets may pay me for the honor! . . .

"You are a fool, sending me romantic letters; if you adore me, find a way to get out of there and come spend a few delicious moments at my side, full of enchantment, beauty, and lofty satisfaction.

"It seems incredible that you haven't figured out that in the carnival of life everything is a lie, honor is a myth, and we must take advantage of our golden age to enjoy worldly delights and inundate ourselves in the sea of happiness of the senses.

"Imbecile, dreamer, sentimentalist—I sneer at you, and hate you!

"Judith."

When she finished writing, Judith put the letter into an envelope, sent it to its destination, and got peacefully into bed.

The subsequent days were daily orgies. Shameless as any hussy, she was descending, descending down into the abyss, to the point of confusing herself with the most miserable prostitutes.

She realized that she was in a compromised state without knowing who might be the father of the child of crime she carried in her breast; and demoralized, she hurled herself, without any restraint or caution or feeling, with the shamelessness of the most vile women, into the putrid foul smelling mire of degradation, into the wretched whirlpool of lust, which, beneath the silk and glitter, oozes moral destitution.

XXIII.

The powerful connections that Ninón had in Mexican society paid off after 14 months of captivity and suffering: the secretary's office granted him full release.

As soon as he was notified, he ran to bid a fraternal goodbye to the captain of the infantry detachment with which he was stationed in the bays of La Ascención and the only friend he had made during his exile. He then was finally and definitively able to leave the company of the rest of the 41 who continued in service, some in the mess halls, others digging trenches and raising light fortifications in the company of the valiant soldiers engaged in the campaign against the Mayas.

And it made one laugh to see the grotesque scene of the popular 41, raising their shovels and pickaxes, sweating, squalid, and crying their eyes out most of the time.

The soldiers gave them a monumental hard time every day, telling them in mocking voices:

"Where are you going in your party dress?"

"Don't work so hard that you throw out your waist, my dear."

"Are you suffocating, pretty boy? Well, use your fan . . ."

And a little refrain also became popular after being published in a metropolitan newspaper of the epoch, which the soldiers would sing when they marched:

"Look at me as I march
with my shako to Yucatán,
where I'll find myself in a convoy
dancing *jota*[9] and can can."

Life for those disgraceful young men was a veritable hell, exposed as they were to the ruthless mockery of the troops, and the hot and unhealthy coastal climate.

Ninón embarked for the port of Progreso, prepared to work and to recover his honor. He needed to purify himself and to be able to raise his head in pride, and the doors of labor would be his only hope for a future of moral rehabilitation.

Once established in Progreso, he dedicated himself to buying and selling henequen; he made contracts with owners of henequen farms, and, although they were short-term, he himself obtained the necessary loans to get started exporting abroad, thereby stimulating his business, and beginning a new era of struggles, but the sweet and serene struggles of honest labor. His rehabilitation had begun and his redemption shone like the first sparkles of the breaking dawn.

One night, while resting at home, the mailman brought him a letter from Judith. He anxiously broke open the envelope and unfolded the letter, and as he read, his facial features broke down and he turned intensely pale.

The reader is already familiar with the contents of Judith's letter.

Resting his elbows on his desk and his head in his open hands, he remained pensive for a long time.

His calm broken, the man of the jungle awoke, and the thirsty beast roared with vengeance . . . Ninón felt the most immense ire and pain in his soul . . . that's how the perjurer pays for all his lost sleep, all his eagerness! . . . he had sacrificed everything for her, even to the point of regenerating himself; and the rehabilitation he offered danced like a sarcasm on Judith's lips, and that impure woman stained it with a shameful declaration.

Antonio, his best friend, ran off with her in order to enjoy a first caress, and then sell her charms to the first upstart who asked.

What misery Judith held in the putrid sewer of her soul!

No! He would not think of her again; the struggle would be hard, bitter, but his conscience, which was beginning to cleanse itself of its gross blemishes, would not be tarnished again.

He adored Judith with a true love, and for her sake he might have committed further insane acts, but now she was a courtesan who offered him shameless, sullied caresses that, once satisfied, would plunge him down once more into disgust and desperation.

He would forget her! He would search, not among the cohort of vain aristocrats, but among the middle class, a little woman full of good qualities, a good daughter, wife, and mother.

He angrily cursed the society in which she lived, that unhealthy society that is all vanity, lies, and dazzle; where love is nothing more than self-interest and degradation; where love is only for gold, and plethoric hearts palpitate in envy, arrogance, autocracy that slithers like a snake, poisoning and strangling . . .

His heart was no longer the whitened sarcophagus that hid immodest matter and slow venom within his breast, no! His noble heart suffered bloodless martyrdoms, but his suffering was God's vapor that prophesied a golden and happy existence, and the palliative that would soon cure the wounds of his soul in this world full of misery and egoism . . .

. . .

Six months have passed since Ninón received Judith's letter.

Moral changes transform men.

Ninón, solitary, sad, and disappointed with his bohemian lifestyle, had established relations with a middle-class Yucatecan family who lived in the port of Progreso.

The family was composed of an honorable married couple who had borne two children: an 18-year-old son and a 16-year-old daughter.

The daughter was named Josefina, a lovely girl in whom the powerful Yucatecan blood had forged a tropical coastal flower.

She was dark skinned, tall, thin, but with irreproachable curves; black sleepy, dreamy eyes trimmed with long, dark lashes. She was modest in dress, in words, and in manner; she had something of a mysterious charm, full of outpourings of poetry and of exuberant, fecund life.

The sloe-colored curls of her long hair that trimmed her dark forehead brought to mind the ringlets of mythological mermaids, and her small mouth, and fine, straight nose seemed modeled after Phidias.[10]

She was neither haughty nor vain; neither envy nor pride nor the preoccupations of flirtation and seduction disturbed the serenity of her sensitive soul.

She was unfamiliar with the demands and formulas of rigorous etiquette, but she knew virtue and modesty; she was educated with a seductive simplicity that enhanced the treasure of her virtue.

She was clean and hard working; she knew how to read and write correctly; she was capable of sustaining a simple conversation, without affectations; she could cook, embroider, paint, and arrange flowers. She didn't play piano, making a show of her execution, but instead would play sweet and gay coastal airs on the mandolin, and her voice, small and delicate but toned, was a delight to those who listened to it.

She was a good daughter; she respected her parents, took care of them, spoiled them with that seductive simplicity of the noble and ingenuous soul of a model daughter.

And Ninón, who observed her, who studied her character, who grasped her virtues and her innocence, one afternoon that they spent at the beach along with her parents, in a moment of opportunity, spoke to her of love, painted her a supreme, holy, unselfish passion.

He told her of his past, his punishment, his remorse, his purification, and he offered to love her, to make her his wife, and to live happily dedicating the hours of his life to her.

Josefina listened to Ninón's story; she sensed a feeling of nobility in his heart, glimpsed a future of rehabilitation for Ninón and began to be impressed by his good and sensitive heart. She replied to him that he should consult her parents and that if their will was not opposed to the idea and she came to love him, she would not mind dedicating herself to him in return.

That same night Ninón had a conference with Josefina's parents, asking them for the hand of their good daughter.

"The young man doesn't seem bad to me," said Josefina's father, "and if my daughter loves him, let them be married, and may the youngsters live happily ever after."

Ninón went to visit daily from then on, growing closer every day to them, and was content and satisfied to have found such a treasure of a woman.

"What an enormous difference!" thought Ninón.

Judith, raised in an atmosphere of luxury and gold, had only acquired pride and vanity, her happiness depending on fashion and the flattery of that horde of ignorant fops who form the court of the most chic of women; and Josefina, his most chaste fiancée, his virtuous Merideña,[11] whose happiness depended solely on pleasing her parents, inspiring him in his task of regeneration, encouraging him for the future with words of love and consolation whispered into his ear like a poem of heavenly delights; he dreamed of that heaven in which his fantasies caressed him like enchanted multicolored butterflies, shimmering in the splendorous light of a smiling future.

Yes, getting married to Josefina would be felicitous; he would look proudly on those despots who sacrifice tenderness for social form; his existence, peaceful and serene, would slip into eternal springtime, and a grandiose spectacle of true joy.

If he had succeeded in marrying Judith, he'd only have constructed a coffin of disappointments, etched with silver and encrusted with diamonds and pearls; he'd have made a colossal bank deal, showing off wealth forged out of many tears, with great imprecation and damnation.

He'd have buried the indestructible coffer of his affection and sentiment beneath an enormous golden cape: his dreams would have dimmed under the glare of a haughty, feigned, hypocritical pomp, forcing his fantasized redemption to succumb.

Josefina was his hope, his soul, his faith; for her sake he had regenerated, for her sake he had suffered a life metamorphosis; into his ears like a celestial chant she whispered, the voice of forgiveness that sweetened the punishment of his past guilt; and she was always friendly, tender, virtuous, nobly embellished by the dignity of her sensitive and honorable soul.

And Judith, who had sown brilliant delusions within his heart, was his implacable executioner.

Ninón imagined her with her bared shoulders and arms, with her raucous laugh, hysterical and burlesque. She gave herself to men voluntarily, like a depraved woman; going back home, to her upright and indignant parents, she would once again profane her nuptial bed with the most horrendous of adulteries.

Judith, like all worldly women, would go back home only wishing to shine, to exhibit her son, looking for a marriage of convenience in order to sustain her whims and mitigate her anxieties.

Josefina reigned in his soul; she had triumphed and Ninón was glad; he was content, and wanted nothing more than to unite himself indissolubly with his loved one.

. . .

And the longed for day finally arrived.

The preparations for the wedding were made: a humble ceremony and a select group of guests chosen for their sentiments, for their honor and simplicity, and for their good faith in wishing immense happiness to the newlyweds.

marriage
↓
solution
↓
escape

In the most humble curacy, Ninón and Josefina were joined forever in matrimony. After the religious ceremony followed a profane feast: a dinner where all guests, those hard-working and sincere sons and daughters of Yucatan, joyful, frank, and sensitive, congratulated the newlyweds, rejoicing in their happiness.

The most cordial congratulations, the most vehement good wishes for their future, in the best order and enthusiasm, constantly interrupted the toasts.

Ninón, his dreams fulfilled at the side of his virtuous and simple wife, embraced his in-laws with filial affection, and toasted his new life, blessing the hour he came to Progreso; and his straightforward speech sincerely paid tribute to the coastal dwellers, who scorned the egoism and dazzle of vanity, in favor of pleasure and the divine expansion of the soul.

When his imagination flew back to his far-off memories, he despised the bastardly actions of Judith and cursed the hypocritical social forms of which he had been a part, that society in which diabolical, criminal, incestuous, and libertine women dance.

Ninón, redeemed, repudiating his flashy social rank, entered into the democratic heart of a society that holds honor, virtue, and work as the norm. The sublime society of the middle class! . . .

. . .

XXV.

In the tempestuous sea of desires, the blazing young men, the immortal 41, were shipwrecked.

Human misery, like an insatiable hunger, thrust its teeth in and tore out shreds, many shreds of horrific wretchedness.

The nervous jolts of their passions, burned up by the voracious fire of their degradation, violated both morality and the law, and mutilated virtue, which in its imperial throne sat erect with the majesty of an immaculate princess.

Prostitution, converted into scum, into a swamp, into pestilent sewage, gathered a bunch of ruffians of the most perverse evil who sunk the dagger of their unruly appetites into the hearts of modesty and shame.

What repulsive and disgusting debauchery of the damned, who supplant women's charms, amid the most contemptible ridicule, and who lost all noble sentiment and proud dignity!

Existence, so beautiful, so harmonious, so sweet and tender for honorable and hard-working men who live a life of activity and growth, for prostituted refined idlers turns into a sarcasm that kills the grandeur of the soul and the potency of the body; and vice, that impure vice that descends to the lowest of the low, drags them into dishonor, hoodwinks their good sense, and the beast appears in its grossest form, with all its virulent and contagious material.

What a disgrace to live degraded, marked, repudiated by all generations, sunken into the cursed cavity of social disrepute, closing their eyes to the divine laws of progress and ears to the sublime and moving accents of morality!

Sloth annihilates the body and spirit; luxury is a fecund misery that only breeds vanities and develops plagues that diminish the pocketbook, that dull thinking and that ruin, morally and physically, the aspirations of the progressive fighter of a man; and vice, that vice that spills over the cup of the most unbridled prostitution, makes slaves of men and denigrates them to the point that they fall into the immoral den of iniquity and corruption, then breaks their bonds into a thousand splinters, that will never again be purified.

Grotesque characters have circulated through the pages of this little novel: some prostituted perhaps because of some defect or special phenomenon, and others nearly always because of lax motivation, and we do not know whether they are worthy of compassion, disdain, or the inflexible chastisement of justice and society.

Some have regenerated and the beginning of their purification has been to invoke the sacred principles of morality, of the honorable life that they must follow and fulfill with duties for which mankind was created.

Judith abandoned her little son, who, lacking his daily bread and maternal love, lies at the mercy of misfortune, while she crosses the seas in pursuit of more fictitious joy, more impure pleasure, and more looseness.

And what has become of Star, Modesty, Virtue, Blanca, Carola, and Margarita? Have they regenerated? Are they perhaps still marching along the path of degradation and vice? What have they been feeling? What have they been thinking on the sweltering shores of Yucatan? What does the future hold for Judith's son?

Life's mysteries! And mysteries, whose secrets the reader will discover in the second part of this little novel, that fueled the fire of social scandal and provided a theme for this humble narration.[12]

In society, uncorrected vices germinate and bear fruit. Fortunately, those degenerating vices will not run rampant in the fertile fields of civilization, which like every titanic force of struggle purifies peoples and individuals: because progress always imposes itself with majesty.

All vices in general are harmful and detrimental; their material, lined with lace and jewels, is a nest of microbes that infect and propagate with rapid growth. When societies annihilate those infectious plagues, the most holy happiness, the most austere joy, the most tranquil consciences arise; and in the home, in that temple of faith's exalted majesty, the angel of conformity penetrates, and the trembling heart of satisfaction beats gloriously in the purity, in the vapor of the soul, with the triumph of the passions, to enjoy, in peaceful hours, in smiling mornings, in golden afternoons and in beautifully mild nights, the tranquil life, poignantly alive in the face of the sublime spectacle of Nature.

Notes

1. The "Mexican Thinker" (*Pensador Mexicano*) was the pseudonym of José Joaquín Fernández de Lizardi, Mexico's first novelist, whose masterpiece, *El Periquillo Sarniento* (The Itching Parrot) [1816] is a classic work of social parody.

2. Emile Zola was a French novelist and social critic; his three novels, *Nana* (1880); *La terre* (1887); and *J'accuse* (1898), make up the trilogy referenced here.

3. Juan Mateos, Emilio Rabasa, Victoriano Salado Álvarez, three Mexican novelists of the era. It is notable that none of these writers reflect *modernista* or *naturalista* trends that were predominant in Mexican literature at the time, but that were considered immoral by some. Nor have any of the three survived as major figures in Mexican literary history. Conspicuously absent from the list are the bestseller Federico Gamboa and the leading *modernista* Amado Nervo.

4. Name of a popular *zarzuela* of the era.

5. Likely refers to a working-class coquette.

6. French prostitutes.

7. Fan, admirer.

8. Fashionable men's haberdashery in Mexico City.

9. Popular Spanish dance of the era.

10. Ancient Greek sculptor.

11. Incorrect qualifier to describe inhabitants of Mérida, Yucatán. The locals refer to themselves as "Meridanos."

12. There is no evidence of a second novel ever being published.

Los Cuarenta y uno:
Novela crítico-social [1906]

Eduardo A. Castrejón

Dos Palabras

El autor de este libro, contando con la benevolencia del público, entrega a nuestra casa editora su primer ensayo en el género de la novela; y la casa lo da a la luz pública por las razones que expondrá someramente.

Con excepción de genios como el de Víctor Hugo, cuya primera obra fue un éxito, porque *Nuestra Señora de París* se lee con creciente interés, puede decirse después de un siglo, todos los escritores han comenzado por ensayos más o menos felices, contando con la ayuda o con los consejos de literatos ya experimentados en el género que se cultiva.

Tal es la sucesión en la cadena interminable de los hombres y de los tiempos: las generaciones tomando lecciones del pasado en su historia de progreso y de adelanto, poniéndose en el medio social para su desarrollo, y la literatura apoderándose del campo de explotación de las ideas nuevas, de los ideales y de las tendencias de una época. Cada sociedad en su momento histórico tiene un gusto particular; y así hemos visto pasar de improviso del clasicismo al romanticismo y hoy al realismo, sin que se pueda explicar el motivo de la evolución, pues intervienen factores imprevistos, circunstancias anómalas y otras causas que determinan el fenómeno, explicado con más o menos acierto en el mundo de las letras.

Pero en lo que están de acuerdo todas las épocas, ya tratándose de la historia o de la literatura, es en la corrección de las costumbres, la condición de los vicios sociales, el anatema a todas las corrupciones, la exaltación de la moral y el anatema a la perversión del sentimiento humano. La mayor parte de las veces, el escritor que hace un rayo de su pluma para aniquilar los crímenes sociales, es la víctima: pero las almas templadas en el fuego sagrado de la verdad, afrontan todas las vicisitudes y las persecuciones de la hipocresía para entrar vencedoras en el campo social. El *Pensador Mexicano* en su obra inmortal el *Periquillo,* puso sobre la plancha a la sociedad antigua, hizo la autopsia y descubrió toda la gangrena que devoraba aquel cuerpo aniquilado, se puso frente a frente de las costumbres, y ora con la palabra vibrante o con lo amargo de la sátira, arrojó los reproches filosóficos en el terreno de la razón y de la verdad.[1] Excomulgado, perseguido, anatematizado y muerto en la lucha, la historia le ha hecho justicia, y su libro será siempre un monumento que perdurará más que sus cenizas que se han perdido para siempre, Eugenio Sué le dio un golpe al jesuitismo con su *Judío Errante,* del cual no se repondrá nunca, así como la trilogía de Emilio Zola que hizo caer sobre su cabeza los rayos de la indignación política y religiosa.[2] Pero en Europa esas obras producen un capital, que no dejan caer al escritor en el abismo de la miseria; pero en nuestro país es al contrario: trae la persecución social, viene el desfallecimiento de la miseria, el hospital y la muerte. Afortunadamente en la actualidad los fanatismos se han apagado hasta cierto punto; la libertad ha conquistado su puesto y sin temor se puede escribir de todo, dejando a la sociedad como juez árbitro de cuanto se escribe.

El autor de la novela que hoy publicamos ha cumplido con un deber social, sea cual fuera el éxito de lo que él llama su novela, y que es el relato fiel de un hecho que produjo el escándalo y que ha dejado en las llamas de la sátira una memoria que durará por muchos años. El autor del libro deja sentir la fuerza de su imaginación, detalla sus cuadros y flagela de una manera terrible un vicio execrable, sobre el cual escupe la misma sociedad, como el corruptor de las generaciones. El autor comienza hoy su carrera y no hay que exigirle la corrección de los autores con los cuales estamos educados, y más en esta época en que la literatura ha dado un paso gigantesco de avance, como lo denuncia esa multitud de novelas bellísimas que forman el encanto de un sinnúmero de lectores.

Entre nosotros comienza a cultivarse el género, y por estar en su cuna debemos impartirle toda protección. Apenas si tenemos novelistas: Mateos, Rabasa, Salado Álvarez y algunos otros que han obtenido el favor público, y cuyas obras son buscadas con empeño y leídas con satisfacción.[3] Es ya tiempo de que florezcan las letras en nuestro país; comenzaremos con deficiencias, como en todas partes, pero pondremos la primera piedra del provenir. Es ya tiempo de iniciar la competencia; no sólo en la historia, en el teatro, sino en la novela, para lo cual cuenta nuestra raza y nuestra índole con fuerzas suficientes para la lucha. Nosotros creemos en el porvenir, y alentaremos a los escritores mexicanos en su penosa carrera, estando dispuestos a editar todas las obras que produzca su ingenio y nos ofrezcan su estudio y su inteligencia en el vasto campo de la literatura nacional.

Los Editores

I.

¡La tarde iba muriendo!... El sol ocultaba su inmensa cabellera rubia, y en el horizonte las nubes amontonadas tomaban un tinte de bronce.

En la casa aristocrática de *Mimí*, adornada con exquisito gusto femenino y en la sala elegantemente amueblada, se esparcen ondas de perfume delicioso.

Mimí está solo!...

En su traje correcto, cortado a la 'Americana', se nota una elegancia exquisita; sus manos, blancas y tersas, juegan con los guantes, y su mirada impaciente mira el reloj, que le parece retarda mucho las horas.

Han dado las siete de la noche.

En la extensa sala, las innúmeras bombillas de luz eléctrica que la alumbran hacen un armonioso conjunto con las pantallas de formas caprichosas, así como con varias estatuas de mármol de Carrara sobre pedestales de bronce.

Un lacayito de quince años, guapo, de ojos azules con mirada voluptuosa y melancólica, con voz ceremoniosa anuncia a *Mimí* que varios jóvenes desean hablarle.

—¡Que pasen, que pasen!—respondió emocionado *Mimí*.

El lacayito abrió las hojas de la vidriera; hizo a un lado los cortinajes de seda, y fueron desfilando varios adolescentes que llamaremos por sus nombres: *Ninón, Estrella, Pudor, Virtud, Carola, Blanca* y *Margarita*.

Todos vestían con elegancia masculina.

Abrazaron a *Mimí* con efusión, se cambiaron algunos eróticos besos y se sentaron en los sillones aterciopelados.

Mimí había cambiado: su tristeza infinita se trocaba en placer; y *Ninón*, un hércules, de rostro seductor y varonil, tomó la mano de *Mimí* depositando un ósculo de amor, un ósculo lleno de fuego, sonoro, rimado por un murmullo interminable.

—¿Ha venido ya la modista con los trajes?—preguntó *Pudor*.

—Aún no,—respondió *Mimí*;—la cité a las ocho y no debe tardar trayendo los vestidos completamente terminados.

El lacayito entró con una bandeja de finos pasteles y varias botellas de champagne que apuraron los convidados.

La voz atiplada de los adolescentes, formando una inmensa algarabía, recorría todos los tonos de la dulzura; y sus modales afeminados daban a la escena un tinte chocarrero y meloso, pareciendo la reunión más bien voces de señoritas discutiendo en el estrado, que de jóvenes barbilindos.

—¿Me quieres?—decía *Ninón* a *Mimí*.

Y *Mimí*, acariciando las mejillas de *Ninón*, se lo juraba entusiasmado.

—¿Fuiste anoche a la ópera?—le decía *Estrella* a *Margarita*.

—¡¡¡Ay . . . sí, cómo no!!!

—¿Y tú, *Blanca*, no fuiste?

—¡¡¡No, tú!!! Estuve un poco enfermo y no quise salir de casa.

—¡Qué onditas tan preciosas tienes en tu peinado, *Margarita*! ¿qué, te las rizaste?

—No, mi vida, si son naturales . . .

—¿Y tus choclitos, *Virtud*, son americanos? . . .

—Sí, *Estrella*, están muy monos con mis calcetines calados, ¿verdad?

—¡¡Chulísimos, *Virtud*, y muy elegantes!!

—Sólo *Pudor* y *Carola* no hablaban; estrechados por amoroso abrazo se contemplaban arrobados pensando en los deleites de la vida, y de cuando en cuando bebían copitas de champagne para refrescar sus labios ardorosos.

A las ocho en punto el lacayito anunció que la modista estaba presente.

Como impulsados por un resorte eléctrico se levantaron todos de sus asientos a un mismo tiempo y corrieron a la puerta.

La Sra. Charmanti, que era la modista encargada de confeccionar los trajes a que hizo referencia *Pudor,* entró a la sala precedida de un criado, quien depositó en una mesa varias cajas de cartón que contenían vestidos de mujer.

—¿Han quedado concluidos?—le preguntó *Mimí* con una dulzura fingida y una mueca seductora.

—Sí, señor—respondió dignamente la modista;—si encuentra Ud. algo que le disguste vendré mañana para arreglarlo.

Apenas se había despedido la Sra. Charmanti se abalanzaron los jóvenes a las cajas, y destapándolas fueron sacando precipitadamente: quien unas faldas, quien un corpiño escotado, quien un camisón sedalito con encajes finísimos de gran *chic.*

Y, como hembras vanidosas que cifran su ventura y su felicidad en la postura y el adorno de un vestido femenino, se dirigieron a un hermoso retrete-tocador; y despojándose del saco, del chaleco, del cuello de la camisa y la corbata, fueron acicalándose corsés elegantísimos y artísticamente trabajados.

Mimí probaba una falda sevillana; *Margarita* un corpiño de baile con luengo escote y una peluca rubia estilo Luis XV; *Carola* unas medias caladas rellenas de algodón; *Blanca* unos choclos bordados de oro; *Estrella* un vaporoso traje de bebé; *Pudor* y *Virtud* trajes de serpentinas, y *Ninón* se afectaba el rostro con polvo blanco y bermellón y se perfumaba los bucles de su negra cabellera.

¡El entusiasmo fue indescriptible entonces!

Se sentían alegres, satisfechos, emocionados, pletóricos de felicidad mirándose vestidos de mujer.

¡Oh y qué de transportes eróticos, qué de venturas, qué de embriagueces . . . al trocar el traje de hombre para convertirse en deliciosas niñas (?), en huríes encantadoras de suaves contornos y de ondulantes líneas seductoras.

. . .

El corazón degenerado de aquellos jóvenes aristócratas prostituidos, palpitaba en aquel inmenso bacanal.

La desbordante alegría originada por la posesión de los trajes femeninos en sus cuerpos, las posturas mujeriles, las voces carnavalescas, semejaban el retrete-tocador a una cámara fantástica; los perfumes esparcidos, los abrazos, los besos sonoros y febriles, representaban cuadros degenerantes de aquellas escenas de Sodoma y Gomorra, de los festines orgiásticos de Tiberio, de Cómodo y Calígula, donde el fuego explosivo de la pasión devoraba la carne consumiéndola en deseos de la más desenfrenada prostitución.

Y en esa insaciable vorágine de placeres brutales han caído, para no levantarse nunca, jóvenes que, en el colmo de la torpeza y de la degradación prostituida, contribuyen a bastardear la raza humana injuriando gravemente a la Naturaleza.

II.

¡*Mimí* estaba espléndido!

Por su físico, de una verdadera hermosura femenina, así como por sus modales fingidos, era el único que parecía una hembra deliciosa; sus ojos negros, con artísticas y bien retocadas ojeras por la pintura, eran el *non plus ultra* de las damitas (?) allí reunidas.

Del retrete-tocador pasaron a la sala, y *Estrella*, que era un buen músico, sin hacerse de rodeos ejecutó con maestría la 'Serenata de Schubert', con tan deliciosa ternura y tan hondo sentimiento, que arrancó lágrimas fingidas a nuestras *bellas damas* (?).

Después tocó un *'Two-Step'* alegre, ejecutado con mucha rapidez, como a impulsos de una inspiración satánica.

¡Y el placer fue inmenso!

Carola, Blanca, y *Margarita* se reclinaron lánguidamente en elegantes *'chaises-longues'*, y *Pudor* y *Virtud, Ninón* y *Mimí,* entusiasmados, se tomaron del brazo alegremente, lanzándose en el torbellino del baile, describiendo siluetas extravagantes, exageradas, hasta caer rendidos por el placer y llenos de enloquecedora y fecunda dicha.

El lacayito anunció que la cena estaba servida y dispuesta para los comensales.

Y alzándose la falda e imitando el paso de reinas triunfadoras, cimbrando airosamente su cuerpo, de dos en dos y abrazados, fueron desfilando hacia el comedor, donde una opípara cena y una buena y magnífica dotación de vinos los esperaba, para terminar aquellos momentos de expansión.

Cada quien tomó asiento indistintamente en la mesa, excepto *Ninón* y *Mimí* que se sentaron a la cabecera presidiendo la reunión, y estrechamente unidos sus asientos como queriendo fundir sus dos cuerpos en una sola alma.

Se cenaba engullendo sendos platos de exquisitos manjares y se escanciaba el vino en boca de buenos bebedores.

El efecto alcohólico triunfaba y aquellos rostros de tan lindos palmitos gesticulaban beodos cantando sentidísimos (?) trozos de las óperas de 'Bohemia' y de 'Tosca'.

Hebe, erigida en altar de flores eróticas sonreía maliciosamente; Baco bendecía aquella excelsa orgía, y Cupido, el traviesuelo chiquitín, hería con sus dardos aquellos corazones sensibleros.

Los brindis, impregnados de fuego, de infinita vehemencia, se sucedían sin interrupción.

El bueno, el transigente de Baco ponía todos sus encantos y toda su poderosa fantasía en los vasos de vino, y todos se sentían satisfechos forjando visiones amorosas en su calenturienta imaginación.

Y aquella asquerosa falange de rufianes de la aristocracia, dignos imitadores de Heliogábalo, poseídos de una colosal ventura en medio de la más nauseabunda crápula, llegaba al período álgido del delirio obsceno.

Mimí, lleno de tan grandiosa dicha, y tan soberano placer, contemplaba extasiado entreabriendo voluptuosamente sus ojos, para acariciar con su mirada el rostro seductor de *Ninón.*

Pudor se sentía inspirado; aquellos momentos de bestial degeneración no le bastaban para saciar sus deseos; vislumbraba todo un cielo de venturas, todo un mundo de placeres sensibles y de nuevos goces; imaginaba verse transportado al país de la eterna felicidad creando placeres interminables de nefandas aberraciones.

Carola, Blanca, Estrella, Virtud y *Margarita*, confundidos en el mismo nivel de bajeza, en esa triste degeneración, en envilecimiento increíble, se abrazaban, se inflamaban al contacto de la suave epidermis ungida de aceites perfumados, y desfloraban sus manos con chasquidos de ardientes y sonoros besos.

Los ojos de *Ninón* relampagueaban de placer; aquella cena suculenta, aquellos vinos añejos y los rostros pintarrajeados de sus compañeros le deleitaban sintiéndose satisfecho.

El rostro afeminado de *Mimí*, su belleza, su cabello rizado cayendo sobre sus mal pintadas mejillas formando bucles sedosos, su cuello escotado y con el vestido de mujer muy ceñido, pronunciando las formas de su cuerpo, era para *Ninón* la meta apetecida y gloriosa de sus más caros ideales.

Ninón, envilecido, en el estado del bruto, en el olvido del honor y del deber, abría el enorme pórtico de su imaginación calenturienta para disipar tontamente en las para él embriagadoras caricias del cuerpo de *Mimí*.

Infeliz relajación . . .

El lacayito, con su mirada dulce y lánguida y balanceándose sobre sus caderas, servía solícito los vasos llenándolos de vino.

El desorden reinaba en todo su apogeo; las botellas vacías y los vasos yacían sobre el pavimento; los manteles, enrojecidos por el vino, parecían empapados en sangre.

Y ebrios, exangües, bostezando aquel núcleo de haraganes y libertinos, con gestos y posturas lúbricas disputaban bebiendo, cantaban y reían obscenamente.

Sólo *Mimí* había permanecido quieto, indolentemente recostado en el respaldo de su silla, mordiéndose los labios, jugando con la falda, contento de aquella orgía placentera, y soñando venturas deliciosas en un mundo lleno de dichas inefables, como los goces excelsos y venerados del Cielo.

Semejaba su postura y su tocado a la de esas '*cocottes de toilette a la pompodour*' y parecía al lado de *Ninón* la favorita del serrallo de su señor y primera mesalina en el emporio de la crápula, donde al iniciarse en él pierde el ser humano su dignidad y su vergüenza para morar en el seno gangrenado de esa comunidad cínica y abyecta, de esa comunidad menguada usurpadora de las funciones reservadas sólo a la mujer.

Tuvo la peregrina ocurrencia de proponer se hiciera un baile regio, elegante, que hiciera época en la fastuosa historia de hombres depravados, y que se participara a toda la cáfila de esos seres bastardos, que concurriesen elegantemente vestidos de mujer, y además convidar a los más prostituidos para darle mayor animación y brillo al *sarao*.

Y tan disparatada proposición fue aceptada.

Las fisonomías afeminadas de los adolescentes se animaron ardientes; surgió el entusiasmo en todo su esplendor, y una salva de aplausos y un hosanna de placer beodo se esparció por los ámbitos del comedor.

Mimí estaba imponente; se había desatado las cintas de su corpiño transparente de seda azul, cubierto de diamantes, y mostraba sus hombros desnudos provocando deseos en los ojos lánguidos del lacayito.

Propuso que en la calle de la Paz alquilaran la casa marcada con el núm. 000, la que se adornaría convenientemente; y que los demás adolescentes se ocuparan en contratar una orquesta de primer orden, y se hicieran tarjetas de invitación para repartirlas entre los parroquianos de confianza.

Y aquellos parásitos que soñaban en coqueterías, se levantaron de sus asientos tambaleándose, se cambiaron el traje femenino por el de hombre, y con voz rastrera y débil, entre besos y abrazos, apretones de manos y juramentos de abominable perversión, se despidieron satisfechos, a las altas horas de la noche, cuando la ciudad dormía aletargada y sólo de cuando en cuando se oía por la calles asfaltadas el silbato de los guardianes somnolientos.

Un hombre, cubierto con el embozo de la capa hasta los ojos, se desprendió del dintel de una puerta cercana a la casa de *Mimí*, donde estaba oculto, y a rápido paso se dirigió a uno de los ebrios barbilindos, y aquel, creyéndolo un amigo del gremio, le ofreció un cigarrillo y le contó todos sus proyectos de bastardía inmunda, sin pensar que era el nuncio de su muerte civil y el prologuista justiciero de aquellos jóvenes inflamables, repudiados, odiosos para el porvenir y por todas las generaciones, escoria de la sociedad y mengua de los hombres honrados amantísimos de las bellezas fecundas de la mujer.

III.

El Bosque de Chapultepec estaba henchido de una concurrencia elegante, espléndida. Centenares de lujosos carruajes circulaban por las frondosas avenidas, llevando en su interior aristocráticas damas, dándole un fausto señorial a la crepuscular barahúnda humana.

En una flamante carretela abierta, Estela y Judith lanzaban miradas fulgurantes y envidiosas a un coupé donde iba muellemente reclinada una feliz pareja.

—¡Qué felices son Leopoldo y Rosaura! ¿Verdad, Judith?—dijo Estela.

—Sí, Estela—respondió Judith emocionada—su luna de miel ha sido una primavera deliciosa donde el amor ha posado sus reales, fructificando en el vergel florido de una felicidad infinita.

—¿Sientes envidia, Judith?

—¿Envidia, Estela? . . . No, no lo creas; cuando mis ojos contemplan la pareja feliz de un incipiente matrimonio, siento una satisfacción que inunda mi alma de alegría al pensar que muy pronto seré feliz.

—Yo pienso diferente a ti—respondió Estela con acento de envidia y de odio;—al contemplar, como tú, una parejita llena de candor y de dicha, en mi alma ruge una tempestad de celos, de envidia, de egoísmo, y sufro mucho al pensar que *Mimí*, que tanto pregona de adorarme, a mí lado es frío, sus palabras son de hielo, ¡de una grande indiferencia! Cuando en mis meditaciones su figura y su rostro me seducen, lo adoro entusiasmada, me forjo ilusiones de tantos goces, que quisiera darle vida a su corazón y poner en su cuerpo las energías viriles e indomables de la juventud, de esa juventud vigorosa que tanto nos entusiasma a las mujeres ardientes.

—Pues en ese caso—respondió Judith—no te envidio, Estela; mi corazón ardiente que se desborda con las ilusiones de una pasión volcánica, en donde mis deseos buscan un ideal perfecto, un ideal sublime, lo encontré en *Ninón*, que es todo amor, todo bondad y corazón.

Joven, vigoroso, amante de primera fuerza, ha rimado en mis oídos palabras divinas de una ternura encantadora; me ha hecho visionaria en mis noches de ensueños vaporosos, y en mis vigilias solitarias donde en cada pensamiento para el porvenir está él, para saciar mis deseos y para coronar el éxito de mis ilusiones futuras.

Su voz fuerte, timbrada, paréceme el sonido de una viola de embelesadoras harmonías; sus modales finísimos me encantan, y su talle gentil y hercúleo llena por completo las ansias de las vírgenes que soñamos con el matrimonio . . .

Y sin embargo, Estela; como tú, yo también soy una infeliz que mendiga sus caricias; he sentido un volcán de celos en mi alma, y más precavida que tú, pago a un hombre que fue agente de la policía, para que siga todos los pasos de *Ninón* y me desengañe por completo.

Esta mañana me entregó una carta mi doncella de parte del agente, y he sido tan cobarde que no me atreví a romper el sobre; quería consultarte y que ambas de acuerdo, según el contenido de la carta, obremos resueltamente.

¡Ay, Estela! Hay grandes dolores en la vida que son incurables, y yo no quiero enfermarme porque detesto el dolor . . . tengo un miedo cerval de abrir la carta . . . me presagia en lo más íntimo de mi alma un cataclismo horrible.

—¡No temas, Judith! ¿No estás al lado de tu amiga? ¿Quieres que yo la abra?

—Sí, Estela—respondió Judith visiblemente emocionada—, pero vámonos a casa pronto; ahí le darás lectura y saldremos por fin de esta ansiedad horrible.

Estela dio órdenes a su cochero de regresar a casa violentamente; los caballos, fustigados por el látigo, se lanzaron en carrera vertiginosa por la Calzada de la Reforma, y llegaron presto.

Estela y Judith bajaron del coche y penetraron en la perfumada y elegante alcoba de la primera, ansiosas de revelarse mutuamente sus impresiones y de saber el resultado de la carta.

. . .

La estancia, alumbrada tenuemente por los últimos resplandores vespertinos, le daba un aspecto melancólicamente poético.

Sentadas frente a frente en mullidos *chaises-longues,* y agitadas por una conversación muy discutida, Estela y Judith formaban sus proyectos, desesperanzadas con noticias mezcladas de fatalismo, de desgracias, de la ruina de un amor que ambas, respectivamente, creyeron perdurable.

—¿Y si en la carta—interrumpió Estela—se nos presentaran pruebas irrecusables, infamantes, condenatorias para *Ninón* y *Mimí,* no vacilarías en vengarte, Judith?

—No lo sé, Estela—respondió gravemente Judith;—abre la carta, dale lectura, y cuando sepamos su contenido te contestaré dignamente.

Entonces Estela, presintiendo grandes dolores, rompió el sobre, desdobló la carta, y con voz vibrante, con esa virilidad femenina que se posesiona en la mujer en un contacto de cólera, fue leyendo claro y pausado:

"Respetable señorita:

Sus temores no han sido infundados.

Paso a paso sigo todos los movimientos del Sr. *Ninón,* convirtiéndome en su más implacable perseguidor. Ud. paga bien mis noticias, y ésta, que seguramente será de gran interés para Ud., espero me la recompensará con liberalidad.

He tenido que pasar grandes apuros para investigar la vida del Sr. *Ninón* y he agotado todos mis *ardides de sabueso,* gastando dinero, cuyo importe lo encontrará Ud. en la detallada que le adjunto.

En el Bosque de Chapultepec, en la 'Maisón Dorée', en los teatros, en los casinos y en las reuniones de más renombre de la aristocracia, llamó muchísimo mi atención que el Sr. *Ninón* sea inseparable del Sr. *Mimí,* a quien Ud. ya conoce.

Aguijoneado por la curiosidad, he averiguado que tienen mala reputación el Sr. *Mimí* y el Sr. *Ninón* entre sus mismos amigos y criados, exceptuando unos cuantos que se hacen llamar por los siguientes pseudónimos, si así se puede llamar, y son los *Señoritos Blanca, Estrella, Virtud, Pudor, Carola* y *Margarita.*

No perdiendo el menor detalle de su vida, y formando consecuencias de los modales y de los gustos de estos caballeritos, he comprendido que el Sr. *Ninón* los aprecia demasiado, mucho; digo . . . los quiere con mucho fuego, con tanto fuego, que temo que se queme y descienda hasta el vicio de que adolecen algunos jóvenes prostituidos de esa sociedad en que Ud. mora.

No soy un embustero, ni un indigno delator de mi triste oficio, como hay muchos compañeros, no, Srita. Judith; no pertenezco tampoco a esa hez de desdichados que manchan y desprestigian reputaciones honradas; pero en este caso, supuesto que Ud. paga con esplendidez, creo, y se lo aseguro afirmativamente, que el Sr. *Ninón* y el Sr. *Mimí* no nacieron para adorar a Ud. y a la Srita. Estela.

Créame Ud. a carta cabal: el Sr. *Ninón* ama con toda la fuerza de su corazón al Sr. *Mimí.*

¿Que veo visiones? . . . ¿Que soy un impostor? . . . No, señorita, digo la verdad con toda su desnudez.

Se abrazan, se besan, se tienen un afecto demasiado fraternal que traspasa todos los límites de la amistad.

Hay todavía más, señorita.

El domingo se reunieron los caballeritos que le nombro, el Sr. *Ninón,* y el Sr. *Mimí;* cenaron alegremente, se tomó muchísimo vino y . . . prepárese Ud. a creerlo: se vistieron de mujer, improvisaron un bailecito tocando en el piano el jovencito *Estrella,* terminando el festincillo a horas muy avanzadas de la noche.

Tambaleándose por los efectos del alcohol, con el rostro pintorreado, salieron de la casa del Sr. *Mimí* aquellos jóvenes, cuando la aurora comenzaba a desperezarse en su lecho sidéreo.

Los espiaba frente a la casa del Sr. *Mimí,* oculto en el obscuro dintel de una puerta, y cuando salieron seguí tras ellos por las calles, y al despedirse uno de los jóvenes para tomar rumbo distinto, le salí al encuentro, haciéndome el conocido, y trabamos conversación.

Me creyó de la cofradía y me contó que habían estado de *juerga,* que habían bailado vestidos de mujer, y que dentro de pocos días darán un grandioso baile en la casa núm. 000 de la calle de la Paz, que está deshabitada, y que harán una rifa de *Art Nouveau,* siendo feliz el que se saque el premio.

Si Ud. hubiera oído con qué entusiasmo hablaba, y el Sr. *Mimí* iba de toda gala femenina, así como el Sr. *Ninón* de rigorosa etiqueta.

No está de más decirle a Ud. que estoy convidado, y que me aprestaré para informar a Ud. el resultado.

Si alguna cosa se le ofrece, ruego ordene a su servidor que besa respetuosamente sus manos.''

'Mano de Alacrán'

—¿Será posible tanta ignominia, Estela?—preguntaba indignada Judith;—¿*Mimí,* ese varón lleno de vida, de felicidad, de dinero; que trueque sus papeles de hombre para convertirse en bestia, por medio de una crápula sucia y degradante? . . .

—Yo concibo—decía Estela desesperadamente—que un hombre como *Mimí,* mimado de la fortuna, aceptado en nuestra alta aristocracia, sea todo lo inconstante con las mujeres; pero que cambie las caricias de la mujer, en quien los hombres cifran toda su delicia, por las groseras aberraciones de los pederastas, eso, Judith, jamás pasó por mi mente ardiente y visionaria.

En mis ensueños, en las ilusiones de mi imaginación siempre me lo figuraba como el hombre que llenaría el mundo de mis deseos y de mis aspiraciones grandiosas.

Su rostro seductor me enorgullecía cuando estaba delante de mis amigas, y creí encontrar una superioridad sin límites soñando en un paraíso terrenal, donde sólo él era el Dios de mis placeres.

Sí, soñaba sólo en él . . . pensaba que mi vida enlazaba con la de *Mimí,* sería una ventura eterna, salmodiada por un coro de arcángeles, el día que en el altar, y cubierto mi cuerpo con un elegante vestido blanco lleno de azahares, exhibiría mi galán prometido ante la multitud, como una adquisición sublime . . .

¡¡Oh!! ¡y qué vergüenza voy a pasar! ¡cuántas murmuraciones vendrán a invadir mis oídos, y cuántas sátiras punzantes me zaherirán! ¡Y mi orgullo caerá lloroso y abatido del pedestal de su grandeza!

¡¡En el orco de la vergüenza y la desesperación irán cayendo mutiladas mis ilusiones placenteras, y las rosas lozanas de los ideales más sublimes de mi existencia, deshojadas y revueltas en el fango donde se revuelca el infame crapuloso!!

¡Ah! pero su muerte civil será eterna; en mi alma ruge la venganza, una venganza muy grande que reduzca a la impotencia al impostor que erigió en lo más profundo de mi alma una pasión insensata! Mi caída moral tiene rehabilitación, y su caída . . . ¡su caída será la más degradante y vergonzosa!

Lo sabrán todos, Judith; les mostraré si se quiere la carta que te manda el agente de policía; haré circular en nuestra sociedad su degeneración hasta reducirlo a la impotencia, hasta que emigre de la ciudad, y entonces, sólo entonces saciaré mi venganza.

¡Cómo nos equivocamos las mujeres por coquetas! Admiramos el exterior, adoramos un rostro seductor, nos deslumbra el oropel, y caemos vencidas cuando debíamos ser las vencedoras.

¡Yo, la mujer eminentemente erótica; yo, que guardaba mis ilusiones amorosas para disfrutarlas a su lado, y que todo el mundo de mi ventura era para él . . . para un afeminado que desprecia mis ternuras supremas por las de esos repulsivos y vergonzantes!

Siento náuseas al pensar en todas las asquerosidades de *Mimí,* y no seré tan baja de tener una entrevista con él. Le escribiré terminantemente para concluir estas relaciones indecorosas, encerrándome en un profundo mutismo; y mi determinación desde ahora es inalterable.

. . .

—¿Y tú, Judith—dijo para terminar Estela, después de un corto momento de silencio;—te vengarás también? ¿Nos unimos para desenmascarar a esos bribones? . . .

—Ya hablaremos largamente sobre el asunto, mi querida Estela—respondió Judith con voz apagada y siniestra;—estoy muy nerviosa, y lo mejor que debo hacer es retirarme a esa casa y mañana nos veremos por la tarde; te contaré el resultado de mi resolución.

—¿Te vas, Judith?

—Sí, Estela, me voy; y sólo te encargo que en estos momentos de tribulación en que nuestro espíritu lucha con la desgracia, que seamos titanes en nuestra fuerza de voluntad, para derribar a esos monstruos que sellaron con un baldón de ignominia nuestra hermosa vida, que surge esplendente en la primavera de nuestras ilusiones juveniles.

IV.

Hemos llegado como un gnomo de la leyenda mitológica, hasta la espléndida alcoba de Judith para ser testigos invisibles de sus pesares dolorosos y de sus pensamientos vengativos.

Una fastuosa alcoba, alegre, risueña y hermosa, con esa hermosura sugestiva y blanca como una aurora serena y límpida; una alcoba como la mansión de las hadas y como el cielo de los querubes de nuestros sueños fantásticos.

Una alcoba decorada al estilo Luis XV; alfombras afelpadas y colgaduras de raso blanco; un tálamo niquelado despidiendo a la luz centelleantes resplandores, y en la superficie del colchón, alba colcha y almohadones de pluma con su funda de seda azul con grandes moños lilas. Un tocadorcito con su luna de Venecia; una mesa de centro artísticamente tallada donde había juguetes de filigrana; un sillón primorosamente tapizado, guarnecido por un dosel de seda blanca, y un secreter de caoba donde estaban guardadas muchas cartas amorosas del prometido *Ninón*.

En el reloj de la próxima iglesia han dado pausadas las nueve de la noche . . .

Judith ha entrado en su alcoba y está sola, llorosa y triste.

Y en el doselito límpido, fingiendo brumas de plata en noches de plenilunio, sentada, recargando un codo mórbido y blanco sobre la felpa del brazal del sillón, la mirada vaga, dibujándose en sus labios carmíneos una sonrisa amarga, Judith se extasiaba en ver los arabescos de la alfombra, y contemplaba a veces un tiesto de porcelana de Sajonia, donde hermosas begonias adornaban la estancia.

En su traje de brocado gris plata se acentuaban las curvas de su cuerpo como de gentil princesa.

De sus ojos caían ardientes lágrimas, y sus húmedas pupilas se alzaban para ver el marco dorado donde estaba el retrato de *Ninón* figurándose que sonreía amorosamente.

Y . . . una a una, con rapidez vertiginosa, como un torrente que se desborda, fueron saliendo aquellas lágrimas entre suspiros ahogados y ayes virginales.

Por su imaginación calenturienta pasaban velozmente, como llevados por un huracán, todos sus recuerdos del pasado, sus ilusiones de placer y sus candorosos idilios.

Su presente era invadido por espesos nubarrones, empañando el cielo de sus venturas; resonaban en el fondo de su alma quejidos dolorosos y suspiros interminables, mientras de sus ojos rodaban lágrimas de fuego.

Y el futuro, ese futuro soñado lleno de encantamientos y realizaciones para su felicidad, moría estérilmente, con un estertor agónico, horripilante, sin brotar ni una nueva ilusión, ni una esperanza, ni una oleada saturada de fe.

La primavera de sus ideales fenecía palideciendo, y llegaba pronto el invierno precedido de fantasmas, de fúnebres delirios, matando los triunfos y las glorias de su alma fogosa, apagando de un solo soplo la luz resplandeciente que alumbraba el edén de todas sus venturas. ¡¡Ah!! . . . pero su alma rugía en Etna, y estallaba formidable para cubrir con cenizas candentes el pasado ignominioso . . .

Mandaría llamar a *Ninón* inmediatamente, y allí, solos frente a frente, lo repudiaría, lo expulsaría lanzando a su rostro el bofetón de la venganza y del desprecio.

Y resuelta a terminar con aquellas relaciones, tocó el timbre, y después de unos cuantos minutos se presentó su doncella.

Judith fue al secreter y sacó una tarjeta perfumada, escribiéndole a *Ninón* que viniera a verla inmediatamente; y entregándosela a su doncella, le dijo: que uno de los mozos lleve esto a la casa del Sr. *Ninón,* diciéndole que lo espero.

Cuando la doncella salió, Judith volvió a sentarse en el sillón, y apoyando su cabeza sobre sus manos lloró amargamente, con ese llanto doloroso, cuando el corazón ensoberbecido de la mujer vanidosa siente lo imposible, lo irremediable, y maldice al infortunio, a la vida, al dolor incurable que hace sollozar como un niño al que tiene el alma llena de grandeza ficticia.

V.

¡Son las once de la noche!

Una noche serena, salpicada la comba etérea de diamantinas estrellas, destacando pálidamente la luna.

En la poética alcoba de Judith hay un torrente de luz eléctrica; ella se ha esmerado en que haya profusión de luces y ha encendido todas las bombillas, como acostumbra hacerlos en los días de grandes recepciones.

¡*Ninón* y Judith están frente a frente!

—Me has llamado urgentemente, Judith,—decía *Ninón* mirándola con ternura,—y aquí me tienes, como siempre, amoroso, dispuesto a probarte que te adoro.

—¿Que me adoras, *Ninón*? . . . respondió con ironía Judith.

—¿Y lo dudas, Judith, si sabes que tú eres mi sola creencia, mi única ilusión? . . .

—¡Mientes, mientes, *Ninón*! . . . exclamó Judith en el paroxismo de la cólera.

—¿Que miento, Judith?—respondió *Ninón* con hipocresía. ¿Acaso no te he dado mil pruebas de mi cariño inefable? ¿No he depositado en ti, sólo en ti todo lo que de más noble, de más grandioso, de más veneración guardaba en mi alma?

. . .

—Eres un impostor, *Ninón;* creíste que por el amor que te profeso, llegarías al fin que te proponías, y que mi nobleza y mi orgullo lo trocarías por el amor de la ramera que vende sus caricias por una de tus sonrisas, por uno de tus suspiros y por una de tus miradas incendiarias.

Pero te equivocaste; ni he caído del alto lugar en que estoy colocada, ni he perdido la dignidad ni el orgullo; ni he sentido por ti, ni por nadie, las ansias del deseo que pierden a la mujer manchando su pureza, no; te adoraba, sí, como pocas mujeres por ardientes que sean, sepan amar; pero busco un hombre que nunca haya caído en el precipicio de la bajeza.

Y tú crees indigno, miserable, degenerado; tus instintos son criminales y bastardos.

Buscas, infame *Ninón,* en orgiásticas cenas, afectos como los de *Mimí, Pudor, Virtud, Estrella* y no sé cuantos más hombres, que trajeron al mundo un signo de desgracia y que te sirven de instrumentos pasivos, a ti, que estás en el vigor de una existencia llena de juventud.

Y manchas y profanas esa vida con hombres como tú, con hombres . . .

—¿Pero qué dices, Judith?—interrumpió *Ninón,*—¿acaso te han predispuesto mis enemigos, los que se muestran amigos y saben que te amo? Pero no . . . no, Judith; no conozco a esos hombres que tú dices, ni siquiera de nombre . . . ¿por qué me dices eso, mi bien? . . .

—Porque lo repito, respondió Judith, eres un impostor, *Ninón;* porque todo lo noble que tenías lo has cambiado por ruines bajezas.

—¡Judith! . . . murmuró suplicante *Ninón.*

—Sí, *Ninón,* prosiguió Judith; voy a ser franca una vez más y para siempre contigo.

Cuando nos conocimos y entablamos nuestras relaciones amorosas, te había creído digno, bueno y noble.

Sabía que habías sido un poco *calavera* y que te gustaban las emociones *donjuanescas,* y aunque en mi pecho sentía el hervor de los celos, te dispensaba todo porque me hacía la cuenta de que algún día, cansado de tus aventuras y galanteos, vendrías a mí, sumiso y amoroso, y tus caricias y tus pensamientos serían para mí sola.

Y te amaba, te adoraba, *Ninón;* a una insinuación tuya, a la primera queja dolorida hubiera besado tu frente y enjugado tus lágrimas; hubiera acallado con mi ternura los latidos de tu corazón decepcionado y harto de tanto placer beodo.

El primer beso que me diste, lo sentí en mis labios como un bálsamo ardiente, erótico, inmaculado; ¡repercutió hasta lo más íntimo de mi alma, haciéndola estremecer de gozo, creyendo que sería el símbolo de la unión indisoluble de nuestras almas!

¡Cuántas veces en mis poderosas soñaciones mi mente rompió las puertas de la realidad y en alas de la fantasía esta alcoba se convirtió en palacio real, y envuelto en blancos cendales bajaba hasta mí el ángel del consuelo trayéndote a su lado, escoltados por un grupo de querubes que imprimían besos castísimos en mi frente, y entonaban un coro bellísimo, tremulante y melodioso como un himno nupcial!

Pero tú rompiste el misterioso encantamiento de mi candor con tus bastardas acciones de impureza.

Has pululado entre el vicio y el crimen exhibiéndote grotescamente entre cómicas y rameras, y no satisfecho, te has prostituido hasta el grado de caer en el pantano donde los cerdos se avergonzarían de tocarlo por miedo de mancharse.

Y no sólo *Mimí* y esos jóvenes, degenerados que dices no conocer, han satisfecho tus venales deseos, sino que hasta prostituyes a tus criados iniciándoles en esa vida de torpeza en que el hombre ha perdido su decoro, su dignidad y su orgullo.

Eres, *Ninón,* el agente de esos desgraciados y usurpadores de la mujer, y el estigma de la deshonra caerá sobre ti . . .

—Óyeme, Judith—suplicaba avergonzado *Ninón;*—¡si yo te amo, si todo es mentira! . . .

—¿Vuelves a repetir que me amas, *Ninón?*—decía colérica Judith.—Si te conozco demasiado; eres tan hipócrita y tan prostituido que necesitabas una coraza donde poder escudarte, y la víctima sacrificada en aras de la vergüenza sería yo.

Querías juntar tu nombre con el mío para realizar un matrimonio que sólo llevara por único fin atesorar mis millones para derrocharlos con esos granujas, y para que mi nombre honroso te sirviera para cubrir la fórmula social y la apariencia en esta sociedad en que vivimos y que desgraciadamente es tan prostituida y tan hipócrita como tú.

Sí, querías que apareciéramos radiantes de felicidad ante la mojiganga de esta sociedad exigente de alcurnia; y en el hogar, donde están amalgamadas las intimidades, donde se desahogan las pasiones, donde se da rienda suelta al dolor y al placer, donde se acarician las almas buenas, no, *Ninón;* ¡allí no habría más que maldiciones; allí estaría mi orgullo abatido por miedo al escándalo social; allí sólo habría infelicidad, adulterio, degradación! . . .

—¡Óyeme, Judith, atiéndeme! Necesito probarte que son mentiras todo . . . que te adoro . . . que . . .

—Basta, *Ninón,* basta de comedias; es inútil que quieras convencerme; desde este instante todo ha concluido entre nosotros . . . ¡Vete, vete, *Ninón!*

—¡Judith, amor mío, óyeme!—volvió a instar *Ninón.*

—¡Sal de aquí, miserable! ¡Sal pronto, o llamo a mis lacayos para que te despidan a latigazos!—dijo Judith con altanería, mientras que sus ojos lanzaban una mirada siniestra.

Y *Ninón,* avergonzado, tembloroso y pálido, salió de aquella estancia con el fardo del desprestigio al hombro, y al dar el último paso en el dintel de la puerta volvió el rostro, y sus ojos se encontraron con los de Judith, que despedían rayos fulgurantes llenos de odio inextinguible.

VI.

Apenas Judith había salido de la casa de Estela, esta última se aproximó a un coquetuelo pupitre y escribió una larguísima carta a *Mimí,* donde le decía todo lo que se sabía, y terminaba repudiándolo y cortando para siempre sus relaciones de amor.

Cuando hubo despachado la carta a su destino dejóse caer sobre un sillón, llevándose las manos a los ojos que lloraban amargamente.

Los efluvios de las bombillas de luz eléctrica le caían de lleno en el rostro, y por la ventana de su alcoba penetraban los rayos de la luna, poetizando aquella elegantísima estancia.

¡Sufría mucho! ¡La herida recién abierta le parecía incurable!

Brotaban de su pecho de soberbia aristócrata un raudal de pensamientos luciferianos, para vengarse de aquella burla sangrienta de su destino.

Las estrofas del poema de sus amores, aquellas estrofas tiernas y dulcísimas, se esfumaban de su vida, surgiendo frases tiranas; hiriendo sus oídos el grito de la horda burlesca de sus amistades que antes la envidiaban.

Sus ensueños opulentos y espléndidos se extinguían ante el desbordamiento de la realidad, y sus misteriosas grandezas se marchitaban como las flores en ese invierno terrible de las supremas decepciones.

Y como un fantasma venía el tedio cabalgando sobre el coloso paquidermo del dolor, sediento de tenebrosos desengaños.

Su vanidad, esa vanidad estúpida de las mujeres, caía mutilada a sus pies; y en el inmenso dolor de su alma maldecía a esa sociedad mil veces fingida, mil veces hipócrita y desleal, que aparecía radiante ante la multitud exigente de alcurnia, y en intimidades ocultaba sus miserias, sus dramas sangrientos, sus tragedias y sus crímenes.

Maldecía con furor la miserable condición humana.

En el roce social del mundo elegante había conocido a *Mimí;* sus amigas lo habían abonado entusiasmadas y todos sabían que lo adoraba.

Y ahora, las burlas más groseras, la murmuración más picante y las hablillas de esas déspotas empingorotadas le vendrían a infestar con su hálito infecto su corazón enfermo.

Esa sociedad nada perdona, porque no tiene sentimientos ni vergüenza.

¡Ay! y el vacío se haría a su rededor . . . mas se conformaba en apurar su dolor a solas, sufriría menos: se vería excluida de esa caravana de vanidosas que bajo los encajes de un vestido de seda ocultan su miseria horripilante, y en cada faceta de sus joyas una perfidia y un delito.

Desaparecería también, al saber su desgracia, esa turba de arlequines, de vagabundos del *boulevard,* ignorantes y petimetres, que le asediaban con sus pretensiones insensatas.

Pero ella era grande, enérgica, insaciable, vengativa.

Comprendía que *Mimí* jamás volvería al redil de la honra, porque todos esos que se prostituyen en el manantial de la depravación, tienen por consecuencia la pereza, el egoísmo y las pasiones desenfrenadas que tiemblan y palpitan con vibraciones de impotencia . . .

Estela, hermosamente pálida, con el reflejo de sus cóleras en su rostro y de sus venganzas soberbias, parecía el ángel apocalíptico que presagiaba el fin vergonzoso de *Mimí.*

Y en la atmósfera vaga de sus ensueños de princesa destronada, encerraba un misterio de desesperación indefinible, que le hacía arrancar en su copioso llanto, gritos lastimeros como un alarido de hiena impotente, sublimada por la ira de sus venganzas.

VII.

La casa marcada con el número 000, en la calle de la Paz, estaba interiormente revestida de gala.

En el patio de la casa hay dos escaleras laterales y una en el centro que dan paso al interior de la misma que se divide en dos viviendas; en el centro del patio hay una fuente de piedra de Chiluca y las piezas son extensas y bien decoradas.

Los pensamientos de las escaleras están adornados con festones, y la pieza interior más extensa con coronas de gardenias y *panneauxs* de margaritas y rosas blancas, así como distribuidas en la pared innúmeras bandoleras de colores.

Ninón y *Mimí,* que eran los directores de la fiesta, estaban suma-
mente alegres y esperaban impacientes que llegara la hora feliz en que
comenzara el bullicio del *sarao.*

Hablaban entusiasmados y se prometían goces inefables y sensa-
ciones excelsas.

—¿Has arreglado todo, *Ninón* mío?—le decía *Mimí* cariñosa-
mente.

—Todo, *Mimí*—respondió amable *Ninón;*—la orquesta, que es
de lo mejor, no debe tardar; las tarjetas de invitación se las di a *Estrella* para los amigos de confianza, y a tu lacayito lo mandé con
otras para que las repartiera en las cantinas entre gente extraña que,
atraída por la novedad, no tendría inconveniente en venir a divertirse
un buen rato.

—¿Y los vinos y los sandwichs, los mandaste ya preparar?—preguntó *Mimí.*

—Todo está listo—respondió *Ninón* muy satisfecho.

—Entonces sólo falta nuestro tocado—dijo *Mimí.*

—¡Oh! ¡y qué elegante te verás con tu falda de princesa y tu corpiño escotado de seda! ¡parecerás una reina, *Mimí* simpático!—dijo
Ninón en tono de lisonja.

—¿Y tú no te resuelves a ponerte uno de los trajes de mujer, bello
Ninón?

—¡No, alma mía! ¿no ves que soy tu maridito?—respondió *Ninón*
con una mueca grotesca.

—Pero te perfumarás tu cabellera y tu sedoso bigotito, ¿verdad,
chiquitito?—dijo *Mimí* entusiasta.

—Si, *Mimí,* por darte gusto haré lo que tú quieras . . .

—¿Me lo prometes, *Ninón?*—preguntó *Mimí* con zalamería.

—¿No te amo—respondió *Ninón*—como se ama a una virgen ante
un cielo sonriente, infinito, lleno de inexplicables placeres?

¿No por ti—prosiguió *Ninón*—he renunciado todo; hasta la mano
de Judith que tanto me adoraba? . . . ¿No estás satisfecho, pre-
ciosísimo *Mimí?*

¡¡¡Ay, Dios mío, qué barbaridad!!!—respondió *Mimí* ruborizán-
dose;—si no merezco tanto, *Ninón;* pero ya sabes que mi amor para
ti es inalterable, inmenso, delicioso . . .

—Por eso te adoro—decía *Ninón;*—por eso te doy gusto; por eso
esta noche feliz sólo tú serás la única parejita que estrechen mis brazos, serás el único que reciba las caricias que siento por ti; pero si una
sonrisa, si una mirada, si una palabra es para otro, . . . entonces,
Mimí . . .

—¿Qué, sientes celos, *Ninón?*

—¿Y cómo no los he de sentir—decía *Ninón* con hipocresía,—si desde ahora tú eres el único afecto que me queda? Las mujeres son malas, vanidosas; por una sonrisa piden un cielo; por un beso un tesoro; y luego, cuando nos aprisionan en sus redes, ya somos los esclavos que inclinamos la testuz perdiendo nuestra libertad, ¡y trocamos nuestro amor en odio!... ¡No así tú, *Mimí,* que eres constante, amoroso, sincero y noble; a cambio de un beso quieres otro; por una sonrisa otra sonrisa; a cambio de mi amor otro amor más grande, más eterno, más real, más poderoso!

¡Pobres mujeres; ilusas orgullosas que buscan sólo esclavos y mendigos de su amor! Terminó diciendo *Ninón* lleno de cólera.

—¡Ay! *Ninón*—le decía *Mimí* para calmarlo.—Por Dios Santo, no te enojes, no te enfurezcas; si estoy a tu lado como siempre, dispuesto a tus caprichos.

Y mientras de los ojos de *Mimí* resbalaba una lágrima de hipocresía, abrazaba con furia a *Ninón,* sintiéndose feliz en los brazos de su prometido [?].

VIII.

Pudor, Virtud, Blanca, Margarita y *Carola* están en la elegante alcoba de *Estrella* haciéndose la *toilette* para concurrir al baile de la calle de la Paz.

Pudor se acicalaba un magnífico traje femenino de seda roja con encajes negros, luciendo un cuello escotado lleno de flacuras donde surgían prominentes las cuerdas de su garganta, y por la espalda, como un promontorio, los omóplatos descarnados embadurnados de albayalde; su peluca rubia empolvada, y un sombrero de enorme ala, con un museo de pájaros cayendo sobre su hombro izquierdo.

Virtud un traje blanco de piel de España con luenga falda y todo lleno de azahares; peluca negra que contrastaba con sus ojos azules; un sombrero lleno de encajes, y sus manos jugueteaban con finísimo abanico.

Blanca un traje crema, transparente, cuajado de listones y encajes lilas; zapatillas bordadas de oro, guante negro, peluca y trenzas rubias, postizas, y sombrero negro; sus hombros regordetes y morenos, su rostro de pequeños ojos, su boca de belfos africanos y su nariz roma, le daban un aire de hembra gorila, bulliciosa y dislocante.

Margarita portaba un traje rameado de seda azul, una bata hermosísima, donde apenas dejaba entrever la punta de un pie calzado con zapatillas del mismo color, con hebillas plateadas y un moñito a la *mignón;* el escote era interesante: exhibía un seno prominente, blanquísimo [por la demasiada pintura], con dos grandes listones que colgaban en los extremos, y resaltando sus enormes ojos negros, su nariz aguileña y su boca diminuta, pintarrajeado el rostro con *mucho arte,* con ese arte maestro que acostumbran las mesalinas, que semejaba a un *clown* de circo de barrio.

Carola tenía puesto un sencillísimo traje de muselina, pero elegantísimo; tras la peluca negra la confía blanca echada hacia atrás; delantal blanco de peto con un cerco de encajes y blondas a la orilla; la falda muy corta para lucir torneadas pantorrillas rellenas de algodón, con medias caladas, choclo de charol con tacón alto y caderas bien puestas; su voz y sus modales femeninos lo hacían ridículo, que al mirarlo no se podía menos de reír y acordarse de alguna escena bufa de la Isla de San Balandrán.[4]

Dejamos a propósito reservado el último lugar para describir la *toilette* y el vestido del jovencito *Estrella,* el espiritual, el núbil, el duquecito pálido como le decían sus compañeros; el infeliz que se iniciaba esa noche en la sociedad de los degenerados, de los prostituidos, de los sinvergüenzas.

Cubría sus rizados cabellos una peluca negra, adornando graciosamente su testa. Sus ojos límpidos, negros, fulgurantes y vivaces le daban un aire encantador de virgen inmaculada. Su boca de labios gruesos con dos hileras de dientes limpios y blancos, y en sus mejillas dos hoyuelos seductores, aquel adolescente imberbe de quince años tenía mucha semejanza femenina. Su cuerpo pequeño y vigoroso cuadraba a su vestido. Un trajecito blanco de bebé; una bata pequeña, alta, de género calado y encajes de Bruselas; un gorro de seda cargado de encajes transparentes; un listón ceñido al cuello y otro muy ancho a la cintura rematando en un gran moño; medias blancas y choclos negros con pompón de seda; los dedos de sus manos con valiosos anillos y un collar de perlas en la garganta.

Su aspecto era de una niña pudorosa, juguetona, inocente y mimada.

Ya listos los jóvenes, y cubriendo sus hombros desnudos con grandes abrigos de elegante corte femenino, bajaron a la puerta y montaron en elegantes carruajes que ya los esperaban impacientes, para conducirlos a la calle de la Paz, a la casa número 000, donde el placer, el aplauso y las caricias los esperaban, y Baco, Cupido y Príapo se aprestaban sonrientes para solemnizar aquella iniciación grandiosa del espiritual (?) *Estrella.*

IX.

¡Don Pedro de Marruecos!
Su solo nombre indica la magnitud de su popularidad.

Alto, fornido, de tez blanca y bigote abundante y rubio, retorcido hacia arriba, era un tipo distinguido.

Inmensamente rico y desposado con una dama bellísima de noble alcurnia, era una de las figuras más prominentes de nuestra historia novelesca.

Hacía derroches de magnificencia; su soberbio tren era de los más elegantes en la Metrópoli; sus caballos de *pur sang* eran los mejores y más lucidos en el Hipódromo de Peralvillo.

En Francia había causado la admiración de los parisienses, y allí, entre derroche y derroche en bacanales exóticas, aprendió mucho, muchísimo, de la más desenfrenada prostitución.

Comenzó por la conquista de la humilde *grisette*[5] y tiró mucho oro.

Siguió escalando las cumbres del placer y puso trenes lujosos y casas magníficas a las explotadoras *cocottes*.[6]

Fue a Italia; y allí, en la tierra del arte y del canto, compró caricias de notables artistas femeninas. Improvisaba *saraos* donde las tiples de voz de arcángel deleitaban sus oídos, mientras él, muellemente recostado en un canapé, veía embelesado con los ojos entreabiertos los movimientos seductores de una soprano, y a veces los cerraba con indolencia para oír la voz de ruiseñor, mientras su imaginación volaba por otros mundos de placer muy grandes.

Visitó España: Andalucía evocó en su imaginación ardiente las delicias del paraíso creado por él, y los bailes voluptuosos, la sal, la alegría de las chicas iberas lo entusiasmaban, y moría, moría lentamente de ilusión, satisfaciendo sus venales deseos y sus arrobamientos de beodo y arruinando su organismo por el exceso de los placeres lúbricos.

Cansado de contemplar la esplendente luz del arte, hastiado del goce en su último grado, vino a México, con la decepción y la muerte prematura de sus ideales, después de haber vivido tan deprisa.

La vida le era insoportable.

Veía a las mujeres como un ser inútil y despreciable, incapaz de crear nuevos placeres para él, y maldecía a la Naturaleza porque las delicias femeninas fueran tan cortas e insaciables.

Su cuerpo impotente pedía a grandes gritos más placer, más ilusión, más deleites inconcebibles.

Y todo fue en vano; de la alta escala fue descendiendo hasta el último nivel de bajeza, hasta el nivel de los brutos.

Ya entonces para él era la mujer un sarcasmo irrisorio y despreciable.

Y faltando a sus deberes, a su dignidad, a su misión de hombre civilizado, fue un esclavo de sus pasiones y de sus apetitos desordenados.

Germinaban en su corazón nuevos deleites; las espantosas ruinas del pasado las veía humeantes, pestilentes, y surgía la bestia ahíta de venganza, ciega, irascible, cayendo por la pendiente criminal de un abismo sin fin de negruras y dolores.

Comenzó por frecuentar círculos secretos de seres degradados y creyó encontrar un mundo nuevo.

Después . . . después fue degenerando, degenerando inevitablemente . . . ¡y cayó en esa vorágine que le atraía como un vértigo! . . . se prostituyó y llegó al fondo del abismo.

La noche de que nos ocupa este párrafo, acicalado con elegancia, perfumado, retorcido el bigote rubio, se hizo conducir en un flamante *coupé* de su propiedad hacia la casa de la calle de la Paz, para disipar su aburrimiento y para caer una vez en la crápula execrable, mientras su noble y buena esposa dormía candorosamente soñando en él, con un mundo de santas ilusiones y de un futuro delicioso en el camino glorioso de su felicidad.

X.

En las mejores y más concurridas cantinas de la Metrópoli recibían algunos parroquianos tarjetas de invitación para un baile y una rifa, de manos de un jovencito de ojos lánguidos, simpático, afeminado y ceremonioso.

La novedad consistía en una rifa de '*Art Nouveau*' y un elegante baile.

Muchos de los jóvenes de consuetudinaria *parranda*, atraídos por el bombo de las tarjetas, entre guasa y guasa, y copa y copa ya en el estómago, tomaban los trenes de la 'Colonia' para dirigirse a la famosa casa de la calle de la Paz.

El salón, adornado con guirnaldas y cortinajes de seda [todo provisional], ya estaba henchido de gente de trueno, extrañándose mucho que ni una sola dama circulaba por el salón.

La orquesta, aunque no de lo mejor pero sí regularcita, compuesta de varios profesores (?) somnolientos, llenaba los ámbitos del salón tocando variadas piezas de baile.

En la próxima habitación, y convenientemente acondicionada, estaba la cantina con un mostrador desvencijado, pletórico de botellas de buenos vinos, varias cajas de *champagne* y una buena dotación de *sandwichs*.

Las diez de la noche serían, aproximadamente cuando llegaron a la puerta de la calle varios carruajes lujosos, de los cuales se bajaron, al parecer, varias damas de vistosos trajes de fantasía.

Eran los jóvenes *Estrella, Pudor, Virtud, Carola, Blanca* y *Margarita.*

En el salón surgió un murmullo de curiosidad y muchos de los circunstantes se dirigieron a la puerta de entrada para contemplar los rostros de las damas (?).

Apenas habían traspasado los dinteles de la puerta para penetrar al salón las seductoras damas (?) y ya la corte de antiguos adoradores los obsequiaba con una ruidosa salva de aplausos, y un viva gutural, aguardentoso y báquico se esparció en ondas sonoras por el salón; a instancias de algunos la orquesta tocó una diana que mereció el *bis* más entusiasta y polichinesco.

Un ajuar de bejuco estaba reservado para asiento de las damas como lugar de preferencia.

Después, a varios intervalos, fueron llegando otras damas (?) aunque no ataviadas con la misma elegancia.

El lacayito, por su parte, entusiasta también y relacionado con toda la servidumbre de aquellos jóvenes, entre la cual había muchos iniciados en el amor secreto, había formado también su escuadrón de seres afeminados.

Llegó en algunas *calandrias* desvencijadas con varios cocheros, lacayos y, en especialidad, camaristas y meseros, que iban a compartir democráticamente con sus amos los goces venerados de su cielo forjado con venturas del nuevo paraíso terrenal, donde ellos formaban parte como plantas estériles para la buena simiente, pero sí productoras de la inmoralidad y el salvajismo.

¡Pobres seres degradados! . . .

Ninguno de los concurrentes convidados por las tarjetas repartidas en las cantinas había notado que se les daba *gato por liebre*, tan bien confeccionados estaban los vestidos y tan bien remedados los ademanes femeninos.

Pero hasta entonces ningún movimiento había sido tan inusitado en el salón como la llegada de un personaje interesante y popular.

¡Don Pedro de Marruecos! gritó una voz fuerte y sonora.

Y a ese grito todos saltaron de sus asientos, se formaron en dos grupos y dieron paso a Don Pedro, que penetró majestuosamente investigando con su mirada el aspecto del salón; y dirigiéndose hacia las damas (?) saludólas con afecto amoroso.

Pero a pesar de la llegada de Don Pedro de Marruecos la nostalgia invadió todos los semblantes, las damas (?) funcionaban cómicamente y las risas *pierrotescas* se esparcían en murmullos alegres.

Faltaba algo en la reunión.

La reina (?) de la fiesta estaba ahí, con su pudoroso vestido blanco de bebé, cortejada por una caravana de jóvenes galantes.

Pero faltaban *Ninón* y *Mimí* que eran los amos de la fiesta.

Estrella era admirado con curiosidad; su candor de virgen atraía irresistiblemente y no escaseaban los galantes que le presentaban copitas de espiritual *champagne.*

Don Pedro de Marruecos fue a sentarse a su lado, acariciándole sus manos con codicia, y le veía fijamente sus ojos como queriéndolo sugestionar con una mirada impregnada de fuego candente, de ese fuego volcánico que hace palpitar el corazón y comprender la inspiración del hombre viciado en todos sus horrores.

XI.

Cuando cintilaban las luces eléctricas en sus bombillas de colores y los candelabros con multitud de esteáricas daban su luz magnífica; cuando los '*panneaux*' de gardenias y margaritas esparcían sus ondas de perfume, y la orquesta preludiaba una marcha, entraron triunfalmente en el salón los amos del *sarao;* el hercúleo *Ninón* y el tímido *Mimí.*

Más unánime, más estruendosa, más prolongada y espontánea fue la ovación con que los recibieron, y la orquesta entusiasmada y burlesca ejecutaba la diana de reglamento.

Mimí, con su porte de princesa, contoneando suavemente las caderas postizas y languideciendo con ternura su mirada de sílfide, penetró del brazo de *Ninón* haciendo caravanas amistosas.

Era el más elegante en su vestido y en su tocado; la luenga cola de su falda, recargada con encajes de Bruselas, se la recogía con la mano izquierda, ciñéndola a su cuerpo, para exhibir sus formas postizas, y apoyándose en *Ninón* recorría la sala sonriendo a sus amiguitos con gracioso ademán.

¡Comenzó el baile! . . .

Es bastonero, de pie en el centro del salón anunció la primera pieza; un vals sonoro, rítmico y bello.

Don Pedro de Marruecos dio el brazo a *Estrella, Ninón* a *Mimí* y raudos, ligeros, se confundieron con los demás bailadores, describiendo vertiginosas volteretas.

Carola, Blanca, Pudor, Virtud y *Margarita,* melindrosos y haciéndose del rogar como púdicas señoritas, cedieron a mil súplicas su mano a simpáticos alentadores del mismo gremio.

—Y el placer era infinito, dulce, satisfactorio.

—La ridiculez con toda su plástica grosera, danzaba allí con inmensa locura.

El salón estaba henchido de espectadores; los que habían concurrido procedentes de las cantinas ávidos de novedad, se iban retirando la mayor parte contrariados, quedando de los mismos uno que otro rezagado, incoherente y beodo, con los apócrifos palmitos.

Despejado un poco el salón por los que se iban retirando, quedando ya casi todos del mismo gremio, y contenta ya la comunidad por encontrarse entre gente de los *suyos*, el *sarao* siguió en todo su apogeo pareciendo un baile pompeyano de la decadencia romana.

Atizando el fuego en que ardían los jóvenes, hacían derroches de movimientos en el baile, y enardecidos como descocadas meretrices exhibían sus encantos postizos con arrebatadora vehemencia en medio de escandalosas impudicias.

El intermedio de las piezas de baile era cubierto por canciones en su mayor parte picarescas; uno que otro acompañado del *maestro del bajo,* cantaba destemplada canción, que al morir la última nota sucedía una salva de aplausos.

Mimí entusiasmado también cantó; su voz atiplada ejecutó una romanza sentidísima y ridícula, que mereció la repetición a instancias de la concurrencia.

Ninón se sentía satisfecho; contemplaba algunas veces a *Mimí* con delicia, y vibraba su juventud robusta; y violando todos los pudores lo abrazaba con efusión, posando sus labios de fuego en los labios frescos de su compañero. Era *Ninón* un famélico insaciable de caricias y de besos . . .

Don Pedro de Marruecos, el elegante *amateur*,[7] sentía una onda incesante de gratas armonías al oír la voz clara y timbrada del jovencito *Estrella*, cuidadosamente embellecido con su traje pudoroso de bebé.

Estrechaba con febril vehemencia las manos de *Estrella;* sentía una atracción satánica cuando el joven vestido de bebé dejaba entrever las morbideces de su cuerpo.

Y con estilo elegante y voz armoniosa, le decía Don Pedro lleno de ternura—¿me amarías, *Estrella?*

Y *Estrella,* como una ninfa tímida, respondió débilmente:—¡Ay! ¡Don Pedro, quién sabe! . . .

—¿Crees que no te haga feliz? insistió Don Pedro.

—No, Don Pedro,—respondió *Estrella;* necesito consultar con mi corazón, y además que haga Ud. méritos . . .

—Te querré mucho, *Estrella;* te adoraré hasta el delirio, tendrás casa, coche, lujo, mucho lujo, muchas comodidades . . . júrame que me amarás, te prometo lo que tú ansíes, lo que tú quieras, vida mía.

Y dialogando al oído de *Estrella,* Don Pedro en murmurios suaves y cadenciosos, entregado con ardientes transportes, estrechaba dulcemente las manos de *Estrella* que oía las declaraciones como un canto de adoración.

La página honrada de la vida de Don Pedro desaparecía bajo una clámide llena de pauperismos, y surgía la página corruptora llena de delincuencias, llena de crispaturas de sus nervios impotentes, entre el desmoronamiento de su vergüenza y de su dignidad para caer una vez más del alto pedestal de su existencia y de su posición social.

¡Hasta dónde conducen los vicios a los hombres!

Besaba los párpados temblorosos de *Estrella*, y en un arranque delirante acercó sus labios quemantes a su rostro y a sus mejillas, y su pasión, más vehemente, se confundió en un abrazo largo, muy largo, inefable, embriagador e histrionesco como la afectación de sus modales.

Entretanto, en el salón crecía el entusiasmo.

Ojos fosforescentes, ojos lúbricos, ojos lánguidos; caderas postizas ondulantes, gráciles con sus irreprochables curvas; rostros polveados, pintarrajeados; pelucas maravillosamente adornadas con peinetas incrustadas de oro y joyas finísimas; pantorrillas bien cinceladas a fuerza de algodón y auténticas de amorfas flacuras; senos postizos, prominentes y enormes pugnando por salir de su cárcel; muecas grotescas y voces fingidas; le daba todo ese conjunto a la orgía algo de macabro y fantástico.

Se acercaba la hora de la rifa, esa hora esperada con impaciencia, con verdadera impaciencia . . .

El prólogo de la fiesta había sido esplendoroso; la apoteosis sería lo más bello, lo más práctico, lo más satisfactorio, y el epílogo cerraría con broche de oro su báquica orgía . . . ¡así pensaban todos los circunstantes!

En el paraíso del amor, las mil gradaciones del brillante ideal de sus sueños, centelleaban fastuosamente.

XII.

Era la madrugada del domingo 17 de noviembre de 1901 . . .

Llegaba por fin el momento supremo y solemne de la rifa deseada.

Colocada sobre una mesa una ánfora de bronce que contenía varios papelitos enrollados, se sacarían uno por uno, y los números del uno al doce, que era el premio gordo, irían depositando besos ardientes que recibiría el jovencito vestido de bebé, o sea el espiritual *Estrella* . . . el número doce se resiste a describirlo la pluma.

La orquesta tocaba danzones veracruzanos cuando la voz de *Ninón* anunció que se daba comienzo a la rifa.

Todos dejaron de bailar; se formaron paralelamente en dos filas, mientras Don Pedro se disponía a sacar los números premiados.

La rifa de '*Arte Nouveau*' que anunciaban las tarjetas que repartieron, no era de algún objeto de arte, ni mucho menos . . .

La prostitución en su último grado se dejaba mutilar ignominiosamente y cerraba los oídos para no oír las protestas de los hombres de conciencia.

¡Lo que a los hombres honrados nos parece el más inmundo de los vicios, el más desenfrenado, el más miserable, para aquellos jóvenes y para aquellos sirvientes de sus amos, era el manjar de sus dioses, y no tenían escrúpulo en sacrificar su pudor, su dignidad, su vergüenza, al vicio deshonesto que, como un sarcasmo, insultaba a la ley, a la vida, a la civilización, al progreso de todo lo humano, a la misma Naturaleza! . . .

Cada número que salía premiado y que Don Pedro anunciaba a los concurrentes, *Estrella* recibía tantos besos como cifra tenía el papelito enrollado.

Faltaba un solo número por salir: el premio gordo, el número doce; todos los semblantes estaban lívidos.

Uno que otro beodo bailaba de placer en su puesto y revisaba su número en las manos.

Estrella también estaba pálido, sereno y satisfecho; esperaba resignado la hora dichosa en que tocaran a gloria y en que el aplauso, los vivas, las dianas y los brindis surgieran crepitantes como una sinfonía triunfal de su degradación.

Al tumulto del placer y de la felicidad sucedió el tumulto del terror.

Don Pedro desenrollaba paulatinamente el último número, cuando entraron corriendo varios cocheros y lacayos gritando espantados, pintando el miedo en sus rostros:

—¡¡La policía . . . !! ¡¡¡Los gendarmes tocan a la puerta . . . !!!

Una bomba de dinamita arrojada en el salón no hubiera causado tanto pánico entre los concurrentes.

Cuarenta y cuatro personas había en el salón que no daban un paso para remediar la situación aflictiva, sin atreverse a abrir la puerta exterior de la casa.

La policía entretanto tocaba con fuerza, con violencia, esperando que abrieran las puertas de la casa para pedir la licencia del baile.

Don Pedro, sin despedirse de nadie y seguido de dos de sus criados, buscó una salida donde poder escaparse, y encontró una escalera de mano recargada en una de las paredes del patio de la casa; treparon por ella hasta la azotea, después bajaron él y uno de sus criados con la misma escalera para el patio de una casa contigua donde estaban los departamentos de los talleres de la "Unión Litográfica" y se perdieron entre la obscuridad.

Entretanto, el otro criado volvió a subir la escalera para colocarla en su sitio, y se quedó en la azotea *a la luna de Valencia,* después de haber salvado a su amo, esperando los resultados y las pesquisas de la policía.

A tanto golpe en la puerta dado por la policía, uno de los menos timoratos se resolvió a abrir, lleno de miedo, castañeteándole los dientes y temblándole las piernas.

Entró por fin la policía, y la mayor parte de la concurrencia se dispersó por las piezas de la otra vivienda de la misma casa.

Unos se escondían detrás de las puertas, otros en los inodoros, otros en el cuarto de baño dentro de una tina volteándola al revés, algunos intentaban meterse dentro de una estufa y otros en la chimenea.

El lacayo de *Mimí,* arrepentidísimo, se santiguaba y le daba vueltas a un rosario en sus manos.

Mimí lloraba amargamente; *Ninón* hacía pucheros y se tronaba las falanges de sus manos enguantadas.

Estrella, cínico, desvergonzado, esperaba con calma, impasible, la terminación del sainete.

Todos abrían desmesuradamente los ojos y proferían exclamaciones afeminadas y grotescas por el tenor siguiente: ¡Ay! ¡Dios mío, y en qué facha nos encuentran! . . . ¡Santa Virgen de los milagros! . . . ¡Milagroso Niño de Atocha! . . . ¡Madre Dolorosa, sálvanos! . . . ¡San Pascual Bailón, Santa Nicomedes, San Cipriano, óyenos Señor! . . .

Un borracho que estaba tendido a lo largo sobre unas sillas y medio dormido, al despertarlo uno de los gendarmes, le echaba la mano al cuello diciéndole, ¿otra copa alma mía, corazoncito de oro? . . .

Los músicos, asustados y confundidos, tomaban sus sombreros y enfundaban sus instrumentos para retirarse.

Pero como el oficial de gendarmes viera que había gato encerrado, dio orden a los gendarmes de aprehender a todos; de la comisaría mandaron refuerzos de agentes de los de imaginaria, y pocos momentos después era registrada toda la casa hasta el último rincón, aprehendiendo a 41 individuos que fueron conducidos a la Demarcación de Policía, entre los cuales iban algunos vestidos de mujer.

El mozo de Don Pedro, que se había quedado en la azotea observándolo todo, al subir por la misma escalera varios policías por donde su amo se había salvado, no tuvo más remedio que hacer el sacrificio de tomar un baño frío, metiéndose dentro de un tinaco que dotaba de agua a la casa, salvándose así milagrosamente.

XIII.

La aurora, esa princesa fantástica mitad sombra, mitad luz suave y vaga, se desperezaba soberbia con sus tonos divinos del alba.

En la comba azulada del cielo parpadeaban tristemente millares de pálidas estrellas, y la luna, con su blancura de desposada se erguía con las últimas ráfagas de su grandeza.

La vigorosa soberanía de la luz del día triunfaba alegremente.

El invierno, ese asesino implacable de la vida, comenzaba a extender su clámide fría llena de cierzos y de nieve.

La inauguración opulenta del inmundo bacanal de la casa de la calle de la Paz, tenía su epílogo tristísimo en el inmundo calabozo de la Demarcación.

¡Enorme transición! De la atmósfera saturada de perfumes, de la estancia adornada, de los rumores de la música, de los besos ardientes y caricias, una atmósfera viciada, infecta, microbicida; rumores tenebrosos, hondos suspiros y copiosos llantos de dolor inmenso.

Un cuadro triste y grotesco; un cuadro de bacantes masculinos maldicientes, detestando a Príapo y a Lampsaco, fumando para consolarse cigarrillos en cuyas volutas de humo iban muchos recuerdos del pasado . . . muchos incendios de deseos eróticos consumados en la depravación.

Uno por uno fueron llamados para declarar, siendo objeto de risas y contumelias por los guardianes que los llevaban del calabozo a la oficina.

Hubo quien se atreviera a llorar delante de los escribientes y pidiera misericordia.

El espiritual *Mimí* lloraba también a lágrima viva; confeso y convicto no le quedaba más remedio que sufrir la enorme vergüenza y el desprestigio. Se cambió el nombre en la Comisaría y esperó, aterido y somnoliento, el fatal desenlace.

Estrella, el rifado *virginal,* reía estúpidamente como esas descocadas mesalinas que desde mucho tiempo han ejercido su *carrera* en el emporio inmenso de la prostitución.

Varios de los que quedaron rezagados en el baile y que los tomaron por tales, eran de los que habían asistido por las invitaciones de tarjeta que les dieron en las cantinas, y protestaban enérgicamente; pero todo era inútil, había que comprobarlo.

Sólo *Ninón* era el que más sufría. Se arrepentía de sus culpas; reconocía que su ambición por el lujo, que la molicie, que el pernicioso influjo de sus amigos lo arrastraba hacía la deshonra.

Resbalaba por la pendiente de sus deseos desenfrenados y furiosos, intentando en vano saciar sus placeres, y le parecía que ya era tarde para lavar las impuras manchas de su vida; sentía anublados sus ojos por el llanto, y en cada lágrima candente la regeneración de su existencia se perdía en las lontananzas de lo ignoto.

En su imaginación, como en un calidoscopio, pasaban vertiginosamente todos sus recuerdos, y veía el rostro de sus padres que, aunque orgullosos y ridículos que soñaban con prosapias y noblezas, siempre lo amaban con ternura infinita.

Su madre, que tanto lo adoraba, cómo iba a llorar; cómo sufriría la vergüenza y la murmuración de la *High-Life*.[8]

Y Judith, la soberbia cortesana que tanto lo había querido, cómo gozaría con sus miserias y su ruina moral; se vengaría terriblemente como se vengan las mujeres heridas y altivas que desprecian al hombre que odian.

Luego se presentaba el futuro y le daba miedo, sentía pavor . . . sí, el futuro tremolaba la bandera negra de sus desgracias irremediables, y el destino espectral de sus temores hincaba su diente insaciable de hiena . . . la desesperación más infinita lo embargaba, cayendo en un letargo insensible, debilitado por la cobardía, por el temor a la vara de la justicia, a esa vara que flagela a los perversos, en nombre de un derecho sagrado, el derecho que tiene la sociedad honrada para que la respeten.

Esta vez mereció un verdadero elogio así de toda la prensa metropolitana como de la sociedad, la energía viril, incorruptible, del Señor Gobernador, que supo castigar a los impostores que desprestigiaban a la buena sociedad y a las buenas costumbres.

Cerca de las diez de la mañana y en traje de carácter, los que iban fantaseados con su elegante traje mujeril, provistos de buenas escobas de vara unos, otros con palas, un barril con agua y una cubeta de lámina para regar, salieron custodiados por un buen número de gendarmes *los lindos señoritos,* para barrer una de las calles de las Artes, cercana a la Demarcación.

¡Y había que verlos qué bien desempeñaban el oficio! Una señorita hacendosa no lo hubiera hecho con tanto arte y con tanta premura.

Los físicos más grotescos se exhibían en la calle, con sus ojos abotagados, la mirada baja, impúdica en algunos; se habían quitado las pelucas y los aretes de brillantes, y provocaba risa contemplar un rostro ajado con bigotito retorcido, falda recogida y choclos bordados con tacón muy alto; y a cada movimiento de la escoba un contoneo exagerado de las caderas, que contribuía poderosamente a dar pábulo a la sátira y los retruécanos más punzantes de algunos espectadores.

—¡Ay, tú! ¿que no te pesa el escobón?—le decía un espectador a otro, como para ridiculizar a los que barrían.

—¡Sí, tú!—respondía el otro.

—¿Dónde vives, Juan de Amor?—les decía alguno.

—¡¡En la calle de la Hortensia número clavel!! respondía con salero fingido algún peladito.

Y por ese tenor recibían los inmortales 41 los dicharachos más festivos y sangrientos.

Una vez que terminaron de barrer la calle fueron conducidos a la cárcel, donde se les abrió partida, y el Sr. Gobernador los juzgó con la prontitud que el caso requería, para acallar la voz de indignación de la sociedad ultrajada.

Algunos que probaron su inocencia y que sólo habían ido por el deseo de bailar ignorando el hecho escandaloso de los afeminados, fueron dados en libertad después de muchas gestiones.

Los demás, obrando la justicia con estricta energía, fueron consignados al servicio de las armas, determinando la Secretaría respectiva que fueran enviados a Yucatán, pero no como soldados, sino como rancheros unos, y los demás para emplearlos en trabajos de fortificaciones ligeras.

Al efecto, todos los consignados fueron llevados el miércoles 20 del mismo mes a la misma Secretaría para que los pasaran por cajas, y llenando ese requisito fueron destinados a uno de los batallones que hacían la campaña contra los indios mayas.

XIV.

El jueves 21 de noviembre de 1901, a las 7 de la mañana y a bordo de un vagón de tercera clase, custodiados por soldados del 24º batallón, iban 19 de los individuos del baile de la casa de la calle de la Paz, rumbo a Veracruz, para después allí ser embarcados en el primer vapor que saliera para las costas de Yucatán.

En la Estación de Buenavista, del Ferrocarril Mexicano, por cuya línea salieron para Veracruz los *maricones,* un numeroso grupo de curiosos se había instalado desde temprano para verlos partir.

Nuestro pueblo es en extremo curioso; cualquier asunto que ha causado sensación le tiene preocupado, y sólo le abandona cuando ya está saciada su curiosidad y se ha dado cuenta de todos los detalles más culminantes.

Estrella, Virtud, Pudor, Blanca, Margarita y *Carola,* marchaban entre los demás, tristes y cabizbajos.

Se despedían con la mirada de su adorado México, de sus familias que también lloraban y en su último adiós derramaban verdaderas y copiosas lágrimas.

¡Dejaban sus comodidades, su lujo, su emporio de placeres, su inmunda cloaca!

. . .

Ya no pasearían por el Bosque de Chapultepec en flamantes carrete-las, ni concurrían a los risibles bailes de formal etiqueta, ni se esta-cionarían en las avenidas de Plateros para exhibirse, en compañía de los vagos petimetres que se ocupaban en murmurar y en hacer saludos a diestra y siniestra, para lucir de figurín a la moda y demostrar con grandes muecas que son los nocivos de las clases privilegiadas.

Ninón y *Mimí,* también abatidos, marchaban maquinalmente.

Cuando el tren partía, oyó *Ninón* un grito doloroso, sofocado, y al volver el rostro, apenas pudo distinguir la hermosa cara de Judith que se llevaba el pañuelo a sus ojos para secar sus lágrimas.

Ninón entonces odió el pasado lleno de ignominia, apretó los dientes convulsivamente y sus ojos llameantes de cólera miraron a *Mimí* que iba a su lado, con la mirada mefistofélica, llena de fuego, en que chisporroteaba el más grande de los desprecios tardíos, irre-mediables . . .

Llegaron a Veracruz, y desde allí fueron conducidos al Castillo de San Juan de Ulúa, donde los incomunicaron de los demás presos para evitar el escándalo soez de las prisiones del crimen.

A los pocos días, el segundo bote de la dotación de la Corbeta Zaragoza los embarcó para llevarlos a bordo del vapor transporte noruega "Mercator," que los debía conducir a Yucatán.

En el Puerto de Progreso, Isla de Mujeres, Puerto de Morelos, donde hizo carbón el "Mercator," Isla de Cozumel y el término de su jornada en las bahías de la Ascensión, fueron objeto de ilimitada curiosidad por la sencilla gente de la costa.

Llegados al campamento donde operaban las fuerzas contra los re-beldes, fueron entregados a los Cuerpos que hacían la campaña, y dis-tribuidos en algunas compañías para confeccionar el rancho a la soldadesca unos, y otros para hacer trabajos de zapa.

La vegetación exuberante, los árboles seculares, la multitud de co-coteros y platanares que le dan sublimidad a la costa, y en que el artista puede soñar en un paraíso ideal, desconsolaba a los jóvenes 41.

La mar, con sus inmensas olas azules, bañaba suavemente la plea-mar sus costas, surcando multitud de embarcaciones veleras que parecían perderse en la inmensidad y entre el oleaje.

Las chozas de palmeras surgentes unas, hundidas otras entre lo más espeso de las arboledas, se antojaban ciudades de la época an-tigua en que Colón descubriera nuestra joven América.

Las fiebres intermitentes, el paludismo y el vómito, eran la pesadilla incesante de los *señoritos,* que lloraban lágrimas de sangre al recordar su bacanal lleno de extravíos y maldecían el destino irónicamente.

El calor excesivo y la plaga de los tábanos les hacía insoportable la vida.

Sus rostros escuálidos, famélicos y enfermizos no tenían ya ninguna semejanza con el físico que tenían en la Metrópoli.

Los marinos de la Corbeta Zaragoza les protegían dándoles a lavar su ropa por unos diez centavos, que siempre iban seguidos del insulto.

Mimí estaba inconocible, desmoralizado; habíale escrito primero a sus padres y éstos permanecieron mudos a su llamamiento. Escribióle después a Don Pedro de Marruecos una carta llena de ternuras dolorosas, de sufrimientos insoportables y horribles martirios; pero Don Pedro había muerto en una orgía a consecuencia de una congestión alcohólica; recurrió a *Ninón* para hacer menos pesado su cautiverio, y éste lo repudiaba; *Ninón,* en cambio, había sufrido una metamorfosis: aparentaba ser el más resignado, pero sentía en el fondo de su alma sus desvíos, deploraba la primera demostración de brutalidad que había infringido y prometíase regenerar, avergonzándose de las torpezas de su pasado en su vida de orgías.

Confidenció con el capitán de un destacamento, y aquel, compadecido, lo quitó de la compañía de los 41, ocupándolo en trabajos de escritorio de la tropa.

Su único ideal era fugarse; buscar una oportunidad, y volver al lado de sus padres que le escribían cartas tristísimas llenas de sanos consejos.

Cuando contemplaba el blanco traje de las costeñas, con su camisón de bordados azules o rojos, y blanca toca de inmensas alas, llenas de simpatía, de donaire y de gracia, pensaba en Judith, en esa mujer ardiente todo fuego, y arrepentido se ensimismaba en una profunda meditación.

Adoraba con más locura a Judith, y desesperado al contemplarla en su imaginación, pura y hermosa, amante y heroína, sentía anublados sus ojos por el llanto y recordaba el último desdén olímpico y aquella mirada de infierno llena de odio inconmensurable.

Intervalo de los traductores

[Desde este momento, el enfoque de la novela vuelve inexplicablemente a las vidas de Estela y Judith. Estela se enamora de un joven de la clase obrera, lo cual va en contra de los deseos de sus padres, cuya opinión cabia cuando él la salva de un incendio. Entonces se casan, con la aprobación de sus padres, y viven una vida feliz.

Entre tanto, la vida de Judith toma otro camino, como se verá en la siguiente parte de la novela. Su decaída le permite al autor seguir criticando el libertinaje de la clase acomodada de la Ciudad de México.

En cuanto a los famosos 41, una vez que son enviados a Yucatán, desaparecen de la narrativa. A pesar del título del libro, no son su enfoque después del capítulo 14, con la excepción de Ninón, cuyo nombre reaparece in el capítulo 22, cuando Judith recibe una carta suya.]

XXII.

. . .

"Adorada Judith," decía *Ninón* en la carta.

"Por el marinero que se prestó bondadosamente para llevarte ésta, supe que estás en Veracruz, al lado de tus padres, pasando una corta temporada.

Recibí tus recuerdos, y cree que te vivo reconocido.

El pan del destierro, amor mío, es el más amargo de los manjares.

El lenguaje de la tristeza es mi único confidente en estas soledades caldeadas por una temperatura ardiente; las bahías son tristísimas: muchos árboles y mucha montaña; un calor sofocante y unos sobresaltos terribles porque pienso en los ataques de los indios mayas.

He buscado en el dolor el olvido de mis remembranzas y lo he encontrado; he sufrido muchísimo y creo que me voy purificando.

Tú no puedes comprender lo que sufro y lo que he sufrido; primero, tu enojo, tu desprecio, tu pérdida; después, la vergüenza, la degradación y el infortunio.

A todas horas tu imagen está grabada en mi mente con caracteres indelebles, siderales, y te amo; sí, te amo, Judith, con toda la expresión sincera de mi alma. Te amo porque sé que en tu corazón sin mancha anida la virtud.

Si no creyera en la nobleza de tus acciones y en tu pudor, ya me hubiera confundido con la canalla de los protervos, de los beodos, o créelo, hubiera buscado mi alivio en el suicidio.

Pero tu corazón es tan grande, tan sincero y tan leal, que no dudo perdonarías los extravíos de mi juventud.

El castigo ha sido inmenso, pero es más inmensa mi regeneración.

Por ti, sólo por ti seré bueno; perdona mis locuras, mis brutalidades de otros tiempos . . . fueron obcecaciones de mi espíritu, de mi inexperiencia, de mi desgracia.

Seré tu esclavo, seré lo que tú quieras, con tal de que tu perdón, impregnado de inmaculada pureza, sea mi salvación. Si tú me perdonas, creeré que será la mano de Dios, la Justicia Divina, la que redime a los hombres cuando el dolor y la desventura los purifica en la atmósfera asfixiante de los más crueles martirios.

Tú que eres tan buena, tan soñadora y tan sublime en tus actos de perdón, rompe la página negrísima del pasado, y abre tus brazos y tu corazón al desdichado que sólo ansía verse alumbrado por la aurora sacrosanta de su redención eterna.

La unión de nuestros seres será la vida deliciosa de mi alma. ¡No desmorones mis castillos de grandeza, no hagas polvo al templo donde te deifico, ni abandones la sementera estéril donde vegeto, que con tu perdón fructificarían mis dichas los anhelos de transfigurarme, y la rehabilitación de mi dignidad y mi honra! . . .

Ninón"

. . .

Terminando la lectura de la carta, Judith se quedó un largo momento pensativa; *Ninón* estaba regenerado, no le cabía duda; pero ella, empujada por el destino, caída en la prostitución, prefería los goces groseros a una rehabilitación honrosa.

Por la noche, y después de haber estado con varios individuos tomando copas de vino, antes de acostarse y casi ebria, le contestó a *Ninón* la siguiente carta:

"*Ninón:*

Soberbia, como toda mujer en quien circula por sus venas la sangre azul, no te perdono nunca.

Con Antonio, el más íntimo de tus amigos, me fugué del hogar paterno, y cuando te mandé mis recuerdos irónicos, estaba con él, en sus brazos, sintiendo la irresistible corriente del diluvio de sus caricias.

¡Al recordarte y leer tu carta prorrumpo en estrepitosas carcajadas de locura, porque te odio con toda la fuerza poderosa de mi alma!

La Judith que tú conociste, ha caído y ha roto en mil jirones su pureza decantada; necesitaba un hombre que mitigara mis ansias; tú fuiste torpe y yo tuve que ceder al primer impulso de la enloquecedora pasión de Antonio.

Necesitaba otro ambiente; parodio esa vida de disipación que tú llevabas, y en la que sentiste el placer forjando en tu cerebro alegrías interminables; borracheras de amor, ligaduras de tus brazos con los brazos de las impúdicas cortesanas, al chocar de las copas rebosantes de vino espumoso. Necesitaba una atmósfera que caldeara mi cuerpo y mi espíritu . . .

Las alas de querube con que vestías mis dorsos ebúrneos en tu exaltada imaginación, han sido desplumadas por la mano de apasionados que me dejaron exangüe y satisfecha de deleites divinos.

He buscado el olvido en la orgía cuotidiana y con el vino he borrado la remembranza de nuestros amores insulsos.

¡El poema inacabable de mis pesadumbres se apagó entre los gritos de la chusma insaciable, de los compradores de mis besos candentes! . . .

Por eso festejo la caída con bacanales de amor, y de fiebre y de vino.

¡Soy la pecadora que se venga de ti; la que gozará hasta saciarse y después volverá al redil para que un imbécil, o un desvergonzado que codicie mi herencia, me cubra la honra! . . .

Eres un sandio con mandarme cartitas románticas; si me adoras, procura fugarte y venir a pasar momentos deliciosos a mi lado, llenos de encantamiento, de belleza, de satisfacción soberana.

Paréceme increíble que no hayas conocido que en el carnaval de la vida todo es mentira, que la honradez es un mito, que debemos aprovechar nuestra edad de oro para gozar de las delicias mundanas, e inundarnos en el agua del mar de las dichas sensibles.

¡Imbécil, soñador, sentimentalista te desprecio y te odio!

Judith"

Cuando terminó de escribir Judith, metió la carta en un sobre, la mandó a su destino y se metió en su lecho durmiéndose tranquila.

Los días subsecuentes eran diarias orgías. Desvergonzada como toda mesalina, fue descendiendo, descendiendo al abismo, hasta llegar a confundirse con las más miserables meretrices.

Se sintió en estado interesante sin saber quién fuera el padre del hijo del crimen que llevaba en su seno; y desmoralizada se precipitó, ya sin freno, sin cautela, sin sentimiento, con el descaro de las más viles mujeres, en el fango putrefacto mal oliente de las degradaciones, en la vorágine miserable del lujo, que tras la seda y los oropeles escurre podredumbre.

XXIII.

Las poderosas influencias con que contaba *Ninón* en la sociedad de México, le valieron para que después de catorce meses de cautiverio y de sufrimientos, en la Secretaría del ramo le expidieran su baja absoluta.

Apenas se lo notificaron corrió a despedirse fraternalmente del Capitán de infantería que estaba con un destacamento en las bahías de la Ascensión, el único amigo que había adquirido en su destierro, y abandonó por fin en lo absoluto la compañía de los 41, que seguían prestando sus servicios, unos como rancheros de la tropa y otros en trabajos de zapa: como abrir brechas y levantar fortificaciones ligeras, en compañía de los valientes soldados que hacían la campaña contra los indios mayas.

Y era de risa ver el cuadro grotesco de los populares 41, levantando la pala y golpeando con el zapapico, sudorosos, escuálidos y llorando las más veces a lágrima viva.

Los soldados les daban todos los días "*latas*" monumentales, diciéndoles con voz fingida:

—"¿Adónde vas con tu traje de gala?"

—"¡No trabajes que te quiebras la cintura, vida mía!"

—"¿Te sofocas, lindo mío? pues carga con el abanico . . ."

Y hasta popular se hizo un estribillo que publicó un diario de la metrópoli en aquella época, y que cantaban los soldados cuando marchaban:

> "*Mírame, marchando voy*
> *con mi chacó a Yucatán,*
> *por hallarme en un convoy*
> *bailando jota⁹ y cancán.*"

La vida para esos desgraciados era un verdadero infierno, expuestos como estaban a las burletas sangrientas de la soldadesca y al cálido y enfermizo clima de la costa.

Ninón se embarcó para el Puerto de Progreso dispuesto a trabajar y a reconquistar su honra. Necesitaba purificarse y levantar con orgullo algún día su frente, y sólo las puertas del trabajo serían en lo porvenir su rehabilitación moral.

Radicado ya en Progreso, se dedicó con actividad a la compra y venta de henequén; hizo contratos con dueños de plantíos, y aunque en corta escala, con créditos que él mismo se abrió, comenzó a exportarlo al extranjero, activando sus negocios, y comenzando para él una nueva vida de luchas; pero luchas serenas dulcificadas por el trabajo. La rehabilitación comenzaba a iniciarse y su redención resplandecía con destellos de aurora.

Una noche, estando descansando en su casa, el cartero le llevó una carta de Judith. Rompió con ansia febril el sobre, desdobló la carta, y a medida que iba leyendo se descomponían sus facciones, tornándose en intensamente pálidas.

La carta de Judith ya la conoce el lector.

Apoyados sus codos sobre su escritorio y su rostro sobre sus dos manos abiertas, quedóse pensativo largo tiempo.

Alterada su calma, despertaba el hombre de las selvas, rugía la fiera sedienta de venganza . . . *Ninón* sentía en su alma la ira y el dolor más inmenso ... ¡así pagaba la perjura todos sus desvelos, todos sus afanes! ... había sacrificado todo por ella, hasta regenerarse; y su rehabilitación ofrecida danzaba como un sarcasmo en los labios de Judith, y la manchaba la impura con una declaración vergonzante.

Antonio, su mejor amigo, la raptaba para disfrutar la primera caricia, y después vendería sus encantos al primer advenedizo que la solicitara.

¡Cuánta miseria encerraba Judith en la pútrida cloaca de su alma!

¡No! no volvería a pensar en ella; la lucha sería fuerte, reñida, pero su conciencia que comenzaba a limpiarse de sus manchas groseras no volvería a empañarse.

Adoraba a Judith con verdadero amor, y por ella tal vez hubiera cometido más locuras pero ahora era la cortesana que le ofrecía desvergonzada caricias mancilladas que, una vez satisfechas, la harían caer una vez más en el hastío y en la desesperación.

¡La olvidaría! Buscaría, no entre la cohorte de aristócratas vanidosas, sino entre la clase media, una mujercita llena de cualidades, que fuera buena hija, buena esposa y buena madre.

Maldecía lleno de ira a la sociedad en que vivía, esa sociedad insana donde todo es vanidad, y mentira y oropeles; donde el amor no es más que interés y degradación; donde sólo se ama el oro y palpitan los corazones pletóricos de envidia, de soberbia, de autocracia que se arrastra como las serpientes que envenenan y ahorcan ...

Su corazón no era ya el sarcófago blanqueado que escondía en su seno materia impúdica y veneno lento ¡no! Su alma noble sufría incruentos martirios, pero su sufrimiento era el hálito de Dios que vaticinaba una existencia áurea y feliz, y el lenitivo que pronto curaría las llagas de su alma en este mundo lleno de miserias y egoísmos ...

...

Han pasado seis meses desde que *Ninón* recibió la carta de Judith.

Los cambios morales transforman a los hombres.

Ninón, solitario, triste y decepcionado en su vida bohemia, habíase relacionado con una familia yucateca de la clase media, radicada en el puerto de Progreso.

Se componía la familia de un matrimonio honrado que tenía por fruto dos hijos: un hombre de dieciocho años y una señorita de dieciséis.

Josefina se llamaba la hija, una niña hermosísima en que la poderosa sangre yucateca había forjado una flor tropical de la costa.

Era morena, alta, delgada, pero de curvas irreprochables; ojos negros, dormidos y soñadores, orlados por largas y obscuras pestañas. Modesta en su traje, en sus palabras y en sus modales, tenía algo de misterioso encantamiento lleno de efluvios, de poesía, de vida exuberante y fecunda.

Los bucles endrinos y crespos de su larga cabellera que orlaban su frente morena, se antojaban a los ensortijados de las sirenas mitológicas, y su boca chica y su nariz recta y fina a las modeladas por Fidias.[10]

No era vanidosa ni altiva; ni la envidia, ni el orgullo, ni las preocupaciones de la coquetería y de la seducción turbaban la serenidad de su alma sensible.

Desconocía las exigencias y las fórmulas de la rigurosa etiqueta, pero conocía la virtud y el pudor; estaba educada con una sencillez seductora que realzaba el tesoro de su virtud.

Era limpia, hacendosa; sabía leer y escribir correctamente; sabía sostener una conversación sencilla, pero sin afectaciones; sabía cocinar, bordar, pintar y hacer flores. No tocaba el piano haciendo alardes de ejecución, pero en la mandolina tocaba aires dulcísimos y alegres de la costa, y su voz, pequeñita pero entonada, hacía delicias de los que la escuchaban.

Era buena hija; respetaba a sus padres, los cuidaba, los mimaba con esa simpatía seductora de las almas nobles y candorosas de las hijas modelos.

Y *Ninón*, que la observaba, que estudió su carácter, que palpó sus virtudes y su candidez, una tarde que paseaban por la playa, al lado de sus padres, en un momento de oportunidad le habló de amores, le pintó una pasión suprema, santa, desinteresada.

Le contó su pasado, su castigo, su arrepentimiento, su purificación, y le ofreció amarla, hacerla su esposa, y vivir muy felices dedicando sus horas de vida para ella.

Josefina oyó la historia de *Ninón;* sintió en su corazón un sentimiento de nobleza, vislumbró un futuro de rehabilitación para *Ninón* y comenzó a impresionarse su alma sensible y buena. Le contestó que se dirigiera a sus padres y que si su voluntad no se oponía y ella llegaba a quererlo, entonces no tendría inconveniente en corresponderle.

Esa misma noche conferenció *Ninón* con los padres de Josefina, pidiéndoles la mano de su buena hija.

—El muchacho no me parece malo—decía el padre de Josefina,— y si mi hija lo quiere pues que se casen, y a vivir felices los chicos.

Ninón concurría ya desde aquel día cuotidianamente, estrechando cada día más sus relaciones, y contento y satisfecho de haber encontrado un tesoro de mujer.

—¡Qué diferencia tan enorme!—pensaba *Ninón*.

Judith, educada en una atmósfera de lujo y de oro, sólo había adquirido orgullo y vanidad, cifrando su ventura en las frivolidades de la moda y en oírse lisonjeada por esa horda de petimetres ignorantes que forman la corte de ciertas mujeres de gran *chic;* y Josefina, su castísima novia, su virtuosa merideña,[11] sólo cifraba su felicidad en agradar a sus padres, en inspirarlo a él en su obra de regeneración, en alentarlo para el porvenir con palabras de amor y de consuelo que murmuraban a su oído como un poema de las delicias del cielo; de ese cielo soñado por él, en que sus ilusiones como encantadas mariposas de múltiples colores, le acariciaban, deslumbrándolo entre la luz esplendorosa de un porvenir risueño.

Sí, casándose con Josefina sería feliz; pasaría orgulloso su vista sobre esas déspotas que sacrifican su cariño a la fórmula social; su existencia, tranquila y serena, se deslizaría como una eterna primavera, y como un espectáculo grandioso de la verdadera dicha.

Si hubiera llegado a realizar su matrimonio con Judith, sólo habría construido un féretro de decepciones, orfebrado y con incrustaciones de diamantes y perlas; habría hecho un colosal negocio de banca, luciendo oropeles forjados con muchas lágrimas, con mucha imprecación y maldiciones.

Habría sepultado bajo una enorme capa de oro el arca indestructible de sus afectos y sentimientos: se hubieran opacado sus ensueños con el deslumbramiento de un fausto soberbio, fingido, hipócrita, haciendo sucumbir su redención soñada.

Josefina era su esperanza, su alma, su fe; por ella se había regenerado, por ella había sufrido una metamorfosis monumental ensanchando sus horizontes de vida; ella murmuraba en sus oídos, como un canto celeste, la voz de perdón, que dulcificaba el castigo de sus culpas pasadas, y siempre era amable, tierna, virtuosa, noblemente hermoseada por la dignidad de su alma sensible y honrada.

Y Judith, que había sembrado su corazón de ilusiones brillantes, era su verdugo implacable.

Se la imaginaba *Ninón* con sus hombros y sus brazos desnudos, con la carcajada estridente, histérica y burlesca. Se entregaba a los hombres voluntariamente, como se entregan todas las mujeres depravadas; al volver a su hogar, al lado de sus consecuentes e indignados padres, volvería a profanar el tálamo nupcial con el más horrendo de los adulterios.

Judith, como todas las mujeres del gran mundo, volvería a su hogar con el único fin de brillar, de exhibir su lujo, buscando un matrimonio de interés para sostener sus caprichos y para mitigar sus ansias.

Josefina predominaba en su alma; había triunfado, y *Ninón* era feliz; vivía contento, sin ambición para más que unirse indisolublemente con su amada.

. . .

El día deseado llegó por fin.

Se hicieron los preparativos para el casamiento: una ceremonia humilde y una concurrencia selecta por sus sentimientos, por su honrada sencillez y por su buena fe para desear inmensas dichas a los nuevos cónyuges.

En el más humilde curato se unieron para siempre *Ninón* y Josefina. Después de la ceremonia donde todos los comensales, esos laboriosos y sinceros hijos de Yucatán, alegres francos y sensibles, felicitaban a los novios gozando con su dicha.

Las felicitaciones más cordiales, los deseos más vehementes para el progreso se interrumpían a cada momento en los brindis y entre el mayor orden y entusiasmo.

Ninón, coronados sus sueños al lado de su virtuosa y sencilla esposa, abrazaba a sus suegros con cariño filial, y brindaba por la nueva vida bendiciendo la hora en que fue a radicarse en Progreso; y su palabra fácil encomiaba sinceramente a los hijos de la costa, que desprecian el egoísmo y los deslumbramientos de la vanidad, por los goces y la expansión divina del alma.

Cuando su imaginación volaba hacia las lejanías del recuerdo, odiaba las acciones bastardas de Judith y maldecía las fórmulas de la sociedad hipócrita a que él había pertenecido, a esa sociedad donde danzan diabólicas mujeres criminales, incestuosas y libertinas.

Ninón, redimido, repudiando su rango oropelado, entraba en el seno democrático de una sociedad que tiene por norma la honradez, la virtud y el trabajo. ¡La sociedad sublime de la clase media! . . .

XXV.

En el mar tempestuoso de los deseos naufragaron los jóvenes inflamables, los inmortales 41.

La miseria humana, como una hambrienta insaciable, hincó sus fauces y arrancó jirones, muchísimos jirones de horripilante bajeza.

Los sacudimientos nerviosos de sus pasiones, abrasados por el fuego voraz de su degradación, falsearon los placeres naturales, violaron la moral y la ley, y mutilaron a la virtud que desde su trono imperial se erguía con su majestad de princesa inmaculada.

La prostitución, convertida en escoria, en pantano, en albañal pestilente, reunió en un hato de rufianes a la maldad más perversa;

que hundía el puñal de los apetitos desordenados en los corazones del pudor y de la vergüenza.

¡Cuánta crápula hedionda y asquerosa de los malditos que suplantan el encanto de la mujer, entre el ridículo más ruin, y que perdieron todo sentimiento noble y toda dignidad altiva!

La existencia, tan bella, tan harmoniosa, tan dulce y tierna para los hombres honrados y trabajadores que llevan una vida de actividad y de engrandecimiento, se convierte para los prostituidos refinados y ociosos, en un sarcasmo que mata la grandeza del alma y la potencia del cuerpo; y el vicio, ese vicio impuro que desciende hasta el último peldaño de la bajeza, los arrastra a la deshonra, les venda la razón, y aparece la bestia con toda su plástica grosera, con toda su materia virulenta y contagiosa.

¡Qué desgracia vivir degradado, señalado, repudiado por todas las generaciones, hundido en el cóncavo maldito de los desprestigiados sociales, cerrando los ojos a las leyes divinas del progreso, y los oídos a los acentos sublimes y conmovedores de la moral!

La pereza aniquila el cuerpo y el espíritu; el lujo es una miseria fecunda que sólo engendra vanidades y desarrolla plagas que menguan el bolsillo, que embotan el pensamiento y arruinan, moral y físicamente, las aspiraciones del hombre progresista y luchador; y el vicio, ese vicio que rebosa en la copa de la prostitución más desenfrenada, es el que hace esclavos a los hombres y los denigra, hasta caer en el antro inmoral del envilecimiento y de la corrupción, que rompe sus lazos en mil añicos, para no purificarse nunca.

Han circulado por las páginas de esta novelita personajes grotescos: unos, prostituidos tal vez por un defecto o fenómeno, y otros por un fin casi siempre relajado, que no sabemos si merecen la compasión, el desprecio, o el castigo inflexible de la justicia y de la sociedad.

Unos se han regenerado, y el comienzo de su purificación ha sido invocar los sagrados principios de la moral, de la vida honrada que debe seguirse y cumplir con los deberes para que el hombre fue creado.

Judith abandonó a su hijito, y falto éste de pan cuotidiano, falto de amor maternal, yace a merced del infortunio, mientras ella cruza los mares en pos de más dicha ficticia, de más placer impuro, de más relajación.

¿Y *Estrella, Pudor, Virtud, Blanca, Carola* y *Margarita*, qué se han hecho? ¿Se han regenerado? ¿Marchan acaso todavía por el sendero de la degradación y el vicio? ¿Qué han sentido, qué han pensado en las abrasadoras costas de Yucatán? ¿Cuál es el porvenir del hijo de Judith?

¡Arcanos de la vida! y sólo arcanos que el lector sabrá en la segunda parte de esta obrita que dieron pábulo al escándalo social y tema para escribir esta humilde narración.[12]

En la sociedad, los vicios sin corrección germinan y fructifican. Afortunadamente esos vicios degeneradores no cundirán en los fértiles campos de la civilización, como todo lo que lucha en titánico esfuerzo purifica a los pueblos y al individuo: porque el progreso siempre se impone majestuosamente.

Todos los vicios, en general, son nocivos y perjudiciales; la materia, forrada de encajes y de joyas, es un foco de microbios que infectan y se propagan con rápidos crecimientos. Cuando las sociedades aniquilan esas plagas infecciosas, surge la felicidad más santa, la alegría más austera, las conciencias más tranquilas; y en el hogar, en ese templo de excelsa majestad de fe, penetra el ángel de la conformidad, y el corazón estremecido de satisfacción late entre la pureza, entre el hálito del alma, gloriosamente, con el triunfo de las pasiones, para disfrutar en horas tranquilas, en mañanas risueñas, en tardes de oro y en noches bellísimas y apacibles, la vida tranquila que palpita y que conmueve ante el espectáculo sublime de la Naturaleza.

Notas

1. El "Pensador Mexicano" era el seudónimo de José Joaquín Fernández de Lizardi, el primer novelista mexicano, cuya obra maestra, *El Periquillo Sarniento* es obra clásica de parodia social.

2. Emile Zola era un novelista y crítico social francés; sus tres novelas: *Nana* [1880]; *La terre* [1887] y *J'accuse* [1898] forman la trilogía aquí referenciada.

3. Juan Mateos, Emilio Rabasa, Victoriano Salado Álvarez, tres novelistas mexicanos de la época. Es notable que ninguno de estos escritores refleje tendencias modernistas o naturalistas, las cuales predominaban en la literatura mexicana durante esta época, pero que era consideradas inmorales por algunos. Ni han sobrevivido como figuras importantes en la historia literaria mexicana. Marcadamente ausentes de la lista están el *bestseller* Federico Gamboa y el modernista Amado Nervo.

4. Nombre de una zarzuela popular de la época.

5. Francesa de clase obrera que se viste en gris.

6. Prostitutas francesas.

7. Admirador, fanático.

8. Salón de moda de ropa masculina en la Ciudad de México.

9. Baile español popular en la época.

10. Escultor griego.

11. Forma incorrecta de describir los habitantes de Mérida, Yucatán. Los lugareños usan el término "meridanos."

12. No hay evidencias de la publicación de la segunda parte.

The 41 and the *Gran Redada*

Carlos Monsiváis

Translated by Aaron Walker

To Robert McKee Irwin and José Quiroga

This is not a dress rehearsal, gentlemen. This is life.

—Oscar Wilde

Notó el gendarme de la 4ª calle de la Paz que en una accesoria se afectuaba un baile a puerta cerrada y para pedir la licencia fue a llamar a la puerta. Salió a abrirle un *ajembrado* vestido de mujer, con la falda recogida, la cara y los labios llenos de afeite y muy dulce y melindroso de habla. Con esa vista, que hasta el curtido guardián le revolvió el estómago, se introdujo éste a la accesoria, sospechando lo que aquello sería y se encontró con cuarenta y dos parejas de canallas de éstos, vestidos los unos de hombres y los otros de mujer que bailaban y se solazaban en aquel antro . . .

[The gendarme on duty on the fourth block of La Paz Street noted that in an annex to one of the houses on the block, a ball was being held behind closed doors, and he knocked on the door to request a proper permit. An effeminate type answered the door dressed as a woman with his skirt gathered up, his face and lips full of makeup, and a very sweet and affected way of speaking. At this sight, which turned the stomach of even this most hardened sentinel, he entered the annex, suspecting what might be going on, and found there 42 such couples, some dressed as men and the others as women, dancing and merry making in that lair . . .]. (*El Popular.* November 19, 1901, Spanish 35; English 21–22, this volume)

ANTECEDENTS:
El Ninfo (THE FAIRY) AMONG THE DAMSELS

In the literature of the nineteenth century, *Chucho el Ninfo* (1871), one of the novelized episodes of José Tomás de Cuéllar/Facundo's *costumbrista* series *La Linterna Mágica*, provides an unexpected treatment of homosexuality. As a novel, *Chucho el Ninfo* is terrifyingly bad, disorganized to the point of annoyance and incomprehension, and bursting with sermons and digressions. Its interest lies in the protagonist, an obvious gay described with resentment, mockery . . . and with care not to offend readers who would not tolerate a published reminder of such aberrations. ("Yes, I already know such things exist, but if I read them, I acquaint myself with them, and that I could not bear.") The determinism of the account obliges the character, from a very young age, to display his preferences: "Chucho . . . estaba muy contento entre las niñas: a que quedó aficionado perpetuamente" [Chucho . . . was very happy among the girls: a comfort of which he remained perpetually fond] (4). Elena, his mother, a premature widow, is a parafreudian dream: devout to her son (who beats her), emotional blackmailer, "un terrón de amores . . . casi tan consentidora y tolerante como la patria" [an earthy clump of affections . . . almost as indulgent and tolerant as the nation] (4,7), and obedient to her son's caprices to the point of ignominy (she pays the mother of another child so that the latter will allow himself to be beaten by Chucho). Elena's pampering turns her son "más bonito cada día" [cuter every day] (9), which is to say, more feminine and feminoid:

> . . . al notar (Elena) que las formas del niño se redondeaban, abandonaba sin dificultad la idea del vigor varonil, tan deseado en el crecimiento del niño, y se inclinaba a contemplarlo bajo la forma femenil.
> Elena había agotado ya todas las modas, y su imaginación se había cansado inventando trajecitos fantásticos para Chucho, hasta que un día le ocurrió vestirlo de mujer. Chucho se exhibió vestido de china.
> Estaba encantadora, según Elena, y como Chucho era objeto de repetidos agasajos en traje de hembra, se aficionaba a esta transformación que halagaba su vanidad de niño bonito y mimado.

> [. . . upon noting that the child's form was becoming rounder, Elena abandoned without difficulty the idea of masculine vigor so coveted during the child's upbringing, and became inclined to contemplate him in the shape of a woman.

Elena had exhausted all the fashions, and her imagination had tired of inventing fantastic little outfits for Chucho, until one day it occurred to her to dress him as a woman. Chucho showed himself off dressed as a *china*.[1]

He was enchanting, according to Elena, and as Chucho was the object of lavish and repeated attention in his female costume, he became fond of this transformation which flattered his vanity of a dainty and spoiled child]. (9)

This description of a gay is very clear, but it is without the details that would call attention to the existence of sodomy. Cuéllar abstains from the fatal word (*maricón*) so as not to label the character who continues to exaggerate his femininity, his dandyism and his speech—presumably that of the homosexuals of the period, who were immersed in the cultivation of a *refinadito* [very refined] appearance and sound:

Chucho tenía siempre los labios entreabiertos, mostrando una parte de los dientes superiores, los que generalmente le ayudaban a su labio superior a pronunciar las bb. Chucho, además, silbaba la ss, y pronunciaba ligeramente las zz; de manera que su pronunciación era dulce, blanda y se alejaba un poco de la manera en que en México se pronuncia el español.

Este modo de hablar de Chucho era nuevo y resultado de un estudio especial: además hablaba muy despacio.

Chucho repugnaba la acentuación varonil y combatía en su fisonomía la venida de esas líneas que deciden el temperamento viril. Chucho deseaba aparecer niño y una mancha en el cutis la hubiera conceptuada como una verdadera desgracia.

El uso del *coldcream* había realizado su ensueño de tener una tez virginal; había logrado mantener arqueadas las pestañas; calentándolas con un instrumento de su invención; se pintaba los labios con carmín y tenía diez preparaciones diversas para conservarse la dentadura.

Había logrado convertir su cabello lacio y opaco en ensortijado y brillante; conocía todas las preparaciones adecuadas al efecto, y empleaba gran número de peines y cepillos en su tocador.

Se hacía servir por un camarista que le ayudaba a desnudarse . . .

[Chucho always held his lips half open, showing part of his upper teeth, those which generally assisted him in pronouncing his b's. Chucho, moreover, whistled his s's, and pronounced his z's lightly; in such a way that his pronunciation was sweet, soft and distanced itself slightly from the manner in which Spanish is spoken in Mexico.

Chucho's way of speaking was new and the result of marked study: moreover he spoke very slowly.

Chucho loathed masculine accentuation and combated the arrival in his physiognomy of those lines that decide the virile temperament. Chucho wished to appear as a child and would have deemed any blemish on his skin a true disgrace.

The use of cold cream had realized his dream of having a virginal complexion; he had managed to maintain his eyelashes arched; heating them with an instrument of his invention; he painted his lips with carmine and had ten different preparations to preserve the teeth.

He had managed to transform the texture of his hair from straight and dull to curly and shiny; he knew all of the right preparations for the effect, and furnished his dressing table with a great number of combs and brushes.

He was waited on by a valet who helped him to undress . . .]. (210–211)

Without the words that publishers would not accept, the "*vicio nefando*" [abominable vice] unfurls itself. In the most daring moment of the novel, Cuéllar mentions *la raza ninfea,* the type of *ninfos* [fairies] or *mujerucos* [men who value feminine over masculine virtues]. And even this is disguised. In one of the final chapters, on being challenged to a duel, Chucho surprisingly acquires a virile energy. "Le faltaba a Chucho este toque característico de la raza ninfea, y holgábase en su interior de la ocasión que le proporcionaba desmentir su fama de afeminado" [Chucho was missing that characteristic touch of the fairy race, and deep within mused about the occasion when he could belie his effeminate reputation].

It is still not yet time for the accusation of sodomy, a conduct that sexual illiteracy and the persecutory manias of conservatism corner into the shadows of *intuition* (which is to say, that which is deliberately described with vague statements so as not to take responsibility for knowledge of the subject). Only in the second half of the twentieth century is homosexuality in Mexico approached from a scientific perspective (or so people claim). Before then, *the masculine* is the living and singular substance of *the national* and *the human,* with *the masculine* understood as the code of absolute *machismo* that does not require definition, *the human* as the fulfillment of obligations in accordance with the myth of the species, and *the national* as the catalogue of possible virtues, which are exemplified by heroes and, in daily life, by the *muy machos.* The boastful tradition of virility derives from both Hispanic heritage and broadly diverse codes of valor, and it judges homophilia as so remote and abject that it is not even mentioned "so as not to stain one's lips." Thus, Guillermo Prieto, the patriarch of Mexican letters, praises Cuéllar, since the name of Chucho el Ninfo evokes a "niño mimado y consentido, entregado a los vicios" [spoiled and coddled child, surrendered into vice] (336). Therefore, the character of the *niño consentido* [coddled child] anticipates and makes secondary the specification of vices.

"Viejo ridículo"

What is known of homosexual life in Mexico before the social and police scandal of the *Baile de los 41?* From the gay perspective, we only have at our disposal the testimony of the writer Salvador Novo (1904–1974) in his sexual memoirs, *La Estatua de sal,* written in 1944 or 1945, and published by Conaculta in 1998. Novo recounts the story of an *aristócrata*, Antonio Adalid, son of a groom to Emperor Maximilian and godson by baptism to the emperors. Nicknamed Toña la Mamonera,[2] Adalid, life of the clandestine parties at the end of the nineteenth century and beginning of the twentieth, evokes "con una risa sus excursiones colectivas y tempraneras a Xochimilco, en tranvía, todos con sacos azules y sombreros de jipijapa" [with a laugh his collective daybreak excursions to Xochimilco by streetcar, with everyone dressed in blue jackets and Panama hats] (109). And Adalid tells, moreover, a love story that he relates to an adolescent Novo:

> Había alcahuetes—¿la propia Madre Meza?—que procuraban muchachos para la diversión de los aristócratas. Una noche de fiesta, Toña bajaba la gran escalera con suntuoso atavío de bailarina. La concurrencia aplaudió su gran entrada; pero al pie de la escalera, el reproche mudo de dos ojos lo congeló, lo detuvo. Parecía apostrofarlo: "¡Viejo ridículo!" Toña volvió a subir, fue a quitarse el disfraz, bajó a buscar al hermoso muchacho que lo había increpado en silencio. En ese momento se ponía al remate al mejor postor la posesión de aquel jovencito. Antonio lo compró.
> Se llamaba también Antonio. No llegaba a veinte años.
> Sea en el famoso baile de los 41, sea en otro, estalló el escándalo. Don José Adalid desheredó y desconoció a este hijo degenerado, mancha de la familia que huyó desconcertado, aturdido, inválido, llegó a San Francisco, California, con unos cuantos dólares en el bolsillo y sin saber qué hacer. Entró en una iglesia, se acercó al confesionario, drenóse de todas sus culpas. "Dios te ha enviado aquí—le dijo el sacerdote—. Necesitamos un profesor de castellano en el St. Mary's College. Te ofrezco un sueldo, un cuarto, comida y ropa limpia." Antonio vio el cielo abierto; empezó a dar clases, desde su buen inglés de Inglaterra, y a rumiar sus recuerdos en la soledad de su pequeño apartamento. Nada sabía, nada quería saber de México. Le parecía haber muerto, o hallarse en medio de una pesadilla.

Una tarde llamaron levemente a su puerta. Abrió. "Aquí estoy"—
le dijo Antonio. "Tú comprendes que desde ese momento . . . no me
separaré nunca de él."

[There were pimps—Madre Meza herself?—who would procure young
men for the diversion of the aristocrats. On the evening of a party, Toña
came down the great staircase in the sumptuous attire of a ballerina.
The guests applauded his grand entrance; but at the foot of the stairs,
the silent reproach of two eyes froze him, arrested him. It seemed to
insult him: "Ridiculous old man!" Toña went back up to take off the
costume, and came back down to look for the handsome young man
who had silently upbraided him. At this moment, that young man was
being auctioned to the highest bidder. Antonio bought him.

He was also named Antonio. He was not yet 20.

Whether in the famous ball of the 41, or in another, scandal
erupted. Don José Adalid disinherited and disowned this degenerate
son, a stain on the family that he fled, bewildered, stunned, disem-
powered; he arrived in San Francisco, California, with a few dollars in
his pocket and without knowing what to do. He entered a church, approached the confessional, and drained himself of all his guilt. "God
has sent you here," the priest told him. "We need a Spanish professor
at St. Mary's College. I can offer you a salary, a room, food and clean
clothes." Antonio saw clear skies ahead; he began to give classes, using
his good English from England, and to rummage through his memories in the solitude of his small apartment. Of Mexico, he knew nothing and did not wish to know anything. It seemed to him to have died,
or to be stuck in the middle of a nightmare.

One afternoon someone knocked lightly at his door. He opened it.
"Here I am," Antonio said to him. "You understand that from that
moment on . . . I would never separate myself from him"]. (109–110)

Up to this moment, nothing is known of gay life in the Porfiriato
other than: "exclusive" parties, cross-dressing without concern for
identity, the raffling off of attractive young men, and, for those "un-
masked" by the scandal, the sense of being "buried alive." Almost all
of the information available relies on the collation of documents from
other societies: liaisons of the bourgeois with soldiers and sailors, adoration of proletarian energy, the impossibility of conceiving an
amorous relation among equals (there is no such thing as a gay couple), identities only negatively defined, the frightening discovery of
sexual inclination, obsessive prayers "so that the Virgin might cure me
of this aberration," the frequenting of certain *cantinas,* parks, and
swimming pools, white lies for the benefit of the confessional priest
("I confess, father, that I like women so much that I can't get married

because I don't know which one to choose"), blackmail, humiliation, the difficult construction of the "tribal family" of friends. And before the *Baile de los 41,* there are only savage jokes or frightened mentions of "inverts," a type that does not even warrant mention in the (very misinformed) psychology books. In England, the trials of Oscar Wilde (1895) divulge the sites, mannered styles, and appearances of "mistaken" young men, and illuminate his pathetic and, in the end, extraordinary defense of the "love that dare not speak its name"; in Mexico, where Wilde's trials are discussed with some detail *after* 1901, it is left to the *Gran Redada* [The Great Raid] to break the silence of traditionalism and its hatred "that does not dare to write the name of the hated beings. They are not even worthy of that."

If inferences are of any use, almost surely a part of the gay minority—on account of its cultural mobility or power of acquisition—is up to date with the culture and/or the fashion of France, even when they do not actually travel there. Because of this, they have heard of the scandals of gay writers, of the cult worship of sailors, of the adoption of the symbol of San Sebastián, and, because of this, they have read Walt Whitman, Wilde, Verlaine, and Huysmans.

The gays of society or of the cultural sector keep up appearances, customarily marrying and having children. A single man does not merely raise suspicions; he also betrays nature that is pure fertility, and thus either professional virginity or whorehouse monomania is demanded of the celibate. And if, despite everything, there are those who opt for this microsociety that, for example, organizes *el Baile de los 41,* it is because of what is evident today: nothing arouses those desiring sex with their own kind more than the thrill of the prohibited, in this context a romantic utopia, however contradictory that may be seen or read. ("They want me to be wretched and I can be but not when I go to bed with other men. Copulation is the only liberty within my reach, so that is where I focus my senses.") If one is attentive to the historical excavations of gay subculture in the United States, England, or France, it is not an exaggeration to affirm that, for Mexican homosexuals of 1901, each sexual act is a feat, especially if, predictably, it is produced in circumstances classified as sordid. In these cases, sordidness means access to the ultimate experience, which, for the same reason, and as a compensatory technique, locates pleasures outside of normality. For those beings stripped of a minimally satisfactory record of their conduct, the orgasm becomes the epic of marginality, and, if this is not conscious, the continuity of the acts demonstrates something: when the act against nature is not enjoyed as an extravagant achievement, the sensation of sin is crushing.

That is to say, each sexual act is "an altar of passage" and each seduction an impetuous flag waving in the presence of the enemy—chastity. Does social censure eliminate instinct? The mere existence of the 41 demonstrates the contrary; they are a window into the second half of the nineteenth century and their taverns, god-forsaken sites, procurers, "rentable" young men, and "specialized" brothels (not fixed places, which would seem impossible but, rather, a labyrinth of trysts). One senses that, for the sexually segregated, the greatest stimulus is the existence of others like themselves: anathema to most but a comfort for the marginalized. In particular, gay traditions are born, develop, and become institutionalized through the play of glances that explains the world through the promulgation of desire and the urge to consummate it immediately. We can guess at the jobs of the very effeminate (domestic posts, restaurants), and we are ignorant of the professions of those gays "susceptible to respectability" as long as their sexual orientation remains unknown. Very probably they are clerics, writers, lawyers, artists, investors. And *el Baile de los 41* casts them into the clarity of scandal, which the bishops and the priests, without mentioning it, exploit in order to moralize and the Jacobins in order to discredit the professional moralizers. Thus, in the anticlerical *El Hijo del Ahuizote* (November 1901), "Chano el Sacristán" jokes:

> Figúrese que entre las mujeres se encontraron al padrecito que recogía las limosnas en todos los jubileos, ese primoroso que tenía cara de San Luis Gonzaga y colectaba tanto dinero y que por eso lo llamaban en todas partes.
>
> Que en el Seminario haya hecho sus cosas, santo y bueno, porque allí todos son harina de un costal y están cortados por una misma tijera, pero eso de andar en bailes y fandango, para exponerse a lo que se expuso, no tiene perdón de Dios.

> [Fancy that among the women they discovered the little priest who collected alms at all of the jubilees, that exquisite man that had the look of San Luis Gonzaga and collected so much money and who, because of this, was in demand everywhere.
>
> It is well and good that he has done his business in the seminary because there they are all flour from the same sack and they are cut from the same mold, but this business of going to dances and fandangos to expose himself to what he exposed himself, does not merit divine pardon.]

Before the *Redada*, it is difficult to even verbalize the abominable sin. To resort to the oft-repeated quotation of Sartre, shame isolates,

and the gays of the time find that the greatest—perhaps the only—
possible solidarity is that of acting ashamed among others, much as
mental health bases itself in the conversion of the ashamed into the
shameless (the oppression is so enormous that cynicism is an act of
civil valor). The community sketches itself around the disciplinary
treatment of its fellows and, for this reason, a ball in 1901 is almost
literally the Gay Pride Parade of 2001. In its own way, what is possible approximates what is desirable.

In the preamble to their community, the excluded rely on the neb-
ulosity of the celibate condition or, in the case of married gays, on
their belonging to the family. In an operation of lies, what finances
the control of patriarchy is the fear of being discovered. Opprobrium
is a penal code in and of itself. Oh, what are you getting all worked
up about, since that guy must have already renounced the advantages
of hypocrisy! (For lack of details of any type, I do not, in these notes,
allude to the urban type that surely existed in the time of the 41: proletarian gays. There is a complete absence of knowledge about them.)

THE FACTS: THE POLICE FIND OUT

At three in the morning, Sunday, November 17, 1901, on a downtown block of La Paz Street (today *calle Ezequiel Montes*), the police
interrupted a gathering of homosexuals, some of them dressed as
women. (In these notes I rely on the excellent periodical research of
Antonio S. Cabrera.) The scene, invented with brio in each journalistic recount, is successively or simultaneously pathetic or apocalyptic
according to the taste of the moralism that selects the victims of law
and disease (one and the same thing). Of the 41, 22 dress as men and
19 as transvestites. This is the attire of those detained, as imagined or
embellished by police gossip (there is no official account): skirts, expensive perfumes, curly-haired wigs, fake hips and breasts, earrings,
embroidered slippers, makeup of white or gaudy colors, flats with
embroidered stockings, fans, and short silk dresses fitted to the body
with corsets. A rag doll lies on the bed in one dressing room. At mid-
night, an elegant boy with the nickname of *Bigotes Rizados* (Curly
Mustache) is raffled off. With incomparable glee, *El Popular* gives its
version of the event:

> ¡Si les hubiéramos visto con su peinado de resplandor, su busto desco-
> tado y con postizos, con sus dormilones de brillantes echando pistas,
> con sus postizos como las *pollas* (señoritas de sociedad) anémicas con
> su talle encorsetado, su falda de bailarina como amapola boca abajo,

sus mallas como las mariposas, sus zapatillas bordadas de canutillo de oro y chaquira, y todos embarrados de blanqueto y colorete, zarandeándose en el fandango con sus lagartijos perfumados y rizados . . .

[If only we had seen them in their resplendent hairdos, their fake cleavage, with their shiny sparkling earrings, with their false breasts like the ones worn by anemic society girls, with their corseted waists, their ballerina skirts like inverted poppies, their butterfly tights, their shoes embroidered with crimped gold thread and colored glass beads, and all of them caked with white powder and rouge, prancing about in the fandango with their perfumed and curled mustaches]. (November 24, 1901; trans. Irwin and Nasser)

Initial reports from the newspapers insist: 42 are detained. Later, the number is adjusted to 41, and that gives life to the rumor (legend; "historical truth"): the man who disappears from the list, who buys his liberty at the price of gold and who flees through the roof, is Don Ignacio de la Torre, the husband of Porfirio Diaz's daughter. More than any other fact, what distinguishes the *Redada* is the presence, certified by massive gossip, of the "First Son-in-law" of the nation. Loyalty to historical memory vouches for this much, despite the imprecision of the news reports, the absence of photos, the very weak rumor that the forty-second participant is a woman, and certainty in the names of no more than three: Jesús Solórzano, Jacinto Luna, and Carlos Zozaya. (The most common trait during the *redadas* is the forgetting of one's identity.) One hundred years after the raid, all certainty has vanished, except for the presence of Nacho de la Torre.

The detention of young men from "well-known families of good standing" is also mentioned. *El Popular* denounces: "además de eso, va resultando que todos son pollos gordos, algunos riquillos que la portan; criados en paños azules" [besides this, it turns out that they are all Big Names, a bunch of little rich boys; raised with silver spoons in their mouths]. Those excluded from the Porfirian elite take advantage of the opportunity and cover with stigma the privileged few who, even after this, do not cease to be so. The exact list of the 41 is never released and no recognizable name is published. The sin is spoken of, but if the guilty have money, their identities circulate only in the generally volatile gallows of gossip. The gays of the elite, "made invisible" by their status, only suffer the snares of rumor, and the exception that breaks the rule is the halo of Nacho de la Torre, whose eccentricities, fortune, ability as a consummate horseman, cutting remarks, and homosexuality are divulged conveniently enough for those in need of instant moral superiority. In *La Feria de La Vida* (1937), José Juan Tablada evokes De la Torre, tells of his relations with Porfirio Diaz, "visiblemente ceremoniosas y tirantes" [visibly ceremonious and strained] (284), and tepidly defends him against his negative prestige: "En cuanto a otros rumores que la envidia desató en torno de aquel personaje, él mismo los invalidaba por los actos bien enérgicos de un cabal *sportman,* entre ellos su decidida admiración por el bello sexo, con todas sus consecuencias" [As far as other rumors that jealousy unleashed around his personage, he himself invalidated them through the vigorous actions of an accomplished sportsman, among them his decided admiration for the gentle sex, with all of its consequences] (284–285).

Tablada also tells how, in his hacienda San Nicolás Peralta, De la Torre showed his guests "todos los zapatos que puedan calzar el pie de un hombre moderno y elegante" [all of the shoes that might grace the foot of a modern and elegant man] (286). A bourgeois man present there exclaimed:

> ¡Pero, válgame, mi señor don Ignacio, ¡qué cantidad de zapatos!
> El prócer sonrió ligeramente y luego, viéndose a nosotros, exclamó como resignado
> ¡Dicen que ésta es . . . mi biblioteca!

> ["But, God help me, my lord don Ignacio! What a quantity of shoes!"
> The nobleman smiled slightly and then, turning his glance toward us, exclaimed in resignation:
> "They say this is . . . my library!"]. (286)

Emiliano Zapata works for some time at Don Nacho's hacienda in Morelos, and—according to the legend—goes to Mexico City for the first time as Don Nacho's groom, and this trip, it is said, increases his homophobia.

The question persists: why did the dictator not manage to eliminate the rumors about his son-in-law? Perhaps because Mexico City is still enough of a small town to be a hotbed for gossip, and because not even supreme power can squelch the subtleties of the oral circuit. And who else is dealt the little miracle of the 41? Besides the case of Antonio Adalid, the information consists in the remnants of hearsay. The journalist Alfonso Taracena resentfully cites the journalist Jesús M. Rábago, and old gossip from Sinaloa points to an *hacendado,* the old bachelor Alejandro Redo, who had an aviary of grand dimensions constructed, where he would pass the afternoons, "el pájaro entre los pájaros" [the bird among birds].

The rest of the "aristocrats of Sodom" very possibly find asylum in marriages or emigrate.

Visibility comes through scandal. In addition to the case of Oscar Wilde, another case also has international repercussions: the German judicial trials and courts-martial (1907–1909), which condemned the homosexual relationship between Berlin's military commander, General von Moltke, and the diplomat Philipp Eulenberg, to whom is also attributed a relationship with the kaiser. *La Redada* of the 41 participates in this upsurge of modern sexual identity that stimulates and structures the public idea of normal and abnormal sexuality. In this order of things, the cultural backwardness of Mexico in relation to England and Germany should be remembered. If Mexico, as is so often said, lacks an equivalent for the European Enlightenment, what space remains for scientific knowledge about the diversity of conduct?

About how not even the *redadas*
of perverts are democratic

When the homosexuals are sent to Yucatán, where they are to pay for their crime with forced labor, their number diminishes considerably. They are only 19. At no risk of slandering the proverbial probity of the judicial apparatus in 1901 Mexico, it can be said for certain that 22 or 23 of the victims of the *Redada* buy their liberty. *El Popular* explains away the decrease without striving to convince:

> Ya escrito el anterior, y con datos adquiridos de buena fuente, sabemos, y esto declaramos porque es honrado hacerlo, que entre muchos de los aprehendidos por la policía en el baile de la 4ª calle de la Paz, había algunos individuos que fueron víctimas de un verdadero chasco pues que, en las primeras horas de la noche del domingo se repartieron en varias cantinas unas tarjetas firmadas por una Sra. Vinchi en las que se invitaba a un baile en la casa citada esa misma noche.
>
> Como era natural, hubo algunos que se supusieron se trataba de uno de tantos bailes que se dan en ciertas casas y acudieron para llevarse el gran chasco que ahora deben lamentar hondamente.

> [Considering the above together with our information acquired from a good source, we know, and this we declare because it is honorable to do so, that among those apprehended by the police on the fourth block of La Paz, were several individuals who were victims of a veritable trick because in the early hours of Sunday night, cards signed by a Sra. Vinchi, which were invitations to a ball in the aforementioned house that same night, were given out.

As was natural, there were some who supposed that this concerned one of so many balls that are held in certain houses and they went only to be tricked, which they now must profoundly regret. (11/24/1901 Spanish 42; English 29, this volume)

How ingenuous is the profit-seeking press! The editor of *El Popular,* well aware that no one will believe him, participates in the scheme: the transvestites alone should be forced to pay the public cost of the *Redada,* which would require a slight bit of compromise, since the thought of the *jotitos* in the army is either bothersome or infuriating. Likewise, the great liberal Daniel Cabrera writes in the article "La aristocracia de Sodoma al servicio nacional" [The Aristocracy of Sodom at the nation's service]:

... pero si podemos decir que hasta hoy las autoridades políticas han considerado el servicio de las armas como un castigo, han confundido los cuarteles con las casas de corrección y con las cárceles y a los abigeos, a los vagos, a los incorregibles, les penan haciéndoles cargar el fusil, como en tiempos atrás se hacía empuñar la pala a los huéspedes de las Acordadas.

El ejército no puede recibir en sus filas a individuos que han abdicado su sexo, la Nación no debe honrar con el ahogo ni a quienes se han degradado con los usos de colorete y los vestidos de las prostitutas, ni a los que les sirvieron de parejas.

Afortunadamente, la mordaza que ponen en nuestros labios el respeto al pudor y a las buenas costumbres, no puede impedirnos protestar por la honra del Ejército, guardián de la paz y parte de la sociedad en que vivimos, contra la consignación de los pederastas al servicio de las armas nacionales.

[... but if we can say that up to now the political authorities have considered military service a punishment, they have confused barracks with corrections houses and prisons, and they punish cattle thieves, idlers, and incorrigibles by making them carry a rifle, just as in times past the guests of the *Acordadas* were forced to use shovels.[3]

The army cannot receive among their ranks individuals who have abdicated their sex, the Nation ought to honor with its uniform neither those who have degraded themselves with rouge and the dresses of prostitutes, nor those who served as their partners.

Fortunately, the gag put to our lips out of respect for modesty and propriety does not impede us from protesting, on behalf of the honor of the Army, the guardian of peace and part of the society in which we live, against the pederasts' consignment to the service of the national army]. (*El Hijo del Ahuizote,* 11/24/1901)

What distance is there between this and the formula set up by Bill Clinton's government in its failure to recognize gays in the American army: "Don't ask, don't tell"? Whatever the case, the protest works and on November 25, *El Popular* publishes a clarification: "Los vagos, rateros y afeminados que han sido enviados a Yucatán, no han sido consignados a los batallones del Ejército que operan en la campaña contra los indios mayas, sino a las obras públicas en las poblaciones conquistadas al enemigo común de la civilización" [The bums, petty thieves, and effeminates who have been sent to Yucatán have not been consigned to army battalions engaged in the campaign against the Mayan Indians but, rather, to public works in the settlements conquered from civilization's common enemies].

THE FAMOUS *jotitos*

A very short time after *el Baile de los 41*, there appears a handbill, from Arsacio Vanegas Arroyo's workshop, with the extraordinary prints of José Guadulupe Posada—and a few atrocious little verses that describe the uproar (see Illustration 1).

Cuarenta y un lagartijos
disfrazados la mitad
de simpáticas muchachas
bailaban como el que más.

La otra mitad con su traje,
es decir de masculinos,
gozaban al estrechar
a los *famosos jotitos.*

Vestidos de raso y seda
al último figurín
con pelucas bien peinadas
y moviéndose con chic.

Sus caras muy repintadas
con albayalde o con cal,
con ceniza o velutina . . .
¡Pues vaya usté a adivinar!

Llevaban buenos corsés
con pechos bien abultados
y caderitas y muslos . . .
postizos . . . pues está claro.

[Forty one *lagartijos* (dandies)
half of them disguised
as nice young girls
danced the night away.

The other half in their costumes,
that is to say the masculine ones,
gratified in embracing
the *famous jotitos.*

Dressed in satin and silk
in the dandiest fashion
with well-combed wigs
and moving with *chic.*

Their faces caked over
with ceruse or with lime
with ash or *velutina* . . .
well you figure it out!

They wore good corsets
with exaggerated breasts
and hips and thighs . . .
fake . . . but of course.]

The gendarmes enter, "alerted by the neighbors," and a scene is
produced that delights the city: some want to run, or "disappear into
the *crowd*," others strip off their clothing or are *frozen stiff* in their
tracks. "They cry, shriek, and even bark," and they are taken straight
to prison.

Al día siguiente ¡oh dolor!
a patinar se los llevan,
con macizas escobotas
que cojer pueden apenas.
¡Qué figuras tan chistosas
los maricones hacían!,
levantándose las naguas,
y barriendo de prisita.

Como era una calle pública
donde hacían la limpieza,
se tapaban las carotas
con sus pañuelos de seda.

[The following day, oh what pain!
They are taken to stumble about
with massive brooms
that they can barely hold.
What laughable figures
the *maricones* made!
lifting up their skirts,
and sweeping in such a hurry.

As it was a public street
where they did the cleaning,
they covered their shameful faces
with silk handkerchiefs.]

The reception committee for twentieth-century homosexuals is made up of the weight of the law, loud guffaws, absolute scorn, and condemnation to forced labor in Valle Nacional, Yucatán, at the time considered a living hell. According to Vanegas Arroyo's handbill, those of the Other Persuasion are going to combat the Mayas.

Ay! pero cuál será el castigo
para *nosotras,* dijeron . . .
—Pues que los van a estacar!
lueguito les respondieron.

[Oh! But what will the punishment be
for *us girls,* they said . . .
"Why you will be impaled!"
was the prompt response.]

What follows is derision, mockery of the *jotitos,* of their cries and moans, of their ill-fated destiny:

Y otros de ellos la comida
irán a hacer a la tropa;
pues pa soldados no sirven,
nada más para la sopa.

Uno de aquellos maricos,
marico de gran vergüenza,
con una aguja intentaba
arrancarse la existencia.

¡Pero qué! No lo dejaron,
y en un baño de regadera,
le dieron para evitarlo
en plenas asentaderas.

[And others of them were going
to make food for the troops;
since as they´re useless as soldiers
they can only serve the soup.

One of those *maricos*
a *marico* full of shame
tried with a needle
to tear out his existence.
But what! They didn't let him,
and in the shower
they gave him a good spanking
on the rear to deter him.]

According to the press, the participants of the "baile singular" [singular dance] are in the majority from "buenas familias" [good families] and this obliges the title of the handbill: "*Aquí están los maricones, muy chulos y coquetones*" [Here are the *maricones,* very cute and flirtatious].

THE BALL OF GOOD HABITS

To understand the hatred of difference in Mexico at the beginning of the century, it is useful to examine the prevailing morality during Porfirio Diaz's dictatorship, which was strict with everyone in the public domain, normal or "abnormal." (Promiscuous heterosexuals do not fare so poorly in private.) This morality provokes indignation, for example, over adultery, over the loss of virginity before matrimony, over sex without reproductive ends, over the exhibition of women's unclothed legs, and over the knowledge of anatomy. Masturbation, it is affirmed, causes irreversible harm, including the sprouting of soft hairs in the palm of the hands. And without any sort of definition, decorum, dignity, modesty, and chastity are praised. The Penal Code of 1871 is, in its own way, a manual of beliefs steeped in hypocrisy. Let us look at the sixth chapter, the one that concerns "Delitos contra el orden de las familias, la moral pública o las buenas costumbres" [Crimes against the order of families, public morality, or good habits].

Capítulo II
Ultrajes a la moral pública, o a las buenas costumbres
Art. 785. El que exponga al público, o públicamente venda o distribuya canciones, folletos u otros papeles obscenos, o figuras, pinturas o dibujos grabados o litografiados que representen actos lúbricos; será castigado con arresto de ocho días a seis meses y multa de 20 a 250 pesos.
Art. 786. La pena que señala el artículo que antecede, se aplicará también al autor de los objetos que en él se mencionan y al que los reproduzca; pero solamente en el caso en que los hayan hecho para que expongan, vendan o distribuyan públicamente, y así se verifique.
Art. 787. Se impondrá la pena de arresto mayor y multa de 25 a 500 pesos, al que ultraje la moral pública o las buenas costumbres, ejecutando una acción impúdica en un lugar público, haya o no testigos, o en un lugar privado en que pueda verla el público.
Se tendrá como impúdica: toda acción que en el concepto público esté calificada de contraria al pudor.
Art. 788. En los ultrajes a la moral pública, o a las buenas costumbres, es circunstancia agravante de segunda clase que se ejecuten en presencia de menores de catorce años.

[Chapter II
Affronts to public morality or to good habits
Art. 785. He who exposes to the public, or publicly sells or distributes, songs, pamphlets, or other obscene papers, or figures, paintings, or engraved prints or lithographs that depict lewd acts will be punished with arrest lasting from eight days to six months and a fine of 20 to 250 pesos.
Art. 786. The punishment indicated by the preceding article will be applied also to the author of the aforementioned objects and to those who reproduce them; but only in cases where they have made them to be exposed, sold or distributed publicly, and such can be proven.
Art. 787. The punishment of greater arrest and a fine of 25 to 500 pesos will be imposed on he who affronts public morality or good habits, by performing an immodest act in a public place, whether or not there are witnesses, or in a private place visible to the public.
Immodest will be considered as: any action that in the public eye is classified as contrary to modesty.
Art. 788. In affronts to public morality, or to good habits, it is an aggravating circumstance of the second degree that they take place in the presence of minors of less than 14 years of age].

The most significant aspect of the *Redada* of the 41 is, to reiterate, the arbitrary detention of a group that enjoyed itself one Saturday evening. In 1901, it was alleged that the 41 "lacked permission," but the newspapers of the period made no mention of the requirement to seek permission or to give previous notification for a gathering. Civil and human rights are inconceivable, and "bad example" is offense enough. Thus, the commentary of Daniel Cabrera, whose phrase explains the strategies of silence surrounding homosexuality: "la mordaza que pone en nuestro labio al respeto al pudor y las buenas costumbres" [the gag that they put to our lips out of respect for modesty and good habits] (*El Hijo Del Ahuizote*, 11/24/1901). To mention the sodomites is not only to concede their existence but also to awaken the curiosity of the young, "ignorant to the perversions of instinct." In Mexico, homosexuality is not prohibited, and this is because of an overflowing admiration for France. In 1791, the Revolutionary Assembly, in explicit rejection of Judeo-Christian prohibitions, suppressed the laws against sodomy. During the Consulate, the first counsel was Napoleon Bonaparte, and the second was Jean-Jacques de Cambacéres, who translated the revolutionary depenalization of homosexuality into the Napeolonic Code, even though detentions for "attempts to commit crimes against decency" persisted in an irregular fashion. The absence of specific mentions of sodomy, besides being influenced by the State's distancing itself from notions of sin and by the presence of Cambacéres who was gay, had to do with the fear of giving a precise description of the "most abominable act":

> When Napoleón was petitioned to judge harshly "a ring" of homosexuals arrested in Chartres, the emperor announced, "We are not in a country where the law should concern itself with these offences. Nature has seen to it that they are not frequent. The scandal of legal proceedings would only tend to multiply them." (White 152)

In Latin America, the adoption of the Napoleonic Code was a great advance. According to Rafael Gutiérrez Girardot in *Modernismo,* this civil code, which liquidated the feudal order, constituted the legalization of bourgeois society, and, at the same time, it was the pinnacle of the rationalization of law and an opposite pole to the theocratic world view. Because of this, Gutiérrez Girardot explains, traditionalism is opposed to the Napoleonic Code adapted for Chile by Andrés Bello in 1854 and later implanted in the rest of the republics (31). In the face of this, traditionalists, with little opposition, established as a means of repression their great persecutory instrument, "las faltas a la moral y las buenas costumbres" [offenses against morality and good habits], a concept that remains undefined to this day and has been drastically applied by the authorities. Let us look at this text from the Procuraduria General de la República in 1932:

> ... hay ataques al pudor—argumenta la Procuraduría General de la República—cuando existe ultraje u ofensa públicos al pudor, a la decencia o a las buenas costumbres, normas rectoras de la vida en la sociedad mexicana; o bien, se excita a la práctica de actos licenciosos o impúdicos, temiéndose, como tales, aquellos que, en el concepto público, estén calificados de contrarios al pudor o representan actos lúbricos. Y el segundo de los instrumentos en cuestión, acoge qué hechos deben ser sancionados, penalmente, por constituir publicaciones u otros actos obscenos.

> [... there are attacks against modesty—argues the Attorney General—when there exists a public affront or offense to modesty, to decency, or to good habits, the ruling norms of Mexican society; or, rather, we are outraged by the practice of licentious or immodest acts, fearing, as such, those who, in the public eye, are qualified as contrary to chastity or perform lewd acts. And the second of the instruments in question covers which acts should receive penal sanction for constituting obscene publications or acts]. (Alfonso Noriega, *Delitos contra la moral pública*)

The former, a judgment from the age of revolutionary radicalism, does not differ in the slightest from the allegations of 1871, and "el concepto público" [the public eye], now exiled into an abstract place, is granted the right to qualify *morality, chastity, decency, lewd acts,* and *obscenity.* This always undefined notion traces the bitter destiny of hundreds of thousands of people through the course of the twentieth century.

"Muy chulos y coquetones"

The oral circuit and, more famously, the eight or ten prints of José Guadalupe Posada, fix the *Gran Redada* in the collective memory (see illustrations 1 through 4). It is evoked in very distinct styles throughout the course of a century, this gathering of "phenomenons," of crudely cross-dressed gentlemen, with mustaches and tiny feet, and of the "beautiful damsels" who accompany them dancing on the road to social pillory. A contemporary book, which would like to be a novel, gives an idea of its impact. In *Los 41. Novela crítico social* (1906), its author, Eduardo A. Castrejón, preaches—in no other way would the novel be published—against the "injuria grave a la Naturaleza" [grave injury to nature] (Spanish 97; English 51, this volume) and invents an abominable soirée:

El corazón degenerado de aquellos jóvenes aristócratas prostituidos, palpitaba en aquel inmenso bacanal.

La desbordante alegría originada por la posesión de los trajes femeninos en sus cuerpos, las posturas mujeriles, las voces carnavalescas, semejaban el retrete-tocador de una cámara fantástica; los perfumes esparcidos, los abrazos, los besos sonoros y febriles, representaban cuadros degradantes de aquellas escenas de Sodoma y Gomorra, de los festines orgiásticos de Tiberio, de Cómmodo y Calígula, donde el fuego explosivo de la pasión salvaje devoraba la carne consumiéndola en deseos de la más desenfrenada prostitución.

[The degenerate hearts of those young prostituted aristocratic men palpitated in that immense Bacchanal.

The overwhelming joy originating out of the possession of women's clothing on their bodies, the womanly postures, the carnivalesque voices, made the dressing room seem like a chamber of fantasies; the disseminating perfumes, the embraces, the sonorous and feverish kisses recalled degrading paintings of those scenes of Sodom and Gomorrah, of those orgiastic parties of Tiberius, of Commodus and Caligula, where the explosive fire of savage passion devoured the flesh, consuming it in desires of the most unbridled prostitution]. (Spanish 97; English 51, this volume)

If Castrejón is not, as might be more fitting to suppose, a gay eager to win space for his obsessions under the pretext of beating them down, he is a moralist without literary talent, preoccupied with the sudden appearance of "jóvenes inflammables, repudiables, odiosos para el porvenir y por todas las generaciones, escoria de las sociedad y mengua de los hombres honrados amantísimos de las bellezas fecundas de la mujer" [inflammable youths, repudiated young men, hated by the future and by all generations, scum of society and discredit to honorable men who are fervent lovers of the fecund beauties of women] (Spanish 100; English 54, this volume). In *Los 41,* Ignacio de la Torre is Don Pedro Marruecos, the axis of this perverted society, and the only one who escapes the *Redada,* whose igneous moment astonishes the narrator:

Entretanto, en el salón crecía el entusiasmo.

Ojos lánguidos; caderas postizas ondulantes, gráciles con sus irreprochables curvas; rostros polveados, pintarrajeados; pelucas maravillosamente adornadas con peinetas incrustadas de oro y joyas finísimas; pantorrillas bien cinceladas a fuerza de algodón y auténticas de amorfias flacuras; senos postizos, prominentes y enormes pugnando por salir de su cárcel; muecas grotescas y voces fingidas; le daba todo ese conjunto a la orgía algo de macabro y fantástico.

[Meanwhile, in the ballroom, the excitement mounted.

Phosphorescent eyes, lewd eyes, languid eyes; false hips, undulant, slender, with their irreproachable curves; powdered painted faces; wigs marvelously adorned with ornamental combs encrusted in gold and fine jewels; calves well chiseled by dint of cotton and authentic amorphous leanness; false breasts, prominent and enormous, struggling to burst out of their prison; grotesque faces and feigned voices; all this together gave the orgy a macabre and fantastic air]. (Spanish 120; English 74, this volume)

Later comes the fall, the shame, the jubilant masses that see the *jotos* depart for Yucatán, to the hell of forced labor.

Y era de risa ver el cuadro grotesco de los populares 41, levantando la pala y golpeando con el zapapico, sudorosos, escuálidos y llorando las más de las veces a lágrima viva.

Los soldados les daban todos los días "latas" monumentales, diciéndoles con voz fingida:

—¿A dónde vas con tu traje de gala?

—¡No trabajes que te quiebras la cintura, vida mía!

—¿Te sofocas, lindo niño? Pues carga con el abanico. . . .

[And it made one laugh to see the grotesque scene of the popular 41, raising their shovels and pickaxes, sweating, squalid, and crying their eyes out most of the time.

The soldiers gave them a monumental hard time every day, telling them in mocking voices:

"Where are you going in your party dress?"

"Don't work so hard that you throw out your waist, my dear."

"Are you suffocating, pretty boy? Well, use your fan . . ."]

(Spanish 131; English 85, this volume)

And a refrain published in a daily of the metropolis at the time becomes popular and the soldiers sing:

Mírame, marchando voy
con mi chacó a Yucatán,
por hallarme en un convoy
bailando jota y cancán.

[Look at me as I march
with my shako to Yucatán,
where I'll find myself in a convoy
dancing *jota*[4] and can can.] (Spanish 131; English 85, this volume)

"Why did you make me like this, God, and not like my sister?"

What do those detained in *el Baile de los 41* think of themselves? At this point it is impossible to interview them and—through the circumstances of the period—impossible not to. They are classified as "hosts of abnormality"—abnormality, a bastion for sinners and an Eden for pleasure-seekers; they live as women trapped in male bodies; they feel like victims of a perverse designation by God; they consider themselves to be moved by an impulse that razes religious controls. Their Catholicism brings them to believe themselves to be on the eve of eternal fire, and they only hope for a last-minute pardon. That is to say, they await the instant of their own agony to repent and save themselves. This is how they were born and have constructed themselves, not as homosexuals (the term does not circulate) but, rather, as a doubly or triply degraded caste: *los maricones,* whether they remain clandestine or already have nothing left to lose. If, in accordance with Didier Eribon, the homosexual learns to speak twice, in their second education the gays of the *Porfiriato* desire an equilibrium between hypocrisy (which is survival) and their sexual appetite, which when unleashed smashes the impositions of Decency to pieces.

The epithet *maricones* is an implacable sentence and, ultimately, is flight through self-parody and orgiastic will. Where pride is not permissible, a desperate humor is exercised that, in and of itself, against the current, puts liberties within reach. This would be the message: "If I do not laugh at myself, I do not reaffirm my humanity." And—in agreement with evidence from the generations to follow—the point of departure for gay resistance is the conversion of determinism into fun, of guilt into a fashion parade, of condemnation into the mockery of idiomatic conventions. In the majority of cases, they speak in the feminine gender, not so much to respect the unanimous dogma ("Las locas están locas" [The queens are queens]) but, rather, to fit language to conduct and to empower themselves linguistically of the heterosexual act's privilege. In other words, if *los maricones* do not scoff at Destiny (which made them as they are), and do not laugh in passing at some of the social axioms that so cruelly vex them, they will never acquire that indispensable identity that is simultaneously the abandonment of hope and the joy of knowing themselves to be alive despite everything. The authorities endorse their moral vocation with arrests, humiliations, and beatings, and *los maricones* gain a stark intuition of their rights thanks to a great and unique resource: the very persistence of their conduct.

In terms of the resonances of the *Gran Redada*, the word *relajo* provides the necessary justification to speak of the subject. Throughout the twentieth century, the number 41 provokes a smile that accompanies the circular joke. *"Vamos a contar: 39, 40, 42"* [Let's count: 39, 40, 42]. *41 . . . zafo* (I'm not included) is the pertinent expression, the substitution of an instantaneous wit for the *albur*,[5] a wit that would be dissipated alongside the self-celebratory guffaws. In *Cancionero folclórico mexicano,* Margit Frenk records two couplets:

a) De aquellos que están allá,
no me parece ninguno:
el uno ya está muy viejo
y el otro es 41.
b) Uno, dos, tres, cuatro, cinco,
cinco, cuatro, tres, dos, uno,
cinco por ocho cuarenta,
con usted cuarenta y uno.

[a) Of those men out there,
not one suits me:
one is already very old
and the other is 41.
b) One, two three, four, five
five, four, three, two, one
five times eight is forty,
plus you forty-one]. (Tomo 4, Copla 9796)

The number isolates and vexes homosexuals—and ultimately exalts them once its meaning is removed from the humors that mock them. *El Baile de los 41* serves also to identify sodomy with transvestism, initiating fear about a practice that, until November 17, 1901, basically seemed a carnivalesque recurrence. In a well-documented article, Alejandro García reports of an undoubtedly formal ball presided over by the governor of the Federal District Pedro, Rincón Gallardo, and attended by the dictator and the Porfirian court. The novelty, as *El Universal* of September 7, 1894, reported, was the presence of various young men costumed as women—such as F. Algara, who arrived as Demoiselle de Compagnie. A similar event, outside the strict carnival season, proved to be impossible after *el Baile.*

"So it is an epidemic"

The religious, social, cultural, and penal powers prohibit the analysis of the *maricón* condition but do not avert the vertigo, the freedom of movement during the hours of the ghetto, the self-lacerating jokes, the fine clothes, and the choreographies of verbal jabs. One's reflection might go something like this: "I am condemned from birth, but my seasons in hell alternate with the successive reprieves of diversion, immoral fun, coitus, and my disguise that is the acquisition, for a few hours, of a second skin, the deeper one, because I chose it." By the law of psychic compensation, the outline of the ghetto is transformed in its hour into a *sui generis* liberatory space. There, humor and the search for style neutralize the severity of condemnatory opinion.

Is it possible to perceive what will be called the "gay ghetto" here? I do not think so. Not even police records are available, and neither diaries nor testimonies of the period are preserved. It is known how the myth of virility is affirmed, but not how some escape from its hegemony. Everything or almost everything must be guessed at: the anxious longing in swimming pools, in *cantinas,* in steam baths, during the carnival season and cruising strolls. But if, before 1918 or 1920, there is not much sense in talking of a ghetto proper, it is appropriate to describe the project, centered in "verbal transvestism," or, so to speak, the implacable use of the feminine gender. Thanks to this, the gays of the end of the nineteenth century and beginning of the twentieth escape the prisons of behavior through language, moments of joy, and the remembrance of those moments. Without the mutation of gender and subsequent feminization of reality, and also without acts of self-denigration, the persecution would be unbearable.

On the difficulties of living the truth of true love

The principle of their identity is the mode by which the 41 are contemplated and judged. As a social entity, the gay is born out of stigma, out of mockery, and in his case the negative images come from—if the metaphor can be accepted—a stagnant pool of inaugural narcissism. A gay man of 1901 perhaps would have said it another way: "I am reflected in the immorality that they attribute to me, the disgust which I provoke, and from my public image, because I cannot avoid it, I extract my own intimate image. I am what they have obliged me to be, and from that point on, mixing pleasure and sadness, I am something different." Without anyone suspecting or becoming concerned, the condition of being expelled from good habits leads, if not to an (unthinkable) criticism of society, then to indifference toward the majority of values in use. According to the testimonies of the next generation, there are no ultrapatriotic gays, nor is there an abundance of those concerned with the development of society.

Although it may not seem so, in a manner of speaking, the *Redada* "invents" homosexuality in Mexico. Those who share such inclinations are aware of their good luck: they might have formed part of the 41, and were saved at least that time. (Thus, the phrase that still circulates in the decade of the 1950s: "De la redada de los 41 te salvaste, manita. Del infierno, todavía no" [You may have been saved from the *Redada* of the 41, sister. But not yet from hell].) By specifying the limits of homosexuality, the *Redada* uncovers the fragilities of determinism. Stigma covers them all, but physical punishments touch only a few, and the rest will not have to sweep the streets at any point in their lives. However much fear they keep inside, however much in secret they guard their orientation, the homosexuals of Mexico City no longer feel alone after the *Redada;* in a certain way, in the spirit of the interrupted party, the 41—the sign of the tribe's existence—accompany them. If the homosexuals are already there—and the *Baile* denounces a minimal but already solid social organization— the *Redada,* by giving a mocking name to the type, imprints onto it a sense of collectivity in the darkness. From the ridicule and the penitentiary threat, the anomalies ascend to the surface and this first visibility is definitive.

On the dehumanization
of the different

In the current perspective of the 41 episode, the outstanding aspect is, of course, the absolute negation of the human and civil rights of the homosexuals. From that moment on, "jurisprudence is felt" and the repressions are legal, not because they correspond to some text but, rather, because they have already once been so. And this promotes incessant *redadas,* police blackmails, tortures, beatings, and detention in prisons and in the penal colony of las Islas Marías, all without any motive. Only one phrase is necessary in the proceedings: "Offenses to morality and good habits." Nothing else is necessary; there are no defense lawyers (not even public defenders in the case of the *jotos*), no trials, merely judicial caprices dictated by "disgust." And society, or those who are aware, finds these proceedings normal and admirable.

La Gran Redada delivers, to the gays of Mexico, the past that is, in synthesis, the interminable negotiation with the present. They emerge from that moment of happiness destroyed by gendarmes, and they are a community despite their burden of being always susceptible to raids. From the early morning of November 17, 1901, to 1978, when a gay contingent paraded in the commemorative march of October 2,[6] gays lived seized by panic from the *Redada;* and the alliance of police abuse and the moral *Redada,* the detentions, the beatings, the insults, the scorn, the wrath, and parental anguish, shows that this is not psychologism. And only when the term gay is popularized is the *Redada* interrupted, not because the persecutory spirit is eliminated, but because the invocation of the law diminishes the raids (with an exception made for transvestites) and prepares for the irruption of a public voice from those who no longer accept silence.

"Your name should go here but I won't put it down because it's a man's name"

On account of the intercession of the 41, homosexuality is constructed on penal and humoristic bases. Also, with the *Gran Redada,* the "secularization" of abnormality is initiated, and a tragic proof in that respect is given by hate crimes, the assassinations of gays "just because," which are so frequent and ultimately so reliant on the tradition of *hogueras* (burning at the stake) that the Inquisition dedicated to *los sométicos* or sodomites. What distance is there from "Let the flames purify your sins" to "I killed him for being a *maricón*"? While the assassins may not know it, they continue to enact the regulations; hate crimes against gays, those orgies of savage cruelty in cheap hotels, in apartments and houses, are the reaffirmation of the theocratic visions that extirpate the sin in exemplary fashion.

The mysteries of semantics: the arrival of the word gay introduces, almost simultaneously, the defense of the human rights of those whom it represents.

Notes

1. *China* as in *china poblana,* refers to a woman dressed in the typical regional costume of the Mexican state of Puebla, which usually consists of a skirt adorned with shiny sequins and the wearing of many necklaces and bracelets. (trans.)
2. The nickname Toña la Mamonera comes from *mamar,* to suck. *"Mamonera"* plays with gender through an overt grammatical feminization of the male subject. Novo recognizes this play in explicitly

physical terms when, in the subsequent passage, he imagines that Adalid received the nickname "por su afición a una caricia que debe de haber sido entonces poco ordinaria, o que Antonio practicaría con mayor europea destreza o predilección" [because of his fondness for a caress that either must have been hardly ordinary at the time, or that Antonio might have practiced with a more European dexterity or predilection] (109). (trans.)

3. *Las Acordadas* were prisons originally founded in 1710 as part of the *Santa Hermandad,* an institution similar to the inquistion, and whose function was to apprehend and judge highway robbers. [trans.]

4. Popular Spanish dance of the era.

5. *Albur*—reference to the Mexican game of *albures*. It consists of, according to Octavio Paz, "el combate verbal hecho de alusiones obscenas y de doble sentido" [verbal combat made up of obscene double *entendres*] (35). One wins when the opponent cannot answer and "traga las palabras del enemigo" [swallows the words of his enemy] (35). For Paz, it is exemplary of the manner in which allusions to "active" homosexuality are tolerated among machos in Mexican culture as long as they violate, figuratively or otherwise, a "passive" agent. Here, Monsiváis creates an opposition between "instantaneous wit" and the fixed or deterministic schemata of the game. [trans.]

6. The date refers to the tenth anniversary of the October 2, 1968, student massacre in Tlatelolco Plaza. [trans.]

Bibliography

Castrejón, Eduardo A. *Los cuarenta y uno. Novela crítico social.* Mexico City: Tipografía Popular, 1906.

Código Penal. México City: Imprenta del Gobierno, 1871.

Cuéllar, José T. de. *Historia de Chucho el Ninfo* y *La Noche Buena.* Mexico City: Editorial Porrúa, 1975.

Frenk, Margit Alatorre. *Cancionero Folklórico de México.* Mexico City: Colegio de México, 1985.

Gutiérrez Girardot, Rafael. *Modernismo.* Bogotá: Fondo de Cultura Económica, 1987.

El Hijo del Ahuizote.

Novo, Salvador. *La Estatua de Sal.* Mexico City: Consejo Nacional para la Cultura y las Artes, 1998.

Paz, Octavio. *El Laberinto de la Soledad.* Mexico City: Fondo de Cultura Económica, 1989.

El Popular.

Prieto, Guillermo. *Obras Completas* Vol. 27. México City: Consejo Nacional para la Cultura y las Artes, 1992.

Tablada, José Juan. *La Feria de la Vida*. Mexico City: Ediciones Botas, 1937.

El Universal.

"Los 41 Maricones: Encontrados en un baile de la Calle de la Paz el 20 de Noviembre de 1901: Aquí están los maricones, muy chulos y coquetones." México City: Arsacio Vanegas Arroyo, no date, no pagination.

White, Edmund. *The Flaneur*. New York: Bloomsbury, 2001.

The Centenary of the Famous 41

Robert McKee Irwin

The Men-Only Ball

In the wee hours of the morning of November 17, 1901, the Mexico City police raided a private party on the fourth block of La Paz Street, arresting all 41 men in attendance, half of whom were dressed as women. The ensuing scandal, played out sensationalistically in Mexico City's newspapers, followed the 41 from their arrest for having a party without proper permission and for their assault on good customs, to their court-ordered public humiliation as they were made to sweep the streets still in drag, to their ultimate embarkment for Yucatán where they were to assist the Mexican army in its war with Maya insurgents as trench diggers and mess hall staff.

While the various newspaper reports, *corridos,* visual caricatures (a series of engravings by the famed Mexican popular artist José Guadalupe Posada), and even a novel (the forgotten *Los 41* by Eduardo Castrejón)[1] were notorious in their contradictions regarding the precise events surrounding the "nefarious ball,"[2] the basic legend is that laid out above. Moreover, a single image has endured, that of the 41 transvestites. As Carlos Monsiváis has observed, "Desde entonces y hasta fechas recientes en la cultura popular el gay es el travesti y sólo hay una especie de homosexual: el afeminado" [From then and until recent times, in popular culture, gay means transvestite and there is only one kind of homosexual: the effeminate man] ("Ortodoxia" 199); in other words, the public scandal of this *baile de sólo hombres* [men-only ball] marks a key moment in the modern construction of male homosexuality in Mexico.[3] Monsiváis, at another moment, elaborates in more detail: "Aunque no parezca, la Redada, por así decirlo, inventa la homosexualidad en México . . . la Redada, al darle el nombre ridiculizador a la especie (Los 41), modifica el sentido de esa colectividad en las tinieblas: de anomalías aisladas ascienden a

la superficie del choteo, y esta primera visibilidad es un paso defini-
tivo" [Although it may not appear to be the case, the Raid, as we
might call it, invents homosexuality in Mexico . . . the Raid, in giving
a ridiculizing name to the species (The 41), modifies the meaning of
this collectivity in the shadows, from isolated anomalies they rise to
the surface of the joke, and this first visibility is a definitive step] ("Los
iguales," no page number).

The *baile clandestino* counted among its guests not only the approximately 19 transvestites but also their servants and various other
men dressed as men, among them a certain number of curiosity seek-
ers who had been recruited at select cantinas. Among the most notorious of the attendees was a group of dandies well known on *los
boulevards* for their flashy elegance.[4] Every afternoon they would
stroll frivolously down Plateros Street, showing off their fabulous
(men's) wardrobe and flirting with ingenuous young ladies. It is said
that among those identified at the ball were lawyers, dentists, and
even priests, but in reality little is known of the identities of the 41,
as even the newspapers reporting lists of names admitted that nearly
all of them were false. Nonetheless, the most famous of the 41 was
really the forty-second *maricón*. The first newspaper reports stated
that the number of men arrested was 42, a figure that mysteriously
became 41 after a few days. The forty-second transvestite had been
surreptitiously deleted from public record when it was discovered
that he was the son-in-law of President Porfirio Díaz.[5]

Another piece of gossip was that the forty-second participant was
in fact a woman, the housekeeper of the building rented for the ball.
A week after the scandal erupted, the not always serious newspaper
El Popular published a dialogue of two *comadritas*[6] in order to better circulate gossip: "Pues oiga, Chanita, yo nada 'vide' ni digo más
que lo que todo el mundo sabe, porque ni me gustan chismes ni me
escandalizo de nada; pero . . . ¡quién se lo había de figurar! Pues, hay
tiene usté nomás, comadrita de mi alma y de mi vida . . ." [Well listen up, Chanita, I ain't seen nothing and I'm not telling you anything more than what everybody knows already, because I don't like
to gossip, and nothing shocks me; but . . . who would have guessed
it? Well, there you have it, my dear *comadrita* . . .]. They go on to
speak of the "vieja . . . que cuidaba el fandango de los 41" [the old
woman who was working the fandango of the 41]: "¡Pero como ha
deshonrado las 'naguas' esa indina bruja de mis pecados! Cosquillas
me hacen las uñas, y Dios no lo 'premito', pero si yo la conociera y
la tuviera al alcance de mis manos, le cortaba las trenzas . . ." [But
what a dishonor this sinful Indian witch is to her race! It makes my

fingernails tremble to think about it, and God would not permit it, but if I knew her and had her within my reach, I'd cut off her braids . . .] (11/24/1901).

Other rumors about the 41 and other scandalous characters of the epoch are brought to light in the one-man play *"Doña Caralampia Mondongo lo sabe y te lo cuenta todo . . . ,"* written and performed by Tito Vasconcelos, the Mexican activist, actor, and entrepreneur (owner of the fashionable nightclub Cabaré-Tito in Mexico City), to launch the Centenary of the 41 in New Orleans. Who better than our *comadrita* Doña Caralampia, cross-dressed alter ego of the turn-of-the-century journalist Ireneo Paz (Nobel Laureate Octavio's grandfather), to whisper to us the most brazen and outrageous secrets of the Porfiriato?

DISCOURSE AND REPRESSION

Of course, the Centenary of the Famous 41 is not a celebration of gossip. The fact that what passed in 1901 for journalistic investigation or social analysis contains no more verifiable "facts" than the gossip of the *comadritas* or of Doña Caralampia Mondongo is emblematic of the problems faced by investigators of sexuality in that period of Latin American history. Homosexuality in 1901 remains basically inaccessible to us. While recognizing that the "evidence of experience" would pose its own problems (Scott), the lack of testimonial evidence on the part of turn-of-the-century homosexuals means that most analysis must limit itself to discourse about sexuality, its assumptions, its biases, and its strategies of social control.

The case of the 41 itself presents us with several curious aspects that reveal that repressive discourse not only makes possible and in some ways promotes its counterdiscourse but also incorporates it, albeit unintentionally. The newspaper articles on the 41, the highlights of which are included in this volume, at times unleash an inexorable and strident indignation at the scandal. Published over a period of three weeks following the ball, they censure the very existence of the 41: they demand and then applaud their punishment, and also ridicule them relentlessly day after day. A similar attitude is seen in the 1906 novel *Los 41* by Eduardo Castrejón in whose introduction his editors promise that the author "flagela de una manera terrible un vicio execrable, sobre el cual escupe la misma sociedad, como el corruptor de las generaciones" [flagellates, in a horrible way, an execrable vice, on which society itself spits, as the corruptor of generations] (Spanish 94, English 48, this volume).[7] In one moment of the novel, all possible discourses of social control are called together to gang up on the 41, who "no tenían escrúpulo en sacrificar su pudor, su dignidad, su vergüenza, al vicio deshonesto que, como un sarcasmo, insultaba a la ley, a la vida, a la civilización, al progreso de todo lo humano, a la misma Naturaleza!" [had no scruples in sacrificing their modesty, their dignity, their shame, to the disgraceful vice that like a sarcasm insulted the law, life, civilization, the progress of all things human, and Nature itself] (Spanish 121, English 75, this volume).

The newspaper reports, at first austere and brief in their prudish condemnation, not daring to disclose details of the case "por ser en sumo asquerosos" [because they are summarily disgusting] (*El Popular* 11/20/1901, Spanish 36, English 22, this volume),[8] in a few days changed their tone. Three days later, the same journal offered to publish "todos los pormenores que se relacionen con este asunto . . . , pues es tiempo de impedir que escenas tan indecentes se repitan" [all details relating to this subject . . . since it is time to prevent such indecent scenes from recurring] (*El Popular* 11/23/1901, Spanish 39, English 25, this volume). The reports ended up mushrooming into an absolute farce. Their ever more frivolous exaggerations and frank inventions reveal more than the disgust of their authors. Their forms are varied. There was the aforementioned gossipy dialogue of the *comadres,* one of whom, on finding out that the 41 will be sent to Yucatán, cries, "Dios de mi vida . . . ¡Pero los Mayas se van a enojar! ¡Ellos no pelean con maricas!" [My dear God . . . But the Mayas are going to be furious! They won't fight with fairies!] and the other replies, "¿Pues, quién les manda? ¡Que se enseñen a hombres!" [Well, who's making them? Let them teach them to be men!] (*El Popular* 11/24/1901). Another journal published a detailed report of the transvestites' public striptease before the military commander who orders them to change into soldiers' uniforms: "Con las lágrimas en los ojos, fueron despojándose de todas sus prendas, suplicando algunos, que se les dejase siquiera sus ropas interiores de fina seda, a lo cual se opuso el Capitán, pues les dijo que allí eran iguales a los demás. Ni los calcetines les permitió y todos comenzaron a llorar cuando se calzaron los zapatos que iban a reemplazar a los monos choclos de glace pasia y charol" [With tears in their eyes, they stripped off all their clothes, some of them begging that they be allowed to at least keep their fine silk undergarments, a request that the captain denied, since, he told them, there they were just the same as everyone else. He didn't even allow them to keep their socks and they all began to cry when they put on the shoes that would replace their pretty patent leather ladies' shoes"] (*El País* 11/23/1901, Spanish 40, English 26, this volume).

Several days later, there appears the collective diary of the perfumed men recounting their voyage to Yucatán, in which they complain because "no sabemos a lo que se atreverán esos marineros, al saber que somos mujeres y solas, y con la seguridad de que no tenemos madre" [we don't know what those sailors might try when they find out that we are women traveling alone, and with the certainty that we have no mother] (*El Popular* 11/29/1901, Spanish 44, English 30, this volume). As a final example, *El Popular* published letters supposedly written by the various transvestites (Concho, Lolito, Carolino) to their lovers (respectively: "Alfredo de mis intestinos" [Alfredo of my intestines], "Mea dorado Luiz" [My golden Luiz] and "Señor Licenciado Triquiñuelas" [Mister Tricky]) about their sufferings, such as the case of poor Carolino: "No puedo estar sin mi hijo. Por señas que me costó diez pesos y lo compré, con muchos sacrificios, en la juguetería de la Palma. Usted no sabe todavía lo que es ser madre" [I can't bear being away from my son. Because he cost me ten pesos and I bought him, by making many sacrifices, in the La Palma toy store. You still don't know what it is to be a mother] (12/1/1901, Spanish 46, English 32, this volume).[9]

But their obsession with details of the transvestites' dress and makeup—for example: "Entre los vestidos de mujer había muchos pintados las caras de blanco y carmín, con negras ojeras, pechos y caderas postizas, zapatos bajos con medias bordadas, algunos con dormilonas de brillantes y con trajes de seda cortos ajustados al cuerpo con corsé" [Among those dressed as women, there were many with faces made up in black and carmine, with black eyeliner, false breasts and hip pads, low heeled shoes with embroidered stockings, several of them with diamond earrings and with short silk dresses tightly fitted to the body with corsets] (*La Patria* 11/22/1901, Spanish 38, English 24, this volume)—their effeminate mannerisms and their daring sexual subversion signals that more avid than their condemnatory aversion was their enthusiastic fascination to imagine, recreate, and feel this new idea of sexuality. Their eagerness to humiliate the 41, publishing lists of their names (most likely invented), turns into a zeal to make up masculinized woman's names for them: Beatrizito, Sofío, Herlindo, Lucrecio, etc. These linguistic games of gender imply less attitudes of disdain than sentiments of gratification. In the same vein, Castrejón's novel alternates between moments of excessive contempt: "En esa insaciable vorágine de placeres brutales han caído, para no levantarse nunca, jóvenes que, en el colmo de la torpeza y de la degradación prostituida, contribuyen a bastardear la raza humana injuriando gravemente a la Naturaleza" [And into that insatiable whirlpool of brutal pleasures have fallen young men who, at the height of crudeness and prostituted degradation, contribute to the bastardization of the human race, gravely injuring Nature itself] (Spanish 97, English 51, this volume), and an apparent and equally exaggerated envy: "¡El entusiasmo fue indescriptible entonces! Se sentían alegres, satisfechos, emocionados, pletóricos de felicidad mirándose vestidos de mujer. ¡Oh! y qué de transportes eróticos, qué de venturas, qué de embriagueces . . . al trocar el traje de hombre para convertirse en deliciosas niñas (?), en huríes encantadoras de suaves contornos y de ondulantes líneas seductoras" [The enthusiasm was indescribable! They felt overjoyed, fulfilled, excited, plethoric with happiness, seeing themselves dressed up as women. Oh! And what erotic transports, what fortune, what raptures . . . trading in their men's suits and turning themselves into delicious girls (?), into enchanting houris of soft curves and undulant seductive lines] (Spanish 97, English 51, this volume).

The schizophrenic character of the discourse on the 41 also can be seen in the visual representations of Posada, in which the 41 *maricones* "muy chulos and coquetones" [very cute and coquettish] are ridiculed, but in an almost endearing way (see illustration 1). Posada cruelly mocks them, but at the same time promotes them affectionately not as detestable criminals but as sympathetic rakes and naughty rascals who are furthermore utterly Mexican. Posada's engravings have come to symbolize the soul of Mexican culture of the era, and there are no images more Mexican than Posada's *calaveras*.[10] The commemoration of the ball of the 41 in Posada's engravings did much more than celebrate it: it immortalized and Mexicanized it. The series of three images published in 1901 recounts the legend in the form of a *corrido*,[11] with illustrations of the ball, the public humiliation of the 41 sweeping the streets, and the 41's ultimate embarkation for Yucatán (see illustrations 1–3). A fourth image from 1907 entitled "El feminismo se impone" [feminism imposes itself] associates the masculinization of the new feminist woman with the feminization (and implicit homosexualization) of the modern man (see illustration 4). Posada's attitude is as always that of the cultural critic, but he presents his criticism in a playful, joking spirit of good humor.

In the end, the apparent discourses of censure often turned out to foment if not homosexuality itself, at least a curiosity about sexual diversity. Their desire to wipe out homosexuality muddled itself with another contradictory desire to explore it and know about it. Their eagerness to denigrate it with humor ended up celebrating it. Finally, their insistence on rejecting it and suppressing it from national culture failed. Although in Argentina sexual subversion was associated with the foreign influences of European immigration, in Mexico homosexuality placed itself agilely into the national landscape and the 41 became national myths.[12] Six years earlier, the newspaper reports on the notorious trials of Oscar Wilde barely stirred up any interest among Mexican readers;[13] it is not English homosexuality that fascinates Mexicans, but their own national homosexuality.

SEXUALITY AND SOCIAL CONTROL

The discourses of social control, then, do not necessarily repress sexuality, and they certainly do not repress interest in sexuality. However, it is also important to bear in mind that they do not express sexuality either. If the Mexican discourses of social control in 1901 attempt to define homosexuality, their definitions are far from believable, because they lacked access to the sexual reality of the sexually subversive. The only aspect of sexuality that they might define with precision is the attitudes of society toward sexual diversity; in other words, they are only capable of defining their own prejudices. Among the most prominent discourses of social control during the Porfiriato: positivist science (the burgeoning fields of criminology, sociology, psychiatry), religion (Catholicism's discourses of morality, sinfulness, and "good customs"), public opinion (newspapers of various political and social ideologies) and law (both criminal statutes and "natural" law), there is none that admits having firsthand access to "abnormal," "perverse," or "depraved" sexuality. The *maricones* (along with prostitutes, syphilitics, onanists, etc.) almost never speak on record. In the case of the 41, there is no interview, no letter of defense, no document of confession, etc. The *científicos*,[14] reporters, state authorities, cartoonists, and novelists charged with representing sexual subversion in their declarations, writings, and cultural productions made no attempt to get to know it up close.

The first representation of Mexican homosexuality of this period, written by an avowed homosexual is *La estatua de sal*, Salvador Novo's memoirs, written in the 1940s and published posthumously in 1998. Novo writes principally of his youthful adventures, the most colorful of which occur around 1920, from which surface gossip about figures as diverse as his friend Xavier Villaurrutia, the scandalous (and inadequately studied) "Ricardo Arenales,"[15] and Novo's one-time mentor Dominican Pedro Henríquez Ureña; but he also mentions the case of Antonio Adalid, known as *el alma* [the soul] of certain balls of "la época en que los exquisitos aristócratas celebraban fiestas: aunque privadas, sin duda trascendidas a la murmuración y el escándalo de una pacata ciudad pequeña: la época, en fin, del famoso baile de los 41" [the epoch in which the exquisite aristocrats threw parties: although private, undoubtedly they evoked whispers and scandal from a prudish small city: that is the epoch of the famous ball of the 41]. Novo goes on, "Había alcahuetes . . . que procuraban muchachos para la diversión de los aristócratas. Una noche de fiesta, Toña [apodo de Adalid] bajaba la gran escalera con suntuoso atavío de bailarina. La concurrencia aplaudió su gran entrada; pero al pie de la escalera, el reproche mudo de dos ojos lo congeló, lo detuvo. Parecía apostrofarlo: '¡Viejo ridículo!' Toña volvió a subir, fue a quitarse el disfraz, bajó a buscar al hermoso muchacho que lo había increpado en silencio. En ese momento se ponía al remate al mejor postor la posesión de aquel jovencito. Antonio lo compró. Se llamaba también Antonio. No llegaba a veinte años. Sea en el famoso baile de los 41, sea en otro, estalló el escándalo. Don José Adalid desheredó y desconoció a este hijo degenerado . . ." [There were pimps . . . who would procure young men for the diversion of the aristocrats. On the evening of a party, Toña [Adalid's nickname] came down the great staircase in the sumptuous attire of a ballerina. The guests applauded his grand entrance; but at the foot of the stairs, the silent reproach of two eyes froze him, detained him. It seemed to insult him: 'Ridiculous old man!' Toña went back up to take off the costume, and came back down to look for the handsome young man who had silently upbraided him. At this moment, that young man was being auctioned to the highest bidder. Antonio bought him. He was also named Antonio. He was not yet 20. Whether in the famous ball of the 41, or in another, scandal erupted. Don José Adalid disinherited and disowned his degenerate son . . .] (109). This little story, repeated second hand decades after it occurred, is the first representation of homosexuality in 1901 not recounted in a homophobic spirit.

Homosexuality, as a new concept in 1901, distinct from the sodomy of a few centuries before, was being defined through the scandal. Still, everyone treated it as if it were a universally well-known concept, without any need of being defined. No one had to explain that transvestitism, superficially merely a practice of dressing up, also implied sexual perversion, yet it was through this new discourse, so often incoherent, of tranvestitism and sexual perversion that these concepts took on a fixed form. Although homosexuality was a new aspect of effeminacy (effeminacy had never suggested sexual deviation in nineteenth-century Mexico),[16] the concept of male effeminacy absorbed it as if it had always been part if it. Sexuality, constructed mainly as a component of nature—although at times a rebellious component, one that "injuria gravemente a la Naturaleza" [gravely injures Nature] (Spanish 97, English 51, this volume)— must find a place to accommodate itself in the Mexican collective habitus, and the preexisting scheme of gender is the place into which it most easily fits.[17]

In Castrejón's *Los 41,* when the young *afeminados* greet each other, it is no surprise that they kiss, nor that their kisses are "erotic" (Spanish 95, English 49, this volume). That transvestitism signals an outrageous sexuality is clear, but how this queer sexuality gets defined is somewhat more blurry. The very prejudices of these voices of authority sometimes entangle themselves in confusion.

A typical case is that of the Mexican criminologist Carlos Roumagnac who, in a series of interviews with prisoners of Mexico's jails, indicates that homosexuality was omnipresent among male inmates.[18] He found, for example, that they even had their own vocabulary to refer to the different roles played by participants in homosexual acts: *caballos* (passive pederasts) and *mayates* (active ones). According to Roumagnac's conclusions, homosexual acts between men follow "un sistema de comunidad" [a system of community] based on gender roles in which *mayates* are men and *caballos* are women. Roumagnac's ideas are not original here. What is interesting is that he finds that "tienen también otras denominaciones" [they also had other denominations] that apparently have little to do with the active/passive scheme. But, as he is less interested in understanding their sexual reality than he is in defining sexual difference in a way that conforms to his preconceptions, he does not even mention what these denominations are (Roumagnac 76–78n1). As for the homosexual acts of women, Roumagnac does not investigate any further than kisses (of course he had no idea what their sexual acts might be).[19] Nevertheless, it can be concluded from his interviews that *las tortilleras*[20] also follow a binary system of sexual relations based on gender roles, as "las que se peinan derecho son hombres" [those who part their hair on the right are men] and those who part it on the other side are women (190–191). It is impossible to know to what extent he discovers new information about the sexuality of prisoners and to what point he simply finds what he is looking for.

In the case of the 41, a review of textual evidence shows a muddle of notions of what homosexuality was. Nonetheless, the number 41 ends up and continues signifying homosexuality and male effeminacy in Mexico. As the revolutionary general Francisco Urquizo pointed out in 1965, "En México el número 41 no tiene ninguna validez y es ofensivo para los mexicanos. . . . Decirle 41 a un hombre es decirle afeminado. Estar bajo lo que ampare a ese número es ser en cierto modo afeminado. La influencia de esa tradición es tal que hasta en lo oficial se pasa por alto el número 41. No hay en el ejército División, Regimiento o Batallón que lleve el número 41. Llegan hasta el 40 y de allí se salta al 42. No hay nómina que tenga renglón 41. No hay en las nomenclaturas municipales casas que ostentan el número 41. . . . No hay cuarto de hotel o de Sanatorio que tenga el número 41. Nadie cumple 41 años. . . . No hay automóvil que lleve placa 41, ni policía o agente que acepte ese guarismo" [In Mexico the number 41 has no validity and is offensive for Mexicans. . . . To call a man 41 is to call him effeminate. To be within what the number harbors is to be somehow effeminate. The influence of that tradition is such that even official numerations skip over the number 41. There is no army Division, Regiment or Battalion that takes the number 41. They go up to 40 and from there skip to 42. There is no roll that has a 41st line. In municipal nomenclatures, there are no houses numbered 41. . . . There are no hotel or hospital rooms with the number 41. No one celebrates a forty-first birthday. . . . There is no automobile with license number 41, nor does any police officer or agent accept that numeral] (quoted in Schneider 69). In recent years, the homosexual milieu has taken control of the number. The first Mexican novel that treated homosexuality as a central theme in a noncondemnatory fashion was Paolo Po's 1963 *41, o el muchacho que soñaba en fantasmas*. Several gay discotheques in Mexico City have used this cultural symbol in their names, sometimes playing with variations: *el 41, el 42, el 14*. A personal anecdote involves a man from the *barrio bravo* of Tepito[21] on vacation with his family in Acapulco who claimed to be 30–11 years old, to avoid saying 41.

The 41 have gone down in history as emblems of Mexican male homosexuality. Yet, the discourse of 1901 did not present any proof that Mexican male sexuality in reality fit the stereotype that is remembered today, namely, a rigid system of gender roles: the active male and the passive female (nor evidence supporting any other fixed stereotype). Nor did these representations of questionable validity present a consistent vision of male homosexuality. The same discourse seems to determine sexuality based on both sexual object and sexual aim; it seems to see it simultaneously as an innate trait and a learned behavior; it appears to understand it as a manifestation of a very strictly defined desire and at the same time as absolute sexual liberty.

From the beginning, there was confusion regarding which of the 41 were homosexuals. At first, the reports indicate that everyone present was guilty and deserving of punishment. And while Posada represented the 41 with moustaches, even in the case of those dressed as women, one newspaper asserts that the guests recruited from *cantinas* were "víctimas de un verdadero chasco" [victims of a real trick], because the transvestites danced "con choclos, medias bordadas de seda, caderas y pechos postizos, pelucas con trenzas, pintados los rostros de blanco, con las picarescas ojeras de ordenanza, en fin, el disfraz tan bien hecho, que era difícil al primer golpe de vista, saber si aquellos individuos eran hombres" [with ladies' shoes, silk embroidered stockings, padded hips and breasts, wigs with braided extensions, faces painted white, with the obligatory picaresquely made up eyes, in short, their disguises so well done that it was difficult to tell at first sight whether those individuals were men] (*El Popular* 11/24/1901, Spanish 42; English 28, this volume). The sources are not in agreement as to the need to punish the men not dressed as women. Were all of them homosexuals, or only half?

There is some incoherence here in the definition of Mexican homosexuality as understood in 1901. Eve Kosofsky Sedgwick, in her book *Epistemology of the Closet*, sees this type of incoherence as emblematic of the Western vision of sexuality, with complications that go well beyond the local scandal. Sedgwick suggests that "many of the major nodes of thought and knowledge in twentieth-century Western culture as a whole are structured—indeed, fractured—by a chronic, now endemic crisis of homo/hetero definition, indicatively male, dating from the end of the nineteenth century" (1). Sedgwick articulates one of the main incoherences as "the contradiction between seeing homo/heterosexual definition on the one hand as an issue of active importance primarily for a small, distinct, relatively fixed homosexual minority (what I refer to as a minoritizing view), and seeing it on the other hand as an issue of continuing, determinative importance in the lives of people across the spectrum of sexualities (what I refer to as a universalizing view)" (1).

In the first case, Sedgwick's "minoritizing view," only effeminate men are homosexuals. Homosexuality is determined by a gender identification. A man who wants to be a woman, who assumes a woman's role, is homosexual. Sexually, this effeminate man has the sexual aim of being penetrated. The 41 ball attendees who had been recruited from *cantinas* and arrived dressed as men, then, were not homosexuals because they demonstrated no desire to be women. Even if they had had sexual relations with the transvestites, they would have done so presumably assuming the role of men. Their sexual aim would have been to penetrate, not to be penetrated.

The "universalizing view" is not based on sexual aim, but on sexual object. In this view, any man who desires or who has sexual relations with another man is homosexual. It does not matter whether he identifies as a woman, whether he wishes to penetrate or be penetrated (or perform some other act). In this case, all of the 41 were homosexuals because they all were there dancing with each other, and implicitly, desiring each other.[22]

In the newspaper reports as well as the novel, the fate of half of the 41 remains in doubt. Were they homosexuals or not? Today only the transvestites are remembered, that is, half of the dancers. Nevertheless, the symbol that has endured in history is the number 41, which refers to all of them.

Another incoherence that can be found concerning sexual definition is that of its etiology. The criminological discourse of the period in Mexico, whose most prolific representative was Carlos Roumagnac, abided by an "eclectic" strategy, according to the historian Robert Buffington (60), taking into account theories that identified the roots of social problems both in biology (discourses on innate criminal instinct, crime and evolution, and social degeneration) and in social environment (discourses on crime's links to education, moral influences, economic class), as well as in chance circumstances. Similarly, homosexuality is understood as an innate or essential trait, a learned habit, and an extemporaneous act, sometimes at the same time. Current-day debates on essencialism versus constructionism (theories of social construction) are often not much different. Many believe simultaneously in both biological and social "origins" of sexuality without realizing the apparent contradiction, while others recognize the importance of both biological and social factors in the formation of sexual identity.[23]

For example, in Castrejón's novel, the sexuality of Ninón, the lover of the ball's host and organizer (a man known by everyone, including inexplicably Estela, his girlfriend, as Mimí) is presented in an inconsistent and incoherent way. When a private detective, contracted by Judith, Ninón's girlfriend, reveals Ninón's clandestine life to her and informs her that Ninón and his intimate friend Mimí "no nacieron para adorar a Usted y a la Señorita Estela" [were not born to adore you and Señorita Estela] (Spanish 103; English 57, this volume), it is implied that homosexuality is not a mere temporary deviation, but an essential condition. This idea is confirmed in the narrator's repeated references to degeneration—with its implications of a deterioration that is not only moral but also biological, functioning as a sort of negative evolution—in describing the transvestites.[24]

However, the novel refers at other moments to some of the transvestites as "iniciados en el amor secreto" [initiates into the secret love]
(Spanish 117; English 71, this volume), and Ninón himself, after being
arrested and humiliated, "se arrepentía de sus culpas; reconocía . . . que
el pernicioso influjo de sus amigos lo arrastraba hacia la deshonra" [re-
gretted his errors; he recognized that his ambition for luxury, his soft
living, and the pernicious influence of his friends dragged him into dis-
honor] (Spanish 123; English 77, this volume) and finally recuperated
his heterosexuality and got married: "Ninón, redimido, repudiando su
rango oropelado, entraba en el seno democrático de una sociedad que
tiene por norma la honradez, la virtud y el trabajo. ¡La sociedad de
clase media!" [Ninón, redeemed, repudiating his flashy social rank, entered into the democratic heart of a society that holds honor, virtue
and work as the norm. The sublime society of the middle class!] (Spanish 135; English 89, this volume). If Ninón is capable of leaving behind his sexual tastes (along with his aristocratic social class), his
sexuality apparently is not a part of his natural essence, but rather an
acquired and temporary vice. As for his friends, as nothing is known of
their end—"¡Arcanos de la vida! y sólo arcanos que el lector sabrá en
la segunda parte de esta obrita . . ." [Life's mysteries! And mysteries,
whose secrets the reader will discover in the second part of this little
novel . . .] (Spanish 136; English 90, this volume); there is no evidence of the publication of this second part—there is no way of knowing whether there was any hope for their reform, or whether, like
Roumagnac's innate criminals, they were lost causes.

This latter example interestingly implies that male effeminacy and
homosexuality are traits of the upper classes. Something similar was
occurring in U.S. culture around the same time. The historian Gail
Bederman explores this "fear that middle class men as a sex had
grown decadent. Working class . . . men, with their strikes and their
'primitive' customs, seemed to possess a virility and vitality which
decadent white middle-class men had lost" (14). This particular view
of gender and class was to figure importantly in Mexican cultural debates following the revolution.[25] Ironically, elite *científicos* such as
Roumagnac see homosexuality as inherent not to the upper or middle classes but to the lower "criminal" classes; writes Buffington, referring to Roumagnac and his contemporaries, "criminals constituted
an identifiable class with distinct traits that included atavistic homosexual tendencies" (130).

Returning to Roumagnac's eclectic ideas, it should be added then
that besides the notions of homosexuality as a trait produced naturally
or socially, there is a third element present in the confused notions of

the era: the idea of homosexuality as an isolated spontaneous act. This third case is not unlike that colonial age notion of sodomy, in which homosexuality was seen as a sinful act, a bad choice, and not as an element of an individual's character. This lack of definition as to what homosexuality meant to Mexicans who wrote about the topic in the early twentieth century allows it to be understood simultaneously as both a profound and established desire emanating from an individual's character and an impulse that comes about as a response to environmental stimuli. In other words, it has its roots in internal conditions and external circumstances.

There is then innate homosexuality, acquired homosexuality, and, also, improvised homosexuality. According to the novel, the men invited from the *cantinas* "se iban retirando la mayor parte contrariados, quedando de los mismos uno que otro rezagado, incoherente y beodo, con más ganas de beber vinos, que divertirse con los apócrifos palmitos" [were departing for the most part, annoyed, leaving just a couple of stragglers here and there, incoherent and drunk, with more interest in drinking wine than in having fun with the apocryphal pretty faces] (Spanish 118–19, English 72, this volume). They were not real homosexuals. Still, they allowed themselves to be carried along by the alcohol and the occasion and as they were still there when the gendarmes arrived; they were presumably punished for their (momentary) homosexuality, just like everybody else.

Finally, there is an inconsistency with regard to the relation between gender and sexuality that goes beyond what has been mentioned thus far. At certain times, there is an implication of a rigidity of sexual definition based on gender identity (as mentioned above). In the novel, when Judith finds out about her boyfriend Ninón's secret life, she upbraids him, "Buscas, infame Ninón, en orgiásticas cenas, afectos como los de Mimí, Pudor, Virtud, Estrella y no sé cuántos más hombres . . . que te sirven de instrumentos pasivos" [You seek, infamous Ninón, in orgiastic dinners, affections like that of Mimí, Modesty, Virtue, Star and I don't know how many more men, who have brought to the world a sign of disgrace and who serve as passive instruments for you] (Spanish 108; English 62, this volume), taking for granted that Ninón, introduced as a "Hercules" (Spanish 101, English 55, this volume), assumes the male (active) role and the more effeminate young men the feminine (passive) role in their "orgiastic" relations. In the newspapers, the sexual jokes are frequent. In their parodic travel diary, the 41, depicted as utterly feminine, sexually speaking, are afraid of rape: "Lo malo es que esta travesía durará tres días . . . y no sabemos a lo que se atreverán esos marineros, al saber que somos mujeres y solas, y con la seguridad de que no tenemos madre" [The worst thing is that this travesty will last three days from here to Progreso, and we don't know what those sailors might try when they find out that we are women traveling alone, and with the certainty that we have no mother] (*El Popular* 11/29/01, Spanish 44; English 30, this volume). Sexuality is clearly defined in these examples with rigidity regarding gender roles, fixed by the act of penetration (which is, in the end, simply the heterosexual model).

At the same time, the idea of orgy defies such inflexibility. Every aspect of the clandestine life appears to have erotic energy. When the 41 greet each other, they embrace "effusively" and exchange "erotic kisses" (Spanish 95; English 49, this volume). Afterward, as they try on their ladies' gowns, they experience "erotic transports" (Spanish 97; English 51, this volume). The expressions that the narrator uses to describe the atmosphere ("immense bacchanal," "orgiastic feasts," "desires of the most unbridled prostitution," "insatiable whirlpool of brutish pleasures," "obscene delirium," "Roman style decadence," "bacchic orgy") point to nothing as strict and orderly as is indicated by a system of desire organized around fixed roles of gender and invariable acts of penetration. At one point, "Carola, Blanca, Estrella, Virtud y Margarita, confundidos en el mismo nivel de bajeza . . . se abrazaban, se inflamaban al contacto de la suave epidermis ungida de aceites perfumados y desfloraban sus manos con chasquidos de ardientes y sonorosos besos" [Carola, Blanca, Star, Virtue, and Margarita, entangled among each other at the same level of lowness, in that sad degeneration, in incredible debasement, embraced each other, inflamed each other with the contact of their soft skin, anointed each other with perfumed oils, and deflowered each other's hands with smacks of ardent and sonorous kisses] (Spanish 99; English 53, this volume). The 41 are, on the one hand, effeminate men who assume the female, passive role, and, on the other, are absolute libertines whose inhibitions have no limits.

The centenary of the 41 is a celebration of the anniversary not of their repression but of the ball that scandalously joined together in the public imagination transvestites, libertines, the sexually curious, and all kinds of horny Mexicans of all social classes under the sign of the 41. It commemorates the disturbing ball that launched the explosion not of simply a repressive discourse but of a dissonance of discourses, many of which were self-contradictory. It recognizes the importance of an event that made possible not only the construction of the homophobic stereotype of the *maricón* but also that of a variety of new non-heteronormative sexualities.[26] This is not to say that the repressive elements of this new discourse were not effective for much of the century that followed. However, it is also important to recognize that a veritable continuum of Mexican masculinities participated in the ball, according to the meager representations that have survived, and these 41 infected the very heart of Mexico, including President Porfirio Díaz's own family. The ball not only Mexicanized homosexuality but also homosexualized Mexico. And Mexico would never be the same.

CONCLUSION

One of the newspaper articles referred to the ball as *"baile estilo nuevo siglo"* [new century - style ball] (*El Popular* 11/25/1901). One hundred years later it can happily be reported that, despite the homophobic intentions of the journalists, medical doctors, criminologists, moralists, literati, politicians, and all the others who conspired against the *maricones,* the Tulane symposium concluded with a closing dinner exactly a century after the date of the original ball, that is, on the night of November 17, 2001. The famous clandestine ball of La Paz did turn out to be an important leit-motif of twentieth-century Mexican culture, eventually transforming itself into an inspiration for resistance to social control. The spirit of the 41 survives, more vigorous than ever, a century later. The homophobia that apparently won out in a battle of "good customs" in 1901 has been losing its power, and one hundred years later it is the 41 whose centenary is being celebrated, and not that of the homophobes. Although silenced in their day, it is the spirit of the 41 *maricones* that has the last word.

NOTES

1. For a chronicle of published materials on the 41, see García. Highlights of the news reports, Posada images, and the novel are published herein. The Castrejón novel is a particular curiosity, since it is utterly ignored by all Mexican literary histories and it appears that only one copy, located in the Rafael H. Valle estate collection at Mexico's national library's *Fondo Reservado,* has survived

2. The press repeatedly calls it "el baile nefando," resuscitating colonial-era rhetoric on sodomy, "the nefarious sin." On colonial discourse on sodomy in Mexico, see Olivier.

3. See Irwin, "The Famous 41," Monsiváis, "The Invention."

4. Moisés González Navarro, the great historian of the Porfiriato, writes that "aun en aristocráticas calles se advertía la presencia de hombres

con traje blanco, choclos del mismo color, pañuelo azul en el bolsillo de la americana, flor roja en el ojal, sombrerito de panamá con listoncito de color, ya fuera rojo o azul o ambos combinados, al caminar procurar exhibir lo más posible el calzado" [even on upper class streets one noted the presence of men in white suits, matching shoes, a blue handkerchief in the jacket pocket, a red flower in the button hole, a little Panama hat with a colored ribbon, whether red or blue or some combination thereof, who while walking would try their best to exhibit their footwear] (410).

5. His name was Ignacio de la Torre; Monsiváis writes, "Según cuenta su amigo José Juan Tablada en *La feria de la vida,* De la Torre, al enseñarles su gran colección de zapatos y botas de montar, se ufana: 'Señores, ésta es mi biblioteca'. Es, además, hacendado en Morelos y entre sus trabajadores se encuentra Emiliano Zapata, que—según la leyenda—viene a México por vez primera en 1910, como caballerango de don Nacho" [According to his buddy José Juan Tablada in *La feria de la vida,* De la Torre, showing off is huge collection of shoes and riding boots boasts: 'Gentlemen, this is my library.' He owns a large ranch in Morelos, where one of his workers is Emiliano Zapata, who—according to legend—comes to Mexico City for the first time in 1910, as don Nacho's groom] ("Los iguales" no page number).

6. The term *"comadre"* is the title of respect used between mothers and godmothers (together they are "co-mothers"); it is also a term of affection used among mature women of the popular classes that evokes a stereotype of middle-aged gossips.

7. References to Castrejón refer to the text and translation as they appear in this volume. The citation for the original text follows the Spanish and the citation for the translation follows the English.

8. References to the newspaper articles refer to the text and translation as they appear in this volume.

9. The same attraction for the idea of the effeminate homosexual man as a mother is found in positivist criminology; Carlos Roumagnac writes of the special section in the Mexico City's Belem Prison for *"pederastas conocidos"* [known pederasts]: "Y era de verse entonces el desfile de esos degenerados sexuales, que pasaban delante de los demás detenidos, sin rubor ni vergüenza, haciendo, por el contrario, alarde de voces y modales afeminados, prodigándose apodos mujeriles, y muchas veces cargando en brazos muñecos de trapo o fingiendo cargarlos, y haciendo alusiones a sus partos recientes" [And the parade of those sexual degenerates was a sight to see as they passed in front of the other prisoners, without blushing or feeling ashamed, but on the contrary making a grand show of themselves with their effeminate voices and mannerisms, lavishing each other with womanly nicknames, and on many occasions carrying rag dolls

in their arms, or pretending to do so, and making allusions to their recent birthings] (77n1).

10. "Calavera" [skull] is the term commonly used to refer both to the skeletons commonly seen in Mexican popular culture, particularly regarding the Day of the Dead, and to a particular sort of rakish Mexican character, usually seen as fun loving, promiscuous, and irresponsible. Skeleton imagery is typical of Posada's work, as are representations of sympathetic rogues.

11. Mexican popular ballad.

12. On Argentina, see Molloy ("Politics"), Salessi; on the 41 as national myth, see Bonfil.

13. The Oscar Wilde scandal received so little coverage in Mexican newspapers that Carlos Monsiváis overlooks 1895 Mexican newspaper reports in his investigations of the era: "un acontecimiento tan importante como el juicio de Oscar Wilde (1895) no recibe comentarios en la prensa. La primera alusión al juicio que localizo es de 1913" [an event as important as the Oscar Wilde trial (1895) did not receive any commentaries in the press. The first allusion to it that I have found is from 1913] ("Ortodoxia" 197). In fact, there are reports in various 1895 newspapers (for example, *El Universal* 4/9/1895, 4/21/1895; *El Nacional* 4/9/1895, 5/3/1895, 5/8/1895, 5/9/1895, 5/25/1895, 5/30/1895, 6/22/1895).

14. Nickname given to the positivist scientists (often social scientists) of the Porfiriato.

15. Pseudonym of Miguel Ángel Osorio, better known by another pseudonym, Porfirio Barba Jacob, the Colombian poet. See Domínguez Rubalcava (79–116), Balderston, "Amistad masculine."

16. See Irwin, "El Periquillo."

17. For a discussion of gender and sexuality as components of the habitus, see Bourdieu (especially 18–33), Lamas.

18. For a detailed analysis of Roumagnac's works, see Buffington 59–86, 130–140.

19. See Irigaray on the problems of representations of female sexuality by men.

20. *Tortillera*, literally a woman who makes or sells *tortillas*, is a slang term frequently used to refer to lesbians.

21. A tough neighborhood known for its high crime rate and smuggler's market in central Mexico City.

22. These same contradictions can be seen in contemporary Mexican culture; see Prieur.

23. For a lucid discussion of these debates in the field of gender studies, see Fuss.

24. According to Lombroso, the innate criminal, the mentally ill, and the morally depraved are all degenerates, born to a race physically infected by anticivilizing forces.

25. For a more in depth discussion of this phenomenon in Mexico, see the introduction by Irwin to *Mexican Masculinities*. See also Balderston, "Poetry."
26. The term "heteronormative" refers to all manifestations of sexuality that conform to the heterosexual norm (Warner).

BIBLIOGRAPHY

Balderston, Daniel. "Amistad masculine y homofobia en 'El hombre que parecía un caballo'." *El deseo, enorme cicatriz luminosa*. Caracas: eXcultura, 1999: 29–26.

———. "Poetry, Revolution, Homophobia: Polemics from the Mexican Revolution." Sylvia Molloy and Robert McKee Irwin, Eds. *Hispanisms and Homosexualities*. Durham, NC: Duke University Press, 1998: 57–75.

Beattie, Peter. "Conflicting Penile Codes: Modern Masculinity and Sodomy in the Brazilian Military, 1860–1916." Daniel Balderston and Donna J. Guy, Eds. *Sex and Sexuality in Latin America*. New York: New York University Press, 1997: 65–85.

Bederman, Gail. *Manliness and Civilization: A Cultural History of Gender and Race in the United States, 1880–1917*. Chicago: University of Chicago Press, 1995.

Ben, Pablo. "Muéstrame tus genitales y te diré quién eres. El 'hermafroditismo' en la Argentina fincsccular y de principios de siglo XX." omar acha y Paula Halperin, Comps. *Cuerpos, género, identidades: estudios de historia de género en Argentina*. Buenos Aires: Ediciones del Signo, 2000: 61–104.

Bonfil, Carlos. "Los cuarenta y uno." Enrique Florescano, Coord. *Mitos mexicanos*. México: Aguilar, 1995: 219–224.

Bourdieu, Pierre. *Masculine Domination* [1998]. Richard Nice, Trans. Stanford: Stanford University Press, 2001.

Buffington, Robert. *Criminal and Citizen in Modern México*. Lincoln: University of Nebraska Press, 2000.

Castrejón, Eduardo. *Los 41*. Mexico City: Tipografía Popular, 1906.

De la Campa, Román. *Latin Americanism*. Minneapolis: University of Minnesota Press, 1999.

Domínguez Rubalcava, Héctor. *La modernidad abyecta: formación del discurso homosexual en Hispanoamérica*. Xalapa: Universidad Veracruzana, 2001.

Escaja, Tina, Comp. *Delmira Agustini y el modernismo: nuevas propuestas de género*. Rosario: Beatriz Viterbo, 2000.

Foucault, Michel. *The History of Sexuality*. Vol. I [1978]. Robert Hurley, Trans. New York: Vintage Books, 1990.

Fuss, Diana. *Essentially Speaking: Feminism, Nature and Difference*. New York: Routledge, 1989.

García, Alejandro. *Los cuarenta y uno: crónica hemerográfica de un baile prohibido*. Unpublished manuscript.

González Navarro, Moisés. *El porfiriato: la vida social.* Daniel Cosío Villegas, Ed. *Historia moderna de México,* Vol. IV. Mexico City: Hermes, 1957.

Green, James Naylor. *Beyond Carnival.* Chicago: University of Chicago Press, 1999.

Irigaray, Luce. *This Sex Which Is Not One* [1977]. Catherine Porter and Carolyn Burke, Trad. Ithaca, NY: Cornell University Press, 1985.

Irwin, Robert McKee. "The Famous 41: The Scandalous Birth of Modern Mexican Homosexuality." *GLQ: A Journal of Lesbian and Gay Studies* 6:3, 2000: 353–376.

———. *Mexican Masculinities.* Minneapolis: University of Minnesota Press, Forthcoming.

———. "El Periquillo Sarniento y sus cuates: el 'éxtasis misterioso' del ambiente homosocial en el siglo diecinueve." *Literatura Mexicana* 9:1, 1998: 23–44.

Lamas, Marta. "Cuerpo: diferencia social y género." *Debate Feminista.* 5:10, 1994: 3–31.

Lombroso, Cesare. *L'uomo delinquente in rapporto all'antropologia, alla giurisprudenza ed alle discipline carcerarie.* Torino: Fratelli Bocca, 1896–1897.

Masiello, Francine. "Estado, género y sexualidad en la cultura del fin de siglo." Josefina Ludmer, Comp. *Las culturas de fin de siglo en América Latina.* Rosario: Beatriz Viterbo, 1994: 139–149.

———. "'Gentlemen,' damas y travestis: ciudadanía e identidad cultural en la Argentina del fin de siglo." Lelia Area and Mabel Moraña, Comp. *La imaginación histórica en el siglo XIX.* Buenos Aires: UNR Editora, 1994: 297–309.

Molloy, Sylvia. "La flexión de género en el texto cultural latinoamericano." *Revista de Crítica Cultural* 21, 11/2000: 54–56.

———. "His America, Our America: José Martí Reads Whitman." Betsy Erkkila and Jay Grossman, Eds. *Breaking Bounds: Whitman and American Cultural Studies.* New York: Oxford University Press, 1996.

———. "The Politics of Posing." Sylvia Molloy and Robert McKee Irwin, Eds. *Hispanisms and Homosexualities.* Durham, NC: Duke University Press, 1998: 141–160.

———. "Too Wilde for Comfort: Desire and Ideololgy in Fin-de-Siècle Latin America." Monica Dorenkamp and Richard Henke, Eds. *Negotiating Lesbian and Gay Subjects.* New York: Routledge, 1985: 35–52.

Monsiváis, Carlos. "Los iguales, los semejantes, los (hasta hace un minuto) perfectos desconocidos (A cien años de la Redada de los 41)." Mexico City: Consejo Nacional para la Cultura y las Artes, Instituto Nacional de Bellas Artes, 2000. Pamphlet.

———. "Ortodoxia y heterodoxia en las alcobas." *Debate Feminista* 6:11, 1995: 183–210.

Montero, Oscar. "Julián del Casal and the Queers of Havana." Emilie L. Bergmann and Paul Julian Smith, Eds. *¿Entiendes? Queer Readings, Hispanic Writings.* Durham, NC: Duke University Press, 1995: 92–112.

————. "Modernismo and Homophobia: Dario and Rodo." Daniel Balderston and Donna Guy, Eds. *Sex and Sexuality in Latin America*. New York: New York University Press, 1997: 101–117.

Moreiras, Alberto. *The Exhaustion of Difference: The Politics of Latin American Cultural Studies*. Durham, NC: Duke University Press, 2001.

Novo, Salvador. *La estatua de sal*. Mexico City: Consejo Nacional de la Cultura y las Artes, 1998.

Olivier, Guilhem. "Conquérants et missionnaires face au 'péché abominable', essai sur l'homosexualité en Mésoamérique au moment de la conquête espagnole." *Caravelle* 55, 1990: 19–51.

Po, Paolo. *41, o un muchacho que soñaba en fantasmas*. Mexico City: B. Costa-Amic, 1964.

Prieur, Annick. *Mema's House, Mexico City: On Transvestites, Queens, and Machos*. Chicago: University of Chicago Press, 1998.

Roumagnac, Carlos. *Los criminales en México*. Mexico City: Tipografía El Fénix, 1904.

Salessi, Jorge. *Médicos, maleantes y maricas*. Rosario: Beatriz Viterbo, 1995.

Schneider, Luis Mario. *La novela mexicana entre el petróleo, la homosexualidad y la política*. Mexico City: Nueva Imagen, 1997.

Sedgwick, Eve Kosofsky. *The Epistemology of the Closet*. Berkeley: University of California Press, 1990.

Warner, Michael. "Introduction." Michael Warner, Ed. *Fear of a Queer Planet: Queer Politics and Social Theory*. Minneapolis: University of Minnesota, 1993.

PART II

SEXUALITY AND SOCIAL CONTROL IN MEXICO, C. 1901

Homophobia and the Mexican Working Class, 1900–1910[1]

Robert Buffington

In his memoirs, *My Last Sigh,* the Spanish émigré filmmaker Luis Buñuel recalls a newspaper story that he read just after his arrival in Mexico City in 1946:

> A man walks into number 39 on a certain street and asks for Señor Sánchez. The concierge replies that there is no Sánchez in his building, but that he might inquire at number 41. The man goes to number 41 and asks for Sánchez, but the concierge there replies that Sánchez lives at number 39, and that the first concierge must have been mistaken. The man returns to number 39 and tells the concierge what number 41 said, whereupon the concierge asks him to wait a moment, goes into another room, comes back with a revolver, and shoots the visitor. (207)

Buñuel adds that "what shocked me more than anything else about this story was the journalist's tone: the article was written as if the concierge's act was perfectly appropriate. Even the headline agreed: *'Lo mata por preguntón'* [He was killed for asking too many questions]." In the memoir, the anecdote serves to illustrate (for a European audience) the surrealistic violence of 1940s Mexico and the macho cult of the pistol, some of whose more notorious adherents included fellow artists Diego Rivera, David Álfaro Siquieros, "El Indio" Fernández, and Pedro Armendáriz. But as any Mexican reader would know, Buñuel's shock is also a sham and a tease (a trio of effects perfected in his Mexican films). No stranger to sexual transgression or to *chilango* humor, he understood perfectly well that the man was killed over a number.

Carlos Monsiváis and Robert McKee Irwin have argued persuasively that the 41 scandal of 1901 marked the birth of modern Mexican homosexuality—that the "shocking" public revelation of flagrant transvestism and elite hanky-panky (which may or may not have included the president's nephew) produced the nation's first homosexual panic and came to represent, as a number, the condition "that dare not speak its name."[2] Buñuel's tongue-in-cheek tale of a man murdered for asking too many questions reminds us that it also marked the birth of modern Mexican homophobia. "As incredible as it seems," Monsiváis asserts, "before [the scandal] there were only fleeting and humorous mentions of 'repugnant youth'" ("El mundo soslayado" 14). Afterward, there were murders.

Challenges to manhood had, of course, been killing Mexican men long before 1901. Most involved cuckoldry and other sorts of honor-related disputes over women. Homophobia may well have skulked anachronistically around the edges of illicit practices such as sodomy and veiled accusations of effeminacy but, like homosexuality—the category that it in fact constructs—it was still a jumble of often contradictory notions about manliness rather than the delimiting mechanism for a state-of-being, masculinity, with recognizable attributes and pretensions to ideological coherence. In Mexico, the 41 scandal changed all that. And as Eve Sedgwick notes for England in the wake of the Wilde trial: "What had been the style of homosexuality attributed to the aristocracy, and to some degree its accompanying style of homophobia, now washed through the middle class, with . . . complicated political effects" (95). Chief among those effects was the deployment of homophobia "as a tool for manipulating the entire spectrum of male bonds, and hence the gender system as a whole" (Sedgwick 16).

Irwin's careful (and delightful) reading of the mainstream literary and press accounts of the 41 scandal has given us a nuanced account of bourgeois homophobia and its construction of the male homosexual as the abjected, feminized Other against which "normal" heterosexual men might measure their claims to manhood. Given the consolidation of bourgeois cultural hegemony under the *pax porfiriana*, it is hardly surprising that these sources would define both normalcy and deviance in decidedly middle-class terms. This is far too neat. After all, as Sedgwick reminds us, "the power of cognitively dividing and hence manipulating the male homosocial spectrum must . . . be understood to be an object of struggle, not something that resides passively in a reified status quo," especially since the "domination offered by this strategy is not only over a minority population, but over the bonds that structure all social form" (86–87). The middle classes were not the only ones with a vested interest in the manipulation of manhood.

This essay, then, examines the construction of homophobia in Mexico City's satiric working-class penny press during the first decade of the twentieth century. Here, too, the 41 scandal proved a watershed. But, unlike the homosexual panic unleashed by the mainstream press and intended to reinforce the heteronormativity of "the class that progresses," penny press editors generally eschewed *nota roja* [tabloid] shock tactics for a more subtle satire that sought to subvert the masculinity of all bourgeois men by portraying them as parasitic *catrines* [dandies] who dozed in a narcissistic haze of self-congratulation and conspicuous consumption while working-class patriots struggled to protect and nurture *la patria* [father/mother land]. For these self-proclaimed spokesmen for the working classes, the homophobic possibilities of the 41 scandal proved a golden opportunity to hoist Porfirian male elites on their own petard—to expose efforts to naturalize a bourgeois hegemony rooted in heterosexual intimacy and nuclear family values as the ideological construct it undoubtedly was (and is), even as they attempted to claim these same values for their own constituents. Like its bourgeois counterpart, working-class homophobia was about much more than just identifying, defining, and naming (with a number) a despised category of nonsubjects; it also was about social domination or, in this case, about the contestation of bourgeois social domination. That purpose gave Mexican working-class homophobia its distinctive contours—contours that are just beginning to adjust to the expansion of middle-class notions of gay identity through mass media, transcultural contacts, and gay rights movements.

Regulatory norms like homophobia, we now recognize, might pretend to novelty but must nevertheless rearticulate elements from existing discourses.[3] That is certainly the case here. Before the 41 scandal, several potentially homophobic notions were already at play in the satiric penny press. To be more precise, four distinct discursive strategies (with only occasional overlap) are in evidence both before and after the scandal itself. Categorized by strategic intent, they look something like this: (1) sticking it to the opposition, (2) cross-dressing the politician, (3) ridiculing the *joto,* and (4) subverting the bourgeois male subject. The last three strategies would form the core of working-class homophobia after 1901; the first would play no obvious role. The reasoning behind these choices was of course political; unpacking the logic behind those politics is the purpose of this essay.

STICKING IT TO THE OPPOSITION

In a previous essay on competing "regimes of truth" in early-twentieth-century Mexican prisons, I argued that, for inmates, the active-passive construction of male sexuality described so vividly by Octavio Paz also served as a political metaphor for lower-class men (Buffington, "Los Jotos").[4] As they saw it, passive acceptance of domination transformed the resistant (if still screwed) *jodido* into a complicit *joto*. Something of this attitude carries over to the satiric penny press. For example, the masthead of *Don Cucufate* depicts the dandified (if disheveled) editor as the *gran chingón* [big fucker]. A long, obviously phallic, quill pen extends from his waist on the upper left-hand side across the top of the page, lording it over some stock Porfirian "types": the *charro* [cowboy], the ballerina, the fashionable bourgeois matron, the respectable gentleman, the policeman, and, last but never least, the *gran caudillo* Don Porfirio himself. A cleric with a protruding tongue, painful grimace on his face, his back to the editor, rides the quill. And if that image weren't explicit enough, the phallic quill parts the upturned legs of a "U" before passing through the enclosed top of the "A" (for *ano* or anus?), while ink drips suggestively at the editor's feet (*Don Cucufate*, July–October 1906)[5] (see illustration 5). The masthead of *El Chile Piquín* (January–July 1905), with its syringe-wielding *campesino*-worker in pursuit of an expanded cast of stock characters, sends a similar if less subliminal message (see illustration 6).

When the subject turned to internal bickering among penny press editors, the penetration metaphor could become rather explicit. In José Guadalupe Posada's cover for the July 7, 1904, edition of *El Pinche*, the editor sticks a pitchfork into a rival editor (of *El Moquete*), causing him to fart (see illustration 7, "El trinche de Pascual Ladrillo" [Pascual Ladrillo's Pitchfork).[6] *El Chile Piquín* covers were less circumspect about the anal aspects of penetration: the February 2, 1905, issue depicts rival *La Guacamaya* as a prostrate, crippled parrot about to receive an enema from the syringe-wielding editor; three weeks later, the February 23 cover applies the same treatment to the editor of *El Moquete*, who is portrayed bent over with his pants around his ankles (see illustration 8, "Primer lavativa a 'La Guacamaya'" [La Guacamaya's first injection], and Illustration 9, "Lavativas" [Injections]).[7] The metaphoric link between chiles and penises in Mexican popular culture is well known. Coupled with verses chiding both papers for betraying their obligation to defend the working class, *El Chile Piquín* implies that this figurative buggering is both punitive and purgative.

Illustration 5. *Don Cucufate*. Courtesy of Benson Latin American Collection, The University of Texas at Austin.

In none of these cases, however, is the penetrated figure feminized. The intention here is to represent the superior power, moral power in these cases, of the penetrator; whatever pleasures he derives from the act of penetration—those telltale fluids as a "remainder"—are his alone.

Cross-Dressing the Politician

Transvestism has a long history in Mexico, especially on the stage. Always considered a bit outré, it was nevertheless accepted by all but the most prudish as permissible practice, at least in the theater. Aside from occasional harassment in the years following the 41 scandal, it has persisted and even thrived into the television age. Whatever the reason, cross-dressing politicians in political cartoons apparently fell within the realm of acceptable editorial practice in an age when slander against a high public official landed many penny press editors in Belem.[8] How else can we explain the July 2, 1900, cover of *El Diablito Rojo*, which portrays president Porfirio Díaz himself as a *zarzuela* [musical theater] heroine surrounded by his *científico* ministers as the eager suitors (see illustration 10, "Zarzuelas populares en la actualidad, La revoltosa" [Current popular operettas, The Seditious One]). The May 23, 1907, cover of *La Guacamaya* extended

Illustration 6. *El Chile Piquín*. Courtesy of Benson Latin American Collection, The University of Texas at Austin.

the same treatment (with newspaper skirts replacing the *gran caudillo*'s fancy ball gown) to the bickering editors of Mexico City's major dailies, *El Diario* and *El Imparcial* (see illustration 11, "Diarios a la greña" [Quarreling dailies]).

In his preface to Salvador Novo's memoirs, Monsiváis argues that the Mexican Revolution sexualized political discourse by mocking "the dignified silences regarding things of the flesh" ("El mundo soslayado" 18). This process began early on as the newly elected, ever-idealistic Francisco Madero loosened government control of the press. Penny press editors responded by cross-dressing him mercilessly. In the September 10, 1911, issue of *El Vale Panchito*, for example, Madero is included in a crowd of vicious hair-pulling, kicking, cross-dressed politicians accompanied by a caption that read: "Así tratan los científicos del día los asuntos del abnegado pueblo mexicano" [That's the way today's technocrats deal with suppressed needs of the Mexican people] (see illustration 12, "La verdulería en el Teatro Hidalgo" [The vegetable stand at the Hidalgo Theater]).[9] *El Charrito*'s issues of October 16 and November 27, 1911, added an overt sexual element missing in previous political cross-dressings. The first cover depicts Madero as a diseased prostitute luring the Mexican people—a working-class man with a sombrero—into an unwholesome alliance; the second shows him in the tight embrace of

Illustration 7. José Guadalupe Posada. "El trinche de Pascual Ladrillo" [Pascual Ladrillo's Pitchfork]. Courtesy of Benson Latin American Collection, The University of Texas at Austin.

Emiliano Zapata as the manly rebel leader attempts to woo him away from a naked, lecherous Uncle Sam (see illustration 13, "Frase del Diputado Bulnes" [Deputy Bulnes's Expression], and Illustration 14, "En el palenque político" [In the political palisade]).[10] Moheno's August 1, 1914, portrayal of Venustiano Carranza as a flirtatious dancing girl in a flouncy dress and high heels and of a swishy Alvaro Obregón modeling his general's uniform give some indication of just how far things had come after only a few years of revolution (see illustration 15, "La revoltosa" [The Seditious One], and Illustration 16, "La hora trágica" [The Tragic Hour]).[11]

Even these more outrageous images, however, were only marginally homophobic. Cross-dressing might feminize politicians in order to represent their weakness for flattery (Díaz), pettiness (mainstream dailies), inconstancy (Madero), or vanity (Carranza and Obregón), but none of these images suggested anything more than a metaphoric connection with "the feminine" and much less overt homosexuality.

Illustration 8. "Primer lavativa á 'La Guacamaya'" [La Guacamaya's first injection].
Courtesy of Benson Latin American Collection, The University of Texas at Austin.

With the possible exception of Madero, all these men were paragons of Mexican manhood, whatever their political failings.

RIDICULING THE *Joto*

Ridiculing the effeminate *joto,* however, was a different kind of strategy altogether. As the most flagrant example of the sexual invert—the categorical predecessor of the homosexual—the *joto* embodied the worst feminine traits in the misogynist canon: vanity, flightiness, self-absorption, and shamelessness. Monsiváis rightly notes that aside from "fleeting and humorous mentions of repugnant youth," references to sexual inversion and homosexuality are mostly absent from nineteenth-century Mexican letters. It's a bit startling, then, to see *jotos* spring fully constituted as a recognizable group (perhaps even a subculture) in a September 17, 1900, editorial from *El Diablito Rojo,* "wiggling their asses like women" and exchanging *flores* [endearments] at the center of Mexican political life—Independence Day celebrations on the Zócalo. "Ya tenemos eléctricos trituradores, agu-

Illustration 9. "Lavativas" [Injections]. Courtesy of Benson Latin American Collection, The University of Texas at Austin.

jeros en las calles, dioses de piedra . . . y hasta científicos pensionados en París de Francia," lamented the editor, "pero si nos faltara ilustración, tenemos ya un síntoma de progreso moral chulísimo" [We already have trolley tracks, potholes, stone idols (statues) . . . and even *científicos* on the dole in Paris, but if we were lacking enlightment, now we have a really cute symptom of moral progress]. And in a classic case of abjection, he goes on to compare *jotos* to adulterated food—rotting meat, microbes in the water, etc.—ignored by a venal Superior Consejo [Public Health Council]. He concludes: "A esos contrabandistas y falsificadores de . . . lo que ustedes quieran, hay que tratarlos como se lo merecen . . . ¡Malditos sean!" [As for these contrabandists and falsifiers of . . . whatever you want to call it, they should be given the treatment they deserve . . . Curses on them!] (The second ellipsis is in the original). Harbingers of a false modernity, *jotos* become, in this vitriolic account, the abject symbols of immorality, degeneration, and dissimulation in a society that prefers images of progress to substantive social improvement.

Illustration 10. "Zarzuelas populares en la actualidad, La revoltosa" [Current popular operettas, The Seditious One]. Courtesy of Benson Latin American Collection, The University of Texas at Austin.

Later references lack the venom of the 1900 *El Diablito Rojo* editorial but carry much the same message. For example, the "street talk" section of *La Guacamaya*'s September 8, 1902, issue includes in its attack on "Spanish" grocers the following exchange between two female busybodies: "Pos él [viejo] está muy entusiasmado a aprender ese baile que dicen se llama *jota* y yo estoy temiendo que se me vaya a golver *joto*" [Well my old man really wants to learn this dance they call the *jota* and I'm afraid he's going to turn *joto*] (italics and deliberate misspellings are in the original). The comment is obviously an *albur* or play on words that conflates the traditional Spanish *jota* (dance) from Aragón and the sexually inverted *joto*. It thus implies dissimulation or betrayal on the part of the crone's husband, who is presumably a working-class Mexican just like the abused clients of the Spanish grocers who employ him. A sarcastic blurb in the August 23, 1906, edition of *La Guacamaya*, by contrast, emphasizes the *jotos'* effeminacy: "Enviamos nuestra más cordial feli-

Diarios á la greña.

No se piensen los lectores
qne es pleito de vecindad,
es tan sólo una eampaña;
mas campaña editorial.

Es un pleito que sostienen
dos diarios de actualidad,
los atletas de la prensa:
"El Diario" y "El Imparcial."

Illustration 11. "Diarios a la greña" [Quarreling dailies]. Courtesy of Benson Latin American Collection, The University of Texas at Austin.

citación a todos las MARIQUITAS y para que no digan que los hacemos menos . . . les deseamos un día de regocijo en compañia de sus mamás, a todos los MARICONES" [We send our most cordial greetings to all the FAIRIES and so that they won't think we're ignoring them . . . we wish a day of rest at home in the company of their mothers to all the FAGGOTS]. The "street talk" section that follows carries the tongue-in-check tone a step further as an apparently confused Don Pitacio toasts Mariquita with "a la suya y porque la goce bien su compañía de su siñora madre y que se busque un hombre que l'haga feliz y se vea rodeada de hartos chimacos que li hagan gozar con sus chillados" [may you enjoy the company of your dear mother and find yourself a man that will make you happy and see yourself surrounded with lots of kids that you can treat to your screaming]. "Muchas gracias" [Mariquita replies], " . . . pero la mera mera neta que no me dan de ala sus deseos" [Thanks a lot . . . but that's not exactly what I had in mind] (upper case and deliberate misspellings are in the original). Dissimulation is still the key to the joke of course,

Illustration 12. José Guadalupe Posada. "La verdulería en el Teatro Hidalgo" [The vegetable stand in the Hidalgo Theater]. Courtesy of Benson Latin American Collection, The University of Texas at Austin.

but in this instance the "betrayal" carries little political baggage beyond the obvious point that sexually inverted men couldn't even manage the principal female role of biological reproduction.

Subverting the Bourgeois Male Subject

Since the French Revolution, productive labor has been the principal hallmark of the worthy national citizen. The nineteenth-century European and American bourgeoisie certainly based their political claims in no small part on their productive importance vis-à-vis decadent aristocrats. For editors of Mexico City's satiric penny press the intimate connection between productivity, political legitimacy, and class status in liberal ideology marked the fracturing point of the Porfirian social order. Mastheads proudly asserted their editors' claims to be "of the people and for the people" or "the defender of the Working Class" and often featured respectable working-class types engaged in productive activities.

Illustration 13. "Frase del Diputado Bulnes" [Deputy Bulne's Expression]. Courtesy of Benson Latin American Collection, The University of Texas at Austin.

Against these images of productive manly workers, penny press editors juxtaposed lazy, effete bourgeois gentlemen. *La Guacamaya*'s cover for September 12, 1907, for example, shows working-class men celebrating while their bourgeois counterparts nap. The poem reads: "El pueblo entusiasmado vitorea a aquellos que nos dieron Libertad . . . en cambio los catrines, los patriotas (?) se entregan a dormir la borrachera y se olvidan de Hidalgo, cuyas gotas de llanto caen sobre la patria tierra" [The enthusiastic people applaud those that gave us Liberty . . . while the dandies, the patriots (?) sleep off their drunk and forget about Hidalgo, whose teardrops fall on the earth of father/mother land] (question mark in original; see illustration 17, "¡Viva la libertad!" [Long live freedom!]). In a similar vein, *El Diablito Rojo*'s September 7, 1908, cover graphic by Posada, "A trabajar los catrines" [Put the dandies to work], depicts two dandies forced to perform manual labor over a poem that declares: "Todo México es testigo,/ pues los ha visto en montón,/ que vagos de profesión/ no más porque tienen pesos,/ cometen miles d'excesos" [All Mexico is a witness/ since it has seen them in abundance/ to those

Illustration 14. "En el palenque político" [In the political palisade]. Courtesy of Benson Latin American Collection, The University of Texas at Austin.

professional vagabonds/ who because they have money/ commit thousands of excesses] (see illustration 18).

These critiques of unproductive bourgeois *catrines* often crossed over into attacks on their manhood. An October 17, 1910, editorial in *El Diablito Rojo* ("El afán de exhibirse") noted that while "sensible men" took walks to relax after a hard day's work, "hay muchos . . . que cuando salen de paseo lo hacen por exhibirse, se les traduce en todo: desde la manera estudiada de ponerse el sombrero, hasta el

Illustration 15. "La Revoltosa" [The Seditious One]. Courtesy of Benson Latin American Collection, The University of Texas at Austin.

modo de andar, siempre tiesos, erguidos, sin mirar a nadie y con la idea fija de que tras de ellos hay murmullos de admiración envidiosa" [there are many that go out only to exhibit themselves, which is evident from everything they do: from the studied manner of putting on their hats, to their way of walking, always rigid, erect, without looking at anybody and with the firm idea that behind them there are mur-

Illustration 16. "La hora trágica" [The tragic hour]. Courtesy of Benson Latin American Collection, The University of Texas at Austin.

murs of envious admiration].[12] This unseemly vanity in men seemed an especially slippery slope towards femininity. *La Guacamaya*'s cover for June 21, 1906, for example, is a Posada print that juxtaposes a trio of fashionable, well-groomed dandies and a pair of dowdy, buck-toothed women with the not-so-subtle implication that the men are considerably prettier and more stylish than their female counterparts (see illustration 19, "Mulas y tarascas" [She-mules and ugly nags]). In this image, the connection between conspicuous consumption, fashion consciousness, and diminished masculinity in elite men is rein-

Illustration 17. "¡Viva la libertad!" [Long live freedom!]. Courtesy of Benson Latin American Collection, The University of Texas at Austin.

forced by the muscular blacksmith who appears above them in the masthead. A February 15, 1909, editorial in *El Diablito Rojo* ("Crónicas de hormiga") explains: "eso de que el hombre, por culto a la moda, se feminice . . . se adorne, se componga a usanza y gusto mujeril, es traición a la nobleza del sexo y, francamente, detestable . . . Aquí y en todas partes, lo cortés no quita la malinche" [this thing

Illustration 18. José Guadalupe Posada. "A trabajar los catrines" [Put the dandies to work]. Courtesy of Benson Latin American Collection, The University of Texas at Austin.

where men, caught up in the fashion of the day, feminize themselves . . . decorate themselves, put themselves together in the manner and style of women, is a betrayal of the nobility of the sex and, frankly, detestable . . . here as everywhere elegance doesn't erase betrayal].[13]

On occasion, the penny press critique of bourgeois manhood made fairly overt references to elite male homosexuality. *El Diablito Bromista*'s cover for September 8, 1907, for instance, features a well-dressed older gentlemen in an overcoat and top hat propositioning a waiter with a not particularly subtle: "Oye, muchacho: te encargo una 'hemosura estragada.' Porque yo soy 'putativo,' ¿sabes?" [Hey young man: I'm attributing to you (begging you for) a "corrupt beauty." Because I have a "reputation." If you know what I mean?] (see illustration 20). The dandy on *El Cabezón*'s September 9, 1917, cover sports a more modern style but a similar inclination. The caption identifies him as "Un fifí de esos fifís que con bastón y paraguas

Illustration 19. José Guadalupe Posada. "Mulas y tarascas" [She-mules an ugly nags]. Courtesy of Benson Latin American Collection, The University of Texas at Austin.

y que llevan la barriga pegadita con las nal . . ." [One of those *fifís* with cane and umbrella who carries his belly stuck to his bu . . .][14] (see illustration 21). Taken as a whole, these frequent attacks on bourgeois manhood might have been diffuse, but, of all the homophobic strategies deployed in the Mexico City penny press, they were the most potentially damaging to the legitimacy of the Porfirian social order. If the bourgeoisie couldn't produce and weren't real men, how could it be expected to lead an unruly country like Mexico? In response to the rhetorical question "¿Cuándo estaremos civilizados?" [When we will be civilized?], an *El Diablito Rojo* (April 16, 1908) columnist responded: "Cuando no haya lagartijos echando flores" [When there are no more dandies throwing flowers].[15]

The 41 Scandal and the Birth of Working-Class Homophobia

Without the 41 scandal, these different strategies might never have developed any real coherence. As it was, the scandal provided a riveting public narrative that could encompass most of them and, more

---Oye, much\\ch\\: te'encargo una «hermosura estragada.» Porque yo soy «putativo,» ¿sabes?

Illustration 20. "Oye, muchacho . . ." [Hey, young man . . .]. Courtesy of Benson
Latin American Collection, The University of Texas at Austin.

important, enhance their explanatory power.[16] And while the penny
press was a secondary venue for that public narrative, it was the place
where its subversive political implications took root. Mainstream
sources, as Irwin shows, produced a homosexual panic that rocked
the complacent Porfirian bourgeoisie. Bourgeois homophobia, however, was an internal policing mechanism for an emerging private
sphere grounded in notions of heterosexual intimacy and nuclear
family values, designed to nurture male citizens, and intended to le-
gitimize the growing influence and power of the "class that progresses." Working-class homophobia, by contrast, sought to subvert
bourgeois hegemony by calling into question these ideological claims
to class superiority.

As a subversive tool, the 41 scandal proved ideal. The first homophobic strategy—sticking it to the opposition—had little resonance
in this context, probably because its metaphoric impact derived from
a graphic portrayal of unequal power relations of a personal rather
than class nature. The "opposition" in most of these cases was someone known to the penetrator and of the same class (in fact, most were

Illustration 21. "Un fifí de esos fifís . . ." [One of those *fifís* . . .]. Courtesy of Benson Latin American Collection, The University of Texas at Austin.

fellow penny press editors). While it's doubtful that anyone was naive enough to believe that penetration wasn't implicit in the 41 scandal, it didn't enter into the public discourse in any obvious way.

Besides, since most penny press editors worked hard to occupy the moral high ground in their competition with mainstream tabloids, an unseemly interest in explicit sexual acts would certainly have exposed them to charges of hypocrisy. This moralistic diffidence is clearly reflected in *La Guacamaya*'s provocative forty-first issue for 1906 (May 17). Under a masthead that features a heterosexual working-class couple in traditional dress surveying the social landscape, the unusually

Illustration 22. "A todos y a ninguno" [To All and to None]. Courtesy of Benson Latin American Collection, The University of Texas at Austin.

stark front page is dominated by a giant 41 and a headline that reads: "A todos y a ninguno" [To All and to None]. A short poem alerts the reader that: "No me refiero a los hombres/ que sin vergüenza y pudor,/ organizaron un baile/ que llamó mucha atención./ Es que ya LA GUACAMAYA/ a este número llegó" [I'm not referring to the men/ who without shame or decency,/ organized a dance/ that called a lot of attention./ It's that now *La Guacamaya*/ has reached this number] (see illustration 22). And, indeed, the issue contains no further references to the scandal (although it certainly testifies to the number's already considerable powers of signification).

By the next year, however, the temptation to expound on the theme proved irresistible. True to form, *La Guacamaya*'s forty-first issue for 1907 (July 25) makes no overt mention of sexual practices like anal penetration. However, the other three homophobic strategies previously deployed by penny press editors, writers, and illustrators—cross-dressing the politician, ridiculing the *joto,* subverting the bourgeois male subject—fit easily into the public narrative of the 41 scandal. It is thus hardly surprising to discover that they structure this "commemorative" issue as well.

Political concerns in the penny press were nearly always connected to current events. In this case, the political scandal *du jour* involved Guatemalan strongman-president Manuel Estrada Cabrera and his minions, Adrian Vidaurre and General José María Lima. According to Mexican authorities, Lima had masterminded the assassination of a Guatemalan exile living in Mexico City two months earlier and they had demanded his extradition. The Guatemalan government denied the request and, following a retaliatory attempt on Estrada Cabera's life, expelled the Mexican ambassador, the novelist Federico Gamboa.[17] Thus, in the opening political commentary, *La Guacamaya*'s indignant editor crossdresses the Guatemalan politicians in order to mark their devious and cowardly behavior. This time, however, he skips over traditional graphic images in favor of a number:

> . . . en Guatemala puede haber **40** ajusticiados inícuamente y **un** Vidaurre ambicioso y con entrañas de Torquemada . . . **40** espías y **un** Lima, dizque **Genral** [*sic*] zapatero y tahur, que paga por que asesinen a indefensos ancianos . . . **40** médicos y un certificado que declaró que varios hombres prominentes habían recurrido al suicidio . . . como responsables del **cuarenta y un** atentado contra el **cuarenta y una** vez tímido Presidente Estrada Cabrera

> [. . . in Guatemala you can have **40** people wickedly murdered and **one** Vidaurre, ambitious and with the disposition of Torquemada . . . **40** spies and **one** Lima, the so-called shoemaker-cardshark **General** who pays for the assassination of defenseless old people . . . **40** doctors and one certificate that declares that various prominent men have had recourse to suicide . . . accused of the **forty-first** attempt on the life of the **forty-one** times timid President Estrada Cabrera] (S. Mero,

"¡¡Presente!!," *La Guacamaya,* July 25, 1907; bold and deliberate misspellings in original).[18]

A "popular dialogue" on the "literary page" adds a humorous touch to this scathing political attack with the following exchange between two friends:

> —Adiós tú, hijo de . . . Lima.
> —vale Ca . . . brera, *gud bay.*
> —Ay no más que no soy de esos . . . *forty uan.*
>
> [—See you later, son of a . . . Lima.
> —Okay, Ca . . . brera, goodbye.
> —Hey, I'm not one of those . . . forty one].

A parting shot dates the dialogue July 41, 1941 (Un moralista, "Diálogo popular," *La Guacamaya,* July 25, 1907; italics in original). In this exchange, the names of Lima and Cabrera are inserted into two standard insults—hijo de puta [son of a whore] and cabrón [cuckold]—both of which carry strong sexual connotations and thus resonate slyly with the implied effeminacy of the number that follows. Moreover, the use of fractured English—*gud bay, forty uan*—highlights Guatemala's subservient position vis-à-vis the United States, a position that is sexualized here by numerical association. If before the 41 scandal cross-dressed politicians were mocked but not emasculated, afterward, the notorious number served to foreground the sexual connotations implicit in the older strategy while still leaving the writer free from charges of slander or salaciousness.

Ridiculing *jotos,* of course, had always implied emasculation. Certainly, their treatment in *La Guacamaya*'s special 41 issue reiterates the mocking condescension typical of most penny press efforts. A dialogue entitled "entre maricones" [between fairies], for example, begins with the following flirtatious exchange:

> —¡Ay Jesús, ay Dios! ¡Vaya unos mecos! ¡Pos no me han echado . . . una flor los muy indinos!
> —La culpa la tienes tú por cocote.
> —¡Ay, tú, Florindo! pero si ni siquiera he movido los ojos pa ver a ese leperote.
> —Pero quien sabe lo que movieras.
> —El chiquito que venía junto a mi, vio que no me metía con el os; pero hay unos hombres muy atrevidos, que porque lo ven a uno del otro sexo, abusan de nuestra debilidad.

[—Oh Jesus, oh God! There go some darkies! Well they haven't even thrown me . . . a flower (paid me a compliment) those little Indians!
—It's your fault for being such a slut.
—Oh, you, Florindo! but if I didn't even move my eyes to see the big bum.
—But who knows what you did move.
—The little one that passed next to me saw that I didn't want to mess with them; but there are some very insolent men, who when they see someone of the opposite sex, take advantage of our weakness] (July 25, 1907; ellipsis and deliberate misspellings in original).

The most famous Posada print of the 41 scandal carried the caption: "Aquí están los Maricones, muy chulos y coquetones" [Here are the Fairies, very cute and flirtatious] (see Illustration 1). The sentiment here is much the same. The two *jotos*, Florindo and Lolito, are represented as classic sexual inverts performing a parody of femininity that serves to heighten their deviance as male members of "the opposite sex." In this instance, however, the performance is public, the protagonists are working-class "mecos" and "maricones," and their interactions are mediated by traditional codes of male honor and female shame. On the street, the writer implies, there are no secrets or pretenses—sexual deviance and the ever-present threat of male violence, certainly, but none of the hypocrisy of bourgeois private parties.

While the cross-dressed politician and the much-maligned *joto* had important roles to play in the working-class homophobia that emerged from the 41 scandal, penny press editors reserved the bulk of their indignation and scorn for the weak, decadent bourgeois male subject. *La Guacamaya*'s July 25, 1907, cover left no room for doubt on this score. As in the previous year's issue, the number 41 leaps out at the reader both from the center-page illustration and the oversized issue number in upper right. This time, however, the headline is unambiguous: "El feminismo se impone" [Feminism imposes itself]. To reinforce the message, Posada's print shows effeminate men in the style of the *maricones* from the 41 scandal images—tiny moustaches, curly hair parted down the middle, women's clothes—performing traditional female tasks. The caption-poem reads:

Mientras la mujer asiste/ al taller y a la oficina,/ y de casimir se viste/ y de la casa desiste/ y entra airiosa a la cantina,/ el hombre barbilampiño/ queda haciendo el desayuno/ cose, plancha y cuida al niño,/ y todos con gran cariño (?)/ le llaman cuarenta y uno

[While the woman goes off/to the workshop and the office/and dresses in cashmere/and abandons the home/and enters freely into bars,/the clean-shaven man/stays [at home] making breakfast/he sews, irons, and cares for the baby,/and all of them with great affection (?)/we call forty-one].[19]

Nearly a hundred years later, the message is still crystal clear. Bourgeois men have grown too soft to control their women, preferring instead to retire to the domestic sphere themselves rather than exercise their male prerogatives and responsibilities. The older whip-wielding plutocrat who challenges the manly blacksmith on the masthead is a formidable if cruel opponent; the younger "sissies" in Posada's print are beneath contempt—hardly the manly progenitors of the self-styled "class that progresses." Parasitic bourgeois *catrines* always had been stock characters in the satiric penny press, but, as with the other homophobic strategies, the numerological possibilities of the number 41 both simplified representation and deepened the critique by linking them to perfidious politicians and ridiculous *jotos* (see illustration 4).

As noted previously, penny press attacks on the bourgeois male subject had considerable subversive potential. That potential was greatly enhanced by the 41 scandal in several ways. The front page of La Guacamaya's 41 issue, with its straightforward feminization of weak-willed bourgeois men, was probably the most obvious. The enduring popularity of Posada's images suggests that it worked quite well. A broadside printed sometime after the 41 bust, for example, reused Posada's print of the first dance, adding in the final strophe of an appended poem: "La jotería es en la época/ Peor que el tifo y gripa fúnebre,/ Peor que la pesta bubónica/ Y los temblors . . . y aun más" [Faggotry is at its height/ worse than typhus and deadly fever/ Worse than bubonic plague/ And earthquakes . . . and even more!] (see illustration 23, "El baile de los 12. Aprehensión de hombres vestidos de mujeres. El pueblo les silba y apedrea" [The dance of the 12. Arrest of men dressed as women. The people whistle and stone them], Imprenta C. Morelos).[20] Illustrated penny press advertisements for the novel based on the incident even added an anticlerical twist.[21] That the message could now be reduced to a number made subversion that much easier.

The new linkages between the 41 scandal and the penny press assault on the bourgeois male subject held out other, more subtle, possibilities as well. A short story entitled simply "Sucedido" [Occurance] from La Guacamaya's 41 issue used the connection to expose the sexual dangers that lurked in the hidden underbelly of respectable bourgeois society. Told in the first person and in high mod-

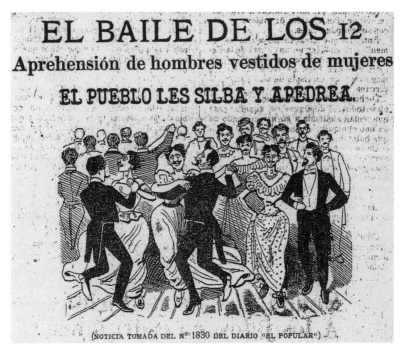

Illustration 23. José Guadalupe Posada. "El baile de los 12. Aprehensión de hombres vestidos de mujeres. El pueblo les silba y apedrea" [The dance of the 12. Arrest of men dressed as women. The people whistle and stone them]. Courtesy of Colorado Springs Fine Arts Center.

ernist style—"templos de Afrodite . . . el traidor Baco . . . Morfeo me adormecío . . . beldad digna del pencil de Miguel Angel" [temples of Aphrodite . . . the traitorous Bacchus . . . Morpheus lulled me to sleep . . . beauty worthy of Michelangelo's pencil]—the story traces the adventure of a decadent young man who indulges in an orgy attended by beautiful priestesses, falls asleep dressed as a woman, and wakes up "indignado y colérico" [indignant and angry] when he is groped by a confused "hombre feo" [ugly man]. Even though the orgiasts quickly gather around "y entre estruendosas y satíricas carcajadas bautizaron al infeliz chasquedo con el nombre de **cuarenta y uno**" [and between thundering and satirical peals of laughter baptize the unhappy fool with the name of **forty-one**] (bold in original), the genderic order is only superficially restored. The air of casual moral degeneracy that suffuses the account suggests that further sexual transgression is inevitable and even encouraged.

The protagonist's age is also significant since his callow tone implicates an entire generation of bourgeois young men. While it's doubtful that penny press editors and illustrators were up on the latest advances in the emerging sexual sciences, Posada's images of the 41 scandal hint at an element of narcissism among bourgeois men that would seem to prefigure Freudian insights into male developmental psychology. According to Freud:

> . . . future inverts, in the earliest years of their childhood, pass through a phase of very intense but short-lived fixation to a woman (usually their mother), and that, after leaving this behind, they identify themselves with a woman and take *themselves* as their sexual object. That is to say, they proceed from a narcissistic basis, and look for a young man who resembles themselves and whom *they* may love as their mothers loved *them*. (*Three Essays* 11–12)

This formative experience, he insists, arrests the psychological development of male inverts, trapping them in an immature and unproductive evolutionary stage characterized by "archaic constitutions . . . primitive psychical mechanisms . . . narcissistic object-choice . . . and a retention of the erotic significance of the anal zone."[22] Whether directly inspired by Freud or not, Posada's images convey much the same message. At one level, the *maricones*' telltale moustaches are an artistic convenience, alerting the reader-viewer that the figures wearing dresses and dancing pumps are indeed men—something that mainstream press accounts admitted was difficult to tell. At another, they expose the narcissism of fashionable bourgeois *catrines* whose self-absorption sends them in search not of real women but of a feminized version of themselves. Either way, the images infantilize both the *maricones* and their partners: the former for renouncing the responsibilities of manhood and the latter for immature object-choice. By extension, neither are fully realized subject-citizens capable of directing Mexico's difficult transition into modernity—a task better left to the manly "class that produces."

The public narrative of the 41 scandal, then, transformed previously distinct homophobic strategies into a coherent working-class homophobia that could conjure up with a magic number a complex web of connotations and insinuations—not enough perhaps to dominate "the bonds that structure all social form" but a formidable disciplinary mechanism nonetheless. Directed at bourgeois men, working-class homophobia functioned as a powerful subversive tool capable of undermining the ideological foundations of a bourgeois authority grounded in heteronormativity and nuclear family values. But homophobia also washed through the working class with "complicated political effects." And the following snippet from an *El Diablito Bromista* column (October 13, 1907), "la calificación en las comisarías" [police station judgments], suggests that it was deployed with some regularity:

[Juez]: Y usted, señora, ¿por qué golpeó al ser de sus entrañas?
[Mujer]: Señor, porque por andar con su garraleta se me ha vuelto de fierro malo.
[Juez]: ¿Y que tiene que ver "eso" para que lo haya descalabrado?
[Mujer]: Es que de palabra se "mechó" a las barbas.
[Juez]: Ah, pues entonces al cuartel.
[Mujer]: No señor, tampoco, no "viusté" que no es de los 41.
[Juez]: Pues por eso le gustan las garraletas; hilo, y cuidado con otra.

[Judge: And you ma'am, why did you strike the fruit of your womb?
Woman: Sir, because his hanging around with that tramp turned me into a wild beast.
Judge: And what does that have to do with you flying off the handle?
Woman: It's that he's really pussy-whipped.
Judge: Ah, then let's send him to the barracks.
Woman: No sir, not that, can't you see that he's not like the 41.
Judge: Well that's why we like tramps; so it's settled, and consider the options].[23]

In this exchange, the complex web of connotations and insinuations surrounding the number 41 informs both juridical relations between judge and accused, and social relations between mother, son, and his female companion. Representing the interests of society as well as the state, the judge gently coerces a reluctant mother to relinquish claims to her son's affections (and probably labor) in the name of heternomativity and nuclear family values (and by extension, social reproduction) by playing off her fears—she's the one who mentions 41—for her son's manhood. Better, the judge hints, that the son be led astray by a loose woman than emasculated by his jealous mother. Better, the subtext implies, that an irresponsible son deprive his mother of financial support than rob the fatherland of his masculine productivity.

There is a subversive element in this story to be sure: both mother and judge see the Porfirian army barracks as a site of transgressive sexuality, the last place either wishes to send the weak-willed son. But, here, social critique is directed at a morally bankrupt political regime unable to prevent the perversion of its most masculine institution, the army. Compulsory heterosexuality and patriarchal authority, by contrast, are endorsed as the guiding principles behind the regulation of juridical and social relations regardless of class position. Sometimes writers even tarred women with the 41 brush. Take, for example, an "Infernal parody" from *El Diablito Bromista* (November 13, 1907) that includes insults like "tortilla dura de maíz azul . . . perra roñosa con garrotillo . . . cloaca apestosa . . . chango postizo de una corista" [hard tortilla of blue corn . . . mangy bitch . . . pestilent sewer . . . performing monkey] and concludes with the damning phrase: "Cuarenta y uno, eso eres tú" [Forty-one, that is you]. Used here to condemn a female betrayer of male affections, the magic number has shaken loose its historical context and come to signify any threat to male subjectivity (whether bourgeois or working class)—to produce, in fact, a numerology of abjection that, as Sedgwick warned, might serve "as a tool for manipulating the entire spectrum of male bonds, and, hence, the gender system as a whole." In *Bodies That Matter*, Judith Butler argues that "femininity is . . . not the product of a choice, but the forcible citation of a norm, one whose complex historicity is indissociable from relations of discipline, regulation, punishment" (232). The same is obviously true of masculinity. And, how better to facilitate the citation of norms than through a number?—a magic number with the power to discipline, regulate, and punish women as well as men, to ensure that no one ask too many questions.

NOTES

1. Special thanks to those whose comments much improved this essay: participants in the Centenary of the Famous 41: Sexuality and Social Control in Latin America Symposium (especially Robert McKee Irwin and Pablo Piccato), participants in the University of Chicago's Latin American History Workshop (especially Everard Meade and Dain Borges), and members of Narrative and Culture Research Cluster of Bowling Green State University's Institute for the Study of Culture and Society.
2. In addition to the essays in the first section of this volume, see Monsiváis, "El mundo soslayado" and Irwin, "The Famous 41."
3. See, for example, Laclau and Mouffe.
4. A slightly amended version of this essay also appears in Buffington, *Criminal and Citizen in Modern Mexico*.
5. The publication dates throughout this essay represent only a best guess based on available issues.

6. The same image appears on the cover of *San Lunes,* December 5, 1907, with the title "Entre la espada y la pared" [Forced to the wall or cornered] as a part of a diatribe directed at elite hypocrites who preach against the drinking habits of lower-class men while surrounding them with cantinas.

7. The word *lavativa,* literally a medical injection or syringe, also is used to mean vexaction or annoynance.—*Eds.*

8. The cross-dressing of prominent politicians was common practice in the bourgeois satiric press as well. See especially Granillo Vázquez, "Masculine and Political Imagery in Mexican Public Opinion, 1898–1900."

9. The word *verdulería,* literally a vegetable stand or store, also refers to an offensive or obscene act.—*Eds.*

10. The caption for the first image translates: "That guy is really taken with the tick (bloodsucker). He'll be sorry someday when he tries to use the urinal."

11. Edited by erstwhile Huertista Querido Moheno, this journal doesn't exactly qualify as working-class penny press—and the Revolution was seriously undermining the genre by blurring class distinctions (at least temporarily)—but reinforces Monsiváis's point about sexualization as well as the notion that cross-dressing didn't necessarily signify homosexuality or even homosexual practices.

12. Words like "*detrás*" [behind] often carried sexual connotations. Buñuel relates a story about Pedro Armendáriz, who, during the filming of *El Bruto,* refused to say the word—"yo no digo detrás" [I don't say behind]—because it might damage his reputation. Again Buñuel is being coy with his readers. In the scene, Armendáriz has a knife sticking out of his back and is supposed to scream "There! Behind! Pull it out!," a line that would surely have elicited laughs had it stayed in the film. The odds that the director was playing with his star (or fabricated the story) are good (*My Last Sigh* 213).

13. The brilliant word play with Cortés and Malinche makes the betrayal explicit: La Malinche was Cortés's translator and concubine during his conquest of the Aztec empire and, in popular parlance, a "malinchista" is someone who sells out Mexico.

14. The ellipsis in the original serves to emphasize (by partial "repression") the suggestive "butt (nalgas)."

15. The word play here is on "echar flores," which can mean both to throw flowers or to toss off compliments. The list holds out little hope for Mexico's social development: the author's final indicator of civilization is "Cuando . . . la rana crie pelos y al sapo le salga cola" [when the frog grows hair and the toad produces a tail].

16. On the power of public narratives to structure perception see Buffington and Piccato.

17. For a short account of the incident, see Iturribarría.

18. The cross-dressing occurs only after the obligatory disavowal that establishes the writer's own manhood—"onque agora me presento haciendo el 14 al revés, no por eso soy defeituosa como aquellos rotos furris que defeicionaron haciéndola de 41" [although now I'm doing 14 in reverse, I'm not defective like those despicable perverts who defected themselves doing the 41].

19. The question mark is in the original and serves to distance the writer from his subjects—something of an obsession as we have seen. The bold is also in the original.

20. The broadside has no date but mentions the 41 incident and was probably published soon after. The ellipsis is in the original.

21. See, for example, "¡¡¡Los cuarenta y uno!!!," *Don Cucufate,* September 3, 1906.

22. The connection is doubtful but not impossible: Freud's pathbreaking *Three Essays on the Theory of Sexuality* was published in German in 1905. Regardless, as Freud himself pointed out, many of his insights were already present in the literature of the period, especially French poetry, which had several direct and indirect lines of transmission to Mexico City.

23. A literal translation of the original would be: "She's really greasing his beard (se mechó a las barbas)." The idiomatic expression reflects the metaphoric connection in Latin American popular culture between a person's face and their public honor, and between men's beards and women's pubic hair. My deliberately "crude" translation of the mother's comment, then, attempts to capture both her concern about her son's humiliation and the implicit sexual innuendo.

BIBLIOGRAPHY

PRIMARY SOURCES

El Charrito
El Chile Piquín
El Diablito Bromista
El Diablito Rojo
Don Cucufate
La Guacamaya
Imprenta de C. Morelos. "El baile de los 12. Aprehensión de hombres vestidos de mujeres. El pueblo les silba y apedrea." n.d.
Moheno
El Moquete
El Pinche
San Lunes
El Vale Panchito

Secondary sources

Buffington, Robert. *Criminal and Citizen in Modern Mexico*. Lincoln: University of Nebraska Press, 2000.

———. "Los Jotos: Contested Visions of Homosexuality in Modern Mexico." *Sex and Sexuality in Latin America*. Daniel Balderston and Donna Guy, Eds. New York: New York University Press, 1997: 118–132.

———and Pablo Piccato. "Tales of Two Women: The Narrative Construal of Porfirian Reality." *The Americas* 55.3 (January 1999): 391–424.

Buñuel, Luis. *My Last Sigh*. Abigail Israel, Trans. New York: Knopf, 1984.

Butler, Judith. *Bodies That Matter: On the Discursive Limits of "Sex."* New York: Routledge, 1993.

Freud, Sigmund. *Three Essays on the Theory of Sexuality*. James Strachey, Trans. and Ed. New York: Basic Books, 1962.

Granillo Vázquez, Lilia. "Masculine and Political Imagery in Mexican Public Opinion, 1898–1900: The Dawn of the Famous 41." Paper delivered at the Centenary of the Famous 41: Sexuality and Social Control in Latin America Symposium held at Tulane University, November 15–17, 2001.

Irwin, Robert McKee. "The Famous 41: The Scandalous Birth of Modern Mexican Homosexuality." *GLQ* 6.3 (2000): 353–376.

Iturribarría, Jorge Fernando. *Porfirio Díaz ante la historia*. Mexico City: Carlos Villegas García, 1967.

Laclau, Ernesto, and Chantal Mouffe. *Hegemony and Socialist Strategy*. New York: Verso, 1985.

Monsiváis, Carlos. "El mundo soslayado (Donde se mezclan la confesión y la proclama)." *La estatua de sal*. Salvador Novo. Mexico City: Consejo Nacional para la Cultura y las Artes, 1998. 11–41.

Sedgwick, Eve Kosofsky. *Between Men: English Literature and Male Homosocial Desire*. New York: Columbia University Press, 1985.

The *Lagartijo* at *The High Life*

MASCULINE CONSUMPTION, RACE, NATION, AND HOMOSEXUALITY IN PORFIRIAN MEXICO[1]

Víctor M. Macías-González

Para R.L.R.

While traditional interpretations of the gendered nature of consumption at the turn of the century would have us believe that the ideal consumer was a married upper-middle-class woman, evidence from advertisements, novels, diaries, and official correspondence suggests that Porfirian Mexico's ideal shopper was the *lagartijo* or elegant middle- to upper-class male.[2] Anglophile gents such as don Guillermo de Landa y Escandón (also known as *de Lana y Algodón*, a pun on his aristocratic last name referring to his favorite fabrics, "Wool and Cotton") and don José de Algara (dubbed the "Mexican Beau Brummell") consumed such great quantities of imported finery that a number of London firms sent agents to Mexico City to take orders and measurements for seasonal wardrobes (Tablada, *Feria* 269–271). Local tailors, department stores such as "El Palacio de Hierro," and fashionable haberdasheries such as "The High Life" kept dandies abreast of fads and sufficiently supplied to enable them to conform to societal conventions of sartorial propriety that demanded as many as three or four daily changes of attire during the high social season.[3] But while some regarded the purchase and display of costly foreign and domestic clothing and other goods as indicative of the country's economic, social, and industrial progress vis-à-vis Western Europe, others saw in the dandy's shopping sprees a sinister feminization of the elite. Public opinion scorned the luxurious lifestyle of fops because they blurred traditional gender boundaries and represented a sterile or unproductive—and, thus, unmasculine—use of capital that violated the values of frugality, modesty, decorum, and capital accumulation that the regime advocated.

This essay focuses on three aspects of masculine consumption. First, it explores the role of elite males as consumers and arbiters of taste. Second, it analyzes how goods offered for sale in gentlemen's magazines allowed men to articulate their notions of racial, ethnic, gender, and class identity. Third, it outlines evidence for the commodification of the male body. In this regard, I explore how Porfirians wrote about the desirability and attractiveness of the European male, a factor that led members of the aristocracy and ruling circle not only to hire and display European male servants but also to whiten themselves. Whereas prescriptive literature and government correspondence provides some insight into the consumer culture of upper-class males, particularly in the matter of taste, gift-giving, and purchases, sources such as diaries, memoirs, travel narratives, and advertisements suggest how Porfirians consumed masculinity. In essence, then, this essay explores upper-class males both as the subject and as the object of consumption, and offers comments on the uses of male consumer culture as a category of historical analysis.

Scholars of Latin America need to give greater attention to male consumer culture because as wealth and the purchasable mass-market image joined (and, to a certain degree, displaced) traditional phenotypical and cultural markers of identity at the turn of the century, evidence suggests that the gendered nature of consumption also evolved and, in so doing, affected individual and collective notions of masculinity. Analysis of male consumer culture is important to better understand the evolving nature of gender in nineteenth-century Mexico, as anthropological research shows that sumptuary goods such as clothing or furniture incorporate "ideas [people] hold about themselves, their relationship to the universe, and the world around them" (Schevill 10). Consequently the study of how male individuals and corporate bodies consumed, displayed, and employed sumptuary objects—including the commodified bodies of other males—sheds great light on how Porfirian society articulated and subjectivized masculinity.

Writing about consumption—whether it is exercised by males or females—forces one to consider issues of morality and moderation. It should not strike us as odd that the words for "lust" and "luxury" in Spanish—*lujuria* and *lujo*—share the Latin root *lux*; it denotes excess and designates, in both cases, the possibility of deviating from the norm (Rey 19). Both can be debauched, fatuous, ostentatious, dissipate, and indulgent of the senses. Similarly, society often has reined in practitioners of *luxury* (and the *lust*-ful). In the case of male consumption, this mitigation keeps the dandy from becoming obscene—or queer. When moderated, the fop's carnal and material indulgence becomes the essence of his *chic*.

Under certain conditions, objectionable excess becomes not only socially acceptable but also economically and politically expedient. When moderated in the guise of good taste, luxury becomes aesthetic and even moral. For early modern Europeans, this moral excess had public utility because it facilitated the expression of traditional hierarchy and divine order (Margairaz 25–29). Hispanic elites employed ornamentation as a weapon of reaction, as a vocabulary of images and spatial relationships that established hierarchy, privilege, and deference to power, while lending oriental opulence and brilliance to the act of astonishing into submission (Maravall 126–145). The desire of Crown and Church to avoid the chaotic mixture of genders, ethnicities, and *calidades* ("the nobility and the luster of their blood"), gave rise to the erection of sartorial barriers of difference (Jovellanos 120, 131–133; Real Academia, II: 67). Concurrently, Spanish sumptuary laws, like those of the Venetian and Genoese Republics, sought to control the representation of social inequalities in an effort to avoid or limit social unrest, focusing on the aristocracy's—and the rising bourgeoisie's—pretensions (Hughes 82–90). During Spain's Golden Age, royal decrees and council legislation also safeguarded the economic interests of the Realm, prohibiting the importation of foreign luxury goods in detrimental competition with national manufactures (Deleito y Piñuela 275–279).

The traditional wariness toward consumption began to change with the Enlightenment, as Spanish reformers elaborated arguments for the social utility of excess. To be certain, writers such as Juan de Sempere y Guarinos advocated an attenuated form of luxury, in which elite purchases would function as the driving force of industry. In New Spain, however, consumption of luxury goods may have been higher than in the Peninsula, because, as the research of Richard Cope and Cheryl English-Martin points out, conspicuous consumption effectively blurred existing racial, ethnic, and class boundaries. By the nineteenth century, the demise of the colonial order, the declining fortunes of the aristocracy, and the rise of the merchant-miner bourgeoisie altered traditional attitudes toward sumptuary legislation. Luxury ceased to be regarded as superfluous or immoral; as bourgeois comfort, excess became socially acceptable. Similarly, the Porfirian ruling circle's adept display and use of imported European finery and sumptuary objects had socially redeeming qualities, because conspicuous consumption—which created an illusion of stability and prosperity—not only enabled Porfirians to lure foreign investment and immigration but also allowed the elite to distance itself from its *mestizo* roots.

The privileged surroundings and education of wealthy young men, often supplemented with extended travel and residence abroad, transformed Mexican dandies into the arbiters of taste. While many grew up in homes housing dozens—if not hundreds—of portraits and landscape paintings, it was during their education at boarding schools in France, Spain, and the United Kingdom that many became assiduous visitors of art galleries and museums. Bernardo Couto Castillo, for example, was said to have become so familiar with the contents of the Louvre that he would often delight his friends by describing from memory any of its galleries (Tablada, *Sombras* 182). Charles de Béistegui, who would subsequently bequeath his famed numismatic collection and dozens of his favorite paintings to French museums, developed his exquisite artistic discernment growing up amid rare bronzes, magnificent paintings, and Flemish tapestries (Montenegro 40–41). American and European museums often consulted with famed Porfirian collectors when adding items to their holdings in Mexican colonial paintings and ceramics.[4] Elegant gentlemen were thus expected to be familiar with the works of great masters and to speak with some authority on different artistic styles. To be truly *chic,* the author of a popular etiquette book noted, one had to "specialize in a particular type of object or period, for this shall make one's conversation easier and more interesting" (Barajas 14–15).

The State also drew on the refined taste of aristocratic males to constitute social hierarchy, state power, and individual identity (Auslander 17–21). Díaz and his collaborators employed objects of everyday life to enhance and construct the power of the state over society and (at a time when the economy required continued infusions of foreign capital) the all-important foreign observer. As I suggest in a forthcoming article analyzing Porfirian ceremony and ritual, Díaz became adept at using light, sound, as well as temporal, spatial, and even emotional mechanisms, to symbolically position himself through ceremonies such as the presidential audience above powerful petitioners whose social status, prestige, and prerogatives would otherwise have outflanked his place in Mexican or global hierarchies (Macías-González, forthcoming).

One of the many cases in which the regime relied on discerning elite male consumers to package and market the country to foreign observers involved preparations for the 1901 Panamerican Conference. Díaz commissioned his dapper chief of protocol—Captain Pablo Escandón y Barrón—to visit the National Portrait Gallery to select artwork with which to decorate the presidential apartments at the National Palace.[5] When the Intendant of the National Palaces decided that the presidential silver service was inadequate for the state dinners planned to fete the visiting dignitaries, dandy diplomats posted to Paris were asked to storm the department stores and silversmith shops to locate the required argentine vessels. The request ruffled the feathers of the aristocratic minister to France, don Sebastián B. de Mier, who noted that the request for so many silver soup tureens—a practice discontinued decades before among the smartest circles in continental society—had raised eyebrows and elicited laughter. At the firm of Boin-Taburet, the silversmiths had irreverently snickered at the order, maliciously implying Mexico was a backward place whose elite behaved like millionaire peasants because they ate vast amounts of the poor man's food out of a rich man's vessels.[6]

Elite males—particularly those residing or studying abroad or serving in the diplomatic corps—thus became purveyors of sumptuary and luxury goods to the State. Their social skills, education, lifestyle, and patterns of consumption made these aristocrats the ideal filter for the introduction of cosmopolitan uses to the highest circles of Porfirian officialdom (Raquillet-Bordry 1–25). From the first lady on down to the cabinet wives, spouses of the ruling clique routinely forwarded shopping lists to dandy diplomats, particularly those posted in Paris and London. "Those with great names" were asked to research and arrange for all types of purchases, ranging from household linens to coronets to automobiles—and even to arrange for gardeners![7] Always stressing their need to have the latest novelties selected "at your discretion and with your good taste," these requests kept the foppish shoppers busy. In the summer of 1902, for example, don Juan Antonio de Béistegui, then attaché at the Mexican Legation in Paris, purchased a pearl necklace, earrings, and a coronet for Limantour's daughter, María Teresa, at a cost of 75,350 French Francs![8] Even the Finance Minister, José Yves Limantour, routinely worked as errand boy for the regime during his frequent trips abroad. In 1907, the first lady asked Limantour to purchase a small, dark-blue, Moroccan leather-upholstered, custom-built, 20-horsepower Renault roadster so that she could enjoy her morning ride about Chapultepec Forest in an exclusive and modern style.[9] Limantour seemed to have been so busy shopping for the regime's matrons that he did not think twice about marshaling the diplomatic corps to do his own personal shopping. In 1903, for example, he asked Miguel de Béistegui, *chargé d'affaires* in London, to procure a large porcelain service for him in France—and to ship it directly to his country chalet outside Mexico City.[10]

Elite males also could give their acts of consumption a patriotic twist. Leading citizens and members of the oligarchy saw it as their civic duty to purchase elegant uniforms for public employees, particularly in small cities and towns. In 1906, for example, don Luis Terrazas donated elegant, gold-trimmed gala uniforms to the Municipal Band of Casas Grandes (Lloyd-Daley 46–48). Such acts were not often easily accomplished. During preparations for the historic Díaz-Taft Summit meeting in 1909, the Jefe Político [prefect] of Chihuahua City, don José Asúnsolo, made plans to provide 25 footmen and coachmen with liveries and plumed top hats. The increasingly worried and time-pressed don José drafted some three dozen letters to department stores and haberdasheries in Chihuahua City, Mexico City, and El Paso (Texas), relating to them that he wanted to receive the presidents with the appropriate protocol. As the day of Díaz's arrival approached, the custom-made outfits, which included plumed top hats, blue overcoats, matching breeches, black-and-white vests, white elk leather gloves, and white-cuffed leather boots, arrived from the Camisería Sucursal de Silvano Coblentz and the firm of Simon Weil in Mexico City, via express shipping.[11]

But in the consumption practices that proclaimed elite males' patriotism and modernity, as well as their class and racial superiority, also lurked the sinister specter of moral danger, for the devotion of dandies' time and resources to conspicuous consumption perilously mimicked what society then considered as strictly feminine behavior. According to the nineteenth-century doctrine of separate spheres, the role of women was to perform within their narrow domestic world the success males attained in the public universe of politics, enterprise, and finance (McCall 1–13). This view of the gendered ordering of bourgeois life maintained that women's leisure activities and preoccupation with shopping were supposed to showcase bourgeois male economic and political achievement; feminine consumption of time and resources were supposed to mark and enhance the male's social status (Montgomery 9). Whereas it may have been the case that elite males may have originally employed women in this fashion, by the fin de siècle, elite Mexicans no longer needed women to showcase their achievement. Thanks to the development of novel forms of consumption, males could project their sense of self-worth

1.—¡Hoy sí que doy el golpe
   por elegante y por guapo!

Illustration 24. Image of *lagartijo* (dandy) about the town. The caption reads: "Today I will impress them with my elegance and my dapper figure!" From the author's private collection. Acquisition and reproduction made possible through a grant from the University of Wisconsin-La Crosse International Development Fund.

without recurring to using women as trophies or display cases. They could show who they were on their own (see illustration 24).

Whereas advertisements, magazines, and literary works are replete with examples of males extremely obsessed with their appearances, it is fascinating to see that the presence (or absence) of women was still required if only to encode the male consumer as heterosexual or as homosexual. Pornographic Spanish magazines published and marketed for the Mexican market, such as *La Vida Galante* and

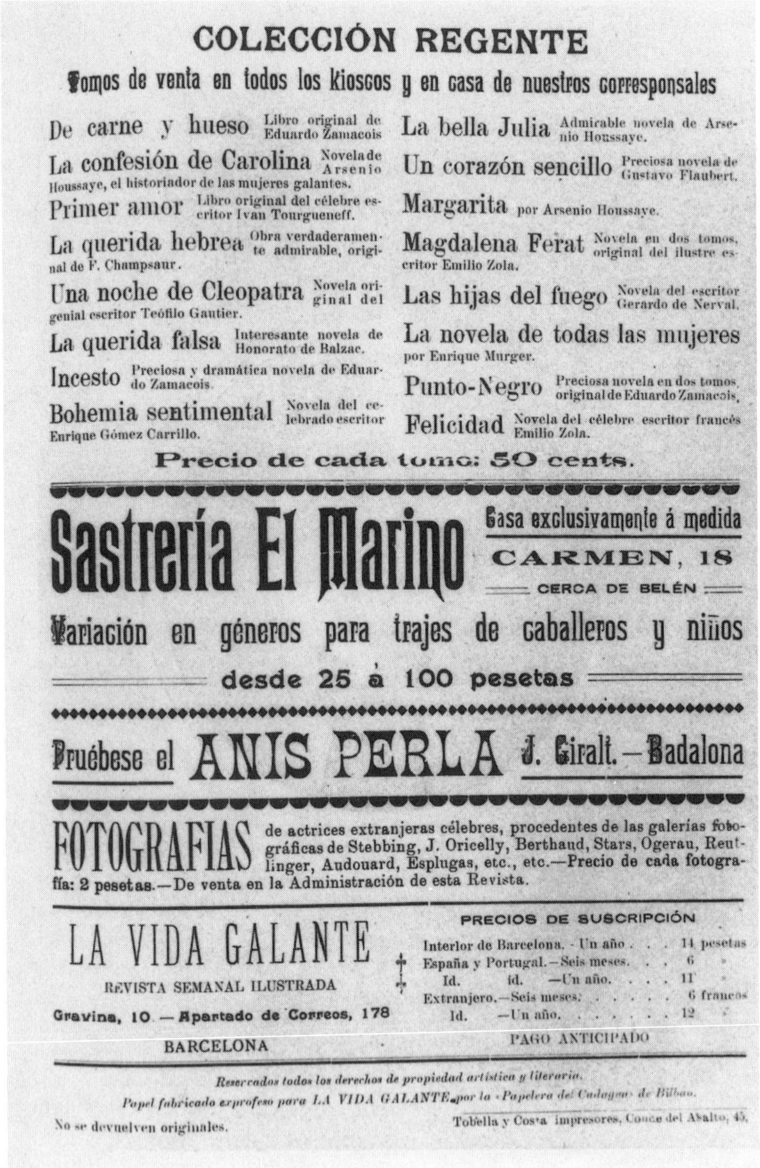

COLECCIÓN REGENTE

Tomos de venta en todos los kioscos y en casa de nuestros corresponsales

De carne y hueso Libro original de Eduardo Zamacois

La confesión de Carolina Novela de Arsenio Houssaye, el historiador de las mujeres galantes.

Primer amor Libro original del célebre escritor Ivan Tourgueneff.

La querida hebrea Obra verdaderamente admirable, original de F. Champsaur.

Una noche de Cleopatra Novela original del genial escritor Teófilo Gautier.

La querida falsa Interesante novela de Honorato de Balzac.

Incesto Preciosa y dramática novela de Eduardo Zamacois.

Bohemia sentimental Novela del celebrado escritor Enrique Gómez Carrillo.

La bella Julia Admirable novela de Arsenio Houssaye.

Un corazón sencillo Preciosa novela de Gustavo Flaubert.

Margarita por Arsenio Houssaye.

Magdalena Ferat Novela en dos tomos, original del ilustre escritor Emilio Zola.

Las hijas del fuego Novela del escritor Gerardo de Nerval.

La novela de todas las mujeres por Enrique Murger.

Punto-Negro Preciosa novela en dos tomos, original de Eduardo Zamacois.

Felicidad Novela del célebre escritor francés Emilio Zola.

Precio de cada tomo: 50 cents.

Sastrería El Marino

Casa exclusivamente á medida

CARMEN, 18

CERCA DE BELÉN

Variación en géneros para trajes de caballeros y niños

desde 25 á 100 pesetas

Pruébese el ANIS PERLA J. Giralt.—Badalona

FOTOGRAFIAS de actrices extranjeras célebres, procedentes de las galerías fotográficas de Stebbing, J. Oricelly, Berthaud, Stars, Ogerau, Reutlinger, Audouard, Esplugas, etc., etc.—Precio de cada fotografía: 2 pesetas.—De venta en la Administración de esta Revista.

LA VIDA GALANTE

REVISTA SEMANAL ILUSTRADA

Gravina, 10.—Apartado de Correos, 178

BARCELONA

PRECIOS DE SUSCRIPCIÓN

Interior de Barcelona.-Un año	14	pesetas
España y Portugal.—Seis meses.	6	»
Id. id. —Un año.	11	»
Extranjero.—Seis meses.	6	francos
Id. —Un año.	12	»

PAGO ANTICIPADO

Reservados todos los derechos de propiedad artística y literaria.

Papel fabricado exprofeso para LA VIDA GALANTE por la «Papelera del Cadagua» de Bilbao.

No se devuelven originales.

Tobella y Costa impresores, Conde del Asalto, 45.

Illustration 25. A virile consumer. Advertisements from *La Vida Galante*. The first ("Colección Regente") and fourth ("Fotografías") sections feature pornographic novels and pinups. Note, however, that the second and third sections feature advertisements for custom-made suits and for a well-known brand of anise liqueur. From the author's private collection. Acquisition and reproduction made possible through a grant from the University of Wisconsin-La Crosse International Development Fund.

Illustration 26. The presence of women dispelled homosexual accusations. Porno-graphic images from *La Vida Galante*. Note the luxurious surroundings. From the au-thor's private collection. Acquisition and reproduction made possible through a grant from the University of Wisconsin-La Crosse International Development Fund.

Barcelona Cómica, featured sexually suggestive and even explicit im-ages and texts portraying women in costly lingerie, smoking and drinking amid ornate furnishings and refined bibelots. It is not with-out reason that often in the pages preceding or following these early centerfolds, the publishers placed advertisements aimed at a refined male shopper. Next to the usual ads for more porn products—taste-fully described as "artistic images of foreign ladies"—were notices marketing wines and fine spirits, bicycles, clothing, and other goods similar to or evocative of those featured in the pornographic texts and images (see illustration 25 and illustration 26).

But perhaps the real reason behind the bathing beauties and inde-cent nudies was, as the cultural critic Barbara Ehrenreich suggests is the case in contemporary issues of *GQ* and *Playboy,* a certain anxiety on the part of genteel, sophisticated male consumers worried about being taken for homosexuals. Similarly, marketers of the Mexican fin de siè-cle employed aggressive heterosexual narrative strategies and represen-tations "to make men feel it was alright to shop for themselves" (Ehrenreich 287). In so doing, they acquired goods that allowed them to explore alternative interpretations of masculinity made possible through social, economic, and political transformations. In the United States, the historians John D'Emilio, George Chauncey, John Donald Gustav-Wrathall, and Gail Bederman have credited the changes stemming from urbanization, the rise of wage labor, the emergence of homosocial institutions such as the YMCA, and the shift in the workplace from manual labor to nonrepetitive, less strenuous, mental tasks with the emergence of a less aggressive, more emotive, urbane, middle-class masculinity as well as with gay identity. Although the same cannot yet be said for Mexico, there are remarkable similarities between urban areas in central and northern Mexico and the United States that would lead us make such an argument.

But what is evident from the advertisements in *La Vida Galante* and *Barcelona Cómica* in 1899 and 1900 is that affluent males in Mexico embraced consumer culture and, in doing so, they were better able to articulate and define their identity as the sum of multiple components inclusive of race, class, and sexuality. For those who wanted to display their personal success, wealth, social arrival, or to simply reassert their privilege, they could purchase costly goods such as crystal and champagne, or visit health spas, arrange for stays in charming country inns, retire to seaside resorts for the weekend, or step into one of the famous cafés to savor delectable French pastries and Italian coffees. Individuals greatly concerned with their image, physique, and health—as well as the occasional hypochondriac—could find some relief in the purchase of the latest medicines, weight-loss programs, antibalding treatments, artificial teeth, breath fresheners, soaps, and colognes. For those men of mixed-race origins or swarthy complexion worried about being perceived as too "Indian-looking"—a category that included the dictator himself—an alternative was any of the products that promised to whiten and soften skin, concerns that we would perhaps expect in the beauty columns of women's periodicals. For those who felt too old and feared that they would be passed up for promotions by younger competitors, there existed lotions that promised to rejuvenate and exfoliate the skin, ridding it of premature age spots and wrinkles. Men with problems in the bedroom could take any of the many tonics that promised "to strengthen [their] virility." Whatever the concern, advertisers promised a product that would alleviate it. *Vanitas, vanitatum!* (see illustration 27).

Ironically, references to similarly refined male consumption in Castrejón's novel *Los 41* encode the finicky consumers not as heterosexuals but as homosexuals. Homosexuality—never spoken about as

HIGIENE Y BELLEZA

Jabon Fluido

Gorgot

NO MAS JABON EN PASTILLAS

EL JABÓN FLUIDO GORGOT,
de **HIEL DE VACA, AFRECHO** y **SALOL,**
no se enturbia ni da escozor á la piel; blan-
quea el cutis y lo conserva terso: suaviza
las manos, quita granos, rojeces, manchas,
y las arrugas prematuras de la cara. Usán-
dolo en e baño, preserva la piel de toda
enfermadad contagiosa, sarampión viruela-
la, etc.—Precio: **3 PESETAS** frasco.

J. GORGOT, Rambla Flores, 8. BARCELONA

Illustration 27. Men also could be vain and beautiful. Advertisement for Gorgo's liq-
uid soap: "Does not sting, whitens and softens your skin and hands, removes pimples,
red spots, specks, and premature wrinkles from your face. When used while bathing, it
protects your skin from all contagious diseases, including measles and smallpox." From
the author's private collection. Acquisition and reproduction made possible through a
grant from the University of Wisconsin-La Crosse International Development Fund.

such but referred to as a perversion, "un vicio execrable, sobre el cual escupe la misma sociedad, como el corruptor de las generaciones" (Spanish 94, English 48, this volume) [execrable vice, on which society itself spits, as the corruptor of generations]—is presented as the feminization of aristocratic males indulgent of elegance and excess (see illustration 28). In the novel's opening scene, the excessive primping and preening of elegant youths overly preoccupied with clothing in a sumptuous setting featuring silken curtains, velveteen sofas, carrara marble statues on bronze pedestals, and electric light bulbs, eating fine pastries and champagne, mark the dapper young men as homosexuals (Spanish 96, English 50, this volume).

Excessive consumption queers the acquisitive elite male. Their proclivity for the "love that dared not speak its name" is established in a campy passage in which the author presents the protagonists in amorous embraces with each other. Describing them as "jóvenes que, en el colmo de la torpeza y de la degradación prostituida, contribuyen a bastardear la raza humana injuriando gravemente a la *Naturaleza*" [fallen young men who, at the height of crudeness and prostituted degradation, contribute to the bastardization of the human race, gravely injuring Nature itself] (Spanish 97, English 51, this volume) Castrejón condemns them of betraying their gender. In the author's mind, the homosexual becomes a prostitute, a claim that echoes the contemporary Mexican usage *puto*—male prostitute—for homosexuals. The epistemic violence is already uttered before the next scene, in which the effete fops begin to try on the stylish custom-tailored women's clothing that they will wear to the infamous 41 drag ball; thoroughly captivated by the womanly finery, their voices become high pitched, sweet-sounding, and fill the house with din. In Castrejón's words, their "modales afeminados daban a la escena un tinte chocarrero y meloso, pareciendo la reunión más bien voces de señoritas discutiendo en el estrado, que de jóvenes barbilindos" [effeminate manners gave the scene a cloying and scurrilous tint, the gathering seeming more like one of young ladies chitchatting in the drawing room than one of dapper young gentlemen] (Spanish 96, English 50, this volume). Unlike the readers of heterosexual pornography who could safely consume effete goods thanks to the presence of nude female images, the homosexual consumer, lacking the reaffirming pornographic presence, becomes feminized and consequently vilified.

Finally, I want to address the issue of males as objects of consumption. Foreign travelers, particularly Anglo-Americans, often were shocked to observe the prevalence of handsome liveried English-speaking servants, primarily as coachmen and butlers, in the

Illustration 28. Las hermanas Monterde, a gender-bending singing duo, embodies late-nineteenth-century Hispanic feminine excess and masculine reserve. Cover art, *La Vida Galante*. From the author's private collection. Acquisition and reproduction made possible through a grant from the University of Wisconsin-La Crosse International Development Fund.

households of elite families. Ethel Brilliana Harley Tweedie noted that "all the great folk . . . had English coachmen and butlers . . . to my intense amazement!" (137, 163–164, 238, and 245). Ignacio de la Torre y Mier, the homosexual son-in-law of Porfirio Díaz, surrounded himself with young, handsome, blond European male servants. In *Los 41,* Eduardo A. Castrejón described how the wealthy homosexual known as "Mimí" kept a young male lackey described as "guapo, de ojos azules con mirada voluptuosa y melancólica" [handsome, blue-eyed, with a voluptuous and melancholic expression] (Spanish 95, English 49, this volume). These men were preferred, a British traveler explained, because their neatness and well-kept appearance lent an air of decency and morality to their place of employment, a task that was difficult to accomplish with Mexican *mozos* [servants] who refused to abandon traditional costume such as *sombreros* and *huaraches* in favor of new goods such as machine-made clothing and Western-style shoes (Martin, I: 209–211).

Novel sartorial consumption may have played an important role in the gradual erosion of social boundaries. Competing with the sartorial sophistication of the foreign clerk or entry-level employee proved costly for Mexicans, even those of the better classes. Youths of good families often found themselves resorting to creative strategies to cover the narrowing consumption gap between them and the rising middle classes. Eduardo Iturbide, who worked as an accountant at the Casa Boker in the 1890s, had to have his father's old suits taken in by an enterprising neighborhood tailor, a practice that he gradually abandoned once he began to work for the Banco Nacional de México. However, despite enjoying the relatively high salary of 175 pesos per month, he still faced difficulties. By 1900, he had become so indebted that he had to abandon Mexico City for the countryside, where, among rustic folk, Iturbide need not have to devote as much of his income to maintain his wardrobe (21–32). Another gentleman, José Juan Tablada—*né* de Aguilar Acuña Tablada y Osuna—also related in his memoirs the great difficulties with which he maintained and renewed his wardrobes. Hardly had he completed paying off a debt of 500 pesos to the Caja de Ahorros on August 19, 1904, when, on August 24, Tablada spent 82 dollars on a sport outfit "for my outdoor exercises next winter" (*Diario* 31–43). While compliance with European fashion may have been a costly endeavor, fashionable outfits functioned as investments that could easily be liquidated at pawnshops in case of economic hardship.[12]

While the country's traditional elites struggled to defend their status from better-clothed social upstarts and foreigners, the government also busied itself in the consumption frenzy for properly attired, European-phenotyped employees. Porfirio Díaz surrounded himself with attractive young men, both as clerks and as presidential guards. In 1900, following an extensive remodeling project of the National Palace and a revision of the presidential ceremonial, newspapers published advertisements for additional staff. After the desirable applicants failed to materialize, the newspapers stressed to readers that only individuals of a "pleasant appearance," defined as "hombres de complexión robusta, de estatura alta, y buena presencia" [men of a vigorous constitution, tall, with a good presence and appearance] need apply.[13] Apparently the right type of men finally applied, as photographs of Díaz with palace guards and aides-de-camp feature attractive young men with pale skin and European phenotypes. Society gossiped about the presidential palace guards' great preoccupation for their appearance. Like debutants, they poured themselves into the tight-fitting dress uniforms and highlighted their small waists and muscled thighs with corsets. Some even dyed their moustaches jet-black, waxed them into gravity-defying, pointy heights, and applied rouge to their lips and cheeks (Novo 89).

I am not suggesting that Díaz was gay. His homophobia is evident in his regime's persecution of homosexual scandals such as the 41 *maricones* or the comic episode that Victoriano Salado Álvarez relates in his memoirs, in which Díaz kissed the German military attaché after he mistook him for a woman at a costume ball. Díaz clearly feared the implications of a Eulenburg Affair - type scandal for his regime.[14] What I am suggesting, however, is that Díaz and his collaborators perceived males of European phenotype to be attractive and, consequently, hired these men to occupy posts of great visibility and prestige. The handsome men of the Iturbide Imperial family, for example, obtained protection and lucrative posts from Díaz and his close friend the Archbishop Eulogio Guillow owing, in large part, to their attractive features. Guillow's memoirs, for example, note that Díaz initially refused to offer Prince Agustín de Iturbide y Green a post as military attaché at the Mexican legation in Berlin or Paris, until Díaz met the Prince. Díaz was supposedly so taken by the prince's "gallant presence" that don Porfirio offered him employment on the spot (Rivera 204). The Iturbides were apparently an attractive bunch, as Prince Agustín's cousin, Prince Salvador, turned many heads during his visit to Pope Pius IX. His Holiness reportedly was so taken by his beauty that he walked around him marveling at his appearance. At the conclusion of the interview, the pontiff helped Prince Salvador to put on his sword belt, and looked admiringly at his long weapon. As the prince exited, the archbishop wrote, the Pope "looked longingly and with much fondness and affection, admiring him justly, for he really was the most beautiful member of the Iturbide family" (Rivera 206).

How did consumption of sumptuary goods, phenotype-altering cosmetics, and leisurely activities—not to mention the possibility of consuming other males—shape the identity of elite Mexican males? If, as contemporary sociologists assure us, consumption patterns allow individuals to explore and express their personal identity, what conjectures can we make about the purchases of elite Porfirians? One could argue that we have evidence of two things. First, it enabled them to show—both to themselves and to others—that they had arrived. Gone were the times of political and economic chaos; the Porfiriato was a time of unparalleled bonanza, relative peace, and stability. Second, for those who had recently risen, such as high-level government employees and the nouveaux riches, the purchase and display of costly goods of European manufacture allowed them to pass, to pose, to construct new identities. By spending time in spas, bathhouses, shopping, visiting a resort, or acquiring a membership at any of the exclusive all-male clubs such as the Jockey Club or the Casino Nacional, elite males engaged in well-choreographed (not to mention well-accessorized) performances of their achievements. As Jennifer Scanlon notes, possessions "can be considered extensions of the self . . . the means of fitting in to a group or a way of distinguishing ourselves in a group" (5). Purchasing and displaying costly imported finery ascribed to the consumer a specific social meaning.

The particular identity that was offered for purchase and that was consumed reveals cultural attitudes and aspirations as well as anxieties. Did the purchase and display of a European appearance—constructed through clothing, but also contrived through cosmetics like skin whiteners—indicate that the average Porfirian, elite male consumer perceived himself as racially inferior, as biologically unmodern? I would certainly say so. Equally important would be to establish whether there are any continuities between the implied intersection of race and consumption in Porfirian Mexico and earlier periods, such as the seventeenth and eighteenth centuries. Were Porfirian notions of racial inferiority any different from those expressed by downwardly mobile hidalgos in the Viceregal period?

In this sense, we also can employ a class-specific analysis of consumer culture that contemplates elites and subaltern classes for evidence of the negotiation and crafting of the imagined community. How linked is consumerism with state-building in nineteenth-century Mexico? It would be interesting to see, based on purchases, how people reacted, resisted, or negotiated imposed messages. Did men use consumer culture in the way that the creators of image and merchandising intended them to use it? Did they employ goods—as I posit that the nascent homosexual community did—to construct alternate models of masculinity? How did "you are what you buy" play out in the end? How did purchases figure into the strategies of self-representation of nonheterosexual men?

In regard to class and ethnicity, there are many more questions that arise. If we study Porfirian sumptuary legislation enforcing the wearing of Western-style clothing and banning traditional costume, will we find evidence of the poor urban and rural population's acceptance or rejection of new consumption patterns? To quote Scanlon again, I believe we can find here how "purchased identities can be oppressive or liberating, passively accepted, or actively pursued" (9). Work needs to be done, along the lines of Daniel Roche's quantitative research on the culture of clothing in Early Modern Paris, analyzing long-term variations in consumption of clothing and other goods as documented in the records of pawnshops or in wills. In doing so, historians also will need to explore whether there are any correlations between the ethnic and class identity that the author claimed in life—a fact that becomes impossible to ascertain after mid-century legislation destroyed the legality of racial and ethnic designation—and the goods that he or she consumed. How did economic, social, and political changes affect Mexican consumption of household goods, for example, over the length of the nineteenth century? How did consumer attitudes and behavior anticipate or reflect political and economic trends?

Although I have touched only superficially on the topic, I also recognize the need for more research on the spatial dimension of consumption and display. Where—and under what circumstances—did men shop? Was the experience of urban male shoppers different from that of rural shoppers? Along these lines, what was the relationship between consumption and the narrative strategies employed by catalogue designers—primarily firms such as "El Palacio de Hierro" and "Casa Boker," which operated successful mail-order departments—to convince consumers to engage in long-distance shopping? How did the development of retail innovations such as mail-order shopping, credit, and layaway allow the male consumer to transcend his class boundaries and ethnic identity, as, increasingly, a person's appearance failed to accurately reflect his class and racial identity? Historians also need to examine the development of elite masculine domestic space, such as rooms for smoking, playing billiards, exercising, working, and displaying arms and hunting trophies. What was the consumer culture that developed around these practices? What image of masculinity did these displays attempt to cultivate and exhibit, and in so doing, what were they trying to cover up? Studies of Porfirian consumer culture also can shed light on the revolution, particularly on the lower classes' delight—not so much for sacking and pillage but, as reported in the case on northern and central haciendas, in the great bonfires of luxury goods, artwork, and furnishings that followed the revolutionary takeover of estates. Did the consuming passions of elites become a target of rites of regime desacralization? It would seem to be the case, especially because, following the defeat of Huerta in 1915, as members of the exile community in the United States and Europe sought to explain "the disaster," critics such as Querido Moheno explained the revolution as the result of the pampered elite's complacency and lack of civic engagement: "cuando los que mandan pierden la vergüenza, los que obedecen pierden el respeto" [when those who command lose their shame, those who obey do not fear them] (150). Moheno and others like Nemesio García Naranjo wrote in the San Antonio-based *Revista Mexicana* and cautioned the exile community to be on guard against the demoralizing influence of U.S. consumer culture and mass media.

Studies of consumer culture, with regard to gender, race, ethnicity, sexuality, and politics, can thus yield light on matters pertaining to Mexican history, and, as these studies are undertaken, they will better enable us to understand the process of individual self-representation and identity politics.

Notes

1. This essay is made possible thanks to a grant from the University of Wisconsin-La Crosse International Travel Fund. I also would like to thank Steven B. Bunker and C. A. Herbert for their comments, suggestions, and friendship.
2. For an overview of traditional interpretations of bourgeois women as the ideal consumer of the late nineteenth century, consult Montgomery (1998) and Beetham (1996).
3. In part, this was because of the elaborate clothing etiquette inherited from the French Second Empire. For examples, consult Comtesse de Tramar, *La moda y la elegancia,* ed. and trans. Marquesa de Fermorán (Paris: Editores-Libreros Garnier Hermanos, N.D.), 85–490 and Anonymous, *Nuevo manual de urbanidad, cortesanía, decoro y etiqueta, ó El hombre fino* (Madrid: Librería de Hijos de D. J. Cuesta, 1889).

4. There are references to Mexican collectors in the scope and content notes of institutional catalogues of the Pennsylvania Museum and others. Consult the works of Barber and Anderson.

5. Porfirio Díaz to Román S. de Lascuráin, Escuela Nacional de Bellas Artes, October 16, 1901, Box 8, Expediente 33, Archivo de la Escuela Nacional de Bellas Artes, Ramo de Instrucción Pública y Bellas Artes, Archivo General de la Nación, Mexico City. Hereafter cited as AENBA-AGN.

6. Sebastián B. de Mier, Mexican Minister to France, Paris, to José Yves Limantour, Mexico City, December 21, 1901, 2nd series, Roll 12, Archivo José Yves Limantour, Centro de Estudios de Historia de México CONDUMEX, Mexico City, hereafter cited as JYL-CONDUMEX.

7. The phrase was employed by Emilio Pardo Sabariego, minister to Belgium and the Low Countries, in a memorandum he wrote Mexican authorities complaining about the difficulty that nonelites faced in trying to break into European aristocratic circles. See Emilio Pardo, Brussels, January 9, 1903, to José Yves Limantour, Mexico City, Roll 18, 2nd Series, JYL-CONDUMEX.

8. The Limantour and Díaz Papers, as well as doña Carmelita's correspondence in the Chousal papers, contain a number of letters regarding the purchase of jewels and clothing. See Juan Antonio de Béistegui, Paris, to José Yves Limantour, Mexico City, July 26, 1902, 1st series, Roll 12, JYL-CONDUMEX; José Yves Limantour, Mexico City, to María Teresa Limantour y Cañas de Yturbe, Paris, May 22, 1907, Roll 45, 2nd series, JYL-CONDUMEX; José Yves Limantour, Paris, to Antonio Álvarez Rul, Mexico City, December 19, 1910, Roll 65, 3rd series, JYL-CONDUMEX; and Pablo Escandón, Paris, to Porfirio Díaz, Mexico City, September 4, 1900, Box 22, Expediente 233, Foja 37, Fondo Documental del Archivo de Rafael Chousal, 1860–1967, Centro de Estudios sobre la Universidad, UNAM.

9. José Yves Limantour, Mexico City, to Miguel de Yturbe, Paris, April 26, 1907, 2nd series, Roll 45, JYL-CONDUMEX.

10. José Yves Limantour, Paris, to Miguel de Béistegui, London, August 2, 1903 and August 8, 1903, Roll 18, 2nd series, JYL-CONDUMEX.

11. Various letters, dated August, September, and October 1909, in *Private and Public Correspondence of José Asúnsolo, Jefe Político of Distrito Iturbide, State of Chihuahua, Mexico* (two hundred-plus unpaginated folios dated 1908–1910 in separate binder, unnumbered frames), in MF 491, The Collection of the Archivo del Ayuntamiento de Ciudad Chihuahua, Chihuahua, Mexico, 1712–1941, Microfilm Collections, Library of the University of Texas at El Paso.

12. "Expediente relativo al remate en el montepío del Sr. Pablo Ybave, Lista de ropa," roll 2 (10 fojas, frames unnumbered), MF 513, Ciudad

Juárez, Chihuahua, Municipal Archives, 1750–1947, Microfilm Collections, Library, The University of Texas at El Paso.

13. The note observed that too many unqualified people had applied and reminded readers of the minimum requirements: "deben tener en cuenta que se necesita gente de complexión robusta, de estatura alta, y buena presencia." See "Los Guardias de la Presidencia," *El Imparcial* 4, No. 1386 (July 6, 1900): 1.

14. Shortly before World War I, a series of homosexual scandals involving friends and close collaborators of Kaiser Wilhelm II—including Minister Eulenburg—seriously compromised public trust of the German ruling circle. Consult James D. Steakley.

BIBLIOGRAPHY

ARCHIVES

AENBA-AGNArchivo de la Escuela Nacional de Bellas Artes, Ramo de Instrucción Pública y Bellas Artes, Archivo General de la Nación, Mexico City.

JYL-CONDUMEXArchivo José Yves Limantour, Centro de Estudios de Historia de México CONDUMEX, Mexico City.

FDARC-UNAMFondo Documental del Archivo de Rafael Chousal, 1860–1967, Centro de Estudios sobre la Universidad, UNAM, Mexico City.

MF 513-UTEPThe Collection of the Archivo del Ayuntamiento de Ciudad Chihuahua, Chihuahua, Mexico, 1712–1941, Microfilm Collections, Library of the University of Texas at El Paso. El Paso, Texas.

MF 491-UTEPThe Collection of the Archivo del Ayuntamiento de Ciudad Chihuahua, Chihuahua, Mexico, 1712–1941, Microfilm Collections, Library of the University of Texas at El Paso. El Paso, Texas.

PERIODICALS

Barcelona Cómica (Barcelona) 1899–1900.
El Imparcial (Mexico City) 1900.
La Vida Galante (Barcelona), 1899–1900.

SECONDARY LITERATURE

Anderson, Laurence. *El arte de la Platería en México, 1519–1936.* New York: Oxford University Press, 1941.

Auslander, Leonora. *Taste and Power: Furnishing Modern France.* Berkeley and Los Angeles: University of California Press, 1996.

Barajas, Hilarión. *Pequeño manual de usos y costumbres de México, y breve colección de algunas frases y modismos figurados, de varios refranes y de muchas otras frases latinas, impuestas unas por el buen gusto e introducidas las otras por el uso y modo común de hablar.* Mexico City: Tipografía Guadalupana de Reyes Velasco, 1901.

Barber, Edwin Atlee. *Maiolica of Mexico: Art Handbook of the Pennsylvania Museum and School of Industrial Art.* Philadelphia: Museum Memorial Hall Fairmount Park, 1908.

———. "Tin Enameled Pottery." *Pennsylvania Museum Art Primer* 5 (July 1906): 110–134.

Bederman, Gail. *Manliness and Civilization: A Cultural History of Gender and Race in the United States, 1880–1917.* Chicago and London: The University of Chicago Press, 1995.

Beetham, Margaret. *A Magazine of Her Own? Domesticity and Desire in the Woman's Magazine, 1800–1914.* London and New York: Routledge, 1996.

Castrejón, Eduardo A. *Los 41. Novela crítico-social.* Mexico City: Tipografía Popular, 1906.

Chauncey, George. *Gay New York: Gender, Urban Culture, and the Making of the Gay Male World, 1890–1940.* New York: Basic Books, 1994.

Cope, R. Douglas. *The Limits of Racial Domination: Plebeian Society in Colonial Mexico City, 1660–1720.* Madison: University of Wisconsin Press, 1994.

Deleito y Piñuela, José. *La mujer, la casa y la moda en la España del Rey Poeta,* 2nd ed. Madrid: Espasa Calpe, 1954.

D'Emilio, John. *Sexual Politics, Sexual Communities: The Making of a Homosexual Minority in the United States, 1940–1970,* 2nd ed. Chicago and London: The University of Chicago Press, 1998.

Ehrenreich, Barbara. "The Decline of Patriarchy." Maurice Berger, Brian Wallis, and Simon Watson, Eds. *Constructing Masculinity.* New York and London: Routledge, 1995: 284–290.

English-Martin, Cheryl. *Governance and Society in Colonial Mexico: Chihuahua in the Eighteenth Century.* Stanford: Stanford University Press, 1996.

Gustav-Wrathall, John Donald. *Take the Young Stranger By the Hand: Same-Sex Relations and the YMCA.* Chicago and London: The University of Chicago Press, 1998.

Hughes, Diane Owens, "La moda proibita: la legislazione suntuaria nell'Italia Rinascimentale." *Memoria: Rivista di Storia delle Donne* 11–12 (1984): 82–105.

Iturbide y Plancarte, Eduardo. *Mi paso por la vida.* Mexico City: Editorial Cultura, 1941.

Jovellanos, Gaspar Melchor de. *Memoria para el arreglo de la Policía de los espectáculos y diversiones públicos, y sobre su origen en España.* José Lage, Ed. Madrid: Ediciones Cátedra, 1979.

Lloyd-Daley, Jane Dale. *El proceso de modernización capitalista en el Noroeste de Chihuahua, 1880–1910.* Mexico City: Universidad Iberoamericana, 1987.

McCall, Laura, and Donald Yacovone, Eds. *A Shared Experience: Men, Women, and the History of Gender.* New York and London: New York University Press, 1998: 1–13.

Macías-González, Víctor M. "Curtsying in the Shadow of the Dictator: Presidential Ritual in Porfirian Mexico." Samuel Brunk and Ben Fallaw, Eds. *Heroes and Hero Cults in Latin America.* Austin: University of Texas Press, Forthcoming.

Maravall, José Antonio. *Culture of the Baroque: Analysis of a Historical Structure.* Terry Cochran, Trans. Minneapolis: University of Minnesota Press, 1986.

Margairaz, Dominique. "La querelle du luxe au XVIIIe siècle." Jacques Marseille, Ed. *Le luxe en France du siècle des "Lumières" à nos jours.* Paris: Association pour le développement de l'histoire économique, 1999: 25–37.

Martin, Percy Falcke. *Mexico of the Twentieth Century,* 2 vols. London: Edward Arnold, 1907.

Moheno Tabares, Querido. "Las clases conservadoras de México ante el desastre nacional." Antimaco Sax, Ed. *Los mexicanos en el destierro.* San Antonio: N.P., 1916: 148–151.

Montenegro, Roberto. *Planos en el tiempo: Memorias de Roberto Montenegro.* Mexico City: Artes de México and Consejo Nacional para la Cultura y las Artes, 1998.

Montgomery, Maureen E. *Displaying Women: Spectacles of Leisure in Edith Wharton's New York.* New York and London: Routledge, 1998.

Novo, Salvador. *La estatua de sal.* Mexico City: Consejo Nacional para la Cultura y las Artes, 1998.

Raquillet-Bordry, Pauline. "Le milieu diplomatique hispano-américain à Paris de 1880 à 1900." *Equipe Histoire et Societé de l'Amérique Latine, Université de Paris I.* Unpublished Manuscript.

Real Academia Española. *Diccionario de la lengua castellana en que se explica el verdadero sentido de las voces, su naturaleza, y calidad, con las frases, o modos de hablar, los proverbios ó refranes y otras cosas convenientes al uso de la lengua.* Madrid: Imprenta de Francisco del Hierro, 1726.

Rey, Alain. "Luxe, le mot et la chose." *Le luxe en France du siècle des "Lumières" à nos jours. Ed. Jacques Marseille.* Paris: Association pour le développement de l'histoire économique, 1999: 17–23.

Rivera G., José Antonio, Ed. *Reminiscencias del Ilustrísimo y Reverendísimo Sr. Dr. D. Eulogio Guillow y Zavalza, Arzobispo de Antequera.* Los Angeles: Imprenta y Linotipía de "El Heraldo de México," 1920.

Roche, Daniel. *The Culture of Clothing: Dress and Fashion in the "Ancien Regime."* Jean Birrell, Trans. Cambridge: Cambridge University Press, 1994.

Salado Álvarez, Victoriano. *Memorias, Tiempo Nuevo.* Mexico City: Edición y Distribución Ibero Americana de Publicaciones, 1946.

Scanlon, Jennifer, Ed. *The Gender and Consumer Culture Reader.* New York City: New York University Press, 2000.

Schevill, Margot Blum. *Costume as Communication: Ethnographic Costumes and Textiles from Middle America and the Central Andes of South America.* Bristol, R. I. : The Haffenreffer Museum of Anthropology of Brown University, 1986.

Sempere y Guarinos, Juan de. *Historia del luxo y de las leyes suntuarias de España,* 2 vols. Madrid: Imprenta Real, 1788.

Steakley, James D. "Iconography of a Scandal: Political Cartoons and the Eulenburg Affair in Wilhelmine Germany," George Chauncey, Jr., Martin Bauml Duberman, and Martha Vicinus, Eds. *Hidden from History: Reclaiming the Gay and Lesbian Past.* New York: New American Library, 1989: 233–263.

Tablada, José Juan. *La Feria de la Vida.* Mexico City: Fondo de Cultura Económica, 1991.

———. *Diario, 1900–1944.* Guillermo Sheridan, Ed. Mexico City: Universidad Nacional Autónoma de México, 1992.

———. *Las sombras largas.* Mexico City: Consejo para la Cultura y las Artes, 1993.

Tweedie, Ethel Brilliana Harley. *Mexico As I Saw It.* London, Edinburgh, Dublin and New York: Thomas Nelson and Sons, 1911.

Interpretations of Sexuality in Mexico City Prisons

A CRITICAL VERSION OF ROUMAGNAC

Pablo Piccato

Para que el cielo de la heterosexualidad exista, se requiere fijar, con saña minuciosa, el infierno de los homosexuales.

—*Carlos Monsiváis,*
Salvador Novo: Lo marginal en el centro

Between 1906 and 1912, Carlos Roumagnac published three books about Mexican criminals based on interviews with inmates of the prisons of Belem and San Lázaro, in Mexico City (*Los criminales en México; Crimenes sexuales y pasionales; Matadores de mujeres*). The books attracted an audience that went beyond the narrow circles of social scientists and, in recent years, have become important documents for our knowledge of everyday life in late Porfirian Mexico. These detailed accounts of inmates' words and deeds exercise a strong attraction because of the rich information they contain and because of their author's ability to condense the ambivalent gaze of criminology toward the everyday life of the urban poor. Roumagnac and other criminologists explored urban life looking for "the criminal"—that creature imagined by the Italian positivist master Cesare Lombroso as the product of immorality and racial backwardness. In Mexico City, amateurs and professionals of criminology, such as Federico Gamboa, Miguel Macedo, and Julio Guerrero, described and speculated about the dark corners of a city that was growing out of the control of Porfirian urban planners and policemen. Criminology provided a scientific vocabulary to document the fascinated wanderings of modern *flâneurs* and customary patrons of the city's seedy night life (Piccato, "Construcción").

The darkest corner of the city was Belem prison. The prevalent view was best portrayed by the verses of one Enrique Valay in *El Diablito Rojo:*

> La humanidad prostituida
> que en tus recintos se alberga,
> adquiere vicios infames
> tras de tus muros de piedra;
>
> En amores asquerosos
> Ofende a Naturaleza,
> y con vil marihuana
> disipa (?) todas tus penas.
>
> Cárcel que guardas al crimen
> entre muros y entre rejas,
> eres del vicio la madre,
> eres infame y abjecta!

[Prostituted humanity / which dwells in your rooms, / acquiring nefarious vices / behind your walls of stone. // In disgusting loves / offends Nature / and with vile marijuana / dissipates (?) your pains. // Jail which keeps crime/ between walls and behind bars, / you are the mother of vice, / you are infamous and abject]. (3, I owe this reference to Robert Buffington)

In a modified version of this perspective, criminologists saw the place as their own laboratory, where the criminal population congregated and immorality ruled (Martínez Baca 5). Over the cranial measurements of the prison population practiced by Lombroso and other Mexican colleagues, however, Carlos Roumagnac, a former journalist, emphasized the direct questioning of inmates. In interviews that followed a common pattern, he asked criminals about their offenses and their past, their inheritance and their beliefs, and registered additional evidence he considered of interest. That was the shortest way, he believed, to get at the heart of "los mundos del delito" [the worlds of crime]—as read the book series title. As an appendix to the first volume, he reproduced pictures of "dos casos de hermafroditismo" [two cases of hermaphroditism]—unrelated to the interviews but sharing the morbid association of deviant sexuality and crime sung by Valay.

Roumagnac, therefore, would have never expected his books to become, 90 years later, primary sources for the history of sexuality.

One can only imagine his surprise in seeing his interviews with characters he considered the basest examples of modern immorality, turned into evidence about the sexual practices of Mexican society at large. Imagine a Belem inmate sitting side by side with the highest point of the moral and sexual pyramid of the Mexican population proposed by Julio Guerrero in *La génesis del crimen en México:* the Creole, faithful, upper-class "señora decente" [decent lady], an exquisite "variedad psíquica de la especie humana" [psychical variety of the human species], the opposite of "the criminal" (111). In 1933, Roumagnac returned to write about Belem for *El Nacional,* and noted without much regret that his criminological writings were now forgotten. In contrast, he fondly remembered his times as a journalist, in the 1880s.[1] Even though his knowledge about "los mundos del delito" still brought him readers in the 1930s, he never overcame the social distance and moral condemnation that were the foundations of positivist criminology.

Yet, *Los criminales en México* and its sequels have become the urtext for recent historical studies that, inspired by Michel Foucault's work, look in penal institutions for the essential machinery of modern power (Sagredo; Barrón; Piccato, *City of Suspects*). From the studies supported by Roumagnac's interviews, those by Robert Buffington and Martin Nesvig deserve particular attention here. They have used Roumagnac with great care to support theses concerning sexual mores and ideologies of national degeneration. Robert Buffington, for example, has built a strong argument about the construction of sexual identities from prisons, focusing on those "heavily stigmatized effeminate sexual inverts" ("Los jotos" 137). Both differ regarding the political meaning of homosexuality, as they present alternative interpretations about the social condemnation of passive and active homosexuality. While Nesvig sees all, active and passive "pederasts," stigmatized by Mexican culture ("Lure"), Buffington understands homosexual relations in prison in the context of the conflation of machismo and political resistance that filtered through inmates' voices. Both agree on "the difficulty of discussing issues like homosexuality," in Buffington's words (140), to the extent that, according to Nesvig, "the historian is obliged to go past textual analysis and attempt to speculate on the nature of the cultural values of Porfirian Mexico"("Lure" 35).

The main goal of this essay is to take a critical look at Roumagnac's interviews as a historical source, particularly as they seek to document "el infierno de los homosexuales" [the homosexual inferno]. The question is not so much whether these interviews are useful (they are) but what can be known through them. The discussion must move away from the common emphasis on the overwhelming success of institutions of social control and look at its resistances and failures—a fruitful perspective on other prison systems (Linebaugh 3; Zedner; Ignatieff). To do so, I will take a close look at prison life in the early twentieth century, with the help of new evidence in the archives of Belem prison, recently made available at the Archivo Histórico del Distrito Federal.

Roumagnac persistently questioned prisoners about sex. He asked them if they masturbated, practiced oral or anal sex, and enquired about their families' mores. (He did not deal with homosexuality as a crime. Scandals such as those of "the 41," he said, "pertenecen más bien al estudio de hábitos y costumbres sociales corrompidos" [rather belong in the study of corrupted habits and customs], to which he promised to devote a future book—to be titled "La mala vida en México," apparently never printed (*Crímenes sexuales* 152).

In some cases, prisoners responded to Roumagnac's prodding and talked about their own experiences and those of fellow inmates. But answers came out reluctantly: the interviewees preferred to accuse than to confess. They were reluctant to talk about sex for the same reasons they refused to debate the crimes of which they had been accused. Judges often deemed confessions enough evidence to convict, never as an extenuating circumstance. Although Roumagnac did not officially represent the judiciary or the police, inmates were right in believing that their statements could become material to further identify them as criminal. Let me reproduce one example of this reticence in the interview with Victoriano A.

> —¿A cuántos años está usted sentenciado?
> —A veinte años.
> —¿Por qué lo sentenciaron?
> —Porque no tuve testigos.
> —¿Por qué?
> —Porque fue de noche.
> —Pero ¿qué?
> —La cuestión.
> —¿Cuál?
> —Por lo que estoy.
> —Pero ¿por qué está usted?
> —Por homicidio

[How many years were you sentenced to? / Twenty years./ Why were you sentenced? / Because I did not have witnesses./ Why? / Because it was at night. / But, what? / The thing. / Which thing? / The thing I am here for. / But, why are you here? / Murder.] (*Los criminales* 244).

This silence, documented also by Federico Gamboa (58, 36), was buttressed by prisoners' lack of adequate legal counsel or even knowledge about the terms of their sentences.

An additional reason for this reluctance was the fact that prisoners shared prevalent notions about the dangers of sexual intercourse. They believed intense sexual activity, including but not limited to homosexual intercourse, was morally wrong, unnatural, and divorced from legitimate heterosexual desire. Juan D. I., 15 years old, declared that he no longer masturbated, because "la naturaleza es como una copa: mientras más se va llenando, más se derrama" [nature is like a goblet: the more it fills, the more it spills] (88). Timoteo Andrade, a prisoner who had had military rank, explained how sexual life in prison could damage the body. In Belem, he told Roumagnac, he "abused" his "access to women," provoking symptoms of impotence and insomnia. Now in the penitentiary, lacking the opportunity to indulge in his desires, he felt better and his health had improved again (339). Rafael N. believed that his grandfather "le gustaban mucho las mujeres y al morir la esposa tomó otra y eso lo mató tal vez" [liked women too much, and took another wife after his first wife died, and that probably killed him] (304). Furthermore, if a man abused homosexual intercourse, said another prisoner, he could suffer "colic" (307).

Both medicine and popular knowledge associated sexual deviance with insanity and disease. According to a Mexican textbook on forensic medicine, hyperesthesia was a common form of alienation that included immoderate sexual activity and masturbation (Ramírez 170–173). Switching sexual roles was a personality disorder, classified among other forms of madness. Suspects could use these notions to their benefit. Alberto T., who participated in an escape attempt in 1887, managed to avoid punishment by faking madness. To do so, he masturbated in public, even during the doctor's visits, and spoke "con verdadero cinismo de su vida íntima" [with true cynicism about his intimate life] (*Crímenes sexuales* 62). This may have been a recourse against prosecution, but it also expressed commonly held beliefs about mental illness, sex, and transgression. The following passage illustrates the guilt that surrounded prisoners' pursuit of pleasure. It comes from the interview with Manuel T.:

T. ha sufrido varios castigos por habérsele encontrado marihuana. Adquirió el vicio en la cárcel, y la primera vez que fumó esa yerba, "sintió una pesadez de cuerpo, no tuvo alientos para nada, tuvo pensamientos, imaginaciones (alucinaciones), figurándose que estaba libre y otras cosas" . . . al principio debe haberse puesto como loco. En una ocasión en que se "descompasó" (se propasó) en fumar, empezó a sentir cosas feas en el cerebro y en la espina y luego sufrió un gran derrame seminal que terminó con algo de sangre; no sabe en qué estado se hallaba y sólo recuerda que se imaginaba efectuar el coito con una mujer. Desde entonces, cree que ha perdido sus facultades genésicas

[T. has been punished several times for possession of marijuana. He acquired the vice in jail, and the first time he smoked this plant "felt his body heavy, lost his breath, had thoughts, imaginations (hallucinations), believing that he was free and other things" . . . at the beginning he must have behaved like an insane person. On one occasion that he smoked too much he began to have disgusting feelings in his brain and spine and then suffered a great ejaculation that ended with some blood. He does not know his state at the time, only remembering that he was fantasizing about having intercourse with a woman. Since then, he believes, he has lost his reproductive ability]. (209–10)

Sex, even imagined sex, was unhealthy. As we will see later, we should not understand these statements as apologies of abstinence. They make sense, I will argue, only when we place them in the context of the lack of hygiene, labor exploitation, and official use of violence that characterized Belem prison.

Venereal diseases were prevalent inside prison. Young Juan D. I., cited above, had blennorrhagia. Other illnesses, such as typhoid fever, were often fatal among prisoners and personnel. The prison flooded and was infested with all kinds of pests. The food was bad and scarce, so most prisoners had to work to pay for meals brought from outside (García Icazbalceta 160–161; Frías 51–54; González de Cosío 849).

The institution's structure only added to these problems. Because of the many rooms, patios, and hallways of the former convent, surveillance was very difficult. The staff was small and poorly paid. To this, authorities responded with a system of vigilance based on the participation of a select group of inmates skilled in the use of violence and closely linked to the warden and guards. They were called *presidentes* (one per each section) and *mayores*. Armed with sticks, they subdued troublemakers and enforced authorities' orders. They were paid less than guards but, as guards, could profit from bribes extracted from prisoners and their families. As guards and the warden, *presi-*

dentes and *mayores* also benefited from the labor of inmates with a percentage of the sales (González de Cosío 866; *Los criminales* 208n). Because vigilance was constructed around close personal relationships between guards and prisoners, the distance that was supposed to separate them was small. Prisoners were divided by social differences marked by their cells' location, property of furniture and other goods, access to authorities and by control, and, in some cases, ownership of prison workshops. These hierarchies also built links across the boundaries established by the law. Guards could have romantic relations with inmates. Journalists, often imprisoned by Porfirio Díaz's regime, could become close friends with the warden. Roumagnac himself is an example: he was imprisoned in the 1880s as a result of the government's pressure against a newspaper he edited. Accompanied by guards, he was able to walk through Belem's sections and explore the world of criminals. Years later, positivist criminology and his work as secretary in police stations only gave a legitimate framework to what was an old curiosity. He returned to prison and methodically compiled the evidence about that world. In 1906, the registry book of Belem shows his name as an inmate again (personal communication, Martín Barrón)—although no specific crime is cited and I have found no additional evidence to corroborate this.

One consequence of this structure of governance was that prisoners had access to drugs, alcohol, and sex. In 1863, Inspector Joaquín García Icazbalceta found that gambling, drinking, and violence were rife in Belem prison. García Icazbalceta, like many later observers, considered Belem a "foco de corrupción" [focus of corruption] and an "escuela de inmoralidad" [school of immorality] (71). In the eyes of penal reformers, the result was the unacceptable fact that prisoners, at least some of them, seemed to enjoy a degree of happiness.

This brings us to an additional reason for inmates' reluctance to talk about their intimate life: sex was both part of prison labor and the most prestigious way to profit from power. Disciplinary and spatial restrictions to sexual activity were not effective, least of all against those among prisoners and staff with resources and influence. Female prisoners were commonly besieged and sexually harassed by employees (who were all male). Resistance only led to solitary confinement or violence.[2] Francisco R. bribed employees and used his position as mayor to be able to meet with female partners after hours at the infirmary or the court offices (*Criminales* 359). Drawing on the same mechanisms as other social interactions, sex often involved money and violence, but also protection.

However strange this may sound, some of these unequal relationships were often articulated as love. Violence could stem from jealousy. A male inmate killed his friend in prison, reported the journalist and inmate Heriberto Frías, because both shared a female lover. Less prejudiced than Roumagnac by scientific views of criminals as immoral beings, Frías saw this and others as crimes of passion (53, 56–60). Roumagnac documented how love, the yearning for stable relationships, mobilized prisoners' emotional and social resources. María Villa, La Chiquita, who was in prison because of her own kind of passion crime (she had killed a fellow prostitute for the love of an upper-class man), had successive relationships with two male inmates. With one of them, María hoped to establish marital life after they left prison. She broke off the relationship, in spite of his promises and threats, when she discovered that he had married another woman, also inside prison. Francisco R., mentioned above, sent María clothes, shoes, and letters. At first, María rejected him because he was "un hombre, de una esfera muy baja, es indigno de mí" [a man of too low a social sphere, not appropriate for me], but finally she gave in to his desires because she felt gratitude for his protection (121–123).

Relationships such as María's were not exclusive to heterosexual couples. Inmate Timoteo A. acquired letters exchanged between "pederasts," to use his vocabulary, in which "besides words of innocent love, they sent each other kisses, by printing their lips with lipstick on the paper." Catalina S. found similar letters in the women's section (330, 190–191).

The parallels between the two sections appear to end there. Homosexuality among men was shrouded by an image of violence that seemed to reduce sex to domination. In the men's department, Manuel T. saw "savage rapes, against poor devils who were first inebriated and then abused by ten or twelve men in front of everyone else in the room!" (210). Same-sex intercourse expressed the subordination of the penetrated partner. It also was a means for guards to obtain money from prisoners. In 1910, two guards were fired because they pimped a "pederasta conocido" [well-known pederast] to other male inmates.[3] According to Juan D. I., older boys had "two or three kids who would allow anyone to perform filthy things on them in exchange for any trifle." They would form a large circle, and have "niños" (boys) masturbate them or endure, as Juan himself did, their "doing it" to them (88, 210; also Frías, "Crónicas" 50–51). In an apparent expression of these uses, male homosexuals there were divided in caballos, the "passive," and *mayates,* the "active" (*Criminales* 77–78n).

I contend, however, that it is possible to go beyond this dichotomy in reading Roumagnac's interviews. Testimonies about love, passivity, or exploitation could not be straightforward, because they seemed to imply subordination and because they confronted negative views about homosexuality. Admitting to homosexual uses could be costly. Even though same-sex intercourse was not prohibited by the 1871 Penal Code, prison regulations established that inmates who were "pederasts," regardless of their legal situation, would be isolated in the section of *separos* and would not be allowed to communicate with other prisoners (González de Cosío 862, 870). Male guards who maintained "intimate relationships" with male prisoners were fired. Such was the case of Pablo Esqueda, a prison guard who was arrested for a month and then fired after he was found to be a "pederast."[4] More important, prisoners' admission into the judicial and penal system placed them in an institutional and discursive context, faithfully reproduced by Roumagnac, that accentuated the immorality and the public nature of their intimacy. Violence, therefore, was a natural companion to male homosexuality. Rape, in particular, seemed the defining practice of "el infierno de los homosexuales" in Belem.

Beyond a first look, however, an emphasis on violence and silence would miss the complexity of relationships and the continuum of experiences and desires that characterized everyday life in prison. Domination and sex were not linked by a blanket condemnation of homosexuality but, to quote Eve Kosofsky Sedgwick, by "the power of cognitively dividing and hence manipulating the male homosocial spectrum" (86, 88–89). Prisoners and guards may benefit from denouncing homosexuals, but they also could build stable relationships, both heterosexual and homosexual, in which protection did not exclude pleasure.

How was the "homosocial spectrum" manipulated in Belem? Male homosexual desire had multiple opportunities to assume a public character. Men spent long hours out in the patios, where washing and doing the laundry made nudity common. If authorities attempted to isolate "known pederasts," they only encouraged the exhibition of transsexual identities. Frías described the *jotos* with an ambivalent mixture of moral condemnation and appreciation for the "rare comradeship" that characterized their relationships:

Abundan estos hombres afeminados en Belem en el patio de años donde, no obstante que se les desprecia, viven con costumbres enteramente femeniles. Tienen la voz tipluda y dan a sus frases una entonación de mujer melindrosa o asustadiza; afectan contorsiones nerviosas—¡oh, muchos las tienen por naturaleza!—, visten lo más

aproximadamente que les es posible conforme a trajes femeninos; llevan alias de prostitutas como: la Diabla, la China, la Pancha, etc., y se
dedican a planchar, lavar, tejer, bordar y guisar.

[There are many of these effeminate men in Belem . . . where, [they]
live with entirely feminized habits. They have soprano voices, and speak
with the intonation of an affected and skittish woman . . . they dress as
much like women as they can; they bear prostitutes' nicknames, like la
Diabla, la China, la Pancha, and devote themselves to ironing, doing
laundry, knitting, embroidering and cooking]. (Frías 61)

This defiant openness could not have survived without some degree of acceptance, perhaps even favor, from the rest of the prison
population. More interestingly, it undermined moral condemnation.
Roumagnac's own detailed description of "el desfile de esos degenerados sexuales, que pasaban delante de los demás detenidos, sin
rubor ni vergüenza, haciendo, por el contrario, alarde de voces y
modales afeminados" [that parade of sexual degenerates, strolling in
front of the arrested, without shame, making feminized voices and
movements] (*Criminales* 77), betrays the success of those inmates in
evoking desirable female bodies. According to Guillermo Mellado,
doing the laundry for male prisoners became a successful business for
los jotos, who even took work from outside the prison (30–33).

In the women's department, the signs of the subversion were less
scandalous. In other words, female homosociability and homosexuality were less explicit in terms of the manifestations of gender roles.
There was no "pederasts" section for women nor, as far as the evidence is available, the public and collective embrace of transgender
images. According to Roumagnac, ever so keen to find taxonomic cri-
teria, female homosexuals who "desempeñan el papel masculino"
[play the male role] parted their hair on the right side, and the others
on the left. Female partners also expressed their love by taking care of
their companions, and fighting for them "con tanta o más furia que
los hombres" [with as much fury, or maybe more, than men]—as
Roumagnac gallantly admitted (174). Yet, the link between sex and
violence seems to have been weaker in the women's section.

The structure of vigilance practiced by male inmates was diluted
among women, and the separation between sentenced and suspects
was not applied. Social life seemed to follow a more consensual
course than in the men's department, and inequality was not so
clearly linked to the use of force. The evidence suggests that authority did not derive exclusively from official patronage. María Villa be-

came mayora of the entire department but, when she was separated from her duty, female inmates rebelled (131). According to Roumagnac, "todos los informes" [all reports] indicated that "practica el safismo con sus codetenidas" [she practices saphism with her fellow inmates] (112).

Relationships between women were formalized through the practice of *madrinazgo*. The *madrina*, or godmother, would sponsor another inmate by placing a scapulary of the Virgen de la Soledad or a *medida*—a ribbon the size of a saint's face—around her neck, and then praying the "Our Father" three times. This ceremony intended to protect the sponsored *ahijada* before she was to appear in court (136). The institution of *madrinazgo* clearly illustrates the reasons and characteristics of solidarity among female prisoners. Relieved from the social condemnation focused on male transgendered identities, women seemed to be better able to avoid the linking of homosexual desire with violence and pathological anomaly. Echoing views about sex and disease cited earlier, María Isabel M. stated that women, after all, were able to resist long years without sexual intercourse because "para nosotros no nos hace mucha fuerza" [we do not have such a strong need] (153). For most male inmates, however, life in prison was not an exploration of the possibilities of sexual desire but a constant defense and negotiation of masculinity. Being in prison radically constrained men's ability to control and exert their normative heterosexual identity. I noted above inmates' fears about sexual activity and disease. Having erections was "lo principal del hombre" [the main thing of a man], according to Manuel T., who had lost that ability in prison (206). More important, male identity was rooted in ideas and practices about "being a man" that brought many of them to prison in the first place. Masculinity obliged one to follow one's desires while fulfilling the expectations of other people—the automatic obedience to violence and desire. Coward, defined Francisco M., "es el que tiene miedo para pegar" [is he who's afraid to hit] (81). Many were in prison because of a scrupulous concern about reputation: Juan D. I. killed a coworker who ridiculed him for returning one peso that he had mistakenly received over his salary (85). Juan A. raped a ten-year-old girl. His justification was that she invited him, and he did not want to "faltar a ser hombre" [avoid being a man], thus following intercourse with the promise of marriage (*Crímenes sexuales y pasionales* 116).

Incarceration undermined the ability to protect attributes of manhood such as the active defense of women and property. A revealing example was a letter, found by the police in a raid against counterfeiters, in which a man who was in Belem warned his wife that he knew that she "lo estaba ofendiendo con otros" [was offending him with other men] and using his tools to produce coins, thus promised to take revenge after he was released (*El Imparcial,* January 22, 1900 3).

Given the limits imposed on legitimate heterosexual relations in prison, most inmates were restricted in their means to be men. Thus, they had to be swift in acting like such. This explains, I believe, why male sexuality in Belem tended to express itself in violent ways and to be closer to the structure of power, and why it was construed by observers as a stark divider between active and passive partners. "Being a man," therefore, also meant projecting male desire—albeit in a swift and brutal way—on other men's bodies. Broad condemnation of homosexuality and the seemingly contradictory acceptance of normal yet secret virility of active homosexuals were reconciled in an ethical obligation to use violence. Placing these reactions in the context of notions of honor and shame offers little help if doing so means referring to general "paradigms" to understand the dichotomy active/passive and ignoring the specific social relations that inform cultural meanings (Nesvig, "Lure" 6–7; Nesvig, "Complicated" 69).[5]

Yet, male violence introduces a deceiving sense of order in our effort to place sex in its context. The distinctions between the modalities of sexual desire were not as neat as they should have been according to scientists, and there were no clear lines between autonomy and obedience, between the dominant and the dominated. In Belem, playing with power was as necessary as playing with gender. As a consequence, the use of gendered dichotomies (homosexual/heterosexual, active/passive) renders a mechanical image of sex and power in prison. Instead of identifying "roles," I contend that looking for individual predispositions toward gender definitions, the cultural conditions of their possibility, and a sharper view of social relations in prison offers a more promising path for research. Thus, I would suggest that, with its emphasis on identities rather than practices, the history of homosexuality, as a field of study, builds artificial boundaries around phenomena that, inside and outside prison, involved broader cultural patterns concerning desire and power.[6]

The contribution of this essay to the growing literature on prison life and sexuality derived from Roumagnac can be summarized in an argument that would seem obvious; namely, that sexuality cannot be studied as pure discourse, even if it is a discourse about identity. Narratives so powerful as those produced by Roumagnac show that practices, no matter how marginal or "immoral," shaped narratives. On the one hand, sexual exchanges were a central component of every-day life in prison and gave a focus to scientific observations. On the other hand, the structure of vigilance and class difference determined the limits and ambivalence of those exchanges and, therefore, our sources.

The sort of contextualization I propose would, perhaps, solve the dilemma faced by the historian Philippe Artières when editing French prisoners' autobiographical writings. After much debating among available interpretations about prison technologies, resistance, and identity, Artières chose simply to publish the documents—as gestures of freedom by men whose crimes had suddenly made their every movement the object of observation. Artières's proposal, in other words, assumes the limits of any historical interpretation, and the darkness at the heart of sources produced by fundamentally strange subjects (13, 25, 36, 422–424, 425). In her own study of interviews between criminological staff and prisoners in the province of Buenos Aires, Lila Caimari is somewhat more positive about the use of this kind of data. She understands interviews in prison "as the point of encounter of two very different symbolic universes," making "the di-alogue . . . itself an eloquent source." Yet, her conclusions do not go beyond that chasm: those "two universes . . . could only see each other partially," as the prisoners selectively appropriated criminolog-ical notions and filtered the information about their lives (5, 23). "Speculation," then, would seem the only solution.

A historical contextualization, I argue, is the only way to transcend the ambivalence that seems to limit the use of prisoners' testimonies. There is no novelty in the method but, at least, a path to build a more constructive dialogue with our sources and with the disciplines, such as criminology, and the institutions, such as prisons, that shape histo-rians' views. Lucia Zedner's study of women in English prisons offers an example of the possibilities at hand. She found guardians and in-mates to be closer, socially and emotionally, than the traditional and revised history of Western prisons had managed to perceive. Their re-lationships, much as those in Belem prison, involved sexual intimacy and "a carefully placed dividing line between emotional attachment and lesbianism" that was "not always easy to discern" (161–162).

There was no "cielo de la heterosexualidad" [heterosexuality heaven] in Belem. There was, however, a systematic effort by au-thorities and educated observers to create a self-contained space in which violence would accompany sex in the "infierno de los homo-sexuales." As I suggested earlier, a careful look at the woman's sec-tion of Belem could shed light on the role of desire and love in relations that, in the men's section, were distorted by cultural views about the risks of sex and the fusion of violence and masculinity.

NOTES

1. Carlos Roumagnac, "Recuerdos de Belem," *El Nacional,* July 23, 1933, second sec., 2. Roumagnac (1869–1937) was born in Madrid and died in Mexico, "in poverty." Alfonso Quiroz Cuarón, *Tendencia y ritmo de la criminalidad en México* (Mexico City: Instituto de Investigaciones Estadísticas, 1939): 129.
2. *Los criminales en México* 191. Yet, for a guard fired for keeping "relaciones ilícitas" with a married female inmate at the boquete, see Dosamantes, August 10, 1901, Archivo Histórico del Distrito Federal, Cárcel de Belén (hereafter AHDF, CB), 31, 1051, and W. Vázquez to Secretario de Gobierno del Distrito Federal, August 3, 1909, AHDF, CB, 31, 1067. On a guard's attempt to rape a female prisoner and his dismissal, see W. Vázquez to Secretario de Gobierno del Distrito Federal, November 14, 1905, AHDF, CB, 8, 282.
3. Unreadable signature to Secretario de Gobierno del Distrito Federal, February 26, 1910, AHDF, CB, 33, 1107.
4. Letter signed by Dosamantes, April 19, 1911, AHDF, CB, 1329.
5. But see Annick Prieur, "Domination and Desire: Male Homosexuality and the Construction of Masculinity in Mexico," in *Machos, Mistresses, Madonnas: Contesting the Power of Latin American Gender Imagery,* ed. Marit Melhuus and Kristi Anne Stolen (London: Verso, 1996), 83–107. For critical views of the Mediterranean model of honor, see David Gilmore, "Introduction: The Shame of Dishonor" in Gilmore, ed., *Honor and Shame and the Unity of the Mediterranean* (Washington, DC: American Anthropological Association, 1987), 3; Michael Herzfeld, "'As in Your Own House': Hospitality, Ethnography, and the Stereotype of Mediterranean Society," in *Honor and Shame,* 75, 87–88.
6. Nesvig, "The Complicated," dismisses the questions raised by violence as part of homosexual practices as the result of "situational homosexuality" in prisons, see page 717. But also see Prieur, *Mema's House.* For a critique of sex role theory, see R. W. Connell, *Masculinities* (Berkeley: University of California Press, 1995); Lynne Segal, *Slow Motion: Changing Masculinities, Changing Men* (New Brunswick: Rutgers University Press, 1990).

BIBLIOGRAPHY

Artières, Philippe, Ed. *Le livre des vies coupables: Autobiographies de criminels (1896–1909).* Paris: Albin Michel, 2000.

Barrón Cruz, Martín Gabriel. "Bosquejo histórico. La cárcel de Belén y el sistema carcelario." Héctor Madrid, Rosa María Luna and Leonor Estevez, Eds. *Catalógo de Documentos de la cárcel de Belén (1900–1910)*, Mexico City: Archivo Histórico del Distrito Federal: 9–89.

Buffington, Robert. "Los Jotos: Contested Visions of Homosexuality in Modern Mexico." Daniel Balderston and Donna Guy, Eds. *Sex and Sexuality in Latin America*. New York: New York University Press, 1997: 118–32.

———. *Criminal and Citizen in Modern Mexico*. Lincoln: University of Nebraska, 1999.

Caimari, Lila. "Remembering Freedom: Life as Seen From the Prison Cell (Buenos Aires Province, 1900–1950)." Paper presented at the conference "The Contested Terrains of Law, Justice, and Repression in Latin American History," Yale University, April 1997.

Frías, Heriberto. "Crónicas desde la cárcel." *Historias* 11 (Oct. - Dec. 1985): 47–71.

Gamboa, Federico. *La llaga*. 1st ed. 1903. Mexico City: Eusebio Gómez de la Puente, 1922.

García Icazbalceta, Joaquín. *Informe sobre los establecimientos de beneficencia y corrección de esta capital; su estado actual; noticia de sus fondos; reformas que desde luego necesitan y plan general de su arreglo presentado por José María Andrade*. Mexico City: Moderna Librería Religiosa, 1907.

González de Cosío, Manuel. *Memoria que presenta al Congreso de la Unión el General . . . Secretario de Estado y del Despacho de Gobernación*. Mexico City: Imprenta del Gobierno Federal, 1900.

Guerrero, Julio. *La génesis del crimen en México: estudio de psiquiatría social*. Paris: Viuda de Charles Bouret, 1901.

Ignatieff, Michael. *A Just Measure of Pain: The Penitentiary in the Industrial Revolution*. London: Penguin, 1978.

Linebaugh, Peter. *The London Hanged: Crime and Civil Society in the Eighteenth Century*. New York: Cambridge University Press, 1992.

Martínez Baca, Francisco, and Manuel Vergara. *Estudios de Antropología Criminal*. Puebla: Benjamín Lara, 1892.

Mellado, Guillermo *Belén por dentro y por fuera*. Mexico City: Cuadernos Criminalia, 1959.

Nesvig, Martin. "The Complicated Terrain of Latin American Homosexuality." *Hispanic American Historical Review* 81:3–4 (2001): 689–729.

———. "The Lure of the Perverse: Moral Negotiation of Pederasty in Porfirian Mexico." *Mexican Studies / Estudios Mexicanos* 16:1 (Winter 2000): 1–37.

Piccato, Pablo. *City of Suspects: Crime in Mexico City, 1900–1931*. Durham: Duke University Press, 2001.

———. "La construcción de una perspectiva científica: miradas porfirianas a la criminalidad." *Historia Mexicana* 187:1 (1997): 133–181.

Prieur, Annick. *Mema's House, Mexico City: On Transvestites, Queens, and Machos.* Chicago: University of Chicago Press, 1998.

Ramirez, Román. *Resúmen de medicina legal y ciencias conexas para uso de los estudiantes de las escuelas de derecho.* Mexico City: Tipografía de Fomento, 1901.

Roumagnac, Carlos. *Crímenes sexuales y pasionales: Estudios de psicología morbosa* vol. 1 *Crímenes sexuales.* Mexico City: Librería de Bouret, 1906.

———. *Los criminales en México: Ensayo de psicología criminal. Seguido de dos casos de hermafrodismo observado por los señores doctores Ricardo Egea . . . Ignacio Ocampo.* Mexico City: Tipografía El Fénix, 1904.

———. *Matadores de mujeres (Segunda parte de "Crímenes Sexuales y Pasionales").* Mexico City: Bouret, 1910.

Sagredo Baeza, Rafael. *María Villa (a) La Chiquita, no. 4002: Un parásito social del Porfiriato.* Mexico City: Cal y Arena, 1996.

Sedgwick, Eve Kosofsky. *Between Men: English Literature and Male Homosocial Desire.* New York: Columbia University Press, 1985.

Valay, Enrique. "A la cárcel de Belem." *El Diablito Rojo,* December 13, 1909: 3.

Zedner, Lucia. *Women, Crime, and Custody in Victorian England.* Oxford, Clarendon Press, 1991.

Beyond Medicalization

ASYLUM DOCTORS AND INMATES PRODUCE SEXUAL KNOWLEDGE AT THE GENERAL INSANE ASYLUM *LA CASTAÑEDA* IN LATE PORFIRIAN MEXICO

Cristina Rivera-Garza

Many of the arguments used to discuss the formation of dominant gender roles and sexual practices in Porfirian Mexico made reference to or directly employed medical language in their quest for validation and legitimacy. The *ángel del hogar,* that cherished image of the Porfirian good woman, not only embodied notions of virtue and morality after all, but, with rosy cheeks and agile limbs, she also personified good health both physical and mental.[1] Likewise, the prostitute, her wicked counterpart, came usually wrapped in images of vice and wretchedness whose ultimate end, and unfathomable source, was disease of both the soul and the body (Rivera-Garza, "Criminalization" 147–180; Bliss 167–194). Constructions of masculinity did not escape this treatment. Productive and moral men were, by definition, healthy. Men of frail physical condition and dubious habits, among which alcohol consumption and masturbation mattered much, had little chance to become role models.[2] Although these kinds of associations between health and morality gained indeed increasing acceptance in Porfirian Mexico—clear indication of the higher levels of professionalization of medicine—little is known, however, about the actual human interaction between doctor and patient from which these concepts came into being. I invite the reader of this essay to enter such space: the observation room of the General Insane Asylum *La Castañeda,* the largest state institution devoted to the care of mentally ill men, women, and children in late Porfirian Mexico,

where prospective inmates and medical interns first faced one another, exchanging information that substantiated or questioned accepted notions of mental illness and mental health in which the issue
of sexuality played a prominent role (Rivera-Garza, *Mad Narratives*).

The possibility to spy over the innuendoes of the psychiatric interview is relevant for studies on Porfirian sexuality for a variety of
reasons. Studies on gender and sexuality in Latin America and
abroad have rightfully resorted to medical writings in order to explore some of the discursive strategies used by professionals and
other social commentators of the era to construct dominant notions
of sexual interchange—notions that came to privilege heterosexuality and monogamy, and to condemn much everything else. Whereas
the medicalization of society involved, in the words of Arthur
Kleinman, a "widespread process in Western societies, whereby
problems previously labeled and managed as moral, religious, or
criminal are redefined as disorder and dealt with through therapeutic technology" (26), it often is assumed that writing doctors, frequently male and middle class, produced that body of knowledge
based on vague, foreign influenced, and heavily ideological notions
of proper female and male behaviors. In this view, an all-powerful,
savvy male physician used patients much in way of parapets—voice-
less and inert, patients were there only to substantiate, whether
through silent acquiescence or senseless stuttering, the medical interpretations that congregated doctor and patient in the first place.
Although this claim is not entirely false, it does miss, however, one
important fact: as aspiring men of science, as positivist thinkers keen
on empirical evidence, doctors required the participation of patients' voices and views in order to produce the knowledge that, according to their own standards and aspirations, would later validate
them as true scientists of the era. Likewise, as people with few opportunities to address the sources and evolution of their physical
and mental conditions, asylum inmates pressed doctors, often suc-
cessfully, to listen to their stories closely. Evidence from the General
Insane Asylum *La Castañeda*, especially the information collected
in the official questionnaire that guided the entry psychiatric interview and that, in conjunction with routine observations made at the
various wards, constituted the medical file, largely confirms this
view. If this is true, as I argue it is in this essay, narrow views of
medicalization processes from the Porfirian era—especially those
defined along rigid lines that assume an ascending dominance of
medical language over and in social understandings of reality—will
require critical reviewing.[3]

Of all the doctor-patient interactions, however, the one taking place at a state asylum is perhaps the least likely to incite in the reader images of dynamism and volatility. Ever since the emergence of the antipsychiatry literature in the early 1970s, a commonly accepted picture of insane asylums depicts them as sites of social control, totalitarian and deeply hierarchical institutions in which all-powerful administrative and medical authorities manipulated powerless inmates more or less at will.[4] Social historians of diverse theoretical persuasions have recently contested this extreme version, exploring instead the complexity of medical and social relations that shaped the internal routine of these institutions.[5] Backed up by evidence from medical files and statistical data from registry books, they have argued that, although designed to both assist and control patients, most large state asylums faced so many challenges and demands from the public that claims of total control, made by either administrative or scholarly authorities, hardly withstand careful scrutiny. That was the case, indeed, of *La Castañeda,* a monumental architectural and medical enterprise designed to confirm the ascending modernity of the regime that, only a couple of months after inauguration in September 1910, suffered from overcrowding, lack of properly trained medical personnel, and physical decay.[6] The outbreak of the Mexican Revolution did not create but certainly aggravated the process that turned *La Castañeda* into a series of scantly funded and loosely interconnected institutions. Soon enough, indeed, the General Asylum became a poorly equipped establishment that provided custodial care for destitute patients suffering from chronic illness; a medical institute in which few doctors paid close attention to promising cases; and a work colony in which able patients performed free labor for the workshops of the asylum. With little funding and half of the number of guards required to function properly, *La Castañeda,* just like most state asylums abroad, could hardly uphold and much less help create the authoritarian and deeply hierarchical structure with which it is often associated.

Much like the general structure of the asylum, the relationship established between doctor and inmate was more conflict-ridden and fluid than is often accepted. As recorded in medical files from the institution, the doctor-inmate interaction was at once less harmonious and less uneven than described in medical exegesis of the era.[7] It was less harmonious because patients' acquiescence to psychiatric diagnosing involved some degree of dissension and friction, and less unbalanced because, even within asylum hierarchies, psychiatrists welcomed, incited in fact, the much-needed participation of patients and their families in the making of the diagnoses. In the intimacy of the inadequately equipped observation room or among many in crowded wards, psychiatrists and patients engaged in a more forceful, quite dynamic, and at times even volatile relation. In strict sense it could be said, with Arthur Kleinman, that patients confined at the state asylum constructed narratives of illness—the way in which the sufferer perceives, lives with, and responds to symptoms—while psychiatrists developed narratives of disease—the recasting of illness in terms of theories of disorder.[8] These divergent views structured the format in which an uneven yet possible interaction took place. Together, crossing frail bridges fraught with misgivings and mistrust, asylum doctors and inmates authored polysemic, multivocal, and heteroglot narratives with which they captured the fluid reality of mental illness, however fleetingly or fragmentarily. These dialogical constructions came out of the tension produced by human contact— as they saw, heard, and evaluated one another more through skillful negotiation than by plain opposition (Bakhtin 282–285).

Medical anthropologists working with live subjects have described, often memorably, the high level of complexity and subtlety involved in psychiatrist-patient interactions—aspects that become only more poignantly bewildering when trying to trace past voices inscribed in clinical histories (Kleinman, *Patients and Healers;* Scheper-Huges, *Death Without Weeping;* Scheper-Hughes, *Saints, Scholars, and Schizophrenics;* Gaines). While medical files from the General Insane Asylum can neither replicate the richness of an ethnographic account nor replace fieldwork, they do contain interpretations of mental illness produced by both asylum doctors and inmates.[9] Because diagnoses constituted then, as they do now, a "thoroughly semiotic activity" involving the "analysis of one symbol system followed by its translation into another," they made evident the distinctive discursive strategies employed by asylum doctors and inmates as they debated the meanings of mental illness in early-twentieth-century Mexico (Kleinman, *Illness Narratives* 16). Indeed, on the one hand, doctors forcefully tried to uplift the scientific status of their profession by committing to a linear narrative in which physical cause and mental effect were linked through the use of psychiatric categories produced in Europe, particularly ideas linked to degeneration theory, later substantiated, and at times recast, by concrete evidence from local cases. Doctors' emphasis on an "order of argumentation" that they saw as replicating an "order of things" only reinforced their faith in the progressive and ascending nature of the modernizing society, whether Porfirian or revolutionary. Inmates, on the other hand, brought with them stories of their lives with illness. Organized in conjunction with doctors and within the narrow confines of the medical questionnaire, these life stories manifested inmates' remarkable impetus to explain why and how their illness began and evolved. If, as the anthropologist Ruth Behar has argued, having both a life story and the willingness to tell it implicitly involves the "ability to rename and remake the world in which [they] were born," such impetus was hardly vacuous (270). As Behar also discovered, when tracing the biography of the determined Mexican peddler Esperanza, the rhetorical devices and plotlines used to organize a life story vary over time, across cultures, and between genders. Indeed, Esperanza told her story divided into three stages, namely suffering, anger, and redemption, which she illustrated through rich vignettes, usually in a dialogue format. Although asylum inmates did not enjoy the flexible arrangement in which Esperanza reconstructed her life, they, too, organized their life stories according to devices that, more often than not, were at odds with doctors' understandings of both what a life was and how such a life should be told. Instead of using a logic of achievement that could replicate the apparent inevitability of progress, they stressed, most tellingly, instances of physical and spiritual suffering in fragmented plot lines dominated by decay. Although actual events varied greatly, most inmates situated suffering at the onset of their lives—a torn home, rampant poverty, alcoholism, domestic violence, and, especially among women, sexual molestation. Illness did not come as breakage point; rather, it was a flash that illuminated ongoing wreckage. Motives fluctuated indeed but most evolved around loss: the death of a child, sudden or long periods of abandonment and neglect, violence inflicted by partners or relatives, the loss of employment, the demise of love. As inmate Olga I. so concisely said, these lives were "bitter"; they were "ditch[es] surrounded by tall walls" ("Olga I.," AHSSA. Box 260, Record 6, 3). They had, thus, a peculiar flavor; they belonged in a distinctive universe of metaphors.

These interpretative theoretical tools will guide the review of one case from *La Castañeda* in which doctor and inmate talked about sex—more specifically, female sexuality—as they discussed the specific nature of mental illness. While I have used portions of this case elsewhere, it is my intention to place specific emphasis now on the dynamic nature of the interaction and how it affected the dialogue about and the production of knowledge on sex (Rivera-Garza, "She Did Not Respect" 653–688). I am here less interested in exploring how these two views came to be divergent and potentially disparaging of one another, and more in how they produced one another in the immediacy of contact within a context they helped create. If metaphors from cultural anthropology must be used, I am more interested in the process of the writing of the cultural text and less in the written text that looms in the imagination as finished and autonomously formed.[10] Implicitly calling for greater emphasis on the "acting and creating of culture," this view also stresses the relevance and complexity of the "contact situation" through which such culture gets created or, as argued by Mikhail Bakhtin, the point (or the concrete utterance of a speaking subject) "where centrifugal as well as centripetal forces are brought to bear" (Bakhtin 272). In the medical case that is discussed in this essay, the *physical* contact situation in which psychiatrist and patient met was a welfare institution, located in the periphery of a city growing exponentially, and in the seams of regimes usually described as antagonistic: the last year of the modernizing administration of Porfirio Díaz and the early phase of revolutionary Mexico. There, within those concentric circles, psychiatrists and patients produced the *semiotic* contact situation: a dialogue—often heated, often interrupted—more accurately described by the Bakhtinian concept of the active understanding that characterizes internal dialogism. In it:

> . . . one assimilates the word under consideration into a new conceptual system, that of the one striving to understand, establishes a series of complex inter-relationships, consonances and dissonances with the word and enriches it with new elements. It is precisely such an understanding that the speaker counts on. Therefore his orientation toward the listener is an orientation toward a specific conceptual horizon, toward the specific word of the listener; it introduces totally new elements into his discourse; it is in this way, after all, that various different points of view, conceptual horizons, systems for providing expressive accents, various social "languages" come to interact with one another (282).

This essay is but an attempt to read one case from the asylum with these theoretical challenges in mind.

The Interrogatory

Life within the General Insane Asylum usually began at seven o'clock in the morning, when the institution's whistle woke up the entire neighborhood (Pensado and Correa 38). Then, administrators and members of the medical staff prepared for a new hard day within asylum walls. The head of the department of admissions opened the doors of his office an hour later and the scrutiny of inmates began.

While the first 848 inmates admitted at *La Castañeda* on inauguration day—430 men and 418 women from the *San Hipólito* and *Divino Salvador* hospitals, respectively—disregarded the official procedure, future incoming inmates were required to present official identification papers, to answer questions included in a medical questionnaire, and to undergo a medical examination on whose results admission was approved or denied (Registry Books, AHSSA).[11] Performed by an asylum intern, this initial routine took place at the observation ward, located in the General Services building that remained the architectural hallmark of the institution through the end. Luz D., the patient I invite the reader to follow closely in this essay, rigorously adhered to this procedure on arrival date ("Luz D. de S.," AHSSA. Box 22; Record 63, 2).

Guided by questions included in the two-page official interrogatory, which both Luz D. and her husband answered, Dr. Agustín Torres gathered that, at 41, Luz D. was older than most inmates—according to a random sample, the average age ranged between 20 and 40 years. She also was among the very few—86 percent of female inmates and 68 percent of male inmates were committed involuntarily, that is as a result of a government order—that came to the institution in company of a family member.[12] In addition, unlike most inmates, she was married (66 percent of women and 78 percent of men were either single or widowed) but, like most (about 68 percent of all inmates), she had immigrated to Mexico City at a young age.[13] A housewife of Catholic religious persuasion, Luz D. also enjoyed a "good" education and "clear" intelligence—aspects that became evident in her reading and writing skills. This, however, went hand in hand with the development of a "violent" temper, which had grown worse in recent times. Nothing in her family background helped explain that twist in her personality for, according to answers recorded in the interrogatory, there were no "nervous, epileptic, crazy, hysterical, alcoholic, syphilitic, or suicidal individuals" in her lineage. One of her three siblings, however, showed symptoms of mental illness; but none of her four children developed similar traits. Luz D. had not suffered from venereal diseases—whose presence always betrayed women of loose morals and men of powerful urges—although she had developed breast cancer, which a surgical intervention allegedly cured. Both Luz D. and her husband agreed, however, on the fact that she had suffered from "nervous afflictions" in the past, which they, in conjunction with the doctor, denominated hysteria, and that, even though she did not smoke or take snuff, she had indeed abused alcoholic beverages over a number of years. They attributed her disease to her "dipsomania" and Dr. Torres limited himself to note that she had experienced a kind of "manic excitement" over the last eight days in the section devoted to describe the "delirium, extravagant behavior, speech and irrational acts, and everything abnormal noticed in the patient" ("Luz D. de S" 1–3).

Luz D., however, still had information to share and later, on an undisclosed date, she used her writing skills to leave note of her experiences with mental illness. It is not clear whether she did it out of her own will—contesting, for example, answers given in the presence of her husband—or whether doctor Torres invited or induced her to write her own version of events. The surviving document, like many barely hidden in the medical files from the General Insane Asylum, constitutes nonetheless an unusual window into the intricacies of the doctor-patient exchange that shaped medical diagnoses at *La Castañeda*. Through this document, the reader has privileged access into the underlying events and practices, aspirations, and frustrations that congregated doctor and inmate in the same place and at the same time.

WHAT DID THEY TALK ABOUT WHEN THEY TALKED ABOUT MADNESS AND SEX?

I have elsewhere related that, on September 28, 1911, Luz D. arrived with her husband at the admission office of the General Insane Asylum *La Castañeda,* the largest state institution devoted to the care of mentally ill men, women, and children in early-twentieth-century Mexico.[14] Following the rules of the establishment, the D.s provided basic identification data before Agustín Torres, an asylum intern, performed a routine physical and psychological examination designed to determine her mental health.[15] Because Luz D.'s affliction did not prevent her from understanding and answering questions, she actively participated in the institutional psychiatric interview—an interrogatory ritual structured around questions included in an official medical questionnaire—that would decide her admission status. Later, as she became an inmate, Luz D. opted for writing the narrative of her illness on her own, on a separate sheet of paper:

My father, Don Vicente D. died when he was 60 years old. My mother was Piedad D. The man, my father, was a very healthy man; he died from bronchitis. My mother was of nervous constitution and very good disposition. She never had seizures and died from the flu, which affected her intestines and her heart.

The man, my husband, married when he was 20 years old. In the 10 years that I lived with him I gave birth to eight children, of whom four survived. Two of them were asphyxiated with the umbilical cord and two were born dead. I also had four abortions due to the hard life I led with the man, my husband.

I was born in 1874. When I was six years old, I suffered from scarlet fever, but I grew up healthy and robust thereafter. When I was 13 years old, I got my period for the first time without derangement. At 15, however, I became nervous. I got married at 17 and I got cured of my nervousness, and so I remained healthy for four years. Then, because of moral pain and physical losses—since I was breastfeeding a very robust girl—I became nervous again from February to August. I was perfectly fine for five years, but I got a case of puerperal fever and, as a result, I was left with an acute nervous condition, which I was able to cure with distractions and short trips. It could be said that at that time I drank alcoholic beverages following medical prescriptions and that, perhaps unconsciously, I abused them.

In 1899, I suffered a sudden case of dipsomania and physician Liceaga convinced me to seek care at the *Quinta de Tlalpan*. At that time I suffered this outburst because of the change in my moral and physical life because the man, my husband, brought a woman to live with him and I did not live intimately with him ever since. The emptiness of my soul was reflected in my physical parts. Then, I did not drink at all until 1901, when I drank for several days, got into *La Canoa*, where I stayed for three months.[16] I got out and was perfectly fine until 1906, a year in which because of excessive work and moral pain and horrible quarrels, I drank again for several days. I went back to *La Canoa* again and remained there for one year and five months. I got out and was again perfectly fine until September 1911, when I drank some cognac and *pulque* while visiting some people. I should warn you that I do not drink unless I get nervous—which happens when the moral pain and physical loses and, above all, when the emptiness of my soul is reflected in my physical aspect—leading me to the first drink. When I am in control of my reason I can bear great pain. I keep the control I must have, given my difficult situation and my exaggerated way of feeling, my exaggerated way of being, when I am overwhelmed by passion and the most complete excitement. (2)[17]

I, however, withheld the fact that, as Luz D.'s own version of her life with illness ended, the diagnosis written by Agustín Torres began:

The information transcribed above was given and written by the patient herself, which shows her clear talent to express her feelings and thoughts through writing. Except for her dipsomania outbursts, which she always relates to her moral pain, she seems to be a moral person. However, a more detailed study unveils a chronic state of maniac excitement, which is more mental than physical (a background of moral insanity). She has new ideas every day, new plans, whether to get out of the asylum or to follow a specific kind behavior with her husband, whom she blames for her condition. Every day, too, she complains about her health, whether a pain in the leg or arm or certain dizziness that causes nausea or a pain in the left ovary or even hiccups. These symptoms make me think of a case of hysteria, which is without doubt present, but they are the result of her chronic mental excitement. We have seen her writing poems for entire days or letters describing her horrible situation to her relatives. Other days, she devotes herself to manual work. But there is no stability in her activities; there is no method. What is pleasant today becomes annoying tomorrow. The patient is aware of her situation and tries to correct herself. She compares herself to a horse that is hard to tame; a horse that does not stop once it starts running.

We have explored her carefully and have noticed only the pain in the left ovary, which speaks in favor of hysteria. There are no signs of alcoholic intoxication. To end this diagnosis, I will point out that she eats and sleeps well, suffering only a slight constipation. Her prodigious memory is rather noticeable." (3)

These two different, yet not completely antithetical, interpretations of an experience with or within the universe of mental illness constitute a Mexican example of what Arthur Kleinman has called illness narratives, that is the series of "plot lines, core metaphors, and rhetorical devices that structure illness [which] are drawn from cultural and personal modes for arranging experiences in meaningful ways and for effectively expressing those meanings" (Kleinman, *Illness Narratives* 49). While divergent indeed, the narratives of illness that shaped Luz D.'s physical and spiritual suffering seem to emerge from an implicit agreement: both patient and psychiatrist—more accurately, in this case, inmate and doctor—spoke of illness as a real experience.[18] Without this tacit yet ubiquitous agreement, the dialogue between Luz D. and Torres could not have taken place. The shifting and, at times, oppositional devices used to describe her ailment, however, indicate that the agreement had limits, which were as real as the unified effort to name her condition. These limits grew out of the specific experiences and meanings that allowed both actors to interpret the medical notion of mental illness—experiences and meanings that developed outside the asylum walls, in a capital city that grew exponentially under the leadership of a president obsessed with the idea of transforming it into a showcase of modernity; in a society of accentuated social contrasts in which men and women were asked to fulfill idealized versions of themselves as homely angels and stern, productive workers; in a time of great volatility that witnessed the fall of a 30-year-old regime and the outbreak of the armed phase of a social revolution that mobilized peasants, workers, and members of the middle classes throughout the abrupt geography of the country. It would be fair to say that the debates about class, gender, and the nation that informed the existence of people living in dramatic transitional times transcended the walls of the asylum, contributing greatly to the identification of what became, at least in the specific instance of Luz D.'s diagnosis, a case of moral insanity.

Defined by James Prichard in 1835 as "a form of monomania in which people recognized the difference between right and wrong, yet lacked the will power to resist evil impulses," this diagnosis opened the door for definitions of "good" and "evil" that clearly induced the use of nonmedical idioms in interpretations of mental derangement—an opportunity that neither Luz D. nor Torres let go unused.[19] In developing a profile of this disorder, they waged their own observations, and their own metaphors to capture such observations, in narratives that emerged as they entered in contact with one another. This was not the case, then, of two ready-made discourses that obliterated each other in sheer opposition—a view often linked, as argued above, to antipsychiatric notions of madness. Instead, a more mobile yet equally relentless strategy of displacement occurred.[20]

In 1911, when the D.s walked under the entrance arch of the General Insane Asylum, Luz had been through the admission process and the initial psychiatric interview at least five previous times. The symptoms of her condition first emerged in 1899, only eight years after marrying Manuel S., when he "brought a woman" to live with him, ceasing physical contact with the patient. Luz D. thus began consuming alcoholic beverages and manifesting the kind of "manic excitement" that would take her back to mental health institutions on repeated occasions. Following the advice from Dr. Liceaga, a prestigious physician and important political player in Porfirian medical circles, she first enrolled at the private clinic *La Quinta de Tlalpan,* of which little is known, owned by Dr. Lavista.[21] Apparently recovered from the dipsomania episode, she led a normal life afterward, although for a very short period of time. Soon enough, at the expressed petition of her husband and with a medical certificate signed by doctors Antonio Romero and Heladio Gutiérrez, she became a patient at *La Canoa,* the common term used to describe the *Divino Salvador* hospital for demented women established in 1571 and located in downtown Mexico City, where she remained for over a year as a paying boarder (Kanarek; Leiby 491–498).[22] According to a report signed by Dr. Herrera, however, medical personnel from *La Canoa* failed to detect the alleged symptoms of her mental illness. She behaved reasonably well, refraining from consuming alcoholic beverages, although she openly and constantly complained about the quality of food and conditions of life at the hospital, something she did orally as well as in writing. In fact, taking advantage of the fact that she knew how to read and write, she took to scribing anonymous notes in which she exposed the detrimental hygienic conditions of wards that soon reached the eyes of higher authorities of the welfare system—a ruse later uncovered by Dr. Francisco Hurtado as he attempted to justify the state of affairs at the hospital. "The anonymous note," he said, "is no longer so since the penmanship and syntax are well known. They belong to Luz D., whom you have met before on one of your visits" (Luz D. 11). In February 1903, and also responding to a petition from her husband, Luz D. was released, "cured of the dipsomania she suffered from" (9–10).

Three years later, on April 19, 1906, Luz D. once again went back to *La Canoa* as a paying boarder because of, in her words, "excessive work, moral pain, and scandalous quarrels." By then, Manuel S. had established his residence separately from hers. In July, when she was released against the expressed wishes of her husband, paperwork for a consensual divorce was initiated. A month later, the *Ministerio Público* began an interdiction trial designed to determine whether Luz D. was mentally sound and could, in consequence, exercise her civil rights.[23] Only two months later, medical experts argued that Luz D. "was under the influence of hysteria, with diminishing sense of will, especially evident in the changeable nature of her ideas and an obvious pathological excitement, shyness bordering on delirium of prosecution, as well as excessive loquacity. For all this, they believed that Luz D. was unable to exercise her civil rights and was not, consequently, responsible for her acts" (20).

Almost a year later, in May 1907, Luz D. became a paying boarder at *La Canoa* once again. This time, however, Manuel S. was unable to fulfill payments according to schedule. He proceeded to ask for a grace period, which was granted to him (17). Only a month later, while she was still in confinement, a second medical team connected to the interdiction trial reviewed her case. Roughly confirming former findings, the team found that Luz D. suffered from a kind of "rational moral insanity and dipsomania with a hysterical background" (21). Based on this and former reports, the lawyer Enrique de la Garza, member of the Fifth Civil *Juzgado* of Mexico City, declared her in "state of interdiction" on November 26, 1907. She was neither legally able to administer her property nor to exercise her civil rights. On the same date, Manuel S. sent a copy of this legal document to the authorities of the hospital, demanding the institution to prevent any further release of his wife. He was not only unable to care for her, he claimed, but he also believed, quite firmly, that her release could be "dangerous for the public" (19). As adamant as his request was, it proved only momentarily successful. It took almost an additional year for the authorities to release Luz D. again on September 29, 1908, on the grounds that she was "cured of her dipsomania" (28).

While living in separate residences and apparently leading separate lives, it was Manuel S., "the man, her husband," who walked with Luz D. under the entrance arch of the recently opened facilities of the General Insane Asylum *La Castañeda* on September 29, 1911. He carried with him a new request, signed once again by licensed doctors, for her confinement. He did not go away when the medical intern Agustín Torres, who came into contact with her for the first time that autumn, initiated the psychiatric interview.

Agustín Torres was by then a young physician in the early stages of his career. As with many asylum doctors in Mexico City, he had taken a couple of elective, upper-level courses on mental illness at the Porfirian School of Medicine, but he would acquire most of his training in the emerging science of Mexican psychiatry through hands-on experience at the facilities of the General Insane Asylum with inmates very much like Luz D. (Rivera-Garza, "Dangerous Minds"; Somolinos). Perhaps this is the main reason why, unlike older and more disgruntled physicians, he paid special and close attention to her case. Judging by his rapidly ascending career, however, it is clear that Torres harbored intellectual and bureaucratic ambitions that clearly surpassed those of his contemporaries from the very beginning. Only two years after his meeting with Luz D. and in the midst of the revolutionary upheaval, for example, Agustín Torres had completed the first section of a study on the classification of mental disease for the Society of Psychiatry and Psychology. The president of this association, Dr. Heladio Gutiérrez, urged him in fact to complete the second section as soon as possible in order "to resolve in a definitive manner the issue of classification of wards at the General Insane Asylum." ("Agustín Torres, expediente personal," AHSSA, Box 45, Record 9, 5). By 1915, the year in which Zapatista and Constitutionalist forces took over Mexico City, Agustín Torres became the head of medical interns, a position from which he was removed shortly thereafter based on information that described him as a "sworn enemy of the revolution" (3). However, only a year later, on November 16, 1916, he became the director of the General Insane Asylum, distinguishing himself as an efficient bureaucrat and active intellectual (6–8). Classificatory issues did not abandon his mind. In fact, writing as both an enlightened physician and a practical director of a large welfare institution, he published a series of articles for the *Encyclopedic Journal of the Public Welfare System,* arguing for the need to change ward nomenclature as well as diagnostic groupings at the establishment (Torres, "Razones por las cuales . . ."; "El estudio y tratamiento"; "El Manicomio General"). His interest in the development of Mexican psychiatry was not short-lived, either. By 1920, Dr. Torres was still teaching a class on psychiatry for the National School of Medicine in Mexico City, in whose syllabus he insisted on the need to combine theoretical knowledge with hands-on practices in each one of the teaching sessions ("Agustín Torres, 1920" AEM, Bundle 201, Record 9, 1).

None of these issues—Luz D.'s past or Agustín Torres's future— appeared in the interrogatory and additional texts in a direct, or overt, manner. However, traces of both, the past and the future, may help explain the peculiar discursive strategies used by both actors. In the document Luz D. elaborated, for example, it is clear that her interpretation of mental illness transcended merely biological readings of mind and body. For Luz D., mental illness, or as she termed it, that "unleashing of passions," came as a result of episodes of great personal pain and suffering in her life, usually in connection with marital disturbances involving infidelity and domestic violence. Mental illness, in her view, did not loom inside lost genes ready to burst open on unexpected dates but presented itself as a natural response against forces seemingly out of or above her control. Mental illness did not break her life but helped illuminate a life already broken. It helped her voice the "emptiness of the soul" left about the lack of intimate, sexual contact with her philandering husband. Mental illness, that "manic excitement" that made her feel like an untamed horse, also helped her talk about her sexual life: the onset of menarche, the first sexual contact, the process of giving birth, the abortions, the sexual neglect. As she pressed these issues, it is also clear that her personal understanding of mental illness evolved in conjunction with, rather than separate from, members of her family, most notably her husband, and the doctors that reviewed her case at both private and public institutions from Porfirian Mexico City. Thus, her personal interpretation, from the start, was at least trivocal, involving contentious perspectives from an unfaithful husband attempting to secure a consensual divorce as well as medical notions from doctors working at the various mental health institutions she entered.

Dr. Torres, by contrast, came with different concerns and perspectives to the psychiatric interview with Luz D. on that September. From what he eventually became, it is clear that working at *La Castañeda* was not, in his unique case, a second or last choice. Unlike most physicians in early-twentieth-century Mexico City, Dr. Torres manifested a sincere intellectual curiosity for and a practical commitment to psychiatry, "the most demanding of medical sciences," that were frankly unusual just then—a fact that became painfully clear in the shortage of medical personnel that affected *La Castañeda* from the start. Intellectual concerns, however, went hand in hand with practical issues in Torres's mind. His etiological study of classificatory issues betrayed indeed an avid reader of foreign literature and a learned physician, but it also shed light on the bureaucrat willing to put to use that theoretical knowledge at the institution for which he worked. Enmeshed in a milieu dominated by the teachings of degeneration theory, Dr. Torres intently sought data that would facilitate a connection between genetic legacies and the outbreak of mental illness. He was, too, however, an empiricist, a positivist thinker concerned with organized information. Perhaps it was all this that invited him to lend an ear—at times, a generous ear—to Luz D.'s medical story.

So, when life took the ambitious young doctor and the enraged woman of unleashed passions to the same room, suspicion and seduction must have played equal roles in the development of their multiple encounters—the suspicion of two who conceived of themselves as utterly different; the seduction of two who perceived themselves as working for a common, and yet not clearly defined, purpose. Simultaneously clashing and negotiating, Luz D. and Agustín Torres produced tense, mad narratives of mental illness—texts of multiple voices in which both actors waged and wove their own relational understandings of body, mind, and society.

Asylum narratives, however, hardly constituted free-flowing constructions of life history. Constrained by an institutional setting that emphasized doctors' authority and a medical questionnaire that provided limited space for inmates' answers, they were based on, and reproduced in turn, the disproportionate access to power that characterized asylum hierarchies. Yet, even in that unevenness, the mad narratives that emerged on asylum grounds incorporated doctors' and inmates' views, and they did it, by necessity, in the friction of its very making. That such views were not isolated entities became clear in Luz D.'s free borrowing of rhetorical devices more often associated with medical interpretations of illness. She showed little hesitation to use, for example, a narrative line that linked her mental derangement with life stages roughly based on a sexual interpretation of the female condition—a connection common in Porfirian medical circles obsessed with their alleged lack of knowledge about the female sex (Rivera Garza, "Criminalization"). Thus, although she noted that menarche did not cause her further complications, she linked the onset of her nervousness with important transitions in her sexual life, most notably with marriage and, later, the conflicts of married life. Yet, even as Luz D. referred to her nervous condition as a phenomena clearly rooted in the reality of her body and, more specifically, of her sexual development and sexual practice, she also, and swiftly, proceeded to place this body in the charged context of daily life through concrete tales of childbirth, conflictive family relations, domestic violence, and, more often than not, suffering and loss. Luz D. thus conceded to medical idioms as much as she maintained her own version of a life with mental illness. And she was not the only one.

Signs of a similar negotiation emerged in Torres's rather pensive, seemingly nonmedical, and even poetic, diagnosis. The word "excitement" with which Luz D. ended her narrative, for example, appeared early in Torres's appended text, serving as a bridge of sorts. No one knows, or will know, who pronounced it first and, thus, who in fact borrowed it from whom, but both used it in conspicuous ways. As expected in a doctor interested in psychiatric science, he disdainfully referred to "what she calls her moral pain," discarding or downplaying the stories of her complicated marital life, which were not included, for example, as valid answers in the official interrogatory. Furthermore, in trying to uphold her medical status, Torres introduced the well-known psychiatric term of "hysteria" (Goldstein; Beizer; Ender), but he did it in a rather haphazard way, relating it in passing with a pain in her ovaries. Much more interesting for him was, however, that she wrote, abundantly and well—a fact that Torres praised in the first sentence of his diagnoses. That he conceded to Luz D.'s interpretations as much as she did became tellingly clear in his use of a metaphor of her own making to describe her—"she compares herself with an indomitable horse." So, even when he could not help but notice a "background of moral insanity" in this patient—his final diagnosis indeed—he likewise could not refrain from expressing his praises for her "prodigious memory." The incorporation of pompous adjectives in a rather nonmedical medical diagnosis shed light on the tenuous terrain both inmates and doctors created—a

view that implicitly questions views of asylums as sites particularly in-
ducing to totalitarian forms of social control and that alerts about the
intricate, and indeed intimate, process involved in the so-called medicalization of sex.

BEYOND MEDICALIZATION

When inmates talked and doctors quoted them they engaged in a relentless strategy of displacement and negotiation.[24] Waging their particular weapons—scientific discourse and progress, on the one hand,
and lived experience, on the other—they clashed indeed, but they also
gave and took. Asylum inmates could have chosen to remain silent—
and some did out of conviction, while others suffered from conditions
that prevented understanding and speech altogether—those who did
not, however, had to find ways to make their stories intelligible. Some,
the most knowledgeable and experienced, went as far as selectively
using medical tropes, dividing the stories of their lives, for example,
according to medical patterns. Most brought tales of suffering and
pain, as if such tales constituted universal, agreed-on nodes of meaning. Likewise, asylum doctors could have chosen to remain listless,
which some most certainly did, but those interested in becoming professionals, in becoming psychiatrists, had to listen. Some, the most
knowledgeable and experienced, even went as far as quoting famous
names or foreign labels to alert readers—medical or otherwise, as it
turned out to be—about the influences that shaped their understanding, making the translation process from illness into disease accessible.
Most brought with them open ears and the willingness to pay attention to the patients' tales of suffering and pain, as if such tales constituted disputed nodes of meaning, rather than faithful reflections of
actual facts. This multilayered and almost intimate relationship cannot
be grasped, much less be understood, within the bifocal axis of opposition. There was too much yearning—for knowledge, for an audience, for validation, for status, for power, for a lending ear—too much
need of one another indeed to call it opposition. There was, above all,
too much complicity, of the forced kind to be sure, between the one
who spoke and the one who recast speech; between the one who was
aware of the recasting and nonetheless kept on speaking and the one
who recast and, for that reason, had to pay close attention to raw
speech in the first place. Interlocked they were, inmate and doctor,
because both needed one another to be and, more fundamentally, to
become one and other. The asylum doctor longed, often ardently, for
the status of a true professional: the psychiatrist. The asylum inmate

longed for the acknowledgment of his or her sufferings, his or her human core. Meeting both aims presented challenges that asylum doctors and inmates met through flexible, yet very tense, strategies of negotiation. Although I am certainly not claiming that all psychiatric interactions developed in such a mobile and spirited manner, the relationship established between Luz D. and Agustín Torres might alert us about the dynamic ways in which patients and doctors coauthored medical explanations of sexuality, and everything else, during this era. Seemingly simple, this warning might compel us to review concepts such as medicalization, a term usually employed to signify the ascendance of medical language vis à vis alternative and/or "popular" views of sexuality. Tracing patients' participation in, rather than against, the growing legitimacy of medical language during the Porfirian era also might compel a review of patients' agency, commonly accepted only when their views appear in opposition to discourses seen, or scholarly construed, as hegemonic or dominant beforehand.

Notes

1. For a historical analysis of Porfirian construction of ideas of female domesticity, see French 529–553; see also Ramos Escandón.
2. Analysis on the making of masculinity often relate to more contemporary times, see Gutmann; Melhaus and Stolen. For a historical analysis indirectly addressing the construction of manhood in early-twentieth-century Mexico, see Buffington 118–132; see also Nesvig. For a more contemporary view, see Prieur.
3. While definitions vary, I take medicalization in the most general of meanings as a "widespread process in Western societies, whereby problems previously labeled and managed as moral, religious, or criminal are redefined as disorder and dealt with through therapeutic technology." See Kleinman, *Illness Narratives* 26.
4. Generally linked to the antipsychiatry movement of the 1970s, the following works constitute representative examples of views of madness and mental institutions from the perspective of social control. See Szasz; Goffman; Scull; Rothman.
5. As research on the history of asylums grows, views of mental health institutions have become more complex. A representative sample of revisionist literature includes Dwyer; Grob; Digby; Goldberg; Sadowsky.
6. For a history of this institution, see Rivera-Garza, *Mad Narratives* and "Becoming Mad."
7. Mexican psychiatrists themselves have done much of this work through memoirs or historical revisions of their professions. See Ramírez Moreno; Calderón Narváez.

8. As Arthur Kleinman has argued, illness and disease are not interchangeable terms. The former refers "to how the sick person and the members of the family or wider social network perceive, live with, and respond to symptoms and disability," whereas the latter relates to "what the practitioner creates in the recasting of illness in terms of theories of disorder" (*Illness Narratives* 4–6).

9. On the uses of memory in both historical and anthropological accounts, see Roseberry and O'Brien. Examples of anthropologically informed histories of modern Mexico include Nugent and Frye.

10. The explicit reference here is to William Roseberry's critique of "the inadequacy of the text as a metaphor for culture. A text is written; it is not writing," and his call for greater emphasis on the "acting, the creating of the cultural forms we interpret" (24).

11. Data on inmates transferred from institutions funded in colonial times to the facilities of the General Insane Asylum comes from the registry books of the institution.

12. According to a sample (50 men and 50 women) taken from the registry books, 86 percent of female inmates and 68 percent of male inmates were committed involuntarily, that is, as a result of a government order.

13. According to a sample of 50 men and 50 women, 66 percent of female and 78 percent of male inmates were either single or widowed. Inmates born in the provinces but residing in Mexico City constituted 68 percent of inmate population.

14. Inmates' last names have been omitted to preserve their privacy.

15. For a historical analysis of the internal regulations and daily routine of the General Insane Asylum, see Rivera-Garza, "Por la salud mental."

16. *La Canoa* was the popular name given to the Divino Salvador, a mental health facility established during the colonial era that served only female patients. For a history of the Divino Salvador hospital, see Kanarek. For a brief history of the other hospital established in colonial times, the San Hipólito hospital, see Leiby.

17. From research conducted at the Archivo Histórico de la Secreataría de Salubridad y Asistencia, Fondo Manicomio General, Sección Expedientes Clínicos, Box 22, Record 63, 2. Hereafter referred to as "Luz D. de S."

18. While this was not always the case at the General Insane Asylum, it was, however, common enough to call it a norm.

19. See Berrios. Definition taken from Gamwell and Tomes 80.

20. I am specifically referring to the strategies analyzed by Michel Foucault in the section "Method" included in *History of Sexuality* 92–102.

21. Little is known about the history of this private clinic where, nonetheless, most Porfirian doctors acquired practical experience treating mental illness. See interview with Mexican psychiatrist Luis Murillo.

22. For a history of mental health institutions in Mexico, see Ramírez Moreno; Calderón Narváez.
23. For information about interdiction trials in Mexico, see Sacristán.
24. I am referring to the strategies analyzed by Michel Foucault in the section on "Method," included in his *History of Sexuality*, Vol. I: 92–102.

BIBLIOGRAPHY

PRIMARY SOURCES

AHSSA: From research conducted at the Archivo Histórico de la Secretaría de Salubridad y Asistencia, Fondo Manicomio General, Sección Expedientes Clínicos and Sección Expedientes de Personal.
AEM: From research conducted at the Archivo de la Escuela de Medicina.

SECONDARY SOURCES

Bachrach, Leona. "Asylum and Chronically Ill Psychiatric Patients," *American Journal of Psychiatry* 141, 1984: 975–978.
Bakhtin, Mikhail. *The Dialogic Imagination: Four Essays*. Austin: University of Texas Press, 1981.
Behar, Ruth. *Translated Woman: Crossing the Border with Esperanza's Story*. Boston: Beacon Press, 1993.
Beizer, Janet. *Ventriloquized Bodies. Narratives of Hysteria in Nineteenth-Century France*. Ithaca: Cornell University, 1993.
Berkstein Kanarek, Celia. *El hospital Divino Salvador*. M.A. Thesis. Universidad Nacional Autónoma de México, 1981.
Berrios, G. E. "Classic Text No. 37. J. C. Prichard and the Concept of Moral Insanity." *History of Psychiatry* X, 1999: 111–126.
Bliss, Katherine. "Guided by an Imperious, Moral Need: Prostitutes, Motherhood, and Nationalism in Revolutionary Mexico." Carlos Aguirre and Robert Buffington, Eds. *Reconstructing Criminality in Latin America*. Wilmington, Del.: Scholarly Resources, 2000: 167–194.
Buffington, Robert. "Los Jotos: Contested Visions of Homosexuality in Mexico," Daniel Balderston and Donna J. Guy, Eds. *Sex and Sexuality in Latin America*. New York: New York University Press, 1997: 118–132.
Calderón Narváez, Guillermo. "Hospitales psiquiátricos de México. Desde la colonia hasta la actualidad." *Revista Mexicana de Neurología y Psiquiatría* 7:3, 1966: 111–143.
Digby, Anne. *Madness, Morality and Medicine: A Study of the York Retreat 1796–1914*. Cambridge: Cambridge University Press, 1985.
Dwyer, Ellen. *Homes for the Mad. Life Inside Two Nineteenth-Century Asylums*. New Brunswick: Rutgers University Press, 1987.

Ender, Evelyne. *Sexing the Mind: Nineteenth-Century Fictions of Hysteria*. Ithaca: Cornell University Press, 1995.

Foucault, Michel. *History of Sexuality*, Vol. I. New York: Vintage, 1981.

French, William. "Prostitutes and Guardian Angels. Women, Work, and the Family in Porfirian Mexico," *Hispanic American Historical Review* 72:4, 1992: 529–553.

Frye, David. *Indians into Mexicans: History and Identity in a Mexican Town*. Austin: University of Texas Press, 1996.

Gaines, Atwood D., Ed., *Ethnopsychiatry: The Cultural Construction of Professional and Folk Psychiatrists*. Albany: State University of New York Press, 1992.

Gamwell, Lynn, and Nancy Tomes. *Madness in America. Cultural and Medical Perceptions of Mental Illness Before 1914*. Ithaca: Cornell University Press, 1995.

Goffman, Erving. *Asylums: Essays on the Social Situation of Mental Patients and Other Inmates*. New York: Anchor, 1961.

Goldberg, Ann. *Sex, Religion, and the Making of Modern Madness: The Eberbach Asylum and German Society, 1815–1849*. New York: Oxford University Press, 1999.

Goldstein, Jan. *Console and Classify: The French Psychiatric Profession in the Nineteenth Century*. Cambridge: Cambridge University Press, 1987.

Grob, Gerald. *The Mad Among Us: A History of the Care of America's Mentally Ill*. New York: Maxwell Macmillan International, 1994.

Gutmann, Matthew C. *The Meanings of Macho: Being a Man in Mexico City*. Berkeley: University of California Press, 1996.

Kleinman, Arthur. *The Illness Narratives: Suffering, Healing, and the Human Condition*. New York: Verso, 1988.

———. *Patients and Healers in the Context of Culture: An Exploration of the Borderland Between Anthropology, Medicine, and Psychiatry*. Berkeley: University of California Press, 1980.

Leiby, John S. "San Hipólito's Treatment of the Mentally Ill in Mexico City, 1589–1650." *The Historian* 54:3, 1992: 491–498.

Melhaus, Marit, and Kristi Anne Stolen, Eds. *Machos, Mistresses, Madonnas: Contesting the Power of Latin American Gender Imagery*. London and New York: Verso, 1996.

Nesvig, Martin. "The Lure of the Perverse: Moral Negotiation of Pederasty in Porfirian Mexico." *Mexican Studies/Estudios Mexicanos* 16:1, 2000: 1–37.

Nugent, Daniel. *Spent Cartridges of the Revolution: An Anthropological History of Namiquipa, Chihuahua*. Chicago : University of Chicago Press, 1993.

Pensado, Patricia, and Leonor Correa. *Mixcoac. Un barrio en la memoria*. Mexico City: Instituto Mora, 1996.

Prieur, Annick. *Mema's House, Mexico City: On Transvestites, Queens, and Machos*. Chicago: University of Chicago Press, 1998.

Ramírez Moreno, Samuel. *La asistencia psiquiátrica en México.* Mexico City: Secretaría de Salubridad y Asistencia, 1950.

Ramos Escandón, Carmen. "Señoritas porfirianas, mujer e idología en el México progresista, 1880–1910." *Carmen Ramos Escandón, et al, Eds. Presencia y transparencia: La mujer en la historia de México.* Mexico City: El Colegio de México, 1987.

Rivera-Garza, Cristina. "The Criminalization of the Syphilitic Body. Prostitutes, Health Crimes, and Society in Mexico City, 1867–1930." Carlos Aguirre, Ricardo Salvatore, and Gilbert Joseph, Eds. *Crime and Punishment in Latin America: Law and Society since Late Colonial Times.* Durham: Duke University Press, 2001: 147–180.

———. "She Did Not Respect nor Obey Anyone: Psychiatrists and Inmates Debate Gender, Class, and the Nation at the General Insane Asylum, Mexico 1910–1930." *Hispanic American Historical Review* 81:3–4, 2001: 653–688.

———. *Mad Narratives: Psychiatrists and Inmates Debate Gender, Class, and the Nation at the General Insane Asylum La Castañeda, Mexico 1910–1930.* Lincoln: Nebraska University Press, forthcoming.

———. "Becoming Mad in Revolutionary Mexico: Mentally Ill Patients at the General Insane Asylum, Mexico 1910–1930." Roy Porter and David Wright, Eds. *The Confinement of the Insane, 1800–1965: International Perspectives.* Cambridge: Cambridge University Press, forthcoming.

———. "Por la salud mental de la nación: Vida cotidiana y Estado en el Manicomio General La Castañeda, Mexico 1910–1930." *Secuencia, Revista de Historia y Ciencias Sociales.* 51, Sept.–Dec. 2001: 57–90.

———. "Dangerous Minds: Changing Psychiatric Views of the Mentally Ill in Porfirian Mexico 1876–1911." *Journal of the History of Medicine and Allied Sciences* 56:I, 2001: 36–67.

Roseberry, William. *Anthropologies and Histories: Essays in Culture, History, and Political Economy.* New Brunswick: Rutgers University Press, 1989: 24.

———, and Jay O'Brien, Eds. *Golden Ages, Dark Ages: Imagining the Past in Anthropology and History.* Berkeley: University of California Press, 1991.

Rothman, David. *The Discovery of the Asylum. Order and Disorder in the Early Republic.* Boston: Little Brown, 1980.

Sacristán, Cristina. "¿Quién me metió al manicomio? El internamiento de enfermos mentales en México, siglos XIX y XX." *Relaciones: Estudios de Historia y Sociedad* 19:74, 1998: 214–20.

Sadowsky, Jonathan. *Imperial Bedlam: Institutions of Madness in Colonial Southwest Nigeria.* Berkeley: University of California Press, 1999.

Scheper-Hughes, Nancy. *Death Without Weeping: The Violence of Everyday Life in Brazil.* Berkeley: University of California Press, 1992.

———. *Saints, Scholars, and Schizophrenics: Mental Illness in Ireland.* Berkeley: University of California Press, 1979.

Scull, Andrew. *Museums of Madness: The Social Organization of Insanity in Nineteenth-Century England.* London: Allen Lane, 1979.

Somolinos D'Arodis, Germán. *Historia de la psiquiatría en México.* Mexico City: Sep-Setentas, 1976.

Szasz, Thomas. *The Myth of Mental Illness: Foundations of a Theory of Personal Conduct.* New York: Harper and Row, 1974.

Torres, Agustín. "El estudio y tratamiento de los enajenados." *Revista Enciclopédica Beneficencia Pública.* 34–35, 1917: 55–57.

————. "El Manicomio General." *Revista Enciclopédica Beneficencia Pública.* 34–35, 1917: 30–32.

————. "Razones por las cuales debe adoptarse la clasificación de enfermedades mentales por el prof. Tanzi en el Manicomio General." *Revista Enciclopédica Beneficencia Pública.* 34–35, 1917: 46–50.

Sentimental Excess
and Gender Disruption

THE CASE OF AMADO NERVO

Sylvia Molloy

Until quite recently, I believed myself immune to the charms of Amado Nervo's poetry. I had never taught it, preferring his unfairly neglected, provocative short fiction. My experience of this poetry was limited, or so I thought, to blurry recollections of books belonging to my parents (more precisely, to my mother: I shall return to this gender marking), among them *Elevación* and *El estanque de los lotos,* which I surreptitiously leafed through, as a child, but never actually read. But this was not all I remembered of Nervo, as I discovered not too long ago. On reading his poetry, I found myself in fact rereading him, found myself remembering poems I had learned by heart at school, both as a child and as an adolescent, poems that I had completely forgotten. Looking through *Cantos escolares,* for example, I rediscovered "Amor filial," and in it, the verses "Yo adoro a mi madre querida, / yo adoro a mi padre también; / Ninguno me quiere en la vida / como ellos me saben querer" [I adore my dear mother,/ I adore father too;/ No one in the world loves me/ As they are wont to do] (OC III: 127),[1] which then lingered in my mind, annoyingly, for hours. And I also found a poem that I had not only memorized as an adolescent but also fully identified with, "En paz," from *Serenidad.* Its last two lines—"Amé, fui amado, el sol acarició mi faz. / ¡Vida, nada me debes! ¡Vida, estamos en paz!" [I loved, was loved, the sun caressed my face,/ Life, you me owe nothing! Life, we are at peace!] (OC XV: 82)—were, I remember, particularly gratifying to my schoolmates and myself, inexperienced teenagers who liked to think they knew all about life. Nervo was clearly the poet of universal truths, one whose life lessons were memorized by schoolchildren not only in Argentina but throughout Latin America: his poetry was a "spiritual pedagogy," to quote the enthusiastic comment of one of his contemporaries, Rafael Cansinos Asséns.

As I was remembering these previous encounters with Nervo, a third memory came to mind, much less remote and more relevant to the topic I am approaching here, that of male sentimental excess. I remembered Alejandra Pizarnik, the Argentine poet, also an unwilling victim of Nervo's "spiritual pedagogy" at school, reciting the poem "Cobardía," strategically replacing certain nouns—say *madre* [mother] in the line "Pasó con su madre" [She went by with her mother], or *alma* [soul] in the line "¡Síguela! gritaron cuerpo y alma al par" [Follow her! Screamed body and soul all at once], or *locura* [madness] in "Pero tuve miedo de amar con locura" [But I was afraid to love unto madness]—with the word *culo* [ass] (OC XI: 153–154), achieving effects that I would not hesitate to call remarkable and even strangely productive.[2]

One rereads Nervo's poetry even as one reads it for the first time, so ingrained is it in Latin American cultural memory. Pizarnik's transgressive gesture appeared to taint its glossy surface, its forgettable yet unforgettable verses popularized through endless recitation and turned into lachrymose clichés. But, for all its easy mischief, its sophomoric scatological thrust, Pizarnik's intervention, I would argue, recognizes a fundamental aspect of Nervo's poetry—its fervor, its excess—and responds by taking that excess even further, to the realm of the outrageous. Hers is not a gratuitous addition; Nervo's poetry as a whole already borders on this outrageousness, sentimental excess, if one (re)reads Nervo with care, coming perilously close to the grotesque.

Who Reads Nervo?

I have deliberately referred to female adolescents, to a woman poet: it is not insignificant, I think, that the above-mentioned fervor, be it mimetic (the case of the schoolgirls) or transgressive (Pizarnik), bears the mark of gender. Nervo writes for women, or rather for (and, I suggest, *from*) a certain figuration of the feminine. Woman and femininity are not synonymous: I shall return to this difference. The criticism of Nervo's contemporaries already confirmed this gender mark. Thus, Luis Berisso writes on the occasion of Nervo's death: "Ningún trovador americano la mimó más [a la mujer], ninguno la elevó tan alto, ni se inclinó a sus plantas más rendido, gentil y caballeresco; pocos penetraron tan hondo en los abismos de su corazón. De ahí el llanto que empaña los ojos de las bellas y deja a su paso una estela de azucenas y un temblor de angustia" [No American troubadour spoiled woman more, none elevated her so high, nor stooped more willingly, gently, chivalrously to the ground she trod; very few penetrated so far into the depths of her heart. Thus, the tears swelling now in the eyes of beautiful women, tears leaving in their path a trail of white lilies and a quiver of grief.] (306).[3] On the same occasion, Fernández Moreno is even more emphatic: "Estáis de luto todas las mujeres" [All you women are in mourning] (308). Years later, in his edition of Nervo's *Obras completas*, Francisco González Guerrero resorts to the same notion: "Por su emotividad profunda y por los aciertos de interpretación del sentimiento amoroso ante el misterio mismo de la muerte, este libro [*La amada inmóvil*] es el más amado por el público femenino. Tiene ya la consagración de un devocionario sentimental que obliga a la repetición de su lectura" [Because of its deep emotion and its keen understanding of amorous feeling when faced with the mystery of death, this book [*La amada inmóvil*] is the one female readers love the most. It is already hailed as a sentimental prayer book, one that calls for repeated readings] (Aguilar OC I: 28).

Nervo himself prepares the way for this reception marked by the feminine, courting his female readers through direct interpellation. The first version (later corrected) of the prefatory poem to his first book, *Mañana del poeta*, reads: "He aquí, mujer, de mi arpa / los cánticos dispersos" [Woman, here from my harp/ I offer you dispersed hymns].[4] The first poem of his last volume, *El arquero divino*, takes up the call: "¡Me clavó con sus flechas el Arquero divino, / y aquí traigo, lectora (trovador vespertino), / más estrofas de amores, con su amargo y su miel!" [The Divine Archer has pierced me with arrows! / Oh, woman, my reader, I bring you once more,/ My crepuscular love songs, both bitter and sweet!] (OC XXVII: 11). Like many turn-of-the-century writers, Nervo deliberately constructs a poetic persona, and that persona is marked by gender—more explicitly, by the dysfunction of gender. Both in his public and his textual displays, Nervo resorts to indefinable malaise, to a vague, hysterical self-figuration that he offers to the reader as a confidence, perhaps as a secret, to be shared. He writes: "Yo soy un alma pensativa. ¿Sabes / lo que es un alma pensativa?—Triste. / Pero con esa fría / melancolía / de las suaves / diafanidades" [I am a pensive soul. Do you know/ How a pensive soul is?—Sad. / With that cold melancholy/ of dying light] (OC IV: 88). Nervo's persona is frail, sickly, helpless. It is an "ave doliente de la espesura, / postrer latido de un corazón" [suffering bird in the thicket,/ The last pulse of a dying heart]

(Aguilar OC II: 1272). He also tells us that "perpetua sombra anida en [su] cerebro" [perpetual shadow dwells in [his] brain] (OC I: 66); that his inspiration is a "pájaro enfermo" [sick bird] (OC I: 93), that his own spirit is "yermo / muy enfermo . . . , muy enfermo . . . , / casi muerto . . . , casi muerto . . ." [wasted/ very sick . . . very sick . . . ,/ almost dead . . . , almost dead . . .] (OC I: 138). In contrast with other self-figurations inspired by disease that become effective tools of inquiry, both social and textual, questioning stereotypical representations of masculinity (I think, for example, of José Asunción Silva's *De sobremesa*), Nervo's pathologized self-figuration is not so much critical as it is emotive. Having chosen confidence as his preferred mode to address the reader—"te lo diré al oído" [I'll whisper it in your ear] (OC XII: 73)—he calls for the reader's pity, even more for her grief, demanding the same teary empathy that Bernardin de Saint-Pierre desired for his *Paul et Virginie* and Jorge Isaacs for his *María*.

Nervo's intimate revelations have their public ceremonies, however, and become spectacles. There are many physical descriptions of Nervo, as if his body were another text to be deciphered, exposed to the *pathos* of his sympathetic and sensitive audience. "Aparentaba edad mayor de la real por la flacura del cuerpo, que parecía extenuado, por la curvatura de la espalda, que se diría cansado por la parsimonia en el andar, que se antojaba fatigado, y por las arrugas de la frente, de contiguo plegada por el enorme abrir de los ojos curiosos; todo ello agravado por la barba en punta, que algunos han comparado con la de Cristo, y que más bien hacía pensar en las que encuadran los rostros macilentos de los taciturnos caballeros que hay en los lienzos del Greco" [He appeared to be older than he was because of the gauntness of his body, which appeared depleted, the curvature of his back, which seemed exhausted, the slowness of his gait, which revealed his fatigue, the furrow in his forehead, always pushed into a frown by his widened, enormously inquisitive eyes; all this was enhanced by his pointed beard, which some have compared to Christ's, but which mostly made one think of the beards framing the pallid faces of the taciturn gentlemen in El Greco's paintings] (Francisco de Olaguíbel, in Mejía Sánchez xix). There also are many descriptions of Nervo's attitudes, his poses, let us say, descriptions of his "manos gesticulantes, expresivas, que se contraían en rígidas crispaduras o se abandonaban a languideces y desmayos elocuentísimos, siguiendo la fulgurante e inagotable verbosidad del poeta" [expressive hands, which contracted and clutched at the air, or let themselves go, languorously, as if in a swoon, in tune with the dazzling, inexhaustible

words of the poet] (Ortiz de Montellano 26–27).[5] His poetry readings, which he relished (for Nervo, proof of a poem's excellence was
that it was "recitable"),[6] were veritable performances, like his last
public appearance in Montevideo, shortly before his death: "Nervo,
emocionadísimo, agradeció el homenaje. Se definió, en ese momento, diciendo que él no era sino un corazón que se había buscado
órganos para caminar por el mundo. Declamó insuperablemente,
como si fuera por última vez, las poesías que todos sus admiradores
saben de memoria. El público quería más; y el poeta, sonriente, con
aquella su inagotable complacencia, recitaba las composiciones que le
indicaba el auditorio, doblando así el programa que había pensado
desarrollar con asombro de los que conocíamos su extenuación"
[Very moved, Nervo acknowledged the homage. At that very moment, he said, he was nothing but a heart which had found itself or-
gans to get around in the world. He recited magnificently well, as if
for the last time, all the poems his admirers knew by heart. The audience wanted more; and the poet, smiling, with his boundless gen-
erosity, recited the compositions requested by the audience, thus
doubling the original program, to the astonishment of those of us
who were aware of his exhaustion] (Belaunde 211). The scene is
oddly memorable: the smiling poet, seeking to satisfy his public (for
Nervo is certainly the most *popular* of the *modernistas*), even as he
feels life draining from him: "casi muerto . . . , casi muerto . . ." [al-
most dead . . . , almost dead . . .] (OC I: 138). Opera could not have
done it better.

To give a textual example of Nervo's pathos, or rather, of the performance of pathos, I briefly call attention to two poems, Darío's
"De invierno" and Nervo's poem XXII in *Perlas negras*. Both poems
posit similar scenes of voyeurism. Inside lies a warm and opulent feminine interior; outside, in the cold, is a male voyeur, looking in. In
Darío's poem, the scene is an exercise in Parisian exotica: a woman,
most likely a courtesan, lounges in her boudoir while her lover, an-
ticipating his pleasure, spies on her before entering the room. In
Nervo, instead, the male subject is a poor and sickly child, a little
street musician who, wistfully peering into a cozy boudoir, only gets
to see the lady's lapdog (and not the lady), comfortably asleep, before collapsing and dying, unattended, on the threshold of the mansion. As Oscar Wilde famously said of Dickens, "One must have a
heart of stone to read the death of Little Nell without laughing."
This is the kind of pathos Nervo delights in, the pathos of the small,
the insignificant, that cloyingly sentimentalized insignificance for
which French has the perfect word—*mièvre*—and Spanish the less

successful *cursi*. This pathos marks both Nervo's tone (those confessions whispered in the reader's ear) as well as his representations: in both cases, it leads to melodrama.[7]

In principle, this pathos can touch both male and female readers. In practice, at the time of Nervo's writing, it is mainly associated with the feminine or, rather, with a certain construction of the feminine, based on emotion, sensibility, and frailty, in a sense an "older" construction of woman, with its aura of nostalgic charm; as John Mullan puts it, "a particular version of the feminine—tearful, palpitating, embodying virtue whilst susceptible to all the vicissitudes of 'feeling'" (218). This construction is remarkably resilient at a time when new subjectivities and new formulations of gender—the "new woman," the homosexual—effectively bring into question facile binarisms and universal heteronormativity. It helps ward off a crisis of representation by postulating the feminine as an unchangeable category: safe, reliable, *certissima*.

The Feminine as Empty Category

I propose that the feminine, in Nervo, is an empty category. Woman is, above all, lack of woman. The possibility of loving her is directly dependant on her absence: on her remoteness, her silence, her death. "Sirena que no cantaba / te podía seducir" [A siren who did not sing/ Could seduce you], writes Alfonso Reyes (Aguilar OC II: 1232). It would perhaps be more apt to say that *only* a siren who did not sing could seduce him. *La amada inmóvil* is obviously the best example of this absence: the book is composed of poems to a dead woman, Anita, the same one that Nervo carefully hid from friends and acquaintances while she was alive. Yet, the construction of woman as absence, as void, is not limited to this autobiographical scene. Reyes deems this construction a constant in Nervo's poetry, even its chief impulse. "Él necesitaba querer así. Su amor era una fabricación secreta . . . Ella, después de la muerte, continúa radiando fulgores" [He needed to love like that. His love was a secret fabrication. . . . After her death, she continues to radiate] (in Durán 75). Present through her very absence, woman, in Nervo, lingers in fetishes. "¡La trenza que le corté / y que, piadoso, guardé / (impregnada todavía / del sudor de su agonía) / la tarde en que se me fue!" [The braid I cut off/ and so piously saved/ on the night she slipped from me,/ even now is drenched/ in the sweat of her death!] (OC XII: 66–67).[8] The fetish—the dead woman's humid braid, the clothes still imbued with her smell—ensures melancholia, the nonclosure of mourning. "¡Hasta sus perfumes duran más que ella! / Ved aquí los frascos, que apenas usó" [Even her perfumes live longer than she did!/ Look at all the vials, which she hardly used] (OC XII: 188), he mourns. Or again, in the introduction to *La amada inmóvil:* "Sus pieles y su blusa negra, pendientes de la percha en que sus manos las colocaron con esa meticulosidad que le era propia y que hacía de ella la *menagère* por excelencia, tienen aún su olor, su tibio olor de mujer limpia, su olor que respiré más de diez años" [Her furs and her black blouse, placed on hangers by her own hands, with that meticulousness that was hers and that made her the perfect *ménagère,* still had her smell, the warm smell of a clean woman, the smell I breathed for more than ten years] (OC XII: 48). The clean smell of the good housekeeper as source for erotica: the middle class never had it so good.

Woman is loved in death, in the vacancy wrought by death: unfilled clothing, half-empty scent bottles. In life, however, woman must be concealed. Again, I draw attention to the introduction of *La amada inmóvil,* in which Nervo details his relation with the woman he calls "la dulce y adorable compañerita de mi vida" [the sweet and adorable little companion of my life] (OC XII: 24), dwelling on the clandestine character of their life together since, for apparently no good reason, they never married:

Como aquel nuestro cariño inmenso no estaba sancionado por ninguna ley . . . no teníamos el derecho de amarnos a la luz del día, y nos habíamos amado en la penumbra de un sigilo y de una intimidad tales, que casi nadie en el mundo sabía nuestro secreto. Aparentemente yo vivía solo, y muy raro debió de ser el amigo cuya perspicacia adivinara, al visitarme, que allí, a dos pasos de él, latía por mí, por mí solo, el corazón más noble, más desinteresado y más afectuoso de la tierra.

Pocas veces, muy pocas, salíamos juntos, evitando las arterias febriles de las metrópolis, donde mi relativa popularidad podía prepararme sorpresas. En cambio, en ciertos viajes nos desquitábamos ampliamente, y, brazo con brazo, enredadas las diestras con una ternura que tenía mucho de fraternal, nos dedicábamos a ese *flaneo* deleitable de París, de Londres, de Bruselas . . . Pero tal persistente secreto fue mi tortura persistente también

[Since our immense love was not sanctioned by any law . . . we did not have the right to love one another in the light of day and had loved in the dark, so cautiously, so intimately, that almost no one in the world knew our secret. I appeared to live alone and very rare was the friend sharp enough to guess, upon visiting me, that there, two steps from him, beat, for me and for me alone, the most noble, most disinterested, most loving heart on earth.

On few occasions, very few, we would go out together, avoiding the frenzied streets of the great cities, where my relative popularity might play me a bad turn. Nevertheless, on certain trips we would fully make up for this, and, arm in arm, our hands entangled with a tenderness that was most fraternal, we gave ourselves over to the delightful *flânerie* of Paris, of London, of Brussels.... But this perpetual secret was also, for me, a perpetual source of anguish] (OC XII: 25).

Anita may have been Nervo's "adorable compañerita de mi vida" [adorable little companion of my life] (OC XII: 24), his "lamparita sana y dulce de mis tinieblas" [pure and sweet little lamp of my darkness] (OC XII: 22), yet, if I'm not mistaken, the terms used by Nervo to describe this relation are rarely used to describe heterosexual love. The relation between Nervo and Anita is secret; it must be concealed (and the concealment is, in itself, a source of pleasure); it is tainted by guilt (lovers love in the dark, "en la penumbra," because they have no right to love openly); it cannot be made manifest and must be displaced, through travel, to the foreign and unfamiliar, where it can be truly enjoyed. Instead of searching for heteronormative reasons to explain this strange relation, as most of his critics have done, one might ask why Nervo resorts to the rhetoric of "the love that dares not speak its name" when referring to a woman. Additionally, one may wonder why Nervo so painstakingly constructs an emblematic space of interdiction, a closet of sorts, wherein to live out this secret relation. Suddenly, a random comment by Manuel Durán acquires unexpected new sense. Nervo, writes Durán, turns woman "en puente para llegar a todo lo demás" [into a bridge to reach everything else] (57).[9] It is that complex "everything else," mediated by the feminine, that I wish to examine now.

The Nunnery

In Nervo, concealment of woman occurs in two ways. Death is the privileged solution, as in *La amada inmóvil,* because it allows Nervo to repress woman and, at the same time, to revel in the pathos of this repression. But there is another solution that I find more productive in that it provides a context for the rhetoric of the closet. I refer to the cloister, both spatially and rhetorically, as the site where some rather remarkable gender transactions are effected.

Cloisters abound in Nervo. There is, of course, biographical evidence: his sister became a nun, Nervo himself was a seminarian and seems to have cultivated a monkish pose, to the point that Darío's nickname for him was "fraile de los suspiros" [sighing monk]. Beyond biography, the cloister first appears in a remarkable short story, *El bachiller,* as the space of gender dysfunction. Before castrating himself for the love of God, the protagonist, torn between God and worldly desires, asks of himself: "¿Qué vas a hacer a un convento? ¿Qué hallarás ahí?" [What will you do in a convent? What will you find there?] (OC XIII: 54). The question is not without significance, given the usual meaning of the word *convent*—primarily a space of seclusion for women. But the choice of the term is not so strange when read in context, since for Nervo, the cloistered space is always identified with the feminine, even better, with the *sororal.* The early poems of *Místicas* stress this identification. The male speaker of "Obsession" is tortured by a ghostly voice, "Hay un fantasma que siempre viste / luctuosos paños, y con acento / cruel de Hamlet a Ofelia triste / me dice: ¡*Mira, vete a un convento!*" [There's a cruel phantom clad in dark garments,/ who quite like Hamlet to sad Ophelia/ says to me: *Listen, go to a convent!*] (OC I: 141–142). (If there is any doubt as to the gendering of *convent,* identification with Ophelia and reference to the nunnery quickly dissipate it.) Through a similar association, the subject of "Gótica" calls out to the dead nuns in the abbey—"Heme aquí con vosotras, las abadesas / de cruces pectorales y de áureo báculo" [See me here in your midst, Oh, abbesses!/ with pectoral crosses and golden crosiers] (OC I: 144)—to become one with them, identifying with their mission: "¡Oh claustro silencioso, cuántas pavesas / de amores que ascendieron hasta el pináculo / donde mora el Cordero, guardan tus huesas . . . ! / Oraré mientras duermen las abadesas / de cruces pectorales y de áureo báculo . . . [Oh silent cloister, how many ashes/ of loves flown high, where dwells the Lamb,/ lie in your graves . . . !/ I pray; they sleep; the abbesses/ of pectoral crosses and golden crosiers] (OC I: 144).

In the cloistered space constructed in these two poems (and there are many other examples of similar constructions throughout Nervo), a striking gender transaction takes place: a male subject enters a locus doubly marked by the sacred and the feminine, not transgressively (there is no profanation in Nervo), but sympathetically, in order to associate with the feminine, to enter into the sorority: to feminize himself. Interestingly, it is said of Nervo, the man, that "se complacía especialmente en la compañía de las mujeres y en los salones le gustaba rodearse de su pequeña corte de admiradoras. Pero por un sentimiento que puede haber sido muestra de timidez o de desgano para entrar en la lucha por la admiración femenina, no le

agradaba que otros hombres se mezclaran a los grupos ocasional-
mente formados a su alrededor; y en los casos en que esto ocurría,
Nervo sabía buscar un pretexto para retirarse discretamente" [He
particularly took pleasure in the company of women and, in drawing-
rooms, liked to surround himself with his small court of female admirers. But due perhaps to timidity, or to a disinclination to enter
into the struggle for feminine admiration, he was displeased when
other men approached the groups that sometimes gathered around
him; on occasions when this happened, Nervo knew how to find a
pretext to withdraw discreetly] (Morgan in Durán 212). In order for
it to be productive, sorority does not tolerate heterogeneity.

Sentimental by Association: Sorority/Fraternity

When I say that by entering into the cloistered feminine space the
male subject feminizes himself, I want to make clear that I do not
mean that he becomes a woman. I return here to the construction of
the feminine typical of the period. A sentimental, excessive construct,
it is an object of curiosity and attraction for the male subject, allow-
ing simultaneously for identification and disidentification because it
is, as Hugo von Hofmannstal famously writes, "what we men love to
call womanly" [*das Frauenhafte*] which "women rarely have" (Molloy 20). It is to this sentimentalized womanliness *that women rarely
have* that Nervo resorts in order to establish relations with what lies
beyond woman, the "everything else" to which woman provides a
"bridge." To be precise: it is from, and through, this displaced feminine that Nervo posits *another* community, the passionate, sentimental brotherhood that marks so many of his pages.

The remarkable letters written by Nervo to his friend Luis Quintanilla constitute one of the most eloquent biographical documents
of that intense brotherhood. Written from Paris and Madrid, routinely dedicated to the "brother"—sometimes "dear brother," often
"beloved brother"—they allow the reader to follow the progress of a
passionate friendship between men that few critics have deemed worthy of comment. Although they are worthy of a more sustained commentary than this one, I do want to point to its more striking
characteristics, and call attention to the profoundly symbiotic nature
of this friendship, the passion of the exchange, and the circulation of
fetishes that sustains it. Nervo wrote from Paris, where he settled for
a time; Quintanilla, who spent some time in Paris, returned to Mexico leaving his friend behind. Acknowledging receipt of a postcard,

Nervo, for example, writes: "Hermano muy amado: Gracias por tu tarjeta. La nube esa es adorable en su *nonchalance*. La he besado" [Very beloved brother: Thank you for your card. That cloud is adorable in its *nonchalance*. I have kissed it] (Aguilar OC II: 1138).

Or, in another letter, staging a veritable scene of amorous recrimination (Nervo is jealous because Quintanilla has written to another compatriot before writing to him), Nervo writes:

Muy querido hermano: Tú eres el único de quien no esperaba un abandono absoluto, tú has sido el único juguete que no se me rompía, y si te dijese que tu olvido no me sorprende mentiría . . . ¡Qué quieres! Yo me imaginaba que estando tú en México y yo en París, los dos estaríamos en las dos partes, que tú serías allá una prolongación de mí mismo. En fin . . . pasemos a otra cosa

[Very dear brother: You are the only one from whom I did not expect total abandonment, you have been my only toy that did not break. But if I told you that your neglect does not surprise me, I would be lying. . . . What did you think? I imagined that you being in Mexico and I in Paris, the two of us would be in both places, and that, over there, you would be an extension of myself. Well . . . let us move on to something else]. (Aguilar OC II: 1152)[10]

Remarkably, both men live with women bearing the same name: Anita. This sentimental triangulation, so provocatively foregrounded by Eve Sedgwick as the basis for homosocial bonding, is eloquently set forth in another of Nervo's letters:

Imagínate dos amigos, dos hermanos como nosotros y entre los dos una amada, por quien los dos están locos—y que enloquece a todo el mundo—. Supongamos luego que uno de esos amigos, por circunstancias imposibles de vencer, ha debido dejar esa amada, que el otro se ha quedado con ella, pero que, forzado por la fatalidad debe abandonarla también, y que entonces el primer amigo le dice al segundo: "Tu amada, es decir, nuestra amada, es muy bella . . . no la abandones"

[Imagine two friends, two brothers like us and between them a beloved over whom both are mad—and over whom everybody is mad. Let us suppose then that one of those friends, due to circumstances impossible to change, has had to leave that beloved; that the other has stayed with her, but, forced by fate, must also leave her, and that then the first friend tells the other: "Your beloved, that is to say, our beloved, is very beautiful . . . do not abandon her]. (Aguilar OC II: 1153)

It is of little importance that the *amada* [loved one] here is not a woman but a city—Paris—where Nervo wishes to stay in order to, he tells Quintanilla, "amarla por ti y por mí" [love her for you and for me] (Aguilar OC II: 1154). What does matter, however, is the presence of a feminine alterity, functioning to strengthen the relation between men; again, serving as a bridge.

Although it would be interesting to follow the manifestations of this male sentimentality on a biographical level, I am more interested in considering its textual representation, observing in Nervo that "change of gears," by which, as Eve Sedgwick notes, "the exemplary instance of the sentimental ceases to be a woman per se, but instead becomes the body of a man who . . . physically dramatizes, *embodies* for an audience that both desires and cathartically identifies with him, a struggle of masculine identity with emotions or physical stigmata stereotyped as feminine" (146). Indeed, if relation with the feminine in Nervo is predicated on absence (woman dead, asleep, remote, cloistered), relation with the masculine, instead, is predicated on presence, on fullness, on a *physicality* in which the subject, delectably, loses himself. "Ven, abad incurable, gran asceta; yo quiero / anegar mis pupilas en las tuyas de acero, / aspirar el efluvio misterioso que escapa / de tus miembros exangües, de tu rostro severo, / y sufrir el contagio de la paz de tu Trapa" [Come, incurable abbot, great ascetic. / I want to plunge my eyes into your steely gaze,/ inhale the dark effluvia that escape/ from your depleted limbs, your severe face,/ and suffer the contagion of your monastic peace] (OC I: 156). While religiosity and mysticism—what Eduardo Colín rather flamboyantly calls "elaciones inmaculadas e infinitas, este aroma santo de lo Absoluto" [immaculate and infinite elations, the holy aroma of the Absolute] (Aguilar OC II: 1252)—channel this male sentimentality, this losing of self in the other, one should not lose sight of the intimate, specifically physical nature of this contact between men, nor of its distinctly abject bent: "Yo soñé con un beso, con un beso postrero/ en la lívida boca del Señor solitario/ que desgarra sus carnes sobre tosco madero/ en el nicho más íntimo del vetusto santuario" [I dreamt of a kiss, of a very last kiss/ on the livid lips of the lonely Lord/ whose flesh tears away from the cragged cross/ in the innermost niche of the dusty church] (OC I: 179). To smell the smell of the leprous abbot's legs and become infected, to kiss the livid lips of Christ as his flesh tears on the cross: of such excesses is this sentimentality made.

From its very beginning, Nervo's writing is marked by gender trouble, starts out with a powerful act the symbolic implications of which are impossible to ignore, the castration of the main character of *El bachiller*. I would propose that all of Nervo's oeuvre, and most especially a considerable portion of his poetry, builds on this excessive gesture. The excision of a genitalized masculinity, having become intolerable, translates into a sentimentality that, not respecting traditional gender assignations, circulating among figurations of masculinity and femininity and, in so doing, rendering them unstable, is, in the final analysis, a liberating gesture. That pathos is the rhetoric of choice for this sentimentality, a pathos that is read today, depending on the reader's perspective, either as *kitsch* or as *camp*, should not obscure its efficacy. On the contrary: as we who cannot erase Nervo from our memories know full well, pathos makes this sentimentality, the gender crossings it spontaneously favors, even the parodic inversions it induces, quite unforgettable.

NOTES

1. Unless otherwise indicated, OC refers to the Biblioteca Nueva's edition of Amado Nervo's *Obras Completas* and Aguilar OC refers the Aguilar 1967 edition of Amado Nervo's *Obras Completas*. All translations into English are mine.
2. The revised poem went more or less like this:

   Pasó con su culo. ¡qué rara belleza
   ¡Qué rubios cabellos de trigo garzul!
   ¡Qué ritmo en el culo! ¡Qué innata realeza
   de culo! ¡Qué formas bajo el fino tul! . . .
   Pasó con su culo. Volvió la cabeza:
   ¡me clavó muy hondo su mirada azul!
   Quedé como en éxtasis . . .
   Con febril premura
   "¡Síguela!," gritaron cuerpo y culo al par.
   . . . Pero tuve miedo de amar con el culo,
   de abrir mis heridas, que suelen sangrar,
   ¡y no obstante toda mi sed de ternura,
   cerrando mi culo, la dejé pasar!

   [She went by with her ass, what a beauty so rare,
   What shining blonde locks like ripening wheat!
   What rhythm in her ass! What innate majesty
   in that ass! What shapes beneath that fine tulle.
   She went by with her ass. Turning her head toward me,
   she pierced me to the core with her deep blue eyes!
   And left me in ecstasy . . .
   With feverish urgency

Follow her! cried body and ass all at once.
. . . But I was afraid to love with my ass,
to reopen my wounds, which so frequently bleed,
and in spite of my consummate longing for tenderness,
closing up my ass, I just let her go by!]

3. The omnipresence of the feminine reappears in Berisso's evocation of Nervo's spectacular funeral: "Su féretro, bañado con las lágrimas de las mujeres,—cuyo imperio conquistó de manera avasalladora, por sobrenatural designio,—fue cubierto materialmente de coronas y de rosas" [His casket, bathed in women's tears,—those women over whom he ruled unchallenged, as if by divine design—was materially covered with wreaths and roses] (307).

4. See Mejía Sánchez xv.

5. Still on the subject of Nervo's hands: "Las manos se movían en la sombra como largas hojas marchitas . . . y al abrirse en cansados gestos, tenían el ademán de bendecir" [His hands moved in the shadows like large, dead leaves . . . and, when they reached out, in weary gestures, they appeared to be imparting a blessing] (Manuel Horta, in Durán 104).

6. "Te acompaño mis últimos endecasílabos. Creo que son muy recitables" [I send you my latest verses. I believe they are quite recitable], he writes Luis Quintanilla on July 7, 1900 (Aguilar OC II: 1138).

7. Peter Brooks speaks of the nineteenth-century novel needing "such theatricality . . . to get its meaning across, to invest in its renderings of life a sense of memorability and significance" (13).

8. In the preface to *La amada inmóvil,* Nervo describes the lover's braid, still humid with her sweat, as "lo sólo material que me queda de la compañera única de mi vida" [the only material thing that remains of the sole companion of my life] (OC XII: 50). But again, fetishistic evocation is not reserved to Anita. Indeed, the very same fetish appears in Nervo's early poetry, practically in the same terms: "Quiero poseer un rizo desprendido/ de esas trenzas que besan en sus giros/ las auras cuando llevan a tu nido/ el lloroso rumor de mis suspiros" [I want to own a severed curl/ from those braids kissed by gently swirling winds,/ that carry to your nest/ the melancholy rumor of my sighs]. Thus begins a poem titled "Un rizo de tu pelo," which concludes: "¡Oh!, dame esos cabellos, que doquiera/ a mi fiel corazón irán opresos;/ y ya los tomarás cuando me muera/ mojados con mi llanto y con mis besos" [Oh! give me those locks, so wherever I go,/ pressed they'll be to my devoted heart;/ when I die they'll finally be yours,/ wet forever with kisses and tears] (Aguilar OC II: 1287).

9. The full context of Duran's unexpectedly accurate phrase is certainly less felicitous if not downright offensive: "Todavía hoy, si se hiciera . . . un análisis de los lectores de Nervo, lo mas probable es

que encontraríamos que una fuerte mayoría de los lectores de Nervo han sido y son del sexo femenino. Las mujeres comprenden instintivamente que hay ciertos hombres, ciertos escritores, que aman a la mujer sin reservas, la convierten en puente para llegar a todo lo demás, en puerta abierta a lo absoluto. Y saben agradecerlo" [Even today, if an analysis were done . . . of Nervo's readers, we would most probably find that a large majority of those readers have belonged and even now belong to the feminine sex. Women understand instinctively that there are certain men, certain writers, who love women without reservations and make them a bridge to reach everything else, a door giving them access to the absolute. And women know how to appreciate that] (57).

10. Nervo's death awakens echoes of that amorous brotherhood. Remembering the poet, Emilio Frugoni, while recognizing Nervo's success with women readers, ultimately privileges a community of loving male readers: "Así se abrió camino entre los corazones; / así llegó a nosotros, preocupados varones, / y nos metió en la límpida onda de sus canciones" [That is how he found a way into our hearts;/ that is how he reached us, worried men,/ and plunged us in the clear flow of his songs]. Those "preocupados varones" [worried men] listen to Nervo, Frugoni contends, because the poet "palpitaba lo mismo que un humano / corazón, y cantaba muy quedamente: 'Hermano'" [throbbed like a human/ heart, softly whispering: "Brother"] (230–231).

BIBLIOGRAPHY

Belaunde, Víctor Andrés. "De la vida de Nervo." *Nosotros,* special issue on the death of Amado Nervo (June–July 1919): 206–211.

Berisso, Luis. "Amado Nervo." *Nosotros,* special issue on the death of Amado Nervo (June–July 1919): 305–307.

Brooks, Peter. *The Melodramatic Imagination: Balzac, Henry James, Melodrama, and the Mode of Excess.* New York: Columbia University Press, 1984.

Cansinos Asséns, Rafael. *Poetas y prosistas del Novecientos (España y América).* Madrid: Editorial América, 1919.

Durán, Manuel. *Genio y figura de Amado Nervo.* Buenos Aires: Eudeba, 1968.

Fernández Moreno, Baldomero. "Amado Nervo." *Nosotros,* special issue on the death of Amado Nervo (June–July 1919): 308.

Frugoni, Emilio. "Al viajero que se va." *Nosotros,* special issue on the death of Amado Nervo (June–July 1919): 230–231.

Mejía Sánchez, Ernesto. "Estudio preliminar." Amado Nervo. *Plenitud. Perlas negras. Místicas. Los jardines interiores. El estanque de los lotos.* Mexico: Porrúa, 1971: ix–xxiii.

Molloy, Sylvia. "Voice Snatching: *De sobremesa,* Hysteria, and the Impersonation of Marie Bashkirtseff." *Latin American Literary Review* 50 (1997): 11–29.

Mullan, John. *Sentiment and Sociability: The Language of Feeling in the Eighteenth Century.* Oxford: Clarendon Press, 1988.

Nervo, Amado. *Obras completas,* Vols. I-XXVIII. Madrid: Biblioteca Nueva, 1920–22.

Nervo, Amado. *Obras completas,* Vols. I and II. Francisco González Guerrero y Alfonso Méndez Plancarte, Eds. Madrid: Aguilar, 1967.

Ortiz de Montellano, Bernardo. *Figura, amor y muerte de Amado Nervo.* Mexico: Xochitl, 1943.

Sedgwick, Eve Kosofsky. *Epistemology of the Closet.* Berkeley and Los Angeles: University of California Press, 1990.

Showalter, Elaine. "Hysteria, Feminism and Gender." *Hysteria Beyond Freud.* Sander Gilman et al, Eds. Berkeley: University of California Press, 1993: 286–344.

CONTRIBUTORS

ROBERT BUFFINGTON, Associate Professor of History at Bowling Green State University, is the author of *Criminal and Citizen in Modern Mexico*, and coeditor (with Carlos Aguirre) of *Reconstructing Criminality in Latin America*. A recent article, cowritten with Pablo Piccato, "Tales of Two Women: The Narrative Construal of Porfirian Reality," won the 2000 Tibesar Prize for the best paper published in *The Americas*.

ROBERT MCKEE IRWIN, Assistant Professor and Director of Undergraduate Studies in the Department of Spanish and Portuguese at Tulane University, is the author of the forthcoming *Mexican Masculinities* and coeditor (with Sylvia Molloy) of *Hispanisms and Homosexualities*. In addition to his work on gender and sexuality in Latin America, he is currently researching Mexican representations of U.S.-Mexico borderlands culture in the late nineteenth century.

VÍCTOR M. MACÍAS-GONZÁLEZ is currently Assistant Professor of History and Director of the Institute for Latino and Latin American Studies at the University of Wisconsin at La Crosse. He previously directed the Oral History Institute and was consultant to the National Museum of Mexican Immigration History at the University of Texas-El Paso. His current research focuses on Mexican elites in Europe in the nineteenth century as well as the art history of Porfirian México.

EDWARD J. MCCAUGHAN, Associate Professor and Chair of Sociology at Loyola University New Orleans, is on the editorial board of *Social Justice*. His books include *Reinventing Revolution: The Renovation of Left Discourse in Cuba and Mexico*, *Latin America Faces the 21st Century: Reconstructing a Social Justice Agenda* (coedited with Susanne Jonas), and *Beyond the Border: Mexico and the U.S. Today* (coauthored with Peter Baird). His articles have appeared in *Latin American Perspectives, Review, Nepantla, Peace Review, Global Development Studies,* and *NACLA's Report on the Americas*. McCaughan is currently writing about art and social movements in Mexico.

CARLOS MONSIVÁIS, one of Mexico's foremost public intellectuals, is author of numerous bestselling books on Mexican and Latin American literature and cultural studies including *Salvador Novo: Lo marginal en el centro*, *Mexican Postcards*, *Aires de familia*, *Los rituales del caos*, *Amor perdido*, *Días de guardar*, *Nuevo catecismo para indios remisos* and *Escenas de pudor y liviandad*.

SYLVIA MOLLOY is Albert Schweitzer Professor in the Humanities at New York University. Among her many publications are the critically acclaimed novel *En breve cárcel* (translated to English as *Certificate of Absence*) and the critical studies *Las letras de Borges* (*Signs of Borges* in English) and *At Face Value: Autobiographical Writing in Spanish America* (*Acta de presencia* in Spanish). She is coeditor of *Hispanisms and Homosexualities* and *Women's Writing in Latin America*.

MICHELLE ROCÍO NASSER is a graduate student in Latin American Studies at Tulane University. She is currently undertaking research on homosexualities and race in Brazilian literature and culture. She was coorganizer of the Centenary of the Famous 41 symposium for which she curated the accompanying exhibition of José Guadalupe Posada broadsides and newspaper stories on the "Famous 41" scandal at Tulane University.

PABLO PICCATO, Assistant Professor of History at Columbia University, is author of *City of Suspects: Crime in Mexico City, 1900–1931* and coauthor of *Hábitos, normas y escándalo: Prensa, criminalidad y drogas durante el porfiriato tardío*. He shared the 2000 Tibesar Prize with Robert Buffington.

CRISTINA RIVERA GARZA, Associate Professor of Mexican history at San Diego State University and head of the Creative Writing Workshop of Centro Cultural Tijuana, is the author of the award-winning historical novel *Nadie me verá llorar* as well as various articles that explore the narratives of insanity produced by psychiatrists and patients at the General Insane Asylum *La Castañeda* in early-twentieth-century Mexico. She is currently completing her book *Mad Narratives: Psychiatrists and Insane Debate Gender, Class, and the Nation in Mexico, 1910–1930*.

AARON WALKER is a translator, Spanish instructor, and sometime graduate student at Tulane University. His academic research focuses on the relationship between anthropology, modernity, and the birth of Afro-Brazilian studies in the first half of the twentieth century.

INDEX